Maker Innovations Series

Jump start your path to discovery with the Apress Maker Innovations series! From the basics of electricity and components through to the most advanced options in robotics and Machine Learning, you'll forge a path to building ingenious hardware and controlling it with cutting-edge software. All while gaining new skills and experience with common toolsets you can take to new projects or even into a whole new career.

The Apress Maker Innovations series offers projects-based learning, while keeping theory and best processes front and center. So you get hands-on experience while also learning the terms of the trade and how entrepreneurs, inventors, and engineers think through creating and executing hardware projects. You can learn to design circuits, program AI, create IoT systems for your home or even city, and so much more!

Whether you're a beginning hobbyist or a seasoned entrepreneur working out of your basement or garage, you'll scale up your skillset to become a hardware design and engineering pro. And often using low-cost and open-source software such as the Raspberry Pi, Arduino, PIC microcontroller, and Robot Operating System (ROS). Programmers and software engineers have great opportunities to learn, too, as many projects and control environments are based in popular languages and operating systems, such as Python and Linux.

If you want to build a robot, set up a smart home, tackle assembling a weather-ready meteorology system, or create a brand-new circuit using breadboards and circuit design software, this series has all that and more! Written by creative and seasoned Makers, every book in the series tackles both tested and leading-edge approaches and technologies for bringing your visions and projects to life.

More information about this series at https://link.springer.com/bookseries/17311.

Mastering Circuit Analysis

Analyzing DC, AC, and Magnetic Circuits

Hubert Henry Ward

Apress®

Mastering Circuit Analysis: Analyzing DC, AC, and Magnetic Circuits

Hubert Henry Ward
Leigh, UK

ISBN-13 (pbk): 979-8-8688-1831-8   ISBN-13 (electronic): 979-8-8688-1832-5
https://doi.org/10.1007/979-8-8688-1832-5

Copyright © 2025 by Hubert Henry Ward

This work is subject to copyright. All rights are reserved by the Publisher, whether the whole or part of the material is concerned, specifically the rights of translation, reprinting, reuse of illustrations, recitation, broadcasting, reproduction on microfilms or in any other physical way, and transmission or information storage and retrieval, electronic adaptation, computer software, or by similar or dissimilar methodology now known or hereafter developed.

Trademarked names, logos, and images may appear in this book. Rather than use a trademark symbol with every occurrence of a trademarked name, logo, or image we use the names, logos, and images only in an editorial fashion and to the benefit of the trademark owner, with no intention of infringement of the trademark.

The use in this publication of trade names, trademarks, service marks, and similar terms, even if they are not identified as such, is not to be taken as an expression of opinion as to whether or not they are subject to proprietary rights.

While the advice and information in this book are believed to be true and accurate at the date of publication, neither the authors nor the editors nor the publisher can accept any legal responsibility for any errors or omissions that may be made. The publisher makes no warranty, express or implied, with respect to the material contained herein.

    Managing Director, Apress Media LLC: Welmoed Spahr
    Acquisitions Editor: Miriam Haidara
    Editorial Assistant: Jessica Vakili
    Copy Editor: Kezia Endsley

Cover designed by eStudioCalamar

Distributed to the book trade worldwide by Springer Science+Business Media New York, 1 New York Plaza, New York, NY 10004. Phone 1-800-SPRINGER, fax (201) 348-4505, e-mail orders-ny@springer-sbm.com, or visit www.springeronline.com. Apress Media, LLC is a Delaware LLC and the sole member (owner) is Springer Science + Business Media Finance Inc (SSBM Finance Inc). SSBM Finance Inc is a **Delaware** corporation.

For information on translations, please e-mail booktranslations@springernature.com; for reprint, paperback, or audio rights, please e-mail bookpermissions@springernature.com.

Apress titles may be purchased in bulk for academic, corporate, or promotional use. eBook versions and licenses are also available for most titles. For more information, reference our Print and eBook Bulk Sales web page at http://www.apress.com/bulk-sales.

Any source code or other supplementary material referenced by the author in this book is available to readers on GitHub. For more detailed information, please visit https://www.apress.com/gp/services/source-code.

If disposing of this product, please recycle the paper

*To my darling wife Ann, who suffers the long hours
of me tap tapping on my laptop,
and to my grandchildren, who might one day
learn from my books.*

Table of Contents

About the Author xix

About the Technical Reviewer xxi

Introduction xxiii

Chapter 1: Electrical Current 1

  The Main Operation of All Electrical Circuits 2

    The Mighty Electron 2

    The Charge C of an Electron 3

    The Sea of Free Electrons 5

    Current Flow 5

  What Is DC? 8

    The Simple Cell, PD, and Voltage 8

    The Dry Cell 9

    Primary and Secondary Cells 10

  The Difference Between EMF and PDs or Voltage 11

    Example 1.1 11

  Connecting Cells in Series and Parallel 13

  Voltage 15

  Energy in Current Flow and the Amp 15

  The Amp/Ampere 17

  Resistance and Resistivity 17

  Current and Charge Calculations 21

TABLE OF CONTENTS

    Example 1.2 21
    Example 1.3 21
    Example 1.4 22
Alternating Current (AC) 23
The Root Mean Square (RMS) 24
Power 27
Resistor Types 29
    The Resistor Colour Coding 30
Chapter 1 Exercises 34
    Exercise 1.1 34
    Exercise 1.2 34
    Exercise 1.3 35
    Exercise 1.4 35
    Exercise 1.5 35
    Exercise 1.6 35
Summary 36

Chapter 2: Fundamental Circuit Theorems 37
Ohm's Law 38
Kirchhoff's Laws 38
    Resistors Connected in Series 38
    Calculating Three Volt Drops 40
Transposing Ohm's Law for Resistance R 41
    The Current Flowing Through a Series Circuit 42
Simulating the Circuit in TINA 44
Kirchhoff's Current Law 47
Series Parallel Combinations of DC Circuits 53

TABLE OF CONTENTS

Engineering Numbers 54
    The Four Main Engineering Numbers 54
The Supply Current 57
    An Alternative Method for Two Components in Parallel 59
The Voltage Divider Rule 63
The Current Divider Rule 73
Chapter 2 Exercises 74
    Exercise 2.1 74
    Exercise 2.2 75
    Exercise 2.3 76
Summary 77
    Answers to Exercise 2.1 77
    Answers to Exercise 2.2 78
    Answers to Exercise 2.3 78

Chapter 3: Further DC Analysis 81
The Kirchhoff's Mesh Currents 81
    KVL Applied to Loop 1 88
    KVL Applied to Loop 2 88
Kirchhoff's Mesh Currents Example 2 89
The Superposition Theorem 93
The Ideal Internal Resistance of a Voltage Source 94
The Ideal Internal Resistance of a Current Source 96
The Voltage V_A Due to $V_{Supply\ 1}$ 96
The Voltage V_A Due to $V_{SUPPLY\ 2}$ 98
    Exercise 3.1 98
    The Voltage VA at Point A 98
    Exercise 3.2 99

TABLE OF CONTENTS

The Maximum Power Transfer Theorem 100
Thevenin's Theorem 102
Thevenin's Equivalent Example 2 106
V_{THEV} Due to the Voltage Source V_1 107
V_{THEV} Due to the Current Source I_{S1} 108
Thevenin's Equivalent Example 3 111
    Exercise 3.3 118
Norton's Theorem 118
The Norton's Resistance (R_N) 119
The Norton's Current 119
Norton's Example 2 122
The Norton's Current Due to V1 122
The Norton's Current Due to I_{S1} 123
    Exercise 3.4 124
Converting from Thevenin's to Norton's 124
    Exercise 3.5 126
Summary 127
    Answers to Exercise 3.2 127
    Answers to Exercise 3.3 127
    Answers to Exercise 3.4 128
    Answers to Exercise 3.5 129

Chapter 4: DC Transients in LR Circuits 131

Inductors 132
Inductors in a Series and in Parallel 132
Transients and Transient Analysis 133
Inductors and Capacitors 134
Current Lag in an Inductor 134

TABLE OF CONTENTS

The DC LR Circuit 136
The Time Constant (Tau) of the LR Circuit 140
Using Laplace Transforms 141
The Time the Circuit Is Switched On 141
    The Applied Voltage V_{Supply} 142
    The Current *i* Used in iR 142
    The Voltage Across the Resistor VR 143
    The Differential of the Current i 143
Partial Fractions 146
Transient Analysis in TINA 155
The Decaying Current 158
The RL Circuit with Some Initial Conditions 164
The Simulation 171
The Voltage Across the Resistor and the Inductor 181
The Voltage Expressions During Decay 182
Supplying the DC LR Circuit with an Irregular Supply 185
The Power and Energy in an Inductor 190
The Car Ignition Circuit 192
Rearrange the Current Growth Expression for Time t 199
Chapter 4 Exercises 202
    Exercise 4.1 203
    Exercise 4.2 204
    Exercise 4.3 204
Summary 204
    Answers to Exercise 4.1 205
    Answers to Exercise 4.2 205
    Answers to Exercise 4.3 205

TABLE OF CONTENTS

Chapter 5: DC Transients in CR Circuits 207
What Is a Capacitor? 208
Example 5.1 210
The Parallel Plate Capacitor 212
Example 5.2 212
Capacitors in Series 212
Example 5.3 213
Example 5.4 213
The Charge on a Capacitor 215
The Impedance of a Capacitor 222
The CR Transient with No Initial Voltage Across the Capacitor 222
Using the Charge Q in a Capacitor 231
Exercise 5.1 232
Example 5.5 232
The Current in the DC CR Transient Circuit 234
Example 5.6 235
Using Laplace Transforms 237
Expressions for Periods of Growth 248
Discharging the Capacitor 250
Example 5.7 254
The CR Transient with Initial Conditions 258
Exercise 5.2 258
Example 5.8 258
Supplying the DC Transient CR Circuit with an Irregular Waveform 262
The Initial 2ms Time Period 262
The First Charge-Up Period 263
The First Discharge Period 263

TABLE OF CONTENTS

The Current Flowing During the First Discharge Period 264

The Second Charge-Up Period 265

The Second Discharge Period 266

Exercise 5.3 269

Summary 271

Answers to Exercise 5.3 272

Chapter 6: The AC Voltage 275

Generating the AC Voltage 275

Generating AC Voltage 279

Calculating the RMS of a Waveform 291

The RMS of a Sine Wave 293

Impedance 297

Argand Diagrams 300

Calculating Z_T Using Trigonometry 303

Calculating the Current and Volt Drops in the Circuit 305

Using Complex Numbers to Represent Phasor Quantities 308

The Value of j 308

j Means Moving Through $90°$ 311

Complex Numbers 313

The Resistor Capacitor Circuit 318

Converting Rectangular to Polar and Polar to Rectangular Formats 321

Example 6.1 323

Example 6.2 324

Adding the Two Volt Drops 329

Example 6.3 331

Using the Complex Conjugate 334

xiii

TABLE OF CONTENTS

    Example 6.4 334
    Example 6.5 335
    Exercise 6.1 340
    Exercise 6.2 343
    Exercise 6.3 343
Rectification 343
Full-Wave Rectification 347
    Full-Wave Rectification Using the Bridge Rectifier 348
Smoothing 349
A Full-Wave Rectifier Power Supply 353
    Exercise 6.4 357
Summary 357
    Answers to Exercise 6.1 357
    Answers to Exercise 6.2 358
    Answers to Exercise 6.3 359

Chapter 7: The Series RLC Circuit 361

The First Circuit in an Audio System 361
The Resonant Frequency of the Series RLC Circuit 362
    Example 7.1 365
Selectivity and Bandwidth 372
The Bandwidth and Selectivity of the Series RLC Circuit 377
The Quality Factor Q in a Series RLC Circuit 379
    Example 7.2 385
The Parallel Circuit at Resonance and Dynamic Impedance 390
    Example 7.3 390
The Currents Flowing in the Parallel Circuit 402

TABLE OF CONTENTS

Example 7.4 402
The Current Through the Capacitor (i_C) 408
Exercise 7.1 411
Exercise 7.2 414
The Quality Factor (Q) of the Parallel RLC Circuit 414
The Tuned Amplifier 416
An Alternative Expression for Z_T 417
Example 7.5 419
Exercise 7.3 423
Exercise 7.4 424
Summary 425
Answers to Exercise 7.3 426
Answers to Exercise 7.4 426

Chapter 8: AC Analysis 427
Example 8.1 427
Thevenin's Equivalent Circuit for a Circuit with Multiple Sources 432
Example 8.2 432
Example 8.3 437
The Maximum Power in the Load 440
Example 8.4 440
Thevenin's Impedance Z_{THEV} 441
The Power in the Load 448
Example 8.5 450
The Superposition Theory 456
Example 8.6 457
Using Thevenin's Theory to Confirm the Result 463
Example 8.7 468

TABLE OF CONTENTS

Splitting a Circuit into Different Sections 475
    Example 8.8 475
An Alternative Approach 479
Converting a Complex Number into Components 484
    Exercise 8.1 485
Norton's Theory 486
    Example 8.9 486
    Exercise 8.2 490
    Exercise 8.3 492
    Exercise 8.4 493
Summary 495
    Answers to Exercise 8.2 495
    Answers to Exercise 8.3 496
    Answers to Exercise 8.4 496

Chapter 9: Magnetism, the Electromagnet, and the Inductor 497

Magnetism 497
Michael Faraday: 1791 to 1867 498
Electromagnetism 498
The Magnetomotive Force (F) 500
Flux Density (B) 500
Nikola Tesla: 1856 to 1943 501
Flux, Flux Density, and the Coil 502
Permeability 504
The Magnetising Force (H) 506
A Basic Electromagnet 507
    Example 9.1 509

xvi

TABLE OF CONTENTS

The Magnetic Circuit 511
Reluctance 513
Comparisons Between Magnetic and Electrical Circuit 518
The B/H Curve 520
Absolute Permeability of the Material 521
Relays 523
Magnetic Calculations Examples 524
    Example 9.2 525
    Example 9.3 525
    Example 9.4 526
    Example 9.5 526
    Example 9.6 528
    Example 9.7 528
Inductance and Magnetism 530
The Impedance of a Coil 532
Lenz's Law 534
The Induced Voltage Across an Inductor 537
The Current Flowing Through an Inductor 544
The Expressions for Inductance (L) 547
Magnetic Fields and Motors 549
The BIL and BLU Laws 553
    Example 9.8 553
    Example 9.9 555
    Example 9.10 556
Generating a Voltage Across a Conductor 557
    Example 9.11 559
    Example 9.12 559
    Example 9.13 560

TABLE OF CONTENTS

    Fleming's Right-Hand Rule 560

    Exercises for Chapter 9 561

        Exercise 9.1 561

        Exercise 9.2 563

        Exercise 9.3 563

        Exercise 9.4 565

    Summary 566

Chapter 10: Using TINA 12 569

    What Are ECAD and TINA 12? 569

    Running the Software 570

    Creating Your First Test Circuit 572

    Running the AC Analysis 578

    Transient Analysis 581

    Using the Oscilloscope 585

    Summary 591

Appendix 1 593

Index 607

About the Author

Hubert Henry Ward has been a college lecturer since 1993 and has over 24 years of experience teaching electrical and electronic engineering for the Higher National Certificate (HNC) and the Higher National Diploma (HND). Hubert has also spent time as a consultant in embedded programming in the assembler and C languages and was the UK technical expert in mechatronics, where he trained the UK team for the Skills Olympics in Seoul in 2001. He is also happily married to his wife Ann, with whom he has two wonderful children, Claire and Vincent.

About the Technical Reviewer

Farzin Asadi received his BS in electronics engineering, his MS in control engineering, and his PhD in mechatronics engineering. Currently, he is with the Department of Computer Engineering at the OSTIM Technical University, Ankara, Turkey. Dr. Asadi has published over 40 international papers and 30 books. His research interests include switching converters, control theory, robust control of power electronics converters, and robotics.

Introduction

This book is intended to be used as a reference for anyone who wants to learn about electrical circuits and how to analyse them. This book assumes that you have no prior understanding of the subject, as it starts with the fundamental principles of current and voltage. As you move through the book, you will learn what DC and AC are, learn about Ohm's Law and all the relevant theorems used to analyse DC, as well as some basic, single-phase AC circuits.

The book leads to the *Mastering Circuit Analysis* book, which covers a more in-depth analysis of AC electrical circuits.

The book is a useful reference for students studying an electrical and electronic engineering course such as ONC or OND or staring out on an HNC or HND. It is also useful reference for anyone working in the field of electrical and electronic engineering.

I hope you find the book informative and useful; thanks for taking the time to read it.

CHAPTER 1

Electrical Current

This chapter explains what electrical current is. It looks at the main building blocks of electrical analysis—Amps, Volts, and resistance. It also looks at some of the common terms, such as DC, PD, AC, and RMS.

The chapter covers three passive components—resistors, inductors, and capacitors. It then looks at the fundamental laws used in electrical analysis—Ohm's Law and Kirchhoff's Laws. Throughout the chapter, and indeed the book, you will use the ECAD software TINA to carry out the laboratory work, which reinforces the concepts in each chapter. Finally, this chapter explains how to use color-coding with respect to resistors.

At the end of this chapter, you will:

- Understand what a "sea of electrons" is and what makes a good conductor and a good insulator.
- Understand what current and voltage are.
- Understand what PD, DC, and AC are.
- Understand what conventional and electron current flow are.
- Understand what makes up a simple DC source.
- Understand the relationship between current I, charge Q, and time t.
- Understand what resistance is and how it is related to the resistivity of a material.

CHAPTER 1   ELECTRICAL CURRENT

- Understand what AC voltage is and what the term RMS means.
- Be able to recognise the value of resistors.

The Main Operation of All Electrical Circuits

The main concept of what engineers are trying to do with electrical circuits is move the energy from the source—be it a DC battery or an AC power source—to a load. With the load, they will convert that energy into something useful, such as sound, light or movement. Electrical current is the medium that carries the energy around the circuit. Therefore, we should start by looking at what *current* is.

The Mighty Electron

The *electron* is at the very heart of electricity. It is the workhorse of all electrical circuits, and I think, it is why we have given the subject the name *elec*tricity. However, the electron is so small that it takes approximately 1 million, million, million, million, million (or $1.098\ E^{30)}$) electrons to make one gram of mass; that's a lot of electrons! Yes, the mass of an electron has been measured. No, we won't be repeating that experiment, as the method scientists used to measure its mass is quite extraordinary and beyond my capability to repeat.

The mass of an electron, given the symbol m_e, has been measured to be:

$$m_e = 9.10939 E^{-31}\ kg$$

I use the capitol E to signify the x10 button, or EXP button, on your calculator when you want to indicate the power of a number. For example.

$$1000 = 1 \times 10^3$$

I will write this as

$$1000 = 1E^3$$

Another example is

$$0.0001 = 100 \times 10^{-6}$$

I will write this as

$$0.0001 = 100E^{-6}$$

One last example is

$$100,000 = 100 \times 10^3$$

I will write this as.

$$100,000 = 100E^3 = 100k$$

I discuss this concept more closely when covering engineering numbers in Chapter 2, especially the difference between scientific notation and engineering numbers.

The Charge C of an Electron

I am not sure what the difference is between *charge* and *energy*; that is probably left to a far more intelligent people than me. I think that an electron has an inherent charge. Then, depending on how we displace electrons, they can possess some form of energy. This can be potential energy (PE), such as when it has the *potential* to move from a negative plate to a positive plate of a battery, using electron flow. Or this can be kinetic energy (KE). as it moves around the circuit. You learn more about these ideas later in this chapter.

CHAPTER 1   ELECTRICAL CURRENT

It was Charles Coulomb, conducting some experiments back in 1888, who discovered that the electron had some form of energy, which he termed *electrical charge*. He named the unit for charge the *Coulomb*, after himself, and he measured the charge on the electron, given the symbol e, as follows:

$$e = 1.6022 E^{-19} \, C$$

Note that the C stands for Coulomb, which is basically why we use the letter *I* for current—not because we can't spell but because C is already taken. I will also add more confusion when we start looking at capacitors, but that's for later.

During these experiments, Charles Coulomb determined that the electron was attracted to the nucleus of an atom, by an invisible force pulling the electron toward the nucleus. If this attraction is compared to the attraction of magnets, then, as with magnets, if like poles repel and unlike poles attract, the electron must be attracted by an unlike or opposite charge on the nucleus.

He used the convention of positive and negative charge and stated that the electron had a negative charge while the nucleus, or rather something inside the nucleus, had a positive charge. The difference in these charges brings the electron close to the nucleus and allows it to settle down into its orbits around the nucleus. The nucleus attracts the electron, and nearby electrons repel the electron, thus holding it in some sort of orbit. When there are enough electrons orbiting the nucleus, the atom is said to be in a stable state, as the positive attractive force of the nucleus is cancelled out by the negative charge of the electrons orbiting the nucleus.

It is the protons inside the nucleus that have a positive charge. There are also neutrons inside the nucleus that have, yes guessed it, a neutral charge on them. One last thing before we leave these atoms—the number of protons in the nucleus gives the elements their numbers on the periodic table.

CHAPTER 1   ELECTRICAL CURRENT

The Sea of Free Electrons

In electrical engineering, we use insulators and conductors. One of the main insulators is ceramics and one of the main conductors is copper. We use copper, because in its normal state there is a continual movement of electrons accelerating away from, and moving to, the nucleus of nearby copper atoms. This is termed a *sea of free electrons* all jumping, or being pushed, from one copper atom to another.

However, you must realise that this movement of electrons is totally random and they are jumping about in all different directions. This is what makes copper a good conductor because, as you will see, it does not need much effort to make these electrons move in a uniform direction and create a flow of current. Indeed, if you studied the copper atom, you would see that it has one lone electron in its outer shell (called the *valence shell*). This lone electron easily moves out of its orbit, which leaves the atom trying very hard to replace the electron it has lost. This is happening all the time, with all the many atoms that make up a length of copper wire, and that is why we say copper has a *sea* of free electrons.

An insulator is a material that is made up of atoms whose electrons are tightly bound to their nuclei, so they are not easily forced out of their orbits. However, the study of electrons is left for another book. This book concentrates on the use of electricity.

Current Flow

Why is the sea of electrons not current flow? The answer is quite simple in that the electrons are moving around in all different directions. The definition of current explains why this is not current flow. We need to change this random movement in the copper wire into current flow. The definition of current flow is as follows:

> *Current flow is the movement of electrons in a uniform direction.*

CHAPTER 1   ELECTRICAL CURRENT

To change this random movement of the sea of electrons in copper into current flow, we need to apply a force that will make the electrons move in a uniform direction. That force comes in the form of an attractive force, as in a voltage. We know that electrons have a negative charge on them and that they can be attracted to move toward a positive charge. That is what we do when we apply a voltage across the copper wire. The positive terminal of the voltage source, which is really a material that has had some electrons stripped from it, creates a massive attractive force that makes the electrons rush toward the positive plate in the voltage source. In this way, we get current flow. One problem is that the current flow would be too great if we just placed a length of copper wire across the voltage source. This is because the electrons would rush to the positive plate, and so we must do something to slow the electrons down. You will learn later in this chapter what we do.

In electrical and electronic engineering, we use two types of current flow:

- Conventional current flow
- Electron flow

I tend to think, and I am not saying it is correct, that engineers first decided that current flowed from a positive potential to a negative or lower potential. However, later it was shown that electrons flow from the negative plate of a source to the positive plate. So, in respect for the early scientist, engineers decided to call the first idea of current flow *conventional current*, as it was the convention to apply this direction of current flow in circuit analysis. They then called the other flow *electron flow*. In this book, we use conventional current flow in all the circuit analyses.

An example of how you use this conventional current flow in circuit analysis is shown in Figure 1-1. I also use Figure 1-1 to explain some of the symbols used in electrical analysis.

CHAPTER 1   ELECTRICAL CURRENT

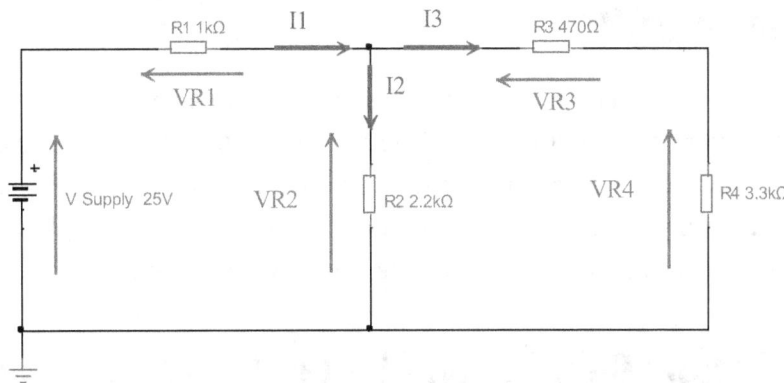

Figure 1-1. *A typical DC circuit using conventional current flow*

The idea of adding the voltage arrows in red, and the current arrows in blue to the circuit drawing helps engineers analyse the circuit. The voltage arrows follow the convention, in that the arrowhead points to the positive end of the volt drop. We use these voltage arrows to help us apply Kirchhoff's Voltage Law, KVL, in Chapter 2.

Using the convention that current flows from positive to negative, you can place the current arrows, in blue, as shown in Figure 1-1. The convention also states that conventional current will always flow into the positive end of a volt drop. Note that V_{supply} is not a volt drop; it is a voltage source, and conventional current will always flow out of the positive end of a voltage source and into the negative end. The current arrows help us apply Kirchhoff's Current Law, KCL, when we use it in Chapter 2. You will use these conventions later in the book when you analyse the electrical circuits.

When scientists realised that electrons flowed in the opposite direction, they simply called this *electron flow* and kept using conventional current flow in their analyses. However, there are some who do adopt the electron flow in their analyses.

7

CHAPTER 1   ELECTRICAL CURRENT

What Is DC?

DC stands for *direct current,* which doesn't really explain what it is. A slightly better name might be *unidirectional current,* UDC, as DC current flows in one direction only. DC sources are normally batteries, although we can use power supplies that usually convert the main AC supply to DC using rectifying circuits that use diodes and other components.

The Simple Cell, PD, and Voltage

The simple cell is probably one of the most basic sources of DC that we used in electrical circuits.

The basic construction of a simple cell is shown in Figure 1-2.

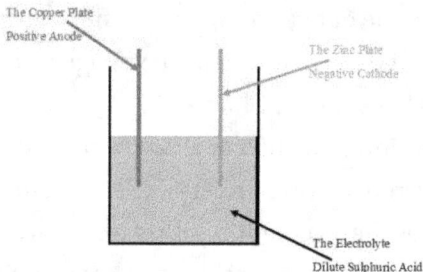

Figure 1-2. The basic wet cell

    This figure shows two electrodes immersed in an electrolyte. I am not a chemical engineer and so I won't be going into a technical description of what happens in a simple cell. I will just say that because of the chemical action electrons are stripped from the copper plate and deposited on the zinc plate. Therefore, the zinc plate has an excess of electrons, which gives it a negative potential. The copper plate has a shortage of electrons, giving it a positive potential. This creates a *potential difference* (PD) or *voltage* across the terminals of the cell. PD is sometimes referred to as EMF, which stands for electro-motive force, as it is the force that motivates electrons to flow in a circuit. Different types of simple or wet cells create different EMFs. For example, zinc/copper in sulfuric acid = 0.75v, nickel/cadmium = 1.3v, and the lead/acid cells = 1.8v. Really though, these are the EMFs produced by a single cell of those materials.

Batteries are a collection of these cells placed in a series to increase the voltage or in parallel to increase the current capability. The term *battery* comes from the naval term, which describes a collection of guns (i.e., a battery of guns). However, nowadays we use the term battery to cover a wide range of voltage sources.

The Dry Cell

The Leclanché cell is an example of a dry cell. Figure 1-3 shows the typical makeup of a Leclanché cell.

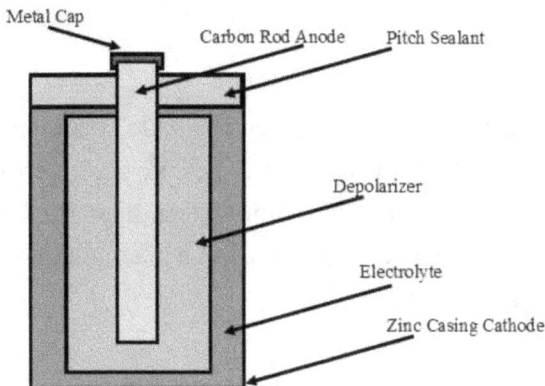

Figure 1-3. *The Leclanché cell*

This is basically a zinc can filled with an *electrolyte* (a substance that conducts electricity through the movement of ions). The electrolyte is typically a paste solution made up of sal ammoniac (ammonium chloride), zinc chloride, and plaster of Paris. The anode, made of a carbon rod, is the positive plate of the cell and the zinc casing is the negative plate.

CHAPTER 1   ELECTRICAL CURRENT

The *depolariser*, made from a paste of ammonium chloride, magnesium dioxide, and powdered carbon, is used to slow down the production of hydrogen on the carbon rod. These cells typically produce an EMF of 1.5V and they are typically known as AA or AAA batteries that we commonly use.

Figure 1-4 shows another dry cell, called the mercury cell.

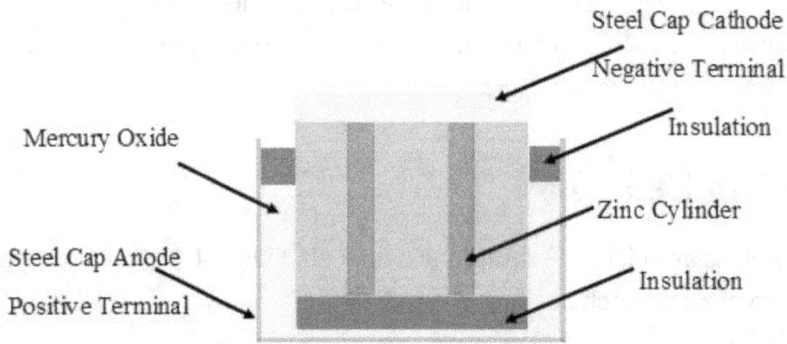

Figure 1-4. *The mercury cell*

The main difference between this cell and the Leclanché cell is that the EMF is typically 1.3V. Also, the outer casing is the positive anode terminal, and the smaller cap is the negative cathode terminal. These mercury cells are smaller than Leclanché cells and are used in smaller devices, such as hearing aids and small toys.

Primary and Secondary Cells

Primary cells cannot be recharged; these are mostly dry cells such as Leclanché and Mercury cells. However, there now exist dry cells that can be recharged, called the nickel cadmium dry cell.

The basic wet cell is a secondary type of cell. It can be recharged. The most common type is the lead acid cell, which is used in the manufacture of car batteries.

CHAPTER 1   ELECTRICAL CURRENT

The Difference Between EMF and PDs or Voltage

The EMFs of the cells I discussed are produced by cells with no circuit or load connected to them. This is sometimes called the *no load potential* or voltage. When a load is connected across the cell, by connecting it to a circuit, a current flows out of the cell. If this current is very small, the potential across the terminals of the battery (termed the PD or potential difference) will be very close to the EMF of the cell. However, if the current starts to increase, the PD will be less than the EMF of the cell. This is because there will be some internal resistance within the cell due to that fact that the chemicals and electrodes don't make perfect connections. That is why, when discussing these cells, we use these terms:

- *EMF* is the no load potential of the cell.
- *PD* is the potential difference across the terminals when a load is connected across the cell.
- *RS* is the internal resistance of the source or cell.

Example 1.1

A cell has an EMF of 1.5V. If it has an internal resistance of 0.1Ω, determine the PD across the terminals if it was connected to a load that demanded 2A from the cell.

In Chapter 2, you will learn about Ohm's Law, but for now you can use one of the relationships from that law that states the following:

$$V = IR$$

This means that as current flows through a resistance, there is a voltage drop across that resistance. This voltage drop is defined as follows:

$$V = 2 \times 0.1 = 0.2V$$

11

CHAPTER 1   ELECTRICAL CURRENT

This means that the PD across the terminals of the cell will be as follows:

$$PD = EMF - IR = 1.5 - 0.2 = 1.3V$$

This can be confirmed by looking at the circuit shown in Figure 1-5.

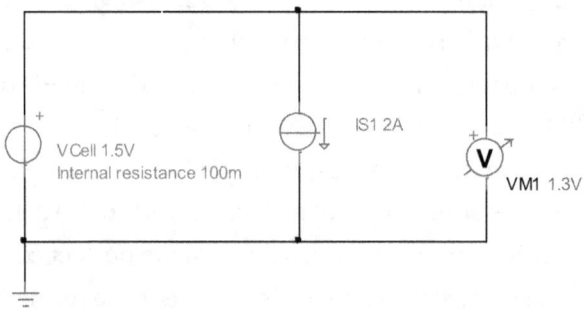

Figure 1-5. *The single-cell DC source with an internal resistance of 0.1Ω*

The single cell shown in Figure 1-5 has an EMF of 1.5V. However, it has an internal resistance of 0.1Ω, which is 100mΩ in engineering format. You can see that when a current of 2A is drawn from the cell, the PD falls to the expected 1.3V.

I am using a simulation from the ECAD software used throughout this book. Chapter 10 explains how to create these circuits and run the simulations using this ECAD software. If you are not experienced with using ECAD software, perhaps you should read some of Chapter 10 now. It takes you through creating the circuits and running the simulation as they are presented in the book. The circuit shown in Figure 1-5 is one of the first circuits described in that chapter.

CHAPTER 1   ELECTRICAL CURRENT

Connecting Cells in Series and Parallel

I stated that a battery is really a collection of connected cells. They can be connected in a series or in parallel. If you connect them in a series, as shown in Figure 1-6, you can see that the voltage at the output is simply the sum of the three EMFs. This is when we limit the current taken from the cells to a very small value of 100µA. However, you should be aware that the internal resistances will also be in a series and so add together as well. Figure 1-7 shows that, when you draw a current of 2A from the cells, the PD reduces due to the voltage drop across the three internal impedances.

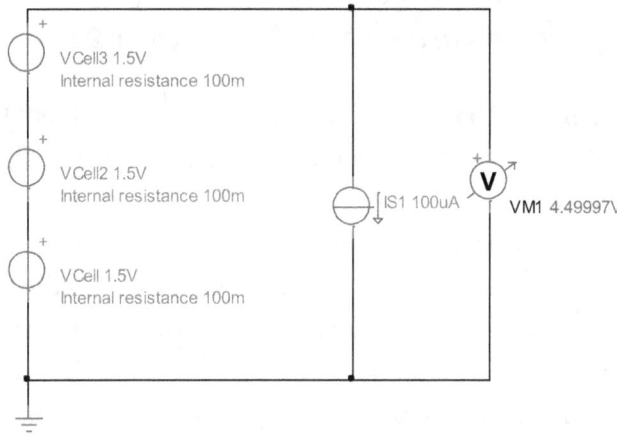

Figure 1-6. *Three cells in a series with no load current*

13

CHAPTER 1   ELECTRICAL CURRENT

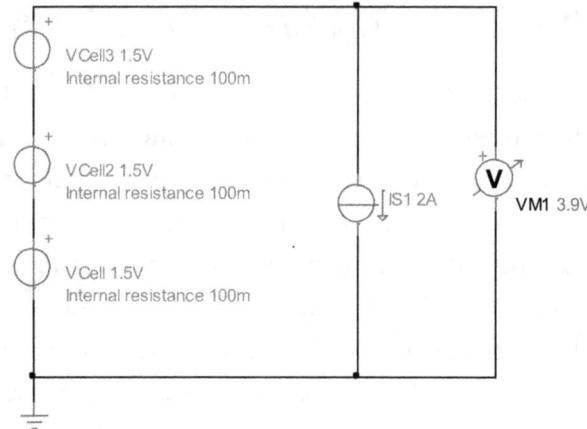

Figure 1-7. *Three cells in a series with a current of 2A*

In Figure 1-6, the PD is very nearly the same as the total EMF of 1.5+1.5+1.5 = 4.5V. However, when the current is 2A, the PD drops to 3.9V, as shown in Figure 1-7.

If you connect the same three cells in parallel, as shown in Figure 1-8, you can see that the PD cannot be greater than the 1.5V of the individual EMFs. However, even with a current of 2A being drawn from the connected cells, the PD is very close to the 1.5V EMF. This because the internal resistances of 0.1Ω are now connected in parallel. This has the effect of reducing the resistance to 0.0333rΩ, which reduces the voltage dropped across the internal resistance to 0.06667V.

Another way of looking at it is that the total current of 2A demanded by the circuit connected to the cells will be shared between the three cells equally. That means that each cell supplies 666.667mA of current. This is confirmed by the results in Figure 1-8.

CHAPTER 1   ELECTRICAL CURRENT

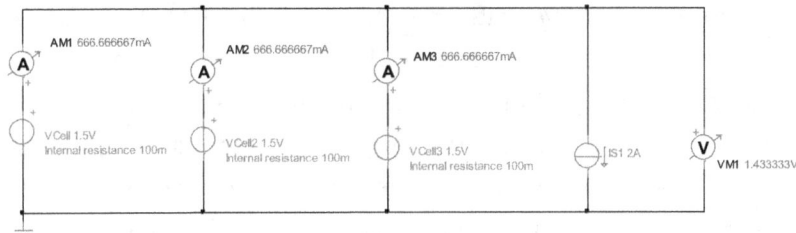

Figure 1-8. *The three cells connected in parallel*

Voltage

The units for EMF and PD are volts, after the Italian physicist Alessandro Volta. His work in the early 1800s, with what is now known as the *voltaic pile,* produced the early type of cell used to produce a voltage. In recognition of his work, the units of volts were named after him. His work and that of others determined a definition for voltage:

1 volt is the usage of 1 Joule of energy per Coulomb of charge.

A simple way of defining voltage is as follows:

Voltage is the force that makes the electrons move in the circuit.

Energy in Current Flow and the Amp

When looking into energy in electrical circuits, we must consider state the *Law of Conservation of Energy,* which states:

Energy cannot be created or destroyed; it can only be converted into another format.

We will consider how the energy changes as the current carries it around the circuit. Originally, we had, with respect to a battery, *chemical energy* in the chemical solution of the battery cells. This energy strips

15

CHAPTER 1 ELECTRICAL CURRENT

electrons from the positive plate and deposits them on the negative plate, thus creating a potential energy difference across the terminals of the battery. This happens with wet cells and dry cells. This means that the chemical energy in the battery changes into potential energy in the electron, because when the electron gets to the negative plate, it has the potential to move around the circuit to the positive plate. The chemical energy of the solution prevents the electron from moving through the battery back to the positive plate unless the battery is flat.

Once the circuit is closed, the potential energy on the electron forces the electron to move. The electron then gains kinetic energy (KE), as the electron has a mass and it is moving. Note that kinetic energy can be expressed as follows:

$$KE = \frac{1}{2}mv^2$$

Where m is the mass of the electron and ' is the velocity of the electron as it moves around the circuit.

The electron then moves around the circuit until it reaches the components in the circuit. It is not the same electron moving all the way around the circuit; it is one electron bumping into another and passing the KE onto the next. If the component is a resistor, the electron will slow down. This slowing down of the electron means that the kinetic energy is reduced. However, using the Law of Conservation of Energy, energy cannot be destroyed—it must be converted into another form. Indeed, the energy is converted into heat energy, which is why resistors get hot.

Other components, such as conductors and capacitors, store energy. Inductors store the energy as a magnetic field around them, and capacitors store it as a charge between the plates of the capacitor. This energy can also be used to create movement, as with motors, or sound, as with speakers.

CHAPTER 1   ELECTRICAL CURRENT

The Amp/Ampere

An electrical circuit must have a *circ*ular path along which *elec*trons are forced to move by a applying a voltage, or an EMF, to the circuit. As the electrons move, they transfer energy from the source to a load. Note that current flow is defined as follows:

Current flow is the movement of electrons in a uniform direction.

The unit of current is an ampere or amp and the one amp is defined as follows:

One amp of current is 1 Coulomb of charge passing a point in one second.

It is the electron that carries the charge, or energy, around the circuit. The charge on an electron has been measured to be $1.602E^{-19}$ Coulombs. Therefore, it takes $6.241E^{18}$ electrons passing a point in one second to constitute a current flow of 1 amp. That is a lot of electrons, but they are very, very small.

Resistance and Resistivity

I mentioned earlier that we could not just put a wire across the voltage supply, as this would end up with the electrons rushing too fast to the positive plate of the voltage source. This means there would be too much current flowing and the wire would most likely burn out or worse. If you were ever foolish enough to try putting a spanner across the terminals of a car battery, you could weld the spanner to the battery. You must not try this as it would be very dangerous—car batteries can supply 80amps and more. It only takes 50mA across your heart to cause it to go into fibrillations, so a car battery can easily kill you. Note that it is current that

CHAPTER 1   ELECTRICAL CURRENT

kills, whereas voltage usually flings you across the room. However, DC voltage could make you stick to the source. All this means is that you must treat voltage and current with respect. A good engineer takes all necessary precautions. A bad engineer thinks they know better and takes shortcuts.

So, what does a resistor do. Well, I think the hint is in the name, as it *resists* current flow. The resistor actually slows down the velocity of the electron, which is why it gets hot. The energy taken from the electron, as it slows down, is converted into heat. All materials have something termed resistivity. A good insulator has a very high level of resistivity whereas a good conductor has a very low level of resistivity. The resistivity is a constant for the material and resistance is related to the cross-sectional area in m² and its length in meters. The longer the length of the wire, the greater the resistance. However, the greater the cross-sectional area of the wire, the easier it is to allow this large number of electrons to pass a point, which means the greater the current flow. The relationship between resistance with resistivity, length, and the cross-sectional area of a material can be expressed as follows:

$$R = \frac{\rho L}{A}$$

Where:

- R is resistance in Ω ohms
- ρ is resistivity also in Ω ohms
- L is length in meters
- A is the cross-sectional area in m²

The resistivity of a range of materials is listed in Table 1-1.

Table 1-1. Resistivity of Various Materials

Material	Resistivity ρ (Ω.m)	Temperature Coefficient α (Ω. °C)
Conductors		
Silver	$1.59E^{-8}$	0.0061
Copper	$1.68E^{-8}$	0.0068
Gold	$2.44E^{-8}$	0.0034
Aluminium	$2.65E^{-8}$	0.0043
Semiconductors		
Germanium	$1E^{-3} - 500E^{-3}$	-0.05
Silicon	0.1 – 60	-0.07
Insulators		
Glass	$10E^{9} - 10E^{12}$	
Hard rubber	$10E^{13} - 10E^{15}$	

This table shows that silver has a lower resistivity than copper, but it is more expensive, so most wires are made out of copper. The table also gives a value for α, which is the temperature coefficient for the materials. This is because the resistance of most materials varies with temperature. A positive coefficient (shown for silver to aluminium) means the resistivity increases with temperature.

When it comes to electrical circuits, as with printed circuit boards, the copper tracks have resistance along their lengths. This means that the resistance at one end of the track could be higher than at the other end. This could be a very small difference, but if a lot of current is flowing through that track, there could be a voltage difference across the length

CHAPTER 1   ELECTRICAL CURRENT

of the track. That is why the thickest track on any PCB is the earth return track, as nearly all the current in the circuit must flow through it. This means that the 0V wanted on the Earth or return track might be slightly different at one end of the track compared to the other end, due to the voltage drop across the track. However, if the track is very thick, the cross-sectional area A could be large and so could keep the resistance of this track to a minimum. More modern PCBs have a whole layer devoted to the Earth track and the same can be done for the power track.

Let's look at the resistance of some typical cables. Typical home electrical circuits are usually 6mm in diameter. The cross-sectional area, CSA, of a wire can be calculated using this equation:

$$CSA = \pi r^2 \text{ or } \frac{\pi D^2}{4}$$

This means that the CSA of a typical cable in the home could be as follows:

$$CSA = \frac{\pi(0.002)^2}{4} = 3.14E^{-6} m^2$$

This means that a 50m length of that wire would have a resistance of:

$$R = \frac{1.68E^{-8} \times 50}{3.14E^{-6}} = 267.38E^{-3} = 267.38 \, m\Omega$$

This may not seem like a lot, but if you had 13amps of current flowing through it, then you would have a voltage drop of 3.48v across just the cable. If the length of the wire increased to 50km, the voltage drop would be in kilovolts. This problem must be addressed when we transmit electricity around the country. You will learn more about how this is overcome later, when we look at transmitting AC around the country.

CHAPTER 1   ELECTRICAL CURRENT

Current and Charge Calculations

I stated that current is the movement of charge over time. You can use the following expression to relate current to charge and time:

$$I = \frac{Q}{t}$$

Where:

- *I* stands for current (remember that *C* is used for Coulombs, which are the units of charge).
- *Q* stands for charge.
- *t* stands for time.

Example 1.2

Calculate how much current is flowing if 26 Coulombs of charge pass a point in two seconds.

This can be calculated as follows:

$$I = \frac{Q}{t} = \frac{26}{2} = 13 \, Amps$$

Example 1.3

Calculate how much charge is being transferred when a battery is connected to a current of 10A for a period of 25 seconds.

To do this, you need to rearrange the expression for *I* into one for *Q*. This means getting the term *Q* on its own. To do this, you need to multiply both sides of the expression by *t*. This gives:

$$I \times t = \frac{Q}{t} \times t$$

CHAPTER 1   ELECTRICAL CURRENT

The two *t*s on the right cancel out and you are left with this:

$$Q = It$$

Putting in the values, you would get:

$$Q = 10 \times 25 = 250 \; Coulombs \; of \; charge$$

Example 1.4

Calculate how long you need to keep a current of 2.5A flowing if you want to pass a charge of 200 C in a circuit.

You first need to transpose the expression for time *t*.

$$I = \frac{Q}{t}$$

To do this, you multiply both sides by *t*, which gives the following:

$$tI = \frac{Q}{t} \times t \quad \therefore tI = Q$$

Now divide both sides by *I* (or multiply both sides by 1/*I*). This gives the following:

$$tI \times \frac{1}{I} = Q \times \frac{1}{I} \quad \therefore t = \frac{Q}{I}$$

Putting in the values results in:

$$t = \frac{200}{2.5} = 80 \; \text{sec}$$

You should be able to transpose a simple three-term expression like this without any problem. As an engineer, you will have to transpose much more difficult expressions as you progress.

CHAPTER 1   ELECTRICAL CURRENT

Alternating Current (AC)

This section takes a brief look at AC. The term AC stands for *alternating current,* as the current alternates; it changes the direction in which it flows around the circuit. At one point in time, it is being forced to move around the circuit in one direction and then at another point in time it is being forced to move in the opposite direction. For that to happen, the supply voltage must change its polarity to push the current in the different direction. However, conventional current can be, and is, applied to AC circuits. This is because the current still flows from the positive terminal toward the negative terminal. We generate this AC type of voltage by rotating a coil inside a magnetic field. This is covered in Chapter 8. For now, we look at a typical AC voltage, shown in Figure 1-9.

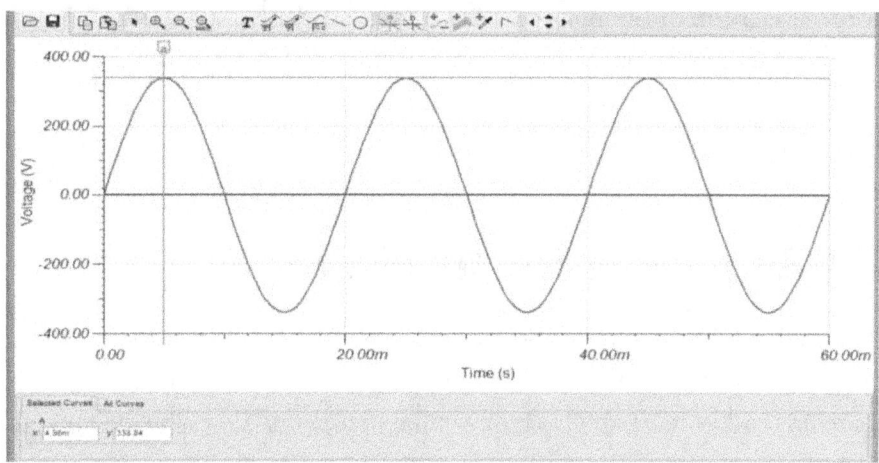

Figure 1-9. *A typical AC voltage*

Figure 1-9 shows what the UK mains voltage would look like if you displayed it on an oscilloscope. I am assuming that the RMS voltage of the UK mains is 240v. (This is what it was when I studied engineering, but now it is more likely to be around 220v.) For an RMS of 240v, the peak voltage would be 339v, as shown in Figure 1-9.

CHAPTER 1   ELECTRICAL CURRENT

In the UK, the turbines that rotate the coil inside the magnetic field rotate at a speed of 3,000 RPM. This produces the frequency of 50Hz, i.e., 50 cycles per second. The periodic time is the time required for the supply to move through one complete cycle, that is, go through all the values it has in its waveform.

$$F = \frac{1}{T} \text{ therefore } T = \frac{1}{F} = \frac{1}{50} = 20ms$$

Figure 1-9 shows that the time to complete one cycle is 20ms. We can see from Figure 1-9 that the voltage starts off at 0 and then rises positively until it reaches the peak of 339. It then reduces to 0 volts. From then on it starts to go negatively until it reaches -339v. Then it starts to rise until it reaches 0. At that point it starts to repeat the process. This happens by rotating a coil through $360°$ or 2π radians inside that magnetic field. Figure 1-9 shows clearly that the polarity of the voltage does change as it completes one cycle. That is why the current alternates, that is, it changes direction during each cycle.

The Root Mean Square (RMS)

You need to be able to describe the voltage of an AC supply by using one value that represents its overall voltage. If you tried to use the average of a sinusoidal AC voltage, to give it one value that would describe the voltage, you would get 0v, which is nonsense. This is because there are as many positive values as there are negative and so when you add the values to get the average, the sum would equal 0.

To get around this problem, we use the RMS value, which stands for *root mean square*. RMS is used to express the voltage of a sinusoidal AC voltage as one value. With the RMS, you square the expression for the voltage, which gets rid of any negative values, as a minus times a minus gives a positive result. This means you can then determine the mean,

CHAPTER 1   ELECTRICAL CURRENT

or average of that squared expression. This gives you a non-zero value. However, to cancel out the squaring of the expression at the beginning, you need to determine the square root of that result. This means you have a value that you can use to describe the AC voltage or quantity.

This may seem a cheat at first but the RMS value of the AC voltage does have a realistic value in that the RMS voltage is the same value of the DC voltage that would be required to get the same power in the load. This suggests that the 240v mains is like having a 240V DC battery in your home. Daft as that might seem, there is a simple experiment that might help you appreciate this concept. If you simulate the circuit shown in Figure 1-10, you could measure the current flowing through the 1kΩ load.

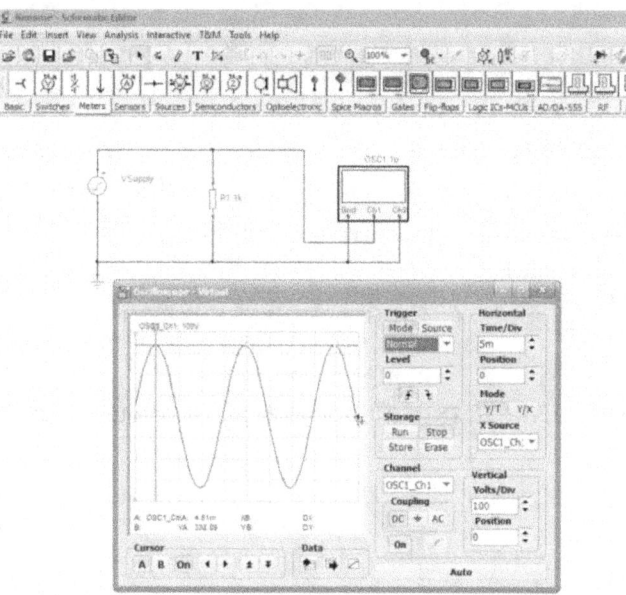

Figure 1-10. Test Simulation to Measure the Current Through R1

An oscilloscope cannot measure current; it can only measure voltage and time. However, you can use those measurements to calculate the frequency of the waveforms measured and, as in this case, the current flowing through the resistor R_1.

25

CHAPTER 1   ELECTRICAL CURRENT

To calculate the frequency, use this expression:

$$f = \frac{1}{T}$$

The term f is for frequency and T is for the periodic time. This is the time the waveform takes to go through one complete cycle that covers all the values the waveform has. This waveform is a simple sinusoidal wave and from the oscilloscope you can see it takes four divisions to complete one cycle. Each division is set to 5ms per division, so it takes 20ms to complete one cycle. Therefore, the value for T is 20ms. You can calculate the frequency as follows:

$$f = \frac{1}{20E^{-3}} = 50 Hz$$

To calculate the current flowing through R_1, you simply need to divide the peak voltage of the waveform by the value of the resistor. This would give you the peak value of the current as follows:

$$i_{Peak} = \frac{338.12}{1E^3} = 338.12 mA$$

Knowing that, the RMS of a sinewave can be calculated as follows:

$$rms = \frac{Peak}{\sqrt{2}}$$

The proof of the expression for the RMS is explained in Chapter 7. You can use that expression to determine the RMS current flowing through R_1, as follows:

$$i_{rms} = \frac{338.12 mA}{\sqrt{2}} = 239.07 mA$$

If a DC voltage of 240V was applied across a 1kΩ resistor, then the current flowing through the resistor can be calculated using Ohm's law, as follows:

$$I = \frac{V}{R} = \frac{240}{1E^3} = 240mA$$

This confirms that the RMS of the AC voltage represents the DC voltage required to get the same power in the load.

Power

Power is a measure of the rate at which we use energy. It has the units of watts. In electrical engineering, the basic expression for power is as follows:

$$P = VI \text{ watts}$$

To be more correct when dealing with AC circuits, the expression for power becomes:

$$P = viCos(\theta)$$

This is because, out of the three basic passive components in electrical circuits, it is only the resistor that dissipates power. The other two components only store the energy.

However, when looking at DC and purely resistive loads, we can ignore the Cos(θ) as θ = 0, and Cos(0) = 1.

Using the standard expression for power, we can develop two more expressions. Using Ohms law, we can express current as follows:

$$I = \frac{V}{R}$$

Substituting this for I in the expression for power, we get:

$$P = V \times \frac{V}{R} \therefore P = \frac{V^2}{R}$$

Also transposing Ohm's law for V, we can say:

$$V = IR$$

If we now substitute this into the expression for power, we get:

$$P = IR \times I \therefore P = I^2 R$$

That is why we sometimes refer to power loss as I²R losses.

There is one final expression you can use to relate power to charge Q. Knowing that we can express current I as follows:

$$I = \frac{Q}{t}$$

We can say:

$$P = V \times \frac{Q}{t} \therefore P = \frac{VQ}{t}$$

Earlier in this chapter, I stated that 1v was 1 Joule of energy per Coulomb of charge. This means that we can express V as follows:

$$V = \frac{Joule}{Q}$$

Which we can transpose for energy (Joule) as follows:

$$Joule = VQ$$

CHAPTER 1 ELECTRICAL CURRENT

This confirms that power is the rate at which we use Joules, as we can say this:

$$P = \frac{VQ}{t} \therefore P = \frac{Joule}{t}$$

Resistor Types

Carbon film resistors are the most common type of resistors by hobbyists and small manufacturers. They come in standard values with different wattage ratings. The E12 is a common standard in the values of resistors. It uses 12 values, hence the series name, going from 1.0 to 8.2 in each decade (i.e., from 1 to 9). It then multiplies these base values by 10 to move to the next decade. In this way, Table 1-2 list the four first decades in the E12 series of resistors.

There are many other types of resistors, but the carbon film types are adequate for most applications. You should always ensure that the wattage rating for the resistor is high enough for your application. The common wattage ratings are $1/8^{th}$, 1/4, ½, and 1 watt. There are higher wattage ratings, but they are more specialised.

Table 1-2. The E12 Series of Resistor Values

1.0	1.2	1.5	1.8	2.2	2.7	3.3	3.9	4.7	5.6	6.8	8.2
10	12	15	18	22	27	33	39	47	56	68	82
100	120	150	180	220	270	330	390	470	56	680	820
1k	1.2k	1.5k	1.8k	2.2k	2.7k	3.3k	3.9k	4.7k	5.6k	6.8k	8.2k
10k	12k	15k	18k	22k	27k	33k	39k	47k	56k	68k	82k

CHAPTER 1   ELECTRICAL CURRENT

The other series split the 1 to 10 range of values according to the number of the series. In this way, we have the following:

- The E3 series uses three values—1.0, 2.2, and 4.7.
- The E6 series uses six values—1.0, 1.5, 2.2, 3.3, 4.7, and 6.8.
- The E24 series uses 24 values—1.0, 1.1, 1.2, 1.3, 1.5, 1.6, 1.8, 2.0, 2.2, 2.4, 2.7, 3.0, 3.3, 3.6, 3.9, 4.3, 4.7, 5.1, 5.6, 6.2, 6.8, 7.5, 8.2, and 9.1.

Other series are E48, E96, and E192

You can get a selection of resistors in dual inline packages, which can have six or eight resistors of the same value. There are also packages of resistors that are in networks that again have number of resistors of the same values but are connected as a bus bar. However, that is for a book on more practical application of electronics.

The Resistor Colour Coding

Resistors have a series of coloured bands around them to indicate their values. The standard resistor was originally four bands but now there are five and six bands. They all use the colours listed in Table 1-3 to represent the numbers.

CHAPTER 1 ELECTRICAL CURRENT

Table 1-3. *The Colours and Their Numbers*

Colour	Number
Black	0
Brown	1
Red	2
Orange	3
Yellow	4
Green	5
Blue	6
Violet	7
Grey	8
White	9

The placing of the bands on the resistor represents their usage. These will be slightly different depending upon the number of bands used. Table 1-4 lists the usage for the bands.

CHAPTER 1   ELECTRICAL CURRENT

Table 1-4. The Usage from the Resistor Bands

Four-Band Resistors

First Band	Second Band	Third Band	Fourth Band
First Number	Second Number	Number of Zeros	Tolerance

Five-Band Resistors

First Band	Second Band	Third Band	Fourth Band	Fifth Band
First Number	Second Number	Third Number	Number of Zeros	Tolerance

Six-Band Resistors

First Band	Second Band	Third Band	Fourth Band	Fifth Band	Sixth Band
First Number	Second Number	Third Number	Number of Zeros	Tolerance	Temp Coefficient

The bands are spaced out to show which end holds the first band. The standard is to place the bands that indicate the numbers of the resistor in a group with closer spacing between them. The group is placed at one end of the resistor with the tolerance and temperature coefficient band placed at the other end of the resistor. The tolerance band uses different colours to represent the tolerance. The tolerance and temperature band colours are listed in Table 1-5

Table 1-5. Colour Codes for Resistors

Colour	Tolerance	Temp Coefficient
Black		250 ppm/K
Brown	±1%	100 ppm/K
Red	±2%	50 ppm/K
Orange		15 ppm/K
Yellow		25 ppm/K
Green	±0.5%	20 ppm/K
Blue	±0.25%	10 ppm/K
Violet		5 ppm/K
Grey		1 ppm/K
Gold	±5%	
Silver	±10%	

Figure 1-11 shows three examples of four-band resistors.

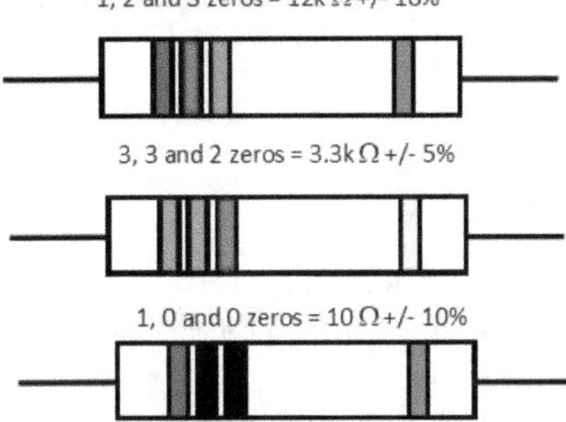

Figure 1-11. Examples of Four-Band Resistor Colours

CHAPTER 1   ELECTRICAL CURRENT

Chapter 1 Exercises

These exercises require the use of the expression for Ohm's Law. You look at this law in Chapter 2, so to be able answer some of these questions, I include the main expression for Ohm's Law and two transpositions of it.

$$I = \frac{V}{R}$$

Transpositions:

$$V = IR \text{ and } R = \frac{V}{I}$$

The answers for the exercise are given in the square brackets at the end of each exercise.

Exercise 1.1

Three primary cells have an EMF of 1.8V. The three cells are connected in series and then reconnected in parallel. If they each have an internal resistance of 0.25Ω, calculate the PD if the current drawn from the battery is 2.25A.

$$[3.7125\,V, \quad 1.6125\,V]$$

Exercise 1.2

If a primary cell with an EMF of 1.3V has a PD of 1.25V when a current of 1.5A is drawn from it, calculate the internal resistance R_S of the cell.

$$[0.0333\,\Omega \text{ or } 33.333\,m\Omega]$$

CHAPTER 1   ELECTRICAL CURRENT

Exercise 1.3

Calculate how much current is flowing if 260 Coulombs of charge passes a point in 22 seconds.

$$[11.818\,A]$$

Exercise 1.4

Calculate how much charge is being transferred when a battery is connected to a current of 15A for a period of 22 seconds.

$$[330\,C]$$

Exercise 1.5

Calculate how long you need to keep a current of 1.5A flowing if you want to pass a charge of 275C in a circuit.

(You need to transpose the expression.)

$$[183.333s]$$

Exercise 1.6

With respect to the resistors shown in Figure 1-12, calculate the current that would flow through them if they were separately connected to a 10V battery.

CHAPTER 1   ELECTRICAL CURRENT

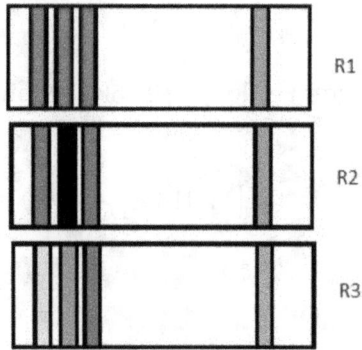

Figure 1-12. *The Resistor for Exercise 1.6*

$[0.00454\ A\ or\ 4.54mA]\ [0.1\ A\ or\ 100mA]\ [0.02128\ A\ or\ 21.28mA]$

Summary

This chapter looked at the principles of current flow and explained how it flows around a circuit. It explained some definitions for DC, AC, voltage, current, and so on. It also explained connecting cells in a series and in a parallel circuit and some useful aspects of using the ECAD software TINA. I hope this has helped set you up for the following chapters, in which you will learn how to analyse different electrical circuits.

In the next chapter, you will start an investigation into the fundamental laws used in electrical analysis, such as Ohm's Law and Kirchhoff's Laws.

CHAPTER 2

Fundamental Circuit Theorems

This chapter explains the three main laws used to analyse electrical circuits. The three laws are:

- Ohm's Law
- Kirchhoff's Voltage Law
- Kirchhoff's Current Law

This chapter concentrates on DC circuits and how to use these laws to analyse them. The circuits will only contain resistors in series, in parallel, and in series parallel combinations.

After reading this chapter, you will have a good understanding of these laws and how to use them. You will also understand the difference between series and parallel circuits and series parallel combination circuits. You will also have studied how to use the ECAD software TINA to carry out circuit simulations on DC circuits. This will enable you to confirm the calculations using the three laws. I hope you will also have an appreciation of how important mathematics is to the engineer.

CHAPTER 2   FUNDAMENTAL CIRCUIT THEOREMS

Ohm's Law

In 1827, George Simon Ohm wrote a pamphlet called *Die galvanische Kette, mathematisch bearbeitet* (*The Galvanic Circuit Investigated Mathematically*). It was a time when the few had the freedom and the income to spend their time investigating the new and exciting field of electricity. It was a time when everything was new and wonderful. What a time it must have been.

With this pamphlet George Simon Ohm wrote about the relationship between the current flowing in a circuit and the voltage and resistance in that circuit. This relationship became the fundamental law we now use in all electrical engineering. He earned the right to name this law after him and so "Ohm's Law" came into being.

Kirchhoff's Laws

Before using Ohm's Law, we will move onto two fundamental laws we use in electrical analysis. We will look at those given to us by Gustav Robert Kirchhoff. These are used when there is more than one resistor in a circuit and when there is more than one section, or loop, in a circuit. This gives rise to the terms *series circuits* and *parallel circuits*. These two terms describe how to connect resistors, and indeed any components, together. I explain Kirchhoff's Laws when I use them in the following examples.

Resistors Connected in Series

A *series circuit* is one where all the components are connected, one after the other end to end, as shown in Figure 2-1.

CHAPTER 2   FUNDAMENTAL CIRCUIT THEOREMS

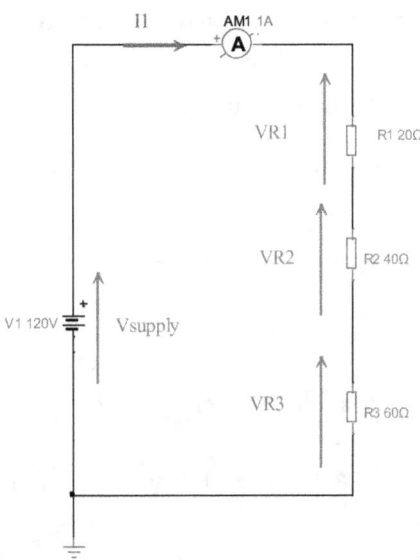

Figure 2-1. *The Series Resistor Circuit 1*

We can apply Kirchhoff's Voltage Law to the series circuit. The law states that:

The algebraic sum of the potential differences in any loop must be equal to 0, as $\Sigma V = 0$.

This maybe a little confusing and I tend to apply the law in a slightly different manner. We can use the voltage arrows drawn on the circuit to apply Kirchhoff's Voltage Law and confirm our calculations for the circuit. This is because, in a closed loop, the sum of the voltage arrows in one direction must equal the sum of the voltage arrows in the other direction. In the circuit shown in Figure 2-1, you can see that the three voltage arrows (V_{R1}, V_{R2}, and V_{R3}) are all in the same direction. This means that we can add their values together and the result will equal the V_{supply} to the loop. This is

39

CHAPTER 2   FUNDAMENTAL CIRCUIT THEOREMS

because the V_{supply} is the only voltage arrow that is in the opposite direction. This will help us interpret Kirchhoff's Voltage Law, KVL. In essence, we can interpret Kirchhoff's voltage as meaning:

> *In a closed loop, the sum of the volt drops around that loop must equal the supply to that loop.*

When we calculate the actual voltage drops, we can use this concept to confirm our calculations.

Calculating Three Volt Drops

We can rearrange Ohm's Law to produce an expression for the volt drop.
Ohm's Law states:

$$I = \frac{V}{R}$$

We can transpose the expression for Ohm's Law to make *V* the subject of the expression. There are those who use a triangular diagram to help transpose this expression. However, transposing expressions is an essential skill for engineers and if you can't transpose a simple three term expression, then I think you are in trouble. There are some simple rules that you must follow when transposing an expression. Then, with enough practice, you can all transpose any formula. In this book, I transpose many more complicated expressions.

The first rule is state exactly what you want to do.
Then state what you must do to achieve that.
Then remember the golden rule, which is:

> *Whatever you do to one side of the equals sign you must do to the other side.*

CHAPTER 2 FUNDAMENTAL CIRCUIT THEOREMS

With this transposition, we want to make V the subject of the expression. This means that we want to get V on its own on one side of the equals sign. This means we need to remove the R in the denominator from the RHS (right side) of the equals sign. The way we do this is to simply multiply the right side R. This works because R is connected to V by division, so we must perform the opposite operation, which is multiplication. Also, we know the following:

$$\frac{R}{R} = 1$$

However, what we do to the right side, we must do to the left side. This means that we must multiply both sides by R. This gives:

$$I \times R = \frac{V}{R} \times R$$

The two Rs on the right cancel out. This gives:

$$V = IR$$

It may be easier to see how the two Rs cancel out if you rewrite the expression in a slightly different manner.

$$I \times R = \frac{V}{R} \times \frac{R}{1}$$

I hope this helps. It works because when we divide anything by 1, we don't change it. I will use this method in some other examples in the book.

Transposing Ohm's Law for Resistance R

We should be able to transpose this expression, $V = IR$, for R as follows. We want to get R on its own. We need to decide what term is connected to R and how it is connected. When we know that we must do the opposite of

CHAPTER 2   FUNDAMENTAL CIRCUIT THEOREMS

how the term is connected to R to both sides. In this expression, we can see that the term I is connected to R and it is connected by multiplication. Therefore, we must divide both sides by I to get R on its own. However, we could also multiply both sides by $\frac{1}{I}$ as this is the same as dividing by I. This gives:

$$V \times \frac{1}{I} = IR \times \frac{1}{I}$$

This may be easier to see if we rewrite it as follows:

$$\frac{V}{1} \times \frac{1}{I} = \frac{IR}{1} \times \frac{1}{I}$$

$$\frac{V}{I} = \frac{IR}{I}$$

Therefore, the two Is cancel out and we get this:

$$\frac{V}{I} = R$$

Which we normally write as follows:

$$R = \frac{V}{I}$$

Hopefully you can see why you don't need a triangular diagram to transpose this simple three-term expression.

The Current Flowing Through a Series Circuit

If we now refer to the series circuit shown in Figure 2-1, we can calculate the current flowing around the circuit. You should always calculate the current flowing through any component in a circuit, as it is the current that can cause the damage. Too much current in any component will destroy it and may cause a fire. As always, use Ohm's Law to calculate how much current will flow through the components. In the series circuit, there is only one circular path for the current to flow out of the supply and back into it.

Note that in all the circuit analysis in this book, I use conventional current, as described in Chapter 1. This flows out of the positive terminal of the battery and back in to the negative terminal. As there is only one loop, or path, it means that the same current flows through R_1, R_2, and R_3. It also flows through the ammeter AM1, as this is also connected in series with the resistors. The ammeter is in the circuit only to measure the current flowing around the circuit, so that we can use TINA to confirm our calculations.

However, what value of resistance is Ohm's Law referring to in this circuit—is it R_1, R_2, or R_3? If we use just R_1 with Ohm's Law, we get this:

$$I = \frac{V}{R} = \frac{120}{20} = 6A$$

However, the simulations shows that the current is 1A, as shown in Figure 2-1. This means that there is more resistance than just 20Ω. Indeed, if we use the expression for R and insert the measured values, we get this:

$$R = \frac{V}{I}$$

If we now put in the values from the simulation (i.e. I = 1A when V = 120V), we get a value for resistance R as follows:

$$R = \frac{120}{1} \therefore R = 120\Omega$$

CHAPTER 2   FUNDAMENTAL CIRCUIT THEOREMS

If we simply add all the values of the resistors in the circuit, we get this:

$$R_1 + R_2 + R_3 = 20 + 40 + 60 = 120 \Omega$$

This would suggest that when resistors are connected in series, we can simply add the individual values together to get a value for the total resistance R_T. Therefore, we can say that in a series circuit, the following is true:

$$R_T + R_1 + R_2 + R_3 + \ldots$$

Simulating the Circuit in TINA

I go through the process of creating the circuit in the ECAD software TINA12 in Chapter 10. If you use a different ECAD software, the process will be similar, so I hope this description will help you. If you are happy using an ECAD software, you can skip the description, but if not, it may help if you read through it now. I normally assume my readers know very little and possibly nothing, so I include these descriptions. I hope after reading that section in Chapter 10, you will be able to create the circuit shown in Figure 2-2.

CHAPTER 2   FUNDAMENTAL CIRCUIT THEOREMS

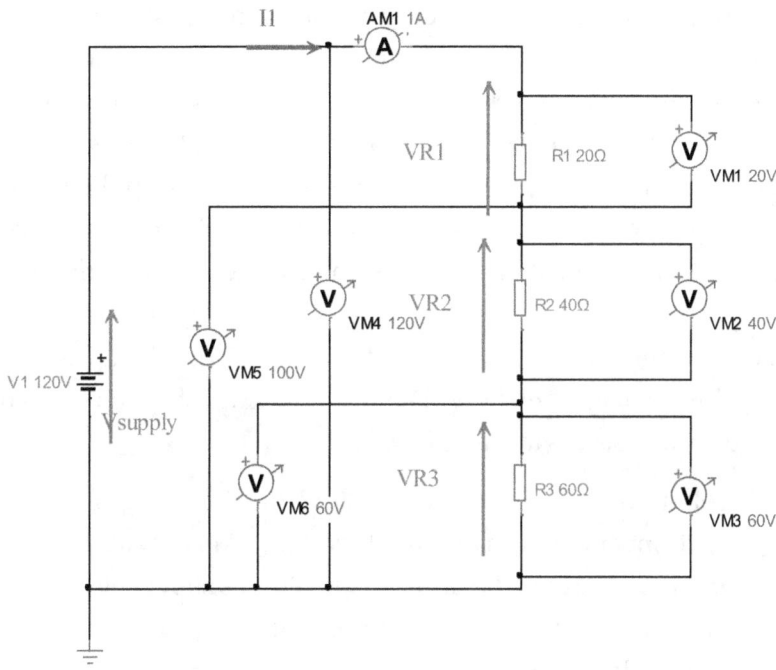

Figure 2-2. *The Simulated Result for Circuit 2*

We can use the simulated results to confirm these calculations. When resistors are connected in series, we can calculate the total resistance R_T in the circuit by simply adding the value of all the resistors in the circuit. With respect to the circuit shown in Figure 2-1, we can now determine the total resistance R_T as follows:

$$R_T = R_1 + R_2 + R_3 = 20 + 40 + 60 = 120 \Omega$$

Now using Ohm's Law, we can say the following:

$$I = \frac{V_{Supply}}{R_T} = \frac{120}{120} = 1\ Amp$$

45

CHAPTER 2   FUNDAMENTAL CIRCUIT THEOREMS

We now know the current flowing through all the resistors in the circuit shown in Figure 2-1 is 1A. When a current passes through a resistor, some force is dissipated across the resistor as the current flows through it. We looked at the energy change when current flows through a resistor in Chapter 1. What I show here is that if there was, say, 120V applied to one end of a resistor, when a current flows through the resistor, the voltage at the other end will be less than 120V, as some voltage will be "dropped" across the resistor.

We can see that the voltage applied to the circuit (i.e., V_{supply}) is 120V. The three voltage meters (VM1, VM2, and VM3) show that the volt drops across the resistors are as follows:

- Volt drop across R_1 (i.e., V_{R1}) is 20V. Note the voltage at the front end of R_1 is the supply voltage VM4 at 120V, and the voltage at the other end is 100V, as shown by the voltmeter VM5. This confirms that we will lose some voltage dropped across a resistor when a current is forced to flow through it.
- Volt drop across R_2 (i.e., V_{R2}) is 40V.
- Volt drop across R_3 (i.e., V_{R3}) is 60V.

If we add the three volt drops together, we can see that the sum equals the supply voltage 120V:

$$V_{R1} + V_{R2} + V_{R3} = 20 + 40 + 60 = 120V$$

This confirms our interpretation of Kirchhoff's Voltage Law in that the sum of the arrows in one direction equals the sum of the arrows in the other direction in a closed loop.

$$V_{supply} = V_{R1} + V_{R2} + V_{R3}$$

CHAPTER 2 FUNDAMENTAL CIRCUIT THEOREMS

We can transpose Ohm's Law to obtain an expression for the volt drop across a resistor. This is as follows:

$$V = IR$$

This means that the voltage across the resistor can be calculated by multiplying the current flowing through the resistor by the value of the resistor.

The simulation shown in Figure 2-2 shows that the current flowing around the loop, and so through all the resistors, is 1A. Now we can calculate each of the volt drops around the circuit as follows:

$$V_{R1} = IR_1 = 1 \times 20 = 20V$$

$$V_{R2} = IR_2 = 1 \times 40 = 40V$$

$$V_{R3} = IR_3 = 1 \times 60 = 60V$$

These calculations agree with the simulation, and more importantly, with our application of Kirchhoff's Law. I say more importantly because we have not always had an ECAD software to simulate circuits, but we have always had Kirchhoff's Laws.

Kirchhoff's Current Law

This is another law that we can use to confirm our analysis of electrical circuits. However, this relates to circuits, where components are connected in parallel. The circuit shown in Figure 2-3 shows a circuit with three resistors connected in parallel.

CHAPTER 2 FUNDAMENTAL CIRCUIT THEOREMS

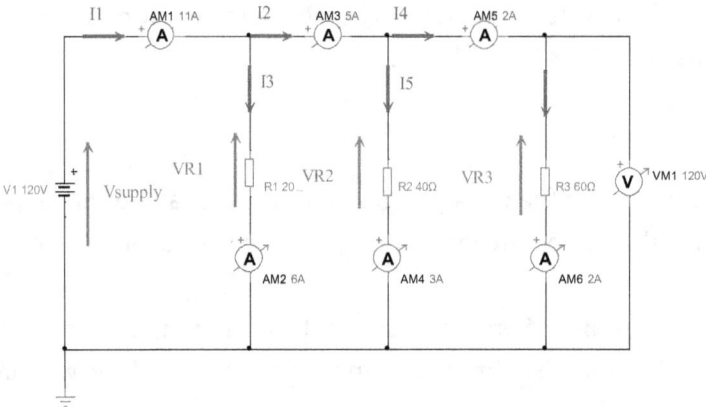

Figure 2-3. *The Simulation of the Parallel Circuit1*

We will use this simulation to interpret what Kirchhoff's Current Law means. I begin by stating the law:

The algebraic sum of all the currents at a node must equal 0.

This is again a rather awkward statement, and I tend to interpret Kirchhoff's current by saying the following:

The sum of the currents flowing into a node must equal the sum of the currents flowing out of the node.

If we look at the simulation in Figure 2-3, we can see that 11A of current is flowing through AM1. We can see that this current flows into a node or junction point in the circuit that has two separate currents flowing out of it (i.e., the two currents flowing through AM2 and AM3).

The two currents are:

- AM2 = 6A
- AM3 = 5A

If we add these two currents together, we get the following:

$$A_{M2} + A_{M3} = 6 + 5 = 11A$$

48

CHAPTER 2 FUNDAMENTAL CIRCUIT THEOREMS

This agrees with the current flowing into the node through AM1. This then agrees with Kirchhoff's Current Law and my interpretation of the law.

We can also carry out some more calculations to see if they all agree with the other calculations and the simulation. We can use Ohm's Law to calculate the current flowing through each resistor. We need to know the voltage across each resistor. However, if we look at the circuit shown in Figure 2-3, note that the voltage across each of the three resistors is the same at V_{supply} (i.e., the 120V supplied to the circuit). This is a common aspect of parallel circuits in that the voltage is the same across all components that are in parallel. However, you must be careful making such general statements. That being the case, we can calculate the three currents through all the resistors as follows:

$$I_{R1} = \frac{V_{R1}}{R_1} = \frac{120}{20} = 6A$$

$$I_{R2} = \frac{V_{R1}}{R_2} = \frac{120}{40} = 3A$$

$$I_{R3} = \frac{V_{R1}}{R_3} = \frac{120}{60} = 2A$$

These results agree with the simulations.

When there are resistors in parallel, we can calculate the value of the total resistance in the circuit, R_T, so that we can calculate the value of the current the circuit will draw from the supply. This is the current I1, as shown in Figure 2-3. When resistors are in parallel, it is a slightly more complicated process. The process is as follows.

To derive the expression for the total resistance in the circuit, we use an old term called *admittance*. This expresses the ability of the circuit, or the paths in a circuit, to admit current to flow through them. This is the opposite of resistance, which expresses the ability of the circuit to resist

49

CHAPTER 2 FUNDAMENTAL CIRCUIT THEOREMS

current flow. We can see from the circuit is Figure 2-3 that there are three paths that will admit current to flow through them. If we added a fourth path to the circuit, this would have its own admittance, and it would increase the total admittance. However, all the currents for the individual paths must come from the supply as the current I1 in Figure 2-3. This means that the total admittance of the circuit is the sum of the individual admittances in the circuit. Admittance uses the units of Siemens S, and it is given the symbol Y. As it is the opposite of resistance, it can be expressed as follows:

$$admittance\ Y = \frac{1}{R}$$

Understanding this concept, we can calculate the admittances of the three paths in Figure 2-3.

$$Y_1 = \frac{1}{R_1}$$

$$Y_2 = \frac{1}{R_2}$$

$$Y_3 = \frac{1}{R_3}$$

This means we can calculate the total admittance in the circuit shown in Figure 2-3 using this approach:

$$Y_T = Y_1 + Y_2 + Y_3$$

$$Y_T = \frac{1}{20} + \frac{1}{40} + \frac{1}{60} = 0.05 + 0.025 + 0.016666r = 0.0.91666r\ S$$

CHAPTER 2 FUNDAMENTAL CIRCUIT THEOREMS

As we know admittance is the opposite of resistance, we can now calculate the total resistance of the circuit using this:

$$R_T = \frac{1}{Y_T} = \frac{1}{0.0916666r} = 10.9091$$

If we use this value for the total resistance, we can calculate the current taken from the supply using this:

$$I = \frac{V_{Supply}}{R_T} = \frac{120}{10.9091} = 10.999999r \; A = 11A$$

This agrees with the ammeter reading, AM1, which measures the current I1 in Figure 2-3. We could use the value of the admittance to calculate the current drawn from the supply using this:

$$Current = voltage \times admittance \; I = V \times Y$$

Therefore:

$$I_1 = 120 \times 0.0916666r = 11A$$

We can use this to calculate the three branch currents as follows:

$$I_{R1} = V_{Supply} Y_1 = 120 \times 0.05 = 6A$$

$$I_{R2} = V_{Supply} Y_2 = 120 \times 0.0125 = 3A$$

$$I_{R3} = V_{Supply} Y_3 = 120 \times 0.01666r = 2A$$

These all agree with the pervious calculations. I hope that this shows that the concept of admittance does work and that the total admittance is the sum of the individual admittances.

CHAPTER 2 FUNDAMENTAL CIRCUIT THEOREMS

Now that we are happy that the expression for the total admittance is valid, we can use it to create an expression for the total resistance, R_T in a parallel circuit.

With respect to the parallel circuit in Figure 2-3, we can say the total resistance is as follows:

$$R_T = \frac{1}{total\ admittance} = \frac{1}{0.0916666r} = 10.9091\Omega$$

$$total\ admittance = \frac{1}{R_1} + \frac{1}{R_2} + \frac{1}{R_3}$$

This means that the process by which we can calculate the total resistance in a parallel circuit is to use the expression for the total admittance and then calculate the inverse of that figure. We can put this concept into a single expression:

$$R_T = \frac{1}{\frac{1}{R_1} + \frac{1}{R_2} + \frac{1}{R_3} + etc}$$

Applying this to the circuit shown in Figure 2-3, we get:

$$R_T = \frac{1}{\frac{1}{20} + \frac{1}{40} + \frac{1}{60}} = \frac{1}{0.05 + 0.025 + 0.016666r} = \frac{1}{0.091666r} = 10.9091\Omega$$

The examples and exercises at the end of this chapter show you how to use this expression. One thing to remember when determining the total resistance in a parallel circuit is:

The result will always be less than the lowest value of resistance in the parallel circuit.

CHAPTER 2   FUNDAMENTAL CIRCUIT THEOREMS

I hope this analysis has shown you how you can use the three laws to calculate and confirm the currents and voltage in a simple DC circuit. I hope it also shows you that you can use the ECAD software to simulate and confirm your calculations.

Series Parallel Combinations of DC Circuits

Now we have looked at series and parallel circuits, we need to move on to a combination of these types of circuits. The first example is shown in the simulation in Figure 2-4. We will develop an approach that enables us to calculate all the values shown in the simulation.

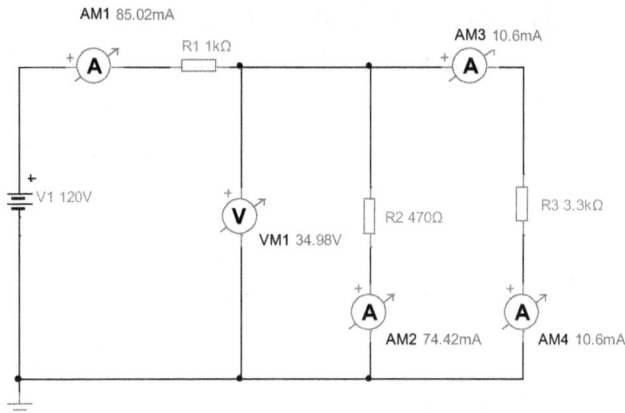

Figure 2-4. The Series Parallel Combination Circuit

I am using more realistic values for the resistors, which will result in smaller values for the currents flowing in the circuit. This could lead to a problem in understanding how we represent these values. Mathematicians use scientific notation, but engineers use engineering notation. The following is my attempt to explain how to create engineering numbers.

53

CHAPTER 2   FUNDAMENTAL CIRCUIT THEOREMS

Engineering Numbers

There will be times when you must write down numbers on a circuit diagram or an engineering drawing. The diagrams will then be photocopied and circulated around the world. People reading the diagram will have to interpret what you have written down correctly. Consider the following set of numbers:

>2000000 0.000002
>
>2000 0.002

With the number 2000000, you could accidentally leave off a 0 or add a 0. If you did, the number will be misread by a factor of 10 or more. The same could be said for the other numbers. Also, the decimal points could be hard to see and the 0.000002 could be a simple 2.

There must be a way of ensuring that the numbers we write on our diagrams cannot be misread. This is where the use of engineering numbers comes in.

The Four Main Engineering Numbers

There is a wide range of engineering numbers to cover the possible range of numbers we might use. To go from one range to another, we increase or decrease by a thousand (i.e., starting from unity 1, the next range is 1000, then 1000000, then 1000000000, and so on). With descending numbers from 1, we go to 0.001, then 0.000001, then 0.000000001, and so on.

Table 2-1 introduces the four main engineering symbols and explains what they mean.

CHAPTER 2   FUNDAMENTAL CIRCUIT THEOREMS

Table 2-1. The Four Main Engineering Symbols

Name	Number	Scientific Notation	Symbol
Mega	1000000.0	$1E^6$	M
Kilo	1000.0	$1E^3$	k
Unity	1.0	$1E^0$	none
Milli	0.001	$1E^{-3}$	m
Micro	0.000001	$1E^{-6}$	μ

Note that the decimal point is indicated with each number. This is to enable you to see that, in order to convert from the actual number to the engineering notation, you move the decimal point, *dp*. Consider converting the number 1000000.0 to 1M.

- Convert the number to engineering notation.
- Replace the E^n part with the equivalent symbol.

For the engineering number, we can only move the decimal point in groups of three places at a time (i.e., either 3, 6, 9 or 12 etc.), but with scientific notation, we are not restricted in the number of places we move the decimal point. In fact, with scientific notation, we move the decimal point, so that there is only one digit in front of the decimal point.

With the number 1000000.0, engineer moves the dp six places to the left. Therefore, we have 1.0. However, we must remember that we have moved the dp. Therefore, we write the number as $1.0E^6$. The 6 stands for the number of places we moved the dp. In Chapter 1 I explained how I use the capitol letter *E* with respect to numbers.

Thus 1000000.0 becomes $1.0E^6$.

We can now replace the E^6 with the appropriate symbol (i.e., *M*).

Thus 1000000.0 becomes 1.0M or 1M.

55

CHAPTER 2   FUNDAMENTAL CIRCUIT THEOREMS

Consider the number 0.000001. Again, we move the dp six places. Therefore, we have 1.0. Again, we must show that we have moved the dp, and this we do by adding the E^n. Therefore, we have $1.0E^6$ Note again the 6 because we moved the dp six places. However, this is the same as before, yet the two numbers are totally different. We need to be able to distinguish between the two numbers. To do this, we use the following rule:

- If the dp is moved to the right, then the *n* is negative.
- If the dp is moved to the left, then the *n* is positive.

Therefore, for the number 0.000001 becomes:

$1.0E^{-6}$

We then replace the E^n with the appropriate symbol.
Therefore, the number 0.000001 becomes 1μ.
Example:

Consider the number 625000.

This is really 625000.0.

We move the dp three places to the left: $625.0E^3$.

We replace the E^3 with k for kilo: 625.0k.

Therefore, 625000 becomes 625k.

Example:

Consider the number 6250000.

This is really 6250000.0.

We move the dp six places to the left: $6.25E^6$.

We replace the E^6 with M for Mega: 6.25M.

Therefore 6250000 becomes 6.25M.

Example:

Consider the number 0.00625.

We move the dp three places to the right: $6.25E^{-3}$.

Note the minus sign, as we have moved the dp to the right.

We replace the E^{-3} with m for milli: 6.25m.

Therefore 0.00625 becomes 6.25m.

Example:

Consider the number 0.00000625.

We move the dp six places to the right: $6.25E^{-6}$.

We replace the E^{-6} with µ for micro: 6.25µ.

Therefore 0.00000625 becomes 6.25µ.

I hope this short explanation has helped you to appreciate how to create and use engineering numbers. I use the capital *E* to describe the exponent. This is because to enter the engineering number into your calculator, you type the numbers, then press the EXP button and enter the exponent power. For example, to enter $625E^3$, you would enter the 625 then press the EXP button then enter the number 3. (Some calculators use a x10 button instead of the EXP button.)

Now that you have a better appreciation of engineering numbers, I will carry on with the analysis of the circuit shown in Figure 2-4.

The Supply Current

The first item to calculate is the current drawn from the supply, as this is the highest amount of current in the circuit. Also, the most important parameter we must calculate in any circuit is the current flowing through

CHAPTER 2   FUNDAMENTAL CIRCUIT THEOREMS

all components. This is because it is the current that can cause the most damage. It is the current that will kill you and the current that will set fire to the circuit board. We cannot just say, well, you can measure the currents because by the time you have turned the circuit on and measured the current the damage would have already been done. That is why the ability to analyse all electrical circuits and calculate all the currents flowing is so important.

To calculate this current, we apply Ohm's Law but use the value for the total resistance R_T. Therefore, use the following:

$$I = \frac{V_{supply}}{R_T}$$

We can see that V_{supply} equals 120V, but what is the value for the total resistance R_T? There is no one simple equation that will give us that result. You have to learn an approach that you can apply to most series parallel combinations that allows you to calculate the value for R_T. The approach is as follows.

Starting with the components that are the farthest away from the supply voltage, we must combine what components, resistors in this case, we can. We start the farthest away from the supply to ensure there are no more components that can be in series or parallel with the ones we are combining. Note that R_3 is the component farthest away from the supply. Also note that the top of R_3 is connected to the top of R_2 and the bottom of R_3 is connected to the bottom of R_2. That is how we can determine that R_3 and R_2 are connected in parallel. If the two tops and the two bottoms of the two components are connected, they must be in parallel. This means that the first thing you do is determine the combined resistance of these two resistors in parallel. We will call that combination R_{COMB1}. Therefore, we can say that:

$$R_{COMB1} = \frac{1}{\frac{1}{R3} + \frac{1}{R2}}$$

Putting the values in, we get:

$$R_{COMB1} = \frac{1}{\frac{1}{3.3E^3} + \frac{1}{470}} = \frac{1}{303.03E^{-6} + 2.128^{-3}} = \frac{1}{2.431E^{-3}} = 411.41\Omega$$

Recall that with resistors in parallel, the combined result is less than the lowest resistor value. We can see that this true here, as $R_{COMB1} = 411.41\Omega$ and R_2 is the lowest of the two resistors in parallel at 470Ω.

An Alternative Method for Two Components in Parallel

Whenever we are dealing with just two components in parallel, we can use the *product*, a posh word for multiplication, over the sum, the simple addition, method to calculate their total value. This means that with respect to R_3 and R_2, we can calculate their combined resistance using the following:

$$R_{COMB1} = \frac{R_3 R_2}{R_3 + R_2} = \frac{3.3E^3 \times 470}{3.3E^3 + 470} = 411.41\Omega$$

I think we should be able to prove any expression we are going to use. This is because when an engineer signs off the design of anything they create, it is their reputation and name they are putting on the line. Therefore, the engineer should not just accept what someone else has told them, or what they have read—they should prove it themselves. There are numerous ways they can prove it and with this expression some simple maths will work. Therefore, I go through the derivation of this expression for calculating the total resistance of two resistors in series.

CHAPTER 2   FUNDAMENTAL CIRCUIT THEOREMS

The expression for two resistors in parallel starts off with this:

$$R_{COMB1} = \frac{1}{\dfrac{1}{R3} + \dfrac{1}{R2}}$$

If we deal with the denominator, we are simply adding two fractions, as follows:

$$\frac{1}{R_3} + \frac{1}{R_2}$$

The first thing we do when adding fractions is create a common denominator by simply multiplying the two denominators together. This gives an approximate result of the following:

$$\frac{1+1}{R_3 R_2}$$

However, because we have changed the denominator, we need to change the numerators to keep the two fractions as they were before we started. This is done by multiplying each numerator by the opposite denominator, which gives the following:

$$\frac{1 \times R_2 + 1 \times R_3}{R_3 R_2} = \frac{R_2 + R_3}{R_3 R_2}$$

If we put this into the expression for R_T, we get the following:

$$R_T = \frac{1}{\dfrac{R_2 + R_3}{R_3 R_2}}$$

When we divide by a fraction, as we are doing here, we can invert the fraction and multiply as follows:

CHAPTER 2   FUNDAMENTAL CIRCUIT THEOREMS

$$R_T = 1 \times \frac{R_3 R_2}{R_2 + R_3} = \frac{R_3 R_2}{R_2 + R_3}$$

I am showing this proof to try and show that, with a bit of patience and some basic maths knowledge, you can derive the expressions you need to use. This is a useful skill for the would-be engineer to develop and so I go through the proofs of other expressions as we come across them in the book. You do can of course just skip them, but I hope you don't, as I am sure you will find that they are not too difficult to do yourself.

This expression for the total resistance only works for two components. When there are more than two, you use the first approach or split them up into groups of two.

Now we that we have calculated the combined resistance of R_2 and R_3, we need to redraw the circuit and replace R_2 and R_3 with R_{COMB1}. This is shown in Figure 2-5.

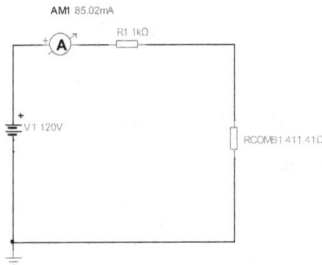

Figure 2-5. *The Circuit with R2 and R3 Replaced with R_{COMB1}*

I hope it is now clear that the two remaining resistors are not in parallel, as their two tops and bottoms are not connected. This means that they are in a series. Therefore, we need only add the two values together to calculate the total resistance of the circuit. If you do this, you will determine that the total resistance R_T is as follows:

$$R_T = R_1 + R_{COMB1} = 1E^3 + 411.41 = 1.411 k\Omega$$

CHAPTER 2   FUNDAMENTAL CIRCUIT THEOREMS

We only need to go to three decimal places for accuracy. As there are no more resistors to consider, we can now calculate the current that will flow out of the voltage supply (i.e., I_{SUPPLY}). This is done using Ohm's Law as follows:

$$I_{SUPPLY} = \frac{V_{SUPPLY}}{R_T} = \frac{120}{1.411E^3} = 85.022 mA$$

If we now simulate the circuit in TINA, we should see that the ammeter confirms our calculation. This is shown in Figure 2-5.

We now need to calculate the currents flowing through R_2 and R_3. The current flowing through both will be caused by the force of the voltage across these two resistors. This will the voltage remaining from what was the 120V supply after the 85.022mA of current has passed through the resistor R_1. We can calculate the volt drop across R_1 (V_{R1}) using the transposition of Ohm's Law as follows:

$$V_{R1} = I_{SUPPLY} R_1 = 85.022E^{-3} \times 1^3 = 85.022V$$

This means that the voltage across the two resistors R_2 and R_3 (call it V_{R2}) can be calculated as follows:

$$V_{R2} = V_{SUPPLY} - V_{R1} = 120 - 85.022 = 34.978V$$

Now we can calculate the currents flowing through R_2 and R_3 as follows:

$$I_{R2} = \frac{V_{R2}}{R_2} = \frac{34.978}{470} = 74.421 mA$$

$$I_{R3} = \frac{V_{R2}}{R_3} = \frac{34.978}{3.3E^3} = 10.6 mA$$

CHAPTER 2   FUNDAMENTAL CIRCUIT THEOREMS

These results agree with the simulated measurements shown in Figure 2-4. However, you won't always have access to an ECAD software and so you need another method by which you can confirm your calculations. You can use Kirchhoff's Laws as an alternative method to confirm your calculations.

Note that the two currents I_{R2} and I_{R3} flow out of the same node into which I_{SUPPLY} flows in. This means that if we add the two currents I_{R2} and I_{R3} together, the result should equal I_{SUPPLY}. Therefore, we can say the following:

$$I_{SUPPLY} = I_{R2} + I_{R3} = 10.6E^{-3} + 74.421E^{-3} = 85.021 mA$$

This is close enough to confirm that our calculations are correct and the simulated measurement, as AM1 in Figure 2-4 measures the supply current.

Finally, we can use Kirchhoff's Voltage Law to confirm our calculation for V_{R2}. Looking at Figure 2-5, we can see that R_1 and R_{COMB1} create a closed loop where the supply is V_{SUPPLY} at 120V. There are two volt drops around that closed loop, and they are V_{R1} and V_{R2}. Therefore, if we add V_{R1} to V_{R2}, the result should be the 120V of V_{SUPPLY}. This means we can say the following:

$$V_{SUPPLY} = V_{R1} + V_{R2} = 85.022 + 34.978 = 120V$$

This does indeed confirm our calculations.

The Voltage Divider Rule

There will be many circuits, or parts of circuits, that have resistors or impedances that are in series with each other. In that situation we could use the voltage divider rule to determine the voltage across anyone of the components. An example to help explain the process is shown in Figure 2-6.

CHAPTER 2   FUNDAMENTAL CIRCUIT THEOREMS

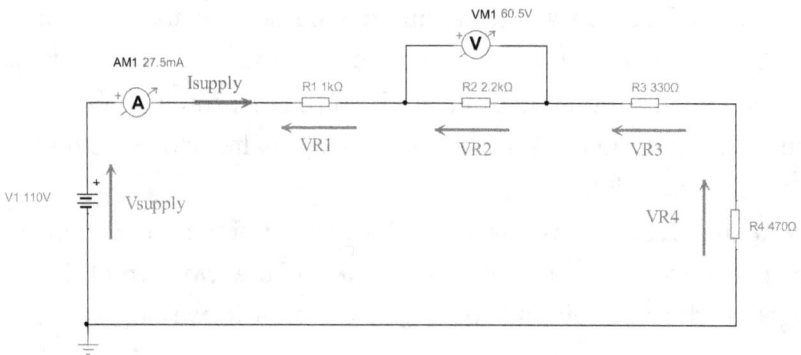

Figure 2-6. *Test Circuit for the Voltage Divider Rule*

We will use the rule to calculate the voltage across the resistor R_2 in the circuit. This is V_{R2} on the circuit diagram. We multiply the resistance, or impedance value in question, by the supply voltage and divide the result by the total resistance or impedance in the loop. Applying the rule gives this:

$$V_{R2} = \frac{V_{SUPPLY} R_2}{R_1 + R_2 + R_3 + R_4} = \frac{110 \times 2.2E^3}{1E^3 + 2.2E^3 + 330 + 470} = 60.5V$$

This is the same voltage as measured by VM1 in Figure 2-6. The expression shows how the four resistors in the loop divide the supply voltage between them. We can use the rule to calculate the voltage V_{R3}. This is done as follows:

$$V_{R3} = \frac{V_{SUPPLY} R_3}{R_1 + R_2 + R_3 + R_4} = \frac{110 \times 330}{1E^3 + 2.2E^3 + 330 + 470} = 9.075V$$

Looking carefully at the rule, we should be able to see that it is using a transposition of Ohm's Law. Using Ohm's Law, we can say that:

$$V_{R2} = IR_2$$

CHAPTER 2 FUNDAMENTAL CIRCUIT THEOREMS

To use this expression, we need to calculate the value of the current, I. We can of course use Ohm's Law for this. With respect to the circuit shown in Figure 2-5, we can say this:

$$I_{SUPPLY} = \frac{V_{SUPPLY}}{R_T} = \frac{V_{SUPPLY}}{R_1 + R_2 + R_3 + R_3}$$

Therefore, we can say the following:

$$V_{R3} = \frac{V_{SUPPLY}}{R_1 + R_2 + R_3 + R_4} \times R_3 = V_{R3} = \frac{V_{SUPPLY} R_3}{R_1 + R_2 + R_3 + R_4}$$

I hope this shows you how the voltage divider rule does use Ohm's Law, but we only use one calculation. We will use the circuit shown in Figure 2-5 as another example of using these laws. We will use Ohm's Law to calculate the value of the supply current, as this is so important to know.

Using Ohm's Law:

$$I_{SUPPLY} = \frac{V_{SUPPLY}}{R_T}$$

As this is a series circuit, we simply add the four resistor values together to calculate the total resistance, R_T.

Therefore:

$$I_{SUPPLY} = \frac{V_{SUPPLY}}{R_1 + R_2 + R_3 + R_3}$$

Therefore:

$$I_{SUPPLY} = \frac{110}{1E^3 + 2.2E^3 + 330 + 470} = 0.0275 = 27.5E^{-3} = 27.5mA$$

CHAPTER 2 FUNDAMENTAL CIRCUIT THEOREMS

This agrees with the value measured by the AM1 ammeter in Figure 2-5. We now calculate each of the four voltage drops across the resistors using the following:

$$V_{R1} = I_{SUPPLY} R_1 = 27.5E^{-3} \times 1E^3 = 27.5V$$

$$V_{R2} = I_{SUPPLY} R_2 = 27.5E^{-3} \times 2.2E^3 = 60.5V$$

$$V_{R3} = I_{SUPPLY} R_3 = 27.5E^{-3} \times 330 = 9.075V$$

$$V_{R4} = I_{SUPPLY} R_4 = 27.5E^{-3} \times 470 = 12.925$$

We can check our calculations using Kirchhoff's Voltage Law. With respect to this circuit, we can say:

$$V_{Supply} = V_{R1} + V_{R2} + V_{R3} + V_{R4}$$

Therefore:

$$110 = 27.5 + 60.5 + 9.075 + 12.925 = 110$$

This shows how using Kirchhoff's Voltage Law, KVL, can confirm your calculations.

Now look at the circuit shown in Figure 2-7.

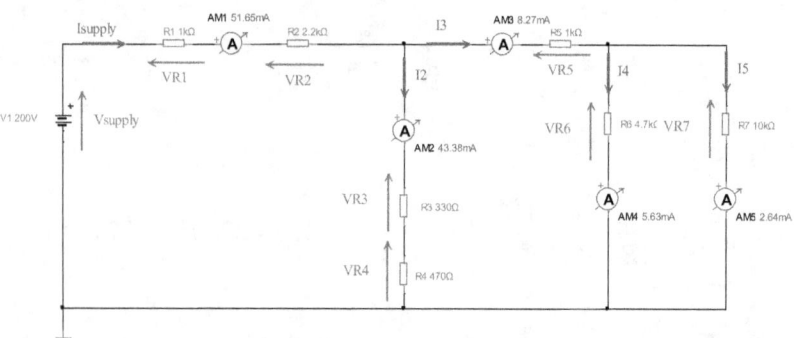

Figure 2-7. Using KVL and KCL

66

CHAPTER 2 FUNDAMENTAL CIRCUIT THEOREMS

There is quite a lot going on with this circuit, but we are trying to study how to use the KVL and KCL and analyse series parallel combination circuits. We will start off by calculating the total resistance, R_T, in the circuit. We need to combine resistors where we can. Firstly, we combine the resistors R_7 and R_6 together. This is because they are the farthest away from the supply and there are no resistors that are in parallel with them. These resistors are in parallel with each other and so, using the product over sum approach, we can say this:

$$R_{COMB1} = \frac{R_6 R_7}{R_6 + R_7} = \frac{4.7E^3 \times 10E^3}{4.7E^3 + 10E^3} = 3197.28\Omega$$

We can now redraw the circuit to make the next step clearer, as shown in Figure 2-8.

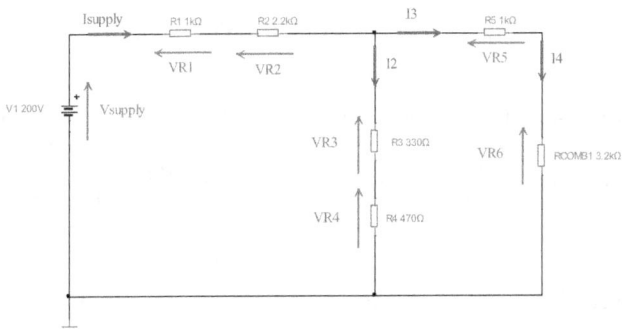

Figure 2-8. *The Circuit with R_{COMB1} Inserted*

I hope you can see that we need to combine R_5 with R_{COMB1} to make R_{COMB2}. As these two resistors are in series, we can say:

$$R_{COMB2} = R_5 + R_{COMB1} = 1E^3 + 3197.28 = 4197.28\Omega$$

CHAPTER 2 FUNDAMENTAL CIRCUIT THEOREMS

The new circuit is shown in Figure 2-9.

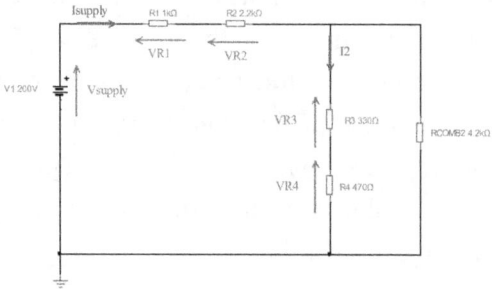

Figure 2-9. *The Reduced Circuit*

I hope you can now see that R_{COMB2} is in parallel with the series combination of R_3 and R_4. So, we need to combine R_3 and R_4 in series as follows:

$$R_{COMB3} = R_3 + R_4 = 330 + 470 = 800\,\Omega$$

We can now combine R_{COMB2} with R_{COMB3} in parallel, as follows:

$$R_{COMB4} = \frac{R_{COMB2} R_{COMB3}}{R_{COMB2} + R_{COMB3}} = \frac{4197.28 \times 800}{4197.28 + 800} = 671.93\,\Omega$$

We can redraw the circuit one more time, as shown in Figure 2-10.

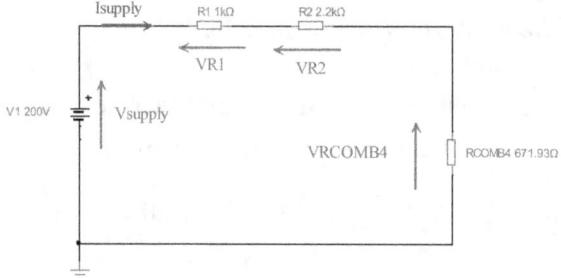

Figure 2-10. *The Final Redrawn Circuit*

CHAPTER 2   FUNDAMENTAL CIRCUIT THEOREMS

You should be able to see that the total resistance R_T is simply the sum of R_1, R_2, and R_{COMB4}, as there are now all in series. Therefore, we can say that:

$$R_T = R_1 + R_2 + R_{COMB4} = 1E^3 + 2.2E^3 + 671.93 = 3871.93 \Omega$$

We can now calculate the supply current, as follows:

$$I_{SUPPLY} = \frac{V_{SUPPLY}}{R_T} = \frac{200}{3871.93} = 0.051654 = 51.654E^{-3} = 51.654 mA$$

This agrees with the measurement of AM1 in Figure 2-7. There is a lot to do before we can calculate the supply current, but as an engineer you will have to carry out many long and complex calculations. As you practice them, they will become more straightforward.

Now that we have calculated the supply current, we can calculate the voltage drops across the resistors R_1 and R_2 and even R_{COMB4} using the circuit shown in Figure 2-10:

$$V_{R1} = I_{SUPPLY} R_1 = 51.654E^{-3} \times 1E^3 = 51.654V$$

$$V_{R2} = I_{SUPPLY} R_2 = 51.654E^{-3} \times 2.2E^3 = 113.638V$$

$$V_{RCOMB4} = I_{SUPPLY} R_{COMB4} = 51.654E^{-3} \times 671.93 = 34.708V$$

We can check these calculations using KVL. Using in the circuit shown in Figure 2-10, we can say:

$$V_{SUPPLY} = V_{R1} + V_{R2} + V_{RCOMB4} = 51.654 + 113.638 + 34.708 = 199.99987 = 200V$$

If you compare the circuit shown in Figure 2-10 with the circuit shown in Figure 2-9, you should be able to see that V_{RCOMB4} is the same as $V_{R3} + V_{R4}$. This is simply because R_{COMB4} is in parallel with the series combination of R_3 and R_4. This can be confirmed because the voltage across the two

CHAPTER 2 FUNDAMENTAL CIRCUIT THEOREMS

resistors, R_3 and R_4, is the supply voltage minus the two voltage drops across the two resistors, R_1 and R_2. This means that the voltage across the two resistors R_3 and R_4 is 34.708V. This means that we can calculate the current I_2 that flows through R_3 and R_4 as follows:

$$I_2 = \frac{V_{RCOMB4}}{R_3 + R_4} = \frac{34.708}{330 + 470} = 0.043385 = 43.385E^{-3} = 43.385mA$$

This agrees with the ammeter measurement AM2 shown in Figure 2-7. We can use KCL to calculate the value of the current I_3. This is because, using KCL, we can say the following:

$$I_{SUPPLY} = I_2 + I_3$$

Therefore, we can say:

$$I_3 = I_{SUPPLY} - I_2 = 51.654E^{-3} - 43.385E^{-3} = 8.269mA$$

This agrees with the AM3 measurement shown in Figure 2-7. We can now calculate the voltage dropped across the resistor R_5 as follows:

$$V_{R5} = I_3 R_5 = 8.269E^{-3} \times 1E^3 = 8.269V$$

We can look at the section of the circuit with R_3, R_4, R_5, R_6, and R_7 as two separate loops, as shown in Figure 2-11.

CHAPTER 2   FUNDAMENTAL CIRCUIT THEOREMS

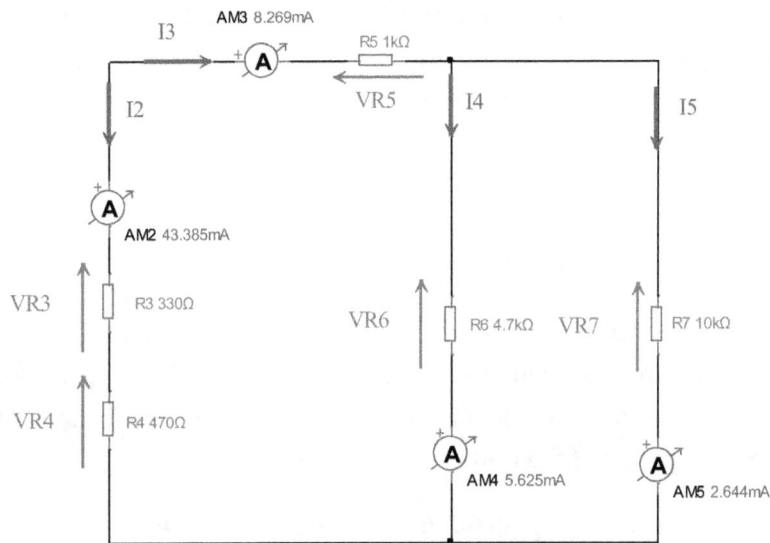

Figure 2-11. *The Separate Loops of R3, R4, R5, R6, and R7*

We can apply KVL to this closed loop to confirm these calculations:

$$V_{RCOMB4} = V_{R3} + V_{R4} = V_{R5} + V_{R6}$$

Therefore, we can say:

$$V_{R6} = V_{COMB4} - V_{R5} = 34.708 - 8.269 = 26.439V$$

Note that you may not have access to an ECAD software so you should practice using KVL and KCL to confirm your calculations.

This means that we can now calculate the current I_4 flowing through the resistor R_6 as follows:

$$I_4 = \frac{V_{R6}}{R_6} = \frac{26.439}{4.7E^3} = 5.625mA$$

71

CHAPTER 2 FUNDAMENTAL CIRCUIT THEOREMS

We can also calculate the current I_5 flowing through the resistor R_7. We know that the voltage across the resistor R_7 is 26.439, the same as V_{R6}, because the two resistors are in parallel with each other; see Figure 2-11. Therefore, we can say that:

$$I_5 = \frac{V_{R7}}{R_7} = \frac{26.439}{10E^3} = 2.644 mA$$

We can check these calculations using KCL. This is because, with respect to the circuit shown in Figure 2-11, we can use the concept from KCL that the sum of the currents flowing into a node equals the sum of the currents flowing out of the node.

$$I_3 = I_4 + I_5 = 5.625E^{-3} + 2.644E^{-3} = 8.269 mA$$

This agrees with our initial calculation of the current I_3.

Before we leave this example circuit, let's explore why it is so important to calculate the current flowing through the components. This is because all components will dissipate some sort of power. This is more important with resistors than it is with capacitors and inductors, as capacitors and inductors don't actually dissipate real power. They use what is termed *reactive power*, something I cover more closely in my next book on AC analysis. However, we know that resistors do dissipate power as they get hot. We can, and should, calculate the amount of power each resistor will dissipate using either:

$$Power = I^2 R \text{ or } Power = \frac{V^2}{R}$$

We can therefore calculate the power dissipated by R_3 as follows:

$$P_{R3} = I_2^2 R_3 = (43.385E^{-3})^2 \times 330 = 0.6211 Watts$$

CHAPTER 2   FUNDAMENTAL CIRCUIT THEOREMS

This means that we should use a 1W rated resistor for R_3. This is quite a high wattage rating, but it shows you how important it is to calculate the current flowing through a resistor. If you used a lower wattage rating for the resistor, there is a very real danger the resistor could set on fire and cause real problems.

This example has shown you how to analyse a series parallel combination circuit and apply the laws you have learnt to calculate the different voltages and currents. It also showed you how to confirm your results using the relevant Kirchhoff Law.

The Current Divider Rule

This is the last circuit analysis rule we look at in this chapter. We can use it to show how a current flowing into a node will split to flow out into different paths in the rest of the circuit. We will use it as an alternative method for calculating the currents, I_4 and I_5, in Figure 2-7. We can see from Figure 2-7 that the current I_3 flows into the node and the currents I_4 and I_5 flow out of it. We will use the current divider rule to calculate the two currents. The current divider rule works in a similar way to the voltage divider rule in that we can calculate the current I_5 as follows:

$$I_5 = \frac{I_3 R_6}{R_6 + R_7}$$

We know I_5 flows through R_7 but we are multiplying I_3, the current flowing into the node, by the opposite resistance of the path from the path the current is actually flowing through. This means you must be careful when applying the current divider rule. Applying this rule with the correct component values gives:

$$I_5 = \frac{8.269E^{-3} \times 4.7E^3}{4.7E^3 + 10E^3} = 2.644E^{-3} = 2.644mA$$

CHAPTER 2   FUNDAMENTAL CIRCUIT THEOREMS

This agrees with the previous calculation for I_5. We could use the current divider rule to calculate the current I_4 which flows through R_6. This is done as follows:

$$I_4 = \frac{I_3 R_7}{R_6 + R_7} = \frac{8.269E^{-3} \times 10E^3}{4.7E^3 + 10E^3} = 5.625E^{-3} = 5.625 mA$$

This agrees with the previous calculation for I_4.

Chapter 2 Exercises

This section includes some exercises for you to try. The answers are at the end of the chapter, after the summary.

Exercise 2.1

With respect to the circuit shown in Figure 2-12, calculate the following using the values in Table 2-2:

- The supply current, I_{SUPPLY}.
- The voltage drops around the circuit—V_{R1}, V_{R2}, V_{R3}, and V_{R4}. Use KVL to confirm your results.
- Use the voltage divider rule to confirm your calculation for V_{R3}.
- Calculate the wattage rating for R_3.

CHAPTER 2 FUNDAMENTAL CIRCUIT THEOREMS

Table 2-2. The Circuit Values for Exercise 2.1

V_{SUPPLY}	R_1	R_2	R_3	R_4
75	1k	220	470	3.3k
125	4.7k	100	1k	220
50	470	3.3K	100	10k

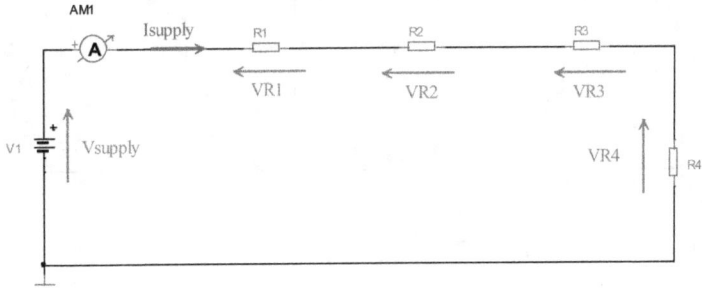

Figure 2-12. The Circuit for Exercise 2.1

Exercise 2.2

With respect to the circuit shown in Figure 2-13, calculate the following using the values in Table 2-3:

- The supply current I_{SUPPLY} and the currents flowing through R_4 and R_5. Use KCL to confirm your results.

- The voltage drops around the circuit—V_{R1}, V_{R2}, V_{R3}, V_{R4}, and V_{R5}. Use KVL to confirm your results.

- Use the voltage divider rule to confirm your calculation for V_{R1}.

CHAPTER 2 FUNDAMENTAL CIRCUIT THEOREMS

- Use the current divider rule to calculate the current flowing through R_3.
- Calculate the wattage rating for R_5.

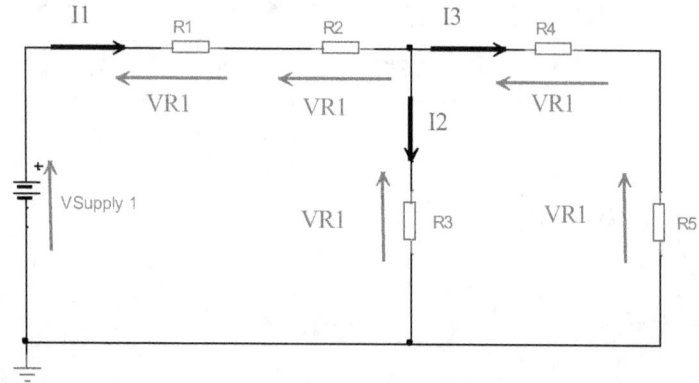

Figure 2-13. *The Circuit for Exercise 2.2*

Table 2-3. *The Circuit Values for Exercise 2.2*

V_{SUPPLY}	R_1	R_2	R_3	R_4	R_5
75	1k	220	470	3.3K	3.3K
125	4.7k	100	1k	220	2.2k
50	470	3.3K	100	10k	1k

Exercise 2.3

With respect to the circuit shown in Figure 2-14, calculate the wattage rating for all the resistors in the circuit and all the volt drops around the circuit.

CHAPTER 2 FUNDAMENTAL CIRCUIT THEOREMS

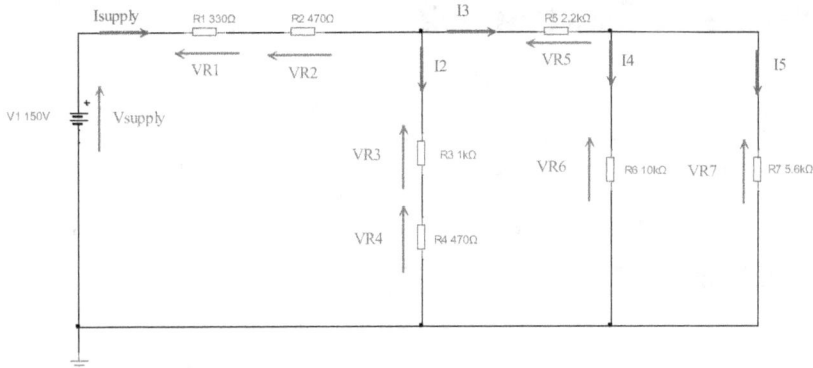

Figure 2-14. The Circuit for Exercise 2.3

Summary

This chapter introduced you to the three fundamental laws of DC circuit analysis. It explained how to use them and showed you that you can, with practice, master these laws to calculate all the quantities in these simple DC resistive circuits.

In the next chapter, we look at three more important theories—Thevenin's, Norton's, and the superposition theory. We also look at using mesh analysis on a circuit with two or more voltage sources.

Answers to Exercise 2.1

Set	I_{Supply}	V_{R1}	V_{R2}	V_{R3}	V_{R4}	R_3 Watt
A	15.03m	15.03	3.307	7.064	49.599	106.17mW
B	20.76m	97.59	2.076	20.76	4.57	431.14mW
C	3.61m	1.69	11.896	360.5m	36.05	1.3mW

CHAPTER 2 FUNDAMENTAL CIRCUIT THEOREMS

Answers to Exercise 2.2

Set	I_{Supply}	V_{R1}	V_{R2}	V_{R3}	V_{R4}	VR5	R_5 Watt
A	45.22m	45.22	9.947	19.838	9.919	9.919	29.81W
B	22.696m	106.67	2.27	16.06	1.46	14.6	96.87mW
C	12.923m	6.074	42.646	1.281	1.164	116.42m	13.55µW

Answers to Exercise 2.3

I_{Supply}	**76.052mA**
I2	60.652mA
I3	15.399mA
I4	5.528mA
I5	9.871mA
V_{R1}	25.097V
V_{R2}	35.744V
V_{R3}	60.652V
V_{R4}	28.507V
V_{R5}	33.879V
V_{R6}	55.28V
V_{R7}	55.28V
W_{R1}	1.909W
W_{R2}	2.718W

(*continued*)

CHAPTER 2 FUNDAMENTAL CIRCUIT THEOREMS

I_{Supply}	**76.052mA**
W_{R3}	3.679W
W_{R4}	1.729W
W_{R5}	521.68mW
W_{R6}	305.559mW
W_{R7}	545.645mW

CHAPTER 3

Further DC Analysis

This chapter covers more analysis theories and rules, including the Maximum Power theory, Thevenin's theory, and Norton's theory. We will also look at how you can use the Superposition rule and mesh analysis on a circuit with two or more sources.

After reading this chapter, you will be able to apply the following theories to DC circuits:

- The Superposition Theorem
- Mesh analysis
- The Maximum Power Transfer Theorem
- Thevenin's Theorem
- Norton's Theorem

We start mesh analysis.

The Kirchhoff's Mesh Currents

We can apply Kirchhoff's Voltage and Current Laws to determine the currents and volt drops in a circuit with more than one source. Such a circuit is shown in Figure 3-1.

CHAPTER 3 FURTHER DC ANALYSIS

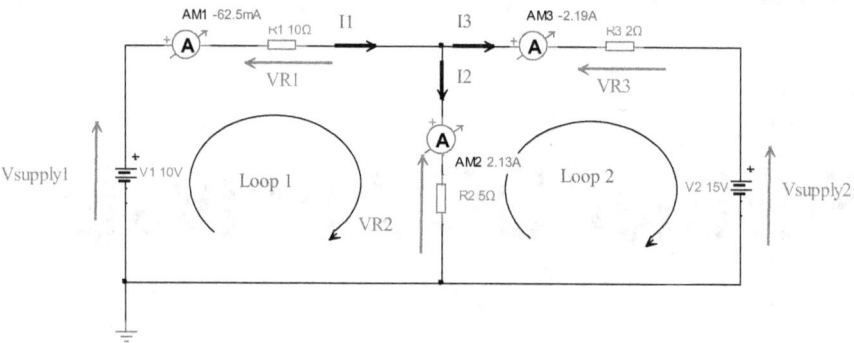

Figure 3-1. *Kirchhoff's Mesh Circuit*

As always, we need to calculate all the currents and volt drops around the circuit so that we can be sure we use the correct gauge of wire and the correct wattage rating for the resistors. The approach is slightly more complex than the previous calculations, but it puts into practice some fundamentals you learnt earlier.

First, we split the circuit up into loops or branches and assume a clockwise direction of the current, as shown in Loops 1 and 2 in Figure 3-1. We could assume an anticlockwise direction, but my preference is clockwise. Note it does not matter if we have assumed the wrong direction for any currents, as the result would be minus, which means the current is flowing in the opposite direction. In assuming a direction of current flow, we dictate what we think will be the positive end of the volt drops, as conventional current flows into the positive end of a voltage or volt drop. That is why I placed the voltage arrows for V_{R1}, V_{R2}, and V_{R3} as shown in Figure 3-1.

Now we need to create the expressions for the voltage sources $V_{SUPLLY1}$ and $V_{SUPPLY2}$. To do this, we can look at the voltage arrows to tell us which voltages add and which oppose each other. Note that if the arrows are in the same direction, the voltages add; if they oppose each other, the voltages subtract. In this case, looking at Loop 1, the arrows for V_{R1} and V_{R2}

CHAPTER 3   FURTHER DC ANALYSIS

are in the same direction, so they add together. However, in that Loop 1, the voltage arrow for $V_{SUPPLY1}$ is in the opposite direction. Therefore, we can say the following:

$$V_{SUPLLY1} = V_{R1} + V_{R2}$$

This agrees with Kirchhoff's Voltage Law, KVL, which states that in a closed loop, all the volt drops add together to equal the supply to that loop. As we are trying to calculate the currents flowing in the circuit, we can apply Ohm's Law to the volt drops in the loop to create expressions for the currents. Using Ohm's Law, we can say:

$$V = IR$$

However, to make it clearer what current we are talking about, we could use the following extension to that expression:

The volt drop across a resistor =
The current flowing through the resistor × the resistor

Knowing that I_1 flows through R_1 and I_2 flows through R_2 we can say:

$$V_{SUPPLY1} = I_1 R_1 + I_2 R_2$$

Looking at Loop 2, we can see that the voltage arrows $V_{Supply2}$ and V_{R3} are in the same direction and they both oppose V_{R2}. Therefore, we can say:

$$V_{SUPLLY2} + V_{R3} = V_{R2}$$

From which we can say:

$$V_{SUPPLY2} = V_{R2} - V_{R3}$$

Applying Ohm's Law, we can say:

$$V_{SUPPLY2} = I_2 R_2 - I_3 R_3$$

CHAPTER 3 FURTHER DC ANALYSIS

We can now put these two expressions together such that:

$$V_{SUPPLY1} = I_1 R_1 + I_2 R_2$$

$$V_{SUPPLY2} = I_2 R_2 - I_3 R_3$$

Putting in the values from the circuit, we have:

$$10 = I_1 10 + I_2 5$$

$$15 = I_2 5 - I_3 2$$

Therefore, we have:

$$10 = 10 I_1 + 5 I_2 \qquad \text{Equation 1}$$

$$15 = 5 I_2 - 2 I_3 \qquad \text{Equation 2}$$

This produces two equations with three unknowns. This would be very difficult to solve as it is. To make it easier, we need to get rid of one of the unknowns (i.e., I_1, I_2, or I_3). From experience, it is easier to get rid of I_3, as it appears only in Equation 2.

Using Kirchhoff's Current Law (KCL) and seeing that I_1 flows into the same node that I_2 and I_3 flow out of, we can say:

$$I_1 = I_2 + I_3$$

Therefore, we can say:

$$I_3 = I_1 - I_2$$

Substituting this for I_3 in Equation 2, we have:

$$15 = 5 I_2 - 2(I_1 - I_2)$$

This gives:

$$15 = 5 I_2 - 2 I_1 + 2 I_2$$

Collecting the like terms gives:

$$15 = -2 I_1 + 7 I_2$$

With this equation, we can now produce a set of simultaneous equations that have just two unknowns, I_1 and I_2. The equations are as follows:

$$10 = 10I_1 + 5I_2 \qquad \text{Equation a}$$
$$15 = -2I_1 + 7I_2 \qquad \text{Equation b}$$

We can solve for these two unknowns by getting rid of another unknown, either I_1 or I_2. Experience tells us to get rid of I_1, as we will be able to add the equations. To get rid of the I_1 term, we must make the coefficients, or the numbers in front of the I_1 terms, the same. This can be done by multiplying (a) by 2 and (b) by 10 as follows (remember that you must multiply everything in the equations):

$$10 = 10I_1 + 5I_2 \qquad \text{-------(x 2)}$$
$$15 = -2I_1 + 7I_2 \qquad \text{-------(x 10)}$$

Which gives:

$$20 = 20I_1 + 10I_2 \qquad \text{Equation c}$$
$$150 = -20I_1 + 70I_2 \qquad \text{Equation d}$$

Note that the coefficients of I_1 in both equations are now 20. We must now add equation d to equation c, because

$$20I_1 + (-20I_1) = 0$$

Adding the two equations together gives us this:

$$170 = 80I_2$$

We can now use the equation to determine a value for I_2 as follows:

$$I_2 = \frac{170}{80} = 2.125 A$$

CHAPTER 3 FURTHER DC ANALYSIS

We can substitute this value for I_2 in Equation a to calculate the value for I_1.

$$10 = 10I_1 + 5I_2 \qquad \text{Equation a}$$

Therefore, we can say this:

$$10 = 10I_1 + 5 \times 2.125 = 10I_1 + 10.625$$

This gives the following:

$$10 - 10.625 = 10I_1$$

Transposing for I_1 gives the following:

$$I_1 = \frac{-0.625}{10} = -0.0625 = -62.5mA$$

The minus sign means that the current is flowing in the opposite direction to what we assumed.

We can check our calculations for I_1 and I_2 by substituting for both in Equation b. You should always check your work before you say it is correct—it is your name that is at stake. This gives the following:

$$15 = -2I_1 + 7I_2$$

Therefore, we have the following:

$$15 = -2 \times (-0.0625) + 7 \times 2.125$$

Therefore:

$$15 = 0.125 + 14.875 = 15$$

This confirms that the values for I_1 and I_2 are correct.
We can now calculate the value for I_3 using:

$$I_3 = I_1 - I_2$$

CHAPTER 3 FURTHER DC ANALYSIS

Therefore, we have this:

$$I_3 = -0.0625 - 2.125 = -2.1875$$

Note that the minus sign means that the direction of the current assumed for I_3 was wrong. To sum up, we can say that the three currents are as follows:

$$I_1 = -62.5 mA$$

$$I_2 = 2.125 A$$

$$I_3 = -2.1875 A$$

If we look at the ammeter readings in Figure 3-1, we see that they agree very closely to these three values.

We can now calculate all the volt drops around the circuit and confirm our calculations using KVL. We can then determine the power dissipated by each of the resistors. However, before we do that, we must redraw the circuit with the current and voltage arrows pointing in the correct directions. This correction is shown in Figure 3-2.

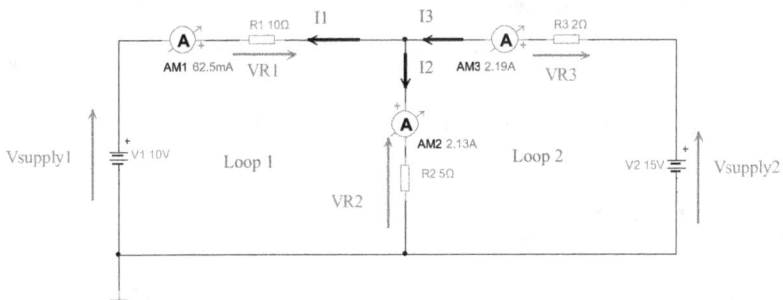

Figure 3-2. *The Voltage Arrows Redrawn Correctly*

The voltage drop, V_{R1}
Using $V_{R1} = I_1 R_1$

$$V_{R1} = 62.5 E^{-3} \times 10 = 0.625 V = 625 mV$$

87

CHAPTER 3 FURTHER DC ANALYSIS

The voltage drop, V_{R2}
Using $V_{R2} = I_2 R_2$

$$V_{R2} = 2.125 \times 5 = 10.625V$$

The voltage drop, V_{R3}
Using $V_{R3} = I_3 R_3$

$$V_{R3} = 2.1875 \times 2 = 4.375V$$

Using the voltage arrows shown in Figure 3-2, we can apply KVL to the two closed loops.

KVL Applied to Loop 1

In this loop, we can see that the voltage arrows for $V_{SUPPLY1}$ and V_{R1} are in the same direction and they both oppose the voltage arrow for V_{R2}. Therefore, we can say that:

$$V_{SUPPLY1} + V_{R1} = V_{R2}$$

Putting the values in, we get:

$$10 + 0.625 = 10.625$$

This is correct and so confirms the values of V_{R1} and V_{R2}.

KVL Applied to Loop 2

In this loop, we can see that the voltage arrows for V_{R2} and V_{R3} are in the same direction and they both oppose the voltage arrow for $V_{SUPPLY2}$. This means that we can say:

$$V_{SUPPLY2} = V_{R2} + V_{R3}$$

Putting the values in gives:

$$15 = 10.625 + 4.375 = 15$$

CHAPTER 3 FURTHER DC ANALYSIS

This is correct and so confirms the values for V_{R2} and V_{R3}.

Finally, the power dissipated in R_2 is calculated using:

$$P = I^2 R = 2.125^2 \times 5 = 22.578W$$

This is a very large wattage rating for a resistor, but then circuits that use resistances of 5 or 10 Ohms are really only for electrical installations. If we were to consider the more common electronic circuits, then we would be dealing with resistance values in the order of k Ohms and so we would use currents in the order of mill amps. This means that we should really work with circuits that use more realistic values for the resistances. The next example of Kirchhoff's mesh currents is more realistic, but the values are more difficult to deal with.

Kirchhoff's Mesh Currents Example 2

The circuit for this example is shown in Figure 3-3.

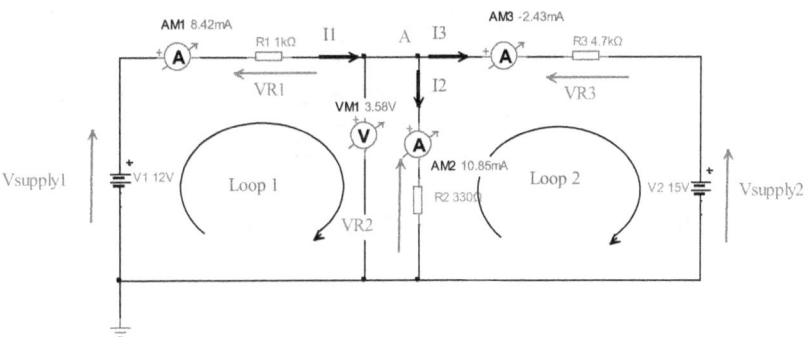

Figure 3-3. *The Circuit for Kirchhoff's Mesh Currents Example 2*

CHAPTER 3   FURTHER DC ANALYSIS

We will use the same approach as in the first example and confirm the currents measured by the ammeters and the voltage at point A as measured by the VM1 voltmeter. After initially assuming a direction of current as shown by the current loops, Loop 1 and Loop 2, we can say that with respect to loop 1:

$$V_{SUPPLY1} = V_{R1} + V_{R2}$$

Therefore, applying Ohm's Law we can say this:

$$V_{SUPPLY1} = I_1 R_1 + I_2 R_2$$

Adding the value of the resistors, we can say:

$$V_{SUPPLY1} = 1E^3 I_1 + 330 I_2$$

Similarly, with respect to Loop 2, we can say:

$$V_{SUPLLY2} + V_{R3} = V_{R2}$$

Which means we can say:

$$V_{SUPLLY2} = V_{R2} - V_{R3}$$

Using Ohm's Law and adding the values of the resistors, we can say:

$$V_{SUPLLY2} = 330 I_2 - 4.7 E^3 I_3$$

Adding the value of the supply voltage, we can say:

$$12 = 1E^3 I_1 + 330 I_2 \qquad \text{Equation 1}$$
$$15 = 330 I_2 - 4.7 E^3 I_3 \qquad \text{Equation 2}$$

Now, applying KVL, we can say that:

$$I_1 = I_2 + I_3$$

Therefore, we can say that:

$$I_3 = I_1 - I_2$$

Substituting for I_3 in the equation for $V_{SUPPLY2}$, we get:

$$15 = 330I_2 - 4.7E^3(I_1 - I_2)$$

Expanding the bracket gives this:

$$15 = 330I_2 - 4.7E^3 I_1 + 4.7E^3 I_2$$

Collecting the like terms gives this:

$$15 = -4.7E^3 I_1 + 5.03E^3 I_2$$

We now have our set of simultaneous equations:

$$12 = 1E^3 I_1 + 330 I_2 \qquad \text{Equation A}$$
$$15 = -4.7E^3 I_1 + 5.03E^3 I_2 \qquad \text{Equation B}$$

We now decide to get rid of the I_1 terms, as this involves adding the two new equations. This means we must make the coefficients of the I_1 terms the same in each equation. Therefore, when we add the two equations, the I_1 terms will cancel out, being equal. The easiest way to make the coefficients the same is to multiply each equation by the coefficient of I_1 in the other equation. This means multiplying all in Equation A by $4.7E^3$ and all in Equation B by $1E^3$. This gives the following two new equations:

$$56.4E^3 = 4.7E^6 I_1 + 1.551E^6 I_2 \qquad \text{Equation C}$$
$$15E^3 = -4.7E^6 I_1 + 5.03E^6 I_2 \qquad \text{Equation D}$$

We now need to add Equation C to D. This gives the following:

$$71.4E^3 = 6.581E^6 I_2$$

Therefore, we can say:

$$I_2 = \frac{71.4E^3}{6.581E^6} = 10.85E^{-3} = 10.85mA$$

CHAPTER 3   FURTHER DC ANALYSIS

This agrees with the AM2 measurement of 10.85mA.

We can now carry on and use Equation A to calculate the current I_1.

$$12 = 1E^3 I_1 + 330 I_2$$

If we substitute the value of 10.85mA for I_2, we get:

$$12 = 1E^3 I_1 + 330 \times 10.85 E^{-3} = 1E^3 I_1 + 3.58$$

Transposing for I1 gives the following:

$$I_1 = \frac{12 - 3.58}{1E^3} = 8.42 E^{-3} = 8.42 mA$$

This agrees with the AM1 measurement of the current, I_1.

We can now calculate the I_3 current using:

$$I_3 = I_1 - I_2$$

Putting the values in gives this:

$$I_3 = 8.42 E^{-3} - 10.85 E^{-3} = -2.43 mA$$

The negative sign for the current I_3 simply means that it is flowing in the opposite direction than we first assumed.

TINA can be used to confirm your calculations, but if you don't have access to an ECAD software, you can check your calculations using Equation 2, as it includes the current I_3. This gives the following:

$$15 = 330 I_2 - 4.7 E^3 I_3$$

Using the values for I_1 and I_3, we get:

$$15 = 330 \times 10.85 E^{-3} - 4.7 \times -2.43 E^{-3}$$

This gives:

$$15 = 3.5805 + 11.421 = 15.0015$$

CHAPTER 3   FURTHER DC ANALYSIS

This is close enough to confirm that our calculations are correct. The small differences are due to rounding errors.

The Superposition Theorem

This theorem is an alternative approach to solving a circuit with multiple sources. We will use it to confirm our work on the circuit shown in Figure 3-3. The theory states that when there are multiple sources in a circuit, we should calculate the unknown quantity with all, but one source is replaced with their ideal internal resistances. This will give multiple values for the unknown. When we get these values, the actual value for the unknown can be determined by adding all the results together. The best way to explain this approach is to go through an example.

With respect to the circuit shown in Figure 3-3, we can calculate the three currents—I_1, I_2, and I_3—using the expression for Ohm's Law. However, if we look at the expression for Ohm's Law, we might need to extend it a little to understand fully how to apply it. The expression for Ohm's Law is:

$$I = \frac{V}{R}$$

However, we need to know what voltage and resistance we should use. To help with this, I extend the expression as follows:

The current flowing through a resistor =
$$\frac{\textit{Voltage at one end of the resistor} - \textit{voltage at the other end}}{\textit{Value of the resistor}}$$

CHAPTER 3   FURTHER DC ANALYSIS

If we apply this description, we can construct an expression for the three currents flowing in Figure 3-3 as follows:

$$I_1 = \frac{V_{SUPPLY1} - V_A}{R_1}$$

$$I_2 = \frac{V_A - 0}{R_2}$$

$$I_3 = \frac{V_A - V_{SUPPLY2}}{R_3}$$

I hope you can see how the extended version of Ohm's Law has helped us construct these three expressions. This means we need to calculate the voltage V_A, the voltage at point A, on the circuit. We can use the Superposition theory to calculate the voltage V_A shown in Figure 3-3. First, we must calculate the voltage with just one source, after replacing all the other sources with their ideal internal resistance.

The Ideal Internal Resistance of a Voltage Source

The purpose of a voltage source is simply to supply a voltage to the circuit that is the same no matter how much current is drawn from it. However, we know that in practice no matter what type of voltage source we are using, the actual voltage at the terminals of the source will be less than its ideal voltage. Also, as we take more current from the source, the voltage at the terminals will reduce. This was discussed in Chapter 1. This means that there must be some internal resistance in the source, as this will produce the voltage drop across this internal resistance as current flows through it. This concept is shown in Figure 3-4.

CHAPTER 3   FURTHER DC ANALYSIS

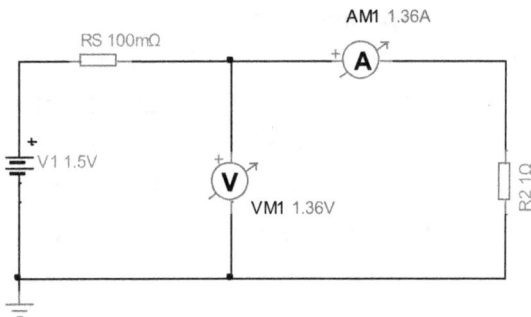

Figure 3-4. *The Internal Resistance of a Voltage Source*

In this circuit, the voltmeter VM1 is measuring the voltage at the output terminals of the voltage source. The V1 is the ideal voltage of the voltage source, a simple battery in this case. The resistance R_S is the internal source resistance, and it is due to the chemicals of the battery not making perfect contact with each other, which causes some voltage to be lost as the current flows through the chemicals. This is the internal resistance that must be present in all voltage sources. If the source was a power supply unit, then the internal resistance is caused by the internal circuitry of the PSU (the *power supply unit*). We set the value of R_S to 0.1Ω, pretty small but hopefully it would be small. The current load value is set at $1k\Omega$. This means that there is about 1.5mA of current flowing out of the voltage source. This flows through R_S before the output terminals of the source, and would inevitably drop some voltage across it. But at 1.5mA this would only be 150µV and so we would not notice this at the output of the source. However, if we reduce the value of the load, R_1, to 1Ω then the current flowing out of the source would increase to around 1.5A. This would have the effect of increasing the voltage lost across the internal resistance R_S to around 150mV. This would have the effect of reducing the voltage at the output of the source to around 1.35V. If you reduce the value of R_1 to 1Ω and simulate the circuit, you will see that the output voltage, as measured by VM1, falls to 1.36V.

CHAPTER 3   FURTHER DC ANALYSIS

I hope that this little experiment and analysis showed you that the only way the battery can give out the expected 1.5V when the current rose the 1.5A is if the internal resistance of the source was 0Ω. This is what the ideal internal resistance of a voltage source is. Therefore, when applying the Superposition theory, we should replace all voltage sources with a short circuit—i.e., a simple wire across the output—as this would have the ideal resistance of 0Ω.

The Ideal Internal Resistance of a Current Source

I am not going through an experiment to show what this would be. Instead, if we appreciate that the use of a current source is to push current into a circuit, then we should appreciate that a current source should not take any current away from the circuit. The only way this can happen is if the ideal internal resistance of a current source was infinity. This means that we should replace all current sources with an open circuit (i.e., simply remove the current source from the circuit).

Now that we have some idea of the internal resistances of a source, we will use the Superposition theory to calculate the voltage at point A in the circuit shown in Figure 3-3.

The Voltage V_A Due to $V_{Supply\ 1}$

There are only two sources in the circuit: $V_{Supply\ 1}$ and $V_{Supply\ 2}$. They are both voltage sources, so their ideal internal resistances are 0Ω. This means we must firstly replace $V_{Supply\ 2}$ with a short circuit. This would produce the circuit shown in Figure 3-5.

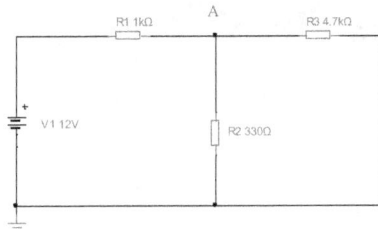

Figure 3-5. *The Circuit with a Short Circuit Replacing $V_{Supply\,2}$*

We see that R_2 and R_3 are now in parallel, as the two tops are connected and the two bottoms are connected. This means that we can replace R_2 and R_3 with a single resistance, R_{COMB1}. The value of R_{COMB1} can be calculated using the product over sum rule, as there are only two resistors:

$$R_{COMB1} = \frac{R_2 R_3}{R_2 + R_3} = \frac{330 \times 4.7E^3}{330 + 4.7E^3} = 308.35\Omega$$

If we redraw the circuit, we'll get Figure 3-6.

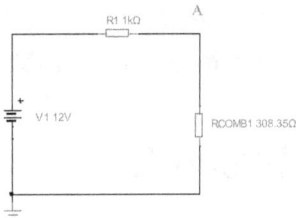

Figure 3-6. *The Circuit Redrawn with R_{COMB1}*

We can now use the voltage divider rule to determine the voltage at point A due to $V_{Supply\,1}$. I hope you can see that the voltage at point A is the same as the volt drop across R_{COMB1}:

$$V_{A\,Due\,to\,Vsupply1} = \frac{V_{Supply1} R_{COMB1}}{R_1 + R_{COMB1}} = \frac{12 \times 308.35}{1E^3 + 308.35} = 2.828V$$

CHAPTER 3   FURTHER DC ANALYSIS

The Voltage V_A Due to $V_{SUPPLY\ 2}$

We need to replace $V_{SUPPLY\ 1}$ with a short circuit. This would produce the circuit shown in Figure 3-7.

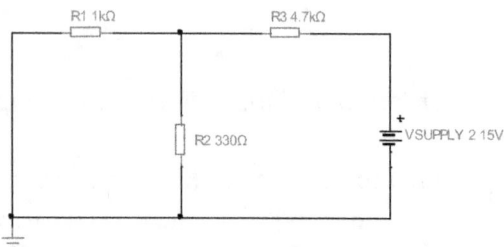

Figure 3-7. The Circuit with a Short Circuit Replacing $V_{Supply\ 1}$

I hope you can see that R_1 is now in parallel with R_2.

Exercise 3.1

As an exercise, calculate the value of R_{COMB2} and show that it is 248.12Ω. Then show that the voltage VA due to $V_{Supply\ 2}$ is 752.165mV.

The Voltage VA at Point A

All we need to do now is add the two results together. This means that:

$$V_A = V_{A\ Due\ to\ Vsupply\ 1} + V_{A\ Due\ to\ Vsupply\ 2} = 2.828 + 752.165 mV = 3.58\ V$$

This value agrees with the voltage measurement of VM1 shown in Figure 3-3. We can now calculate the value of the three currents.

Current I_1

This can be calculated using:

$$I_1 = \frac{V_{Supply\ 1} - V_A}{R_1}$$

Putting the values in gives this:

$$I_1 = \frac{12 - 3.58}{1E^3} = 8.42 mA$$

Current I_2

This can be calculated using:

$$I_2 = \frac{V_A - 0}{R_2}$$

Putting the values in gives this:

$$I_2 = \frac{3.58 - 0}{330} = 10.848 mA$$

Current I_3

This can be calculated using:

$$I_3 = \frac{V_A - V_{Supply\ 2}}{R_3}$$

Putting the values in gives this:

$$I_3 = \frac{3.58 - 15}{4.7E^3} = -2.43 mA$$

Again, the negative value for I_3 simply means it is flowing in the opposite direction than what we assumed. These values agree with the simulation and the values calculated using Kirchhoff's mesh circuit. We will use both approaches in more detail when we move on to AC analysis in Chapter 8.

Exercise 3.2

With respect to the two circuits shown in Figure 3-8, use Kirchhoff's mesh circuits and the Superposition theory to calculate the three currents flowing in the circuit and determine the wattage rating for the resistor R_2 in circuit a and R_5 in circuit b.

CHAPTER 3   FURTHER DC ANALYSIS

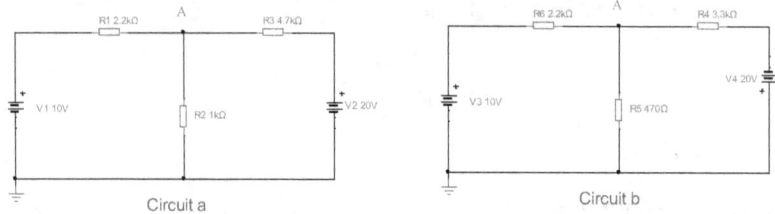

Circuit a   Circuit b

Figure 3-8. *The Two Circuits for Exercise 3.2*

The answers are given at the end of this chapter, after the summary.

The Maximum Power Transfer Theorem

One of the main purposes of an electrical circuit is to deliver power to a load. Mostly, when considering the power dissipated in a load we think about the resistance in the load. This is because a resistor is the only component that dissipates real power. Both inductors and capacitors don't dissipate real power they use what can be considered reactive power. That being the case, we will use a simple DC resistive circuit to investigate this theory of maximum power in the load. The circuit we use to investigate the theory of maximum power is shown in Figure 3-9.

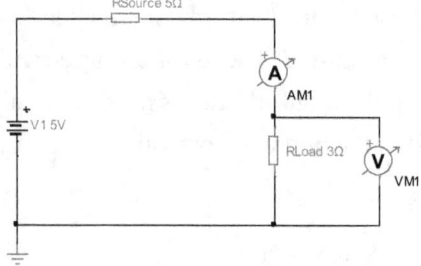

Figure 3-9. *The Test Circuit for the Maximum Power Theory*

100

CHAPTER 3   FURTHER DC ANALYSIS

The idea behind the test circuit is that any source, be it a battery or a power supply, will have an ideal voltage with some internal resistance in series with it. The output voltage is obtained from the terminals after the series internal resistance. In Figure 3-9, the ideal voltage source is the 5V battery and the internal resistance is the R_{Source} set at 5Ω in series with it. The experiment will vary the resistance of the load, R_{Load}, from 3 to 7 Ohms in steps of 1Ω. We will measure the current in the circuit and the voltage across the load for each change in R_{Load}. We will also calculate the power dissipated across the load. The results are recorded in Table 3-1.

Table 3-1. Results for the Maximum Power Theory Experiment

R_{Load} Ohms	Current mA	Voltage Across the Load (Volts)	Power Dissipated in the Load (Watts)
3	625	1.88	1.1719
4	555.56	2.22	1.235
5	500	2.5	1.25
6	454.44	2.73	1.239
7	417.67	2.92	1.221

If we examine the power dissipated, we can see that the maximum power recorded was when the load resistance was set to 5Ω. This is the same value of the source resistance, R_{Source}. This agrees with the theory. The maximum power theory states that:

We will reach the maximum power in the load when the load resistance is equal to the resistance of the circuit that is feeding the load.

This means that it would be useful to be able to determine the internal resistance of a circuit feeding a load. The problem arises because most circuits are very complex. There are two theories that could help in that process.

CHAPTER 3   FURTHER DC ANALYSIS

Thevenin's Theorem

Most electrical circuits are used to deliver power to a load. We should always try to ensure the circuit delivers the maximum amount of power to the load. The maximum power theory tells us that we will reach the maximum power in the load when the load resistance is equal to the resistance of the circuit that is feeding the load. However, most electrical circuits are complex, with lots of series and parallel branches. Therefore, it is very difficult to determine the resistance of the circuit feeding the load. That is where Thevenin's theory comes into play. The theory states that:

> *Any circuit, no matter how complex, can be replaced by a simple circuit that has just a single resistance in series with a single voltage source that feeds the circuit.*

This means that any circuit, no matter how complex, can be replaced with Thevenin's equivalent circuit that has a Thevenin's voltage source in series with a Thevenin's resistance. To ensure that the maximum power is then delivered to the load, the resistance of the load must be the same as the Thevenin's resistance. To help appreciate this theory, we will consider the simple DC circuit shown in Figure 3-10.

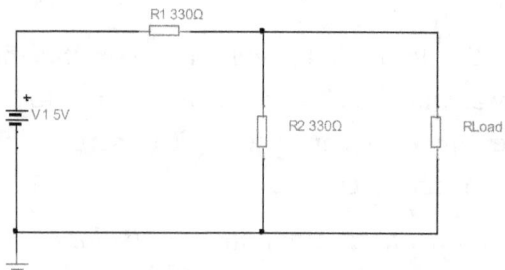

Figure 3-10. *The DC Circuit for Example 1 for Thevenin's Theory*

CHAPTER 3   FURTHER DC ANALYSIS

We need to determine the value of the load resistance for maximum power in the load. We will have to replace the complex circuit made up of the voltage source V_1 and the two resistors R_1 and R_2 with a Thevenin's equivalent circuit. The circuit is not very complex in this first example.

We will calculate the Thevenin's resistance first. As this is a resistive circuit, this will be a Thevenin's resistance, which we call R_{THEV}. To determine R_{THEV}, we must remove the load from the circuit and replace all sources with their ideal internal resistance, then calculate the resistance we would see looking back into the circuit. As there is only one voltage source, we need to replace V_1 with a short circuit. This would produce the circuit shown in Figure 3-11.

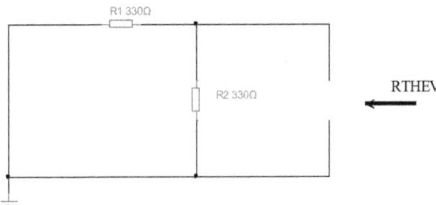

Figure 3-11. *The Thevenin's Resistance R_{THEV}*

I hope it is clear that R_1 is now in parallel with R_2. This means that we can calculate R_{THEV} using the product over sum rule as follows:

$$R_{THEV} = \frac{R_1 \times R_2}{R_1 + R_2} = \frac{330 \times 330}{330 + 330} = 165\Omega$$

I chose the values of R_1 and R_2 to be equal to show you that when two resistors that are in parallel have the same values, the combined resistance will be half the value of resistor's value. This is quite a useful concept to remember.

Now we calculated the Thevenin's resistance, we need to calculate the Thevenin's voltage, V_{THEV}. This will be the voltage that appears across the terminals from where the load resistance has been removed. It is sometimes called *the open circuit voltage*. We can use the circuit shown

CHAPTER 3   FURTHER DC ANALYSIS

in Figure 3-10 to determine this. Note that if the load resistance has been removed, V_{THEV} will simply be the voltage across the resistor, R_2. We can use the voltage divider rule to calculate this, as follows:

$$V_{THEV} = \frac{V_1 \times R_2}{R_1 + R_2} = \frac{5 \times 330}{330 + 330} = 2.5V$$

We can now create the Thevenin's equivalent circuit, as shown in Figure 3-12.

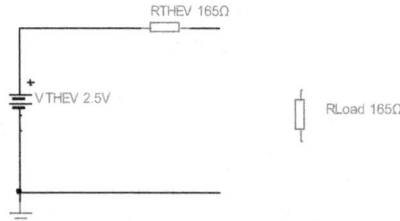

Figure 3-12. *Thevenin's Equivalent Circuit*

This means that to get the maximum power in the load, we must make the load resistance equal to the Thevenin's resistance. In this case, we make $R_L = 165\Omega$. If we did this, we could calculate the current flowing through the load resistance R_L, as follows:

$$I_L = \frac{V_{THEV}}{2 \times R_{THEV}} = \frac{2.5}{2 \times 165} = 7.576 mA$$

This means that the power in the load can be calculated as follows:

$$P_{Load} = I_L^2 R_L = \left(7.576E^{-3}\right)^2 \times 165 = 9.47 mW$$

Now we confirm that this is the maximum power by increasing the load resistance to 200Ω and calculating the power in the load. Then we will reduce the load to 100Ω and calculate the power in the load.

When $R = 200\Omega$.

CHAPTER 3 FURTHER DC ANALYSIS

We need to calculate the current flowing through the load. This would be as follows:

$$I_L = \frac{V_{THEV}}{R_{THEV} + R_L} = \frac{2.5}{165 + 200} = 6.849 mA$$

Therefore:

$$P_{Load} = I_L^2 R_L = (6.849E^{-3})^2 \times 200 = 9.38 mW$$

When R = 100Ω.

We need to calculate the current flowing through the load. This would be as follows:

$$I_L = \frac{V_{THEV}}{R_{THEV} + R_L} = \frac{2.5}{165 + 100} = 9.434 mA$$

Therefore:

$$P_{Load} = I_L^2 R_L = (9.434E^{-3})^2 \times 100 = 8.9 mW$$

These two results help confirm the maximum power theory.

To show that the Thevenin's equivalent circuit, shown in Figure 3-12, is equivalent to the real circuit, we will simulate the circuit shown in Figure 3-13, which is the original circuit with a load resistance of 165Ω.

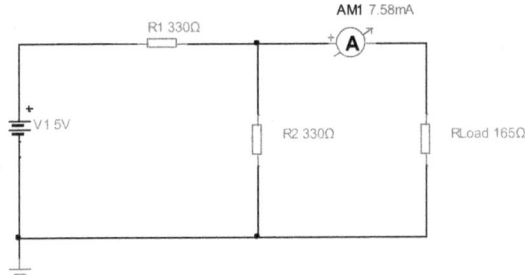

Figure 3-13. *The Original Circuit with R_L Set to 165W*

105

CHAPTER 3   FURTHER DC ANALYSIS

The current in the load is the same as the current calculated using the Thevenin's equivalent circuit. I hope this helps you appreciate that the theory works. However, the Thevenin's equivalent circuit can only be used as an aid to calculations. It cannot be used as a circuit to replace the original circuit, as it will not work practically in the same way.

Thevenin's Equivalent Example 2

We will look at a slightly more complex circuit, in that it has more resistors and a current source. The circuit is shown in Figure 3-14.

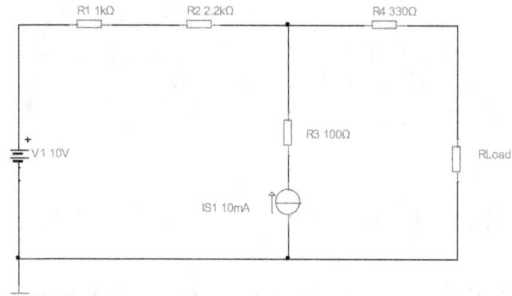

Figure 3-14. *Thevenin's Example 2 Circuit with the Current Source I_{S1}*

We will calculate the Thevenin's resistance, R_{THEV}, first. To do this, we must replace the voltage source V1 with a short circuit and the current source I_{S1} with an open circuit, after removing the load resistance R_L from the circuit. This will produce the circuit shown in Figure 3-15.

106

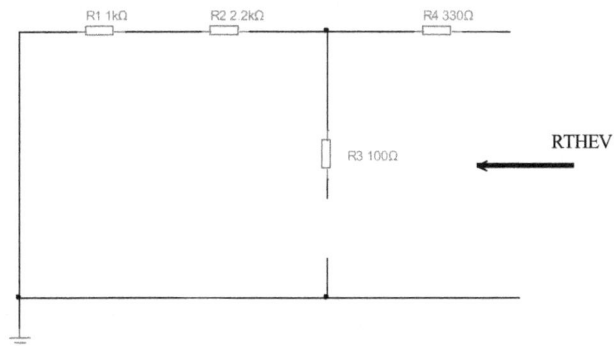

Figure 3-15. *The Thevenin's Resistance R_{THEV}*

I hope you can see that the R_3 resistance has no effect on the Thevenin's resistance, R_{THEV}. This is because it is neither in series nor in parallel with the other resistors in the circuit. You should be able to see that the resistance measured across the output terminals, called R_{THEV}, would be R_1, R_2, and R_4 in series with each other. This means that R_{THEV} is:

$$R_{THEV} = R_1 + R_2 + R_4 = 1E^3 + 2.2E^3 + 330 = 3.53E^3 = 3.53k\Omega$$

Next, we need to determine the Thevenin's voltage, V_{THEV}. This is the open circuit voltage (i.e., the voltage that would appear across the terminals where the load has been removed). As there are two sources that can contribute to this voltage, we can use the Superposition theory to determine this V_{THEV}.

V_{THEV} Due to the Voltage Source V_1

We must replace the current source with its ideal internal resistance, which is basically an open circuit, as no current flows through the source. This circuit is shown in Figure 3-16.

CHAPTER 3 FURTHER DC ANALYSIS

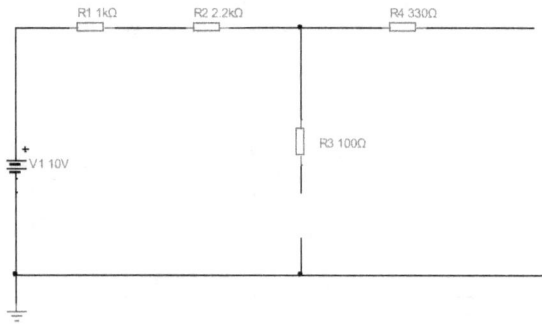

Figure 3-16. *The Circuit for V_{THEV} Due to V_1*

We can see that no current can flow through R_3 and so that plays no part in the circuit. Also, because the load has been removed, leaving an open circuit, there is no path for any current to flow through the circuit. This means that there can be no voltage dropped across any of the resistors and so the open circuit voltage will be the same as V_1. This means that V_{THEV} due to V_1 is 10V.

V_{THEV} Due to the Current Source I_{S1}

We must replace the voltage source with a short circuit, and this will produce the circuit shown in Figure 3-17.

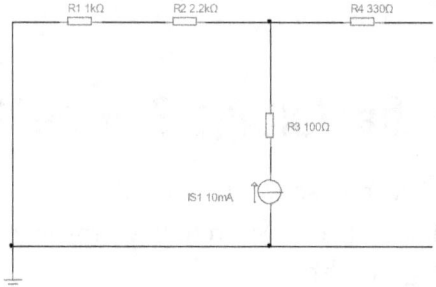

Figure 3-17. *The Circuit for V_{THEV} Due to the Current Source I_{S1}*

108

CHAPTER 3   FURTHER DC ANALYSIS

The purpose of the current source is to force the 10mA into the circuit. This current will flow up through R_3 to the junction of R_2 and R_4. However, as the load is an open circuit, no current can flow through R_4. However, the voltage source has been replaced by a short circuit, so this 10mA can flow through R_2 and R_1. This will create two voltage drops across R_2 and R_1. Using Ohm's Law, we can say that:

$$V_{R2} = I_{S1} \times R_2 = 10E^{-3} \times 2.2E^3 = 22V$$

Also:

$$V_{R1} = I_{S1} \times R_1 = 10E^{-3} \times 1E^3 = 10V$$

This means the total volt drop is 32V. We can see that the voltage at the bottom of R_1 is connected to the reference ground, which is 0V. A total of 32V is dropped across R_1 and R_2, which means that the voltage at the junction of R_2 and R_4 is 32V. As no current flows through R_4 the open circuit voltage due to the current source is the 32V.

To calculate the actual Thevenin's voltage V_{THEV}, we simply need to add these two results together. This gives:

$$V_{THEV} = V_{Thev\ Due\ to\ V1} + V_{Thev\ Due\ to\ IS1} = 10 + 32 = 42V$$

If we use a voltmeter to measure the open circuit voltage with both sources connected, as shown in Figure 3-18, we will see that the voltmeter reads the same—42V.

CHAPTER 3 FURTHER DC ANALYSIS

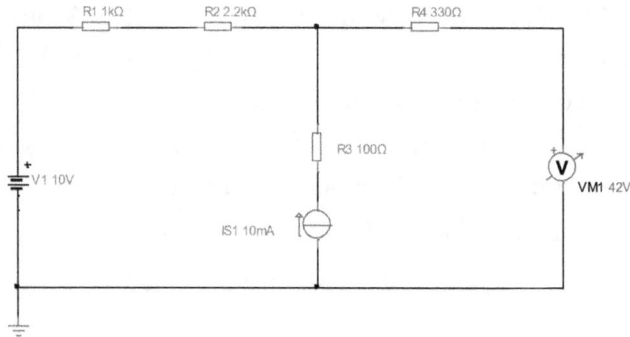

Figure 3-18. *Measuring the Open Circuited Voltage to Confirm Our Calculations*

This analysis to determine the Thevenin's voltage V_{THEV} shows us that we need to interpret how the currents flow around a circuit and how the voltages are dropped across the components of the circuit. This is a skill that you will need to develop, and it will take a lot of time and practice to get it right. I hope the chapter examples and exercises help you start developing this skill.

Now we can create the Thevenin's equivalent circuit, which will be a single voltage source set to the Thevenin's voltage V_{THEV} in series with a single resistance set to the value of R_{THEV}. This equivalent circuit is shown in Figure 3-19.

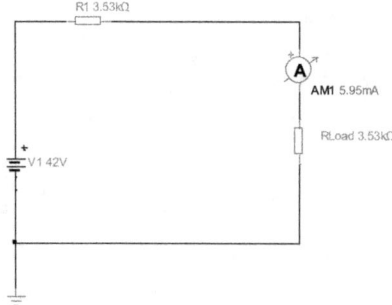

Figure 3-19. *The Thevenin's Equivalent Circuit*

110

CHAPTER 3   FURTHER DC ANALYSIS

The circuit shown in Figure 3-19 shows that the load resistance has already been added. For maximum power in the load, the resistance value is the same as R_{THEV}. We can calculate the current flowing through the load for maximum power as follows:

$$I_{Load} = \frac{V_{THEV}}{2 \times R_{THEV}} = \frac{42}{2 \times 3.53E^3} = 5.949E^{-3} = 5.95mA$$

This agrees with load current measured in Figure 3-19. If we change the value of the load resistance in the original circuit to R_{THEV} (i.e. 3.53kΩ), and then measure the current in the load resistance, as shown in Figure 3-20, we will see that it has the same value as the equivalent circuit shown in Figure 3-19.

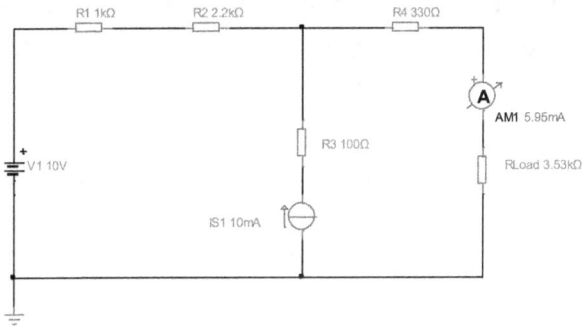

Figure 3-20. Confirming the Calculation of the Load Current

Thevenin's Equivalent Example 3

This example looks at a slightly more complex circuit, shown in Figure 3-21.

111

CHAPTER 3   FURTHER DC ANALYSIS

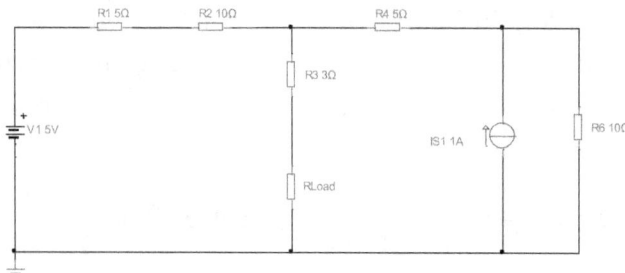

Figure 3-21. Thevenin's Example 3 Circuit

I am using this circuit to illustrate another example of how to develop these skills. That is why we are using simple resistor values. The load is placed in a rather awkward position, which makes it more difficult to analyse. We will create a Thevenin's equivalent circuit so that we can determine the value of the load resistor, R_{Load}, that will dissipate most power in the load. The first thing to do is remove the load resistor. Then, after replacing the sources with their ideal internal resistance, we determine the Thevenin's resistance, R_{THEV}. We redraw the circuit as shown in Figure 3-22.

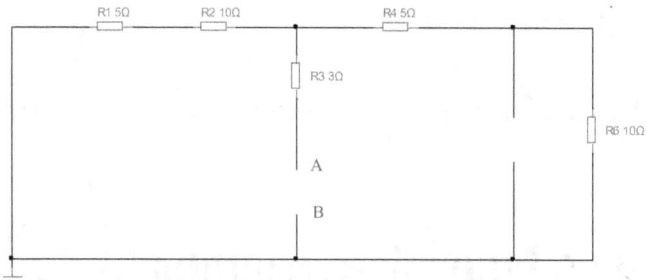

Figure 3-22. The Circuit Redrawn with Load and the Sources Replaced with Their Ideal Internal Resistances

The points A and B are the terminals that the load resistor was removed from. It is across these terminals that we will be taking the output of the circuit. This means that we need to determine the resistance as seen

112

CHAPTER 3   FURTHER DC ANALYSIS

looking back into the circuit from these terminals (i.e., as if we placed an ohm meter across the terminals A and B). If we consider point B, we can see that we could move to the left or the right, but we would be at the ground or 0V in both directions. When looking at point A, we must move up to one end of R_3. As we leave R_3, we come to a junction, which means we can go left or right. If we go to the right, we go through the series combination of R_5 and R_6 and then go to ground. If we go to the left, we must go through the series combination of R_2 and R_1 and then go to ground. This means that from point A, we have a series resistor R_3 and then we have two paths to ground—one going through the series combination of R_5 and R_6 and the other going through the series combination of R_2 and R_1. This means that the series combination of R_5 and R_6 is in parallel with the series combination of R_2 and R_1. Therefore, we can redraw the circuit as shown in Figure 3-23.

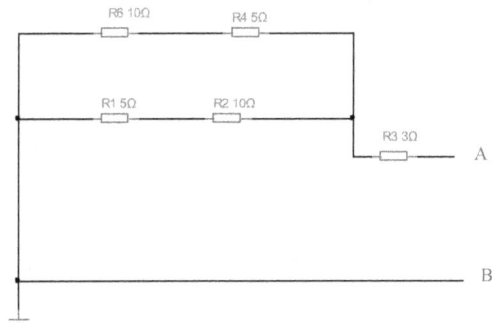

Figure 3-23. *The Circuit Redrawn to Help Calculate R_{THEV}*

Using this circuit, we can see that R_3 is in series with the parallel combination of two 15Ω series combinations. This means that we can combine these two parallel combinations into a single resistor termed R_{COMB1}. We can calculate R_{COMB1} as follows:

$$R_{COMB1} = \frac{15 \times 15}{15 + 15} = 7.5\Omega$$

113

CHAPTER 3   FURTHER DC ANALYSIS

This is shown in Figure 3-24.

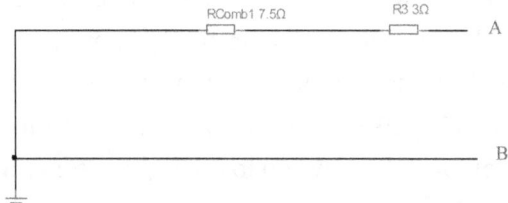

Figure 3-24. *The Circuit to Calculate R_{THEV}*

This shows that R_{THEV} is 10.5Ω. Now we need to calculate the Thevenin's voltage, V_{THEV}. This will be the open circuit voltage (i.e., the voltage across the terminals A and B where the load has been removed). Because there are two sources, the voltage source V1 and the current source I_{S1}, we will use the Superposition rule to determine V_{THEV} due to the separate sources. To calculate V_{THEV} due to V1, we can use the circuit shown in Figure 3-25.

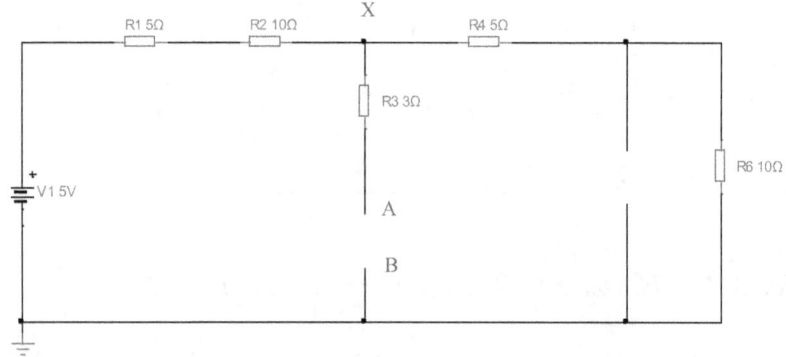

Figure 3-25. *The Circuit to help Calculate V_{THEV} Due to V1*

This shows the circuit with the load removed at terminals A and B as well as the current source replaced with the ideal internal resistance of the current source. We can see that the voltage at terminal B is simply 0V, as it is connected to the ground. This means we only need to calculate

CHAPTER 3   FURTHER DC ANALYSIS

the voltage at the terminal A. Again, from the circuit, we can see that the voltage at the terminal A will be the same as the voltage at the point X in the circuit, as no current can flow through the resistor R_3. The circuit has four resistors in series, but we can think of the circuit as just two 15Ω resistors on either side of the point x in the circuit. We can use the voltage divider rule to calculate this voltage at point x as follows:

$$V_x = \frac{V_1 \times (R_4 + R_6)}{(R_1 + R_2) + (R_4 + R_6)} = \frac{5 \times 15}{15 + 15} = 2.5V$$

Because there is no current flowing through R_3, this is the same as the voltage at terminal A. As terminal B is at ground, the open circuit voltage is 2.5V. This shows that V_{THEV} due to V1 is 2.5V.

Now we calculate V_{THEV} due to the current source, I_{S1}. We use the circuit shown in Figure 3-26 to do this.

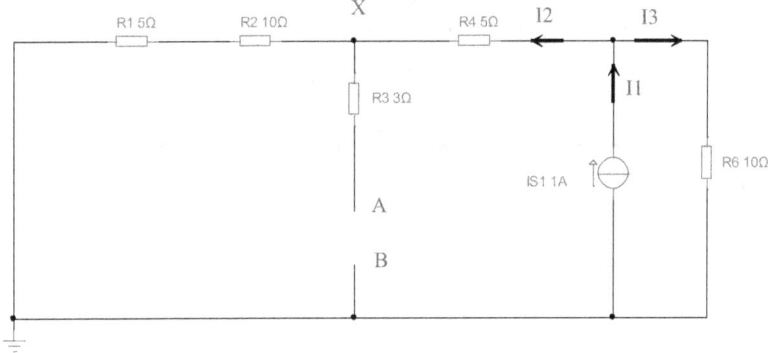

Figure 3-26. *The Circuit Redrawn to Help Calculate V_{THEV} due to I_{S1}*

I replaced the voltage source V1 with a short circuit. We can see that the current source will push 1Amp of current to flow into the node at the junction of R_4 and R_6. The current will then split—some current will flow as

115

CHAPTER 3 FURTHER DC ANALYSIS

I_3 through R_6 and the rest will flow as I_2 through the resistors R_1, R_2, and R_4. If we can calculate the value of I_2, we can calculate the voltage at point X in the circuit. This would simply be as follows:

$$V_X = I_2(R_1 + R_2)$$

We can use the current divider rule to calculate the current I_2. This would give the following:

$$I_2 = \frac{I_1 R_6}{R_1 + R_2 + R_4 + R_6} = \frac{1 \times 10}{30} = 0.333333 rA$$

This means that we can calculate V_X as follows:

$$V_X = I_2(R_1 + R_2) = 0.333333r(5+10) = 5V$$

We can now simply add the two voltages together to get the voltage at point X in the circuit, which, because no current flows through R_3, is the Thevenin's Voltage V_{THEV}. This means that:

$$V_{THEV} = 2.5 + 5 = 7.5V$$

We can now create the Thevenin's equivalent circuit, which is shown in Figure 3-27.

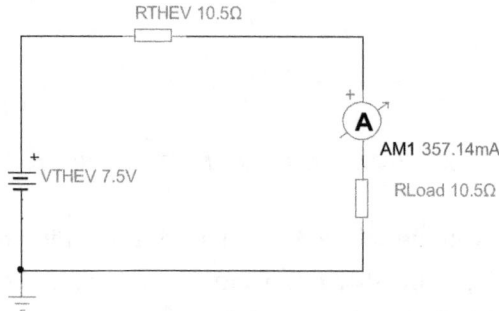

Figure 3-27. *The Thevenin's Equivalent Circuit with R_{Load} Changed to 10.5Ω*

116

CHAPTER 3   FURTHER DC ANALYSIS

The load resistor has been changed to be the same as R_{THEV} so that we will get the maximum power in the load. We can calculate the current flowing through the load resistor as follows:

$$I_{Load} = \frac{V_{THEV}}{R_{THEV} + R_{Load}} = \frac{7.5}{10.5 + 10.5} = 357.143E^{-3} = 357.143mA$$

If we replace the load resistor in the original circuit with the 10.5Ω resistor and measure the current flowing through the load, we get the measurement shown in Figure 3-28.

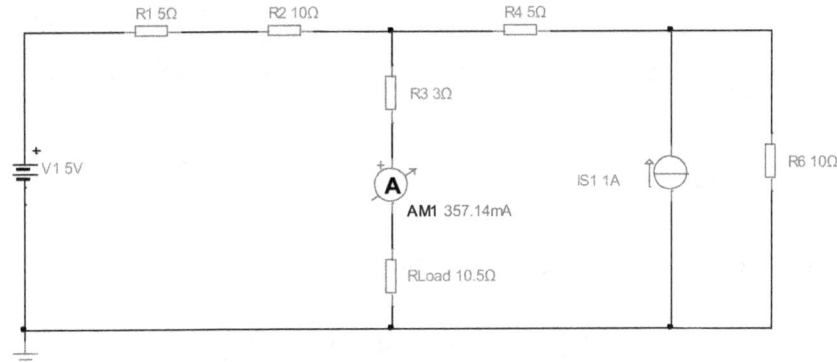

Figure 3-28.   The Complete Circuit with R_{Load} Set to 10.5Ω.

This measurement agrees with the 357.14mA measured in the Thevenin's equivalent circuit shown in Figure 3-27 and with our calculated value.

I hope this example shows you how, by considering carefully how components are connected in a circuit, you can correctly interpret the circuit values. It should also show you that a Thevenin's equivalent circuit can be useful in designing electrical circuits.

CHAPTER 3   FURTHER DC ANALYSIS

Exercise 3.3

Create the Thevenin's equivalent circuits for the three circuits shown in Figure 3-29.

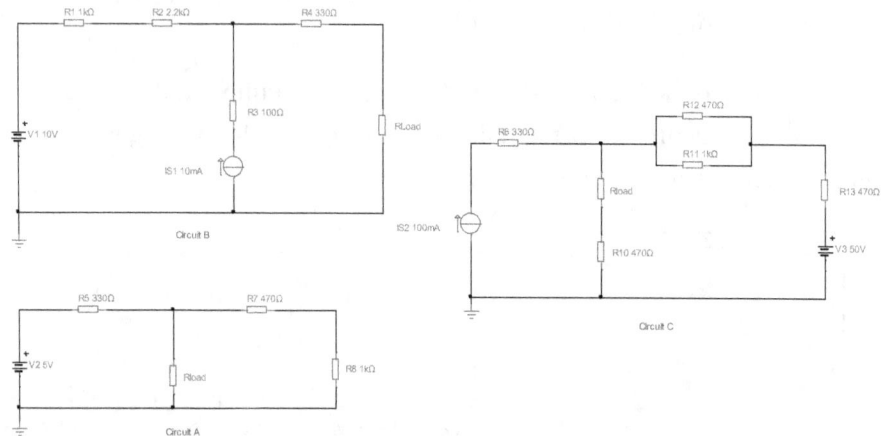

Figure 3-29. *The Three Circuits for Exercise 3.3*

The answers are at the end of this chapter, after the summary.

Norton's Theorem

This is a similar theory to Thevenin's in that Norton's Theory states:

> Any circuit, no matter how complex, can be replaced by a Norton's equivalent circuit, which is a circuit with a single current source that has a single resistance in parallel with it.

We will use Norton's Theory on the circuit shown in Figure 3-10 and confirm the calculations of the Thevenin's theory.

118

CHAPTER 3   FURTHER DC ANALYSIS

The Norton's Resistance (R_N)

The process of determining the Norton's resistance is the same as the Thevenin's resistance; therefore, we can say $R_N = R_{THEV}$. In this case then, $R_N = 165\Omega$.

The Norton's Current

This is the current that will become the current source in the Norton's equivalent circuit. The Norton's current is the current that will flow through a short circuit across the output terminals of the circuit where the load has been removed. In this first example, the circuit to calculate this Norton's current is shown in Figure 3-30.

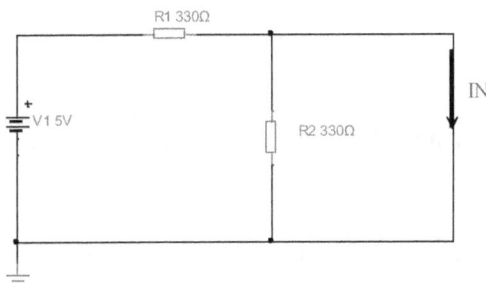

Figure 3-30. The Norton's Current I_N in Norton's Example 1

Note that the conventional current used to analyse electrical circuits flows out of the positive terminal of the source and returns to the supply at the negative terminal. More importantly, the current will always flow through the easiest path to get back to the supply. This means that when the current comes to the junction of R_2 and the short circuit placed across the output, no current flows through resistor R_2 and all the current flows through the short circuit. If you try to use the current divider rule, you will see that no current will flow through R_2. This means that the resistor R_2

CHAPTER 3   FURTHER DC ANALYSIS

plays no part in the circuit, as it is shorted out by the short circuit placed across it. This means that the only resistance in the circuit is that of R_1. Therefore, the Norton's current I_N can be calculated as follows:

$$I_N = \frac{V_1}{R_1} = \frac{5}{330} = 15.152 mA$$

The Norton's equivalent circuit can now be created, as shown in Figure 3-31.

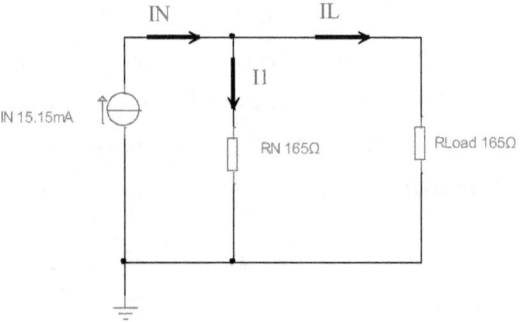

Figure 3-31. *The Norton's Equivalent Circuit with the Load for Maximum Power*

The Norton's equivalent circuit is the current source of I_N in parallel with the Norton's resistance, R_N. The load has been added to the circuit using the value for maximum power (i.e., we set the load resistance to equal the source resistance which, in this case, is the Norton's resistance). We need to know what current will flow through the load. There are two ways to calculate this current—one using Ohm's Law and the other using the current divider rule.

To use Ohm's Law, we need to know the voltage across the load resistance. This will be due to the current source pushing the Norton's current into the combined resistance of R_N in parallel with R_L. As there are only two resistors in parallel, this combined resistance can be calculated using the product over sum rule, as follows:

$$R_{COMB1} = \frac{R_N R_L}{R_N + R_L} = \frac{165 \times 165}{165 + 165} = 82.5\Omega$$

Note that this agrees with the principle that if the two resistors in parallel have the same value, then their combined resistance will simply be half the value of the resistors.

We can now calculate the voltage across the load V_L as follows:

$$V_L = I_N R_L = 15.15E^{-3} \times 82.5 = 1.25V$$

We can now use Ohm's Law to calculate the current flowing through the load as follows:

$$I_L = \frac{V_L}{R_L} = \frac{1.25}{165} = 7.575mA$$

As an alternative method, or a way of confirming this calculation, we could use the current divider rule to calculate this load current I_L, because we know the Norton's current will be split between I_1 and I_L in the two paths that provide a route back to the supply. As current flow depends upon the resistance of the path, and because both paths have the same resistance, they would divide the current equally between them. This means that:

$$I_L = \frac{I_N}{2} = \frac{15.15E^{-3}}{2} = 7.575mA$$

However, we should be able to show how the current divider rule works and gives the same result. When applying the current divider rule, we multiply the current being divided by the resistance of the opposite path and divide the result by the sum of the resistances of the two paths. This means that the load current can be calculated as follows:

$$I_L = \frac{I_N R_N}{R_N + R_L} = \frac{15.15E^{-3} \times 165}{165 + 165} = 7.575mA$$

CHAPTER 3   FURTHER DC ANALYSIS

Both these results are the same and both give the same result calculated using Thevenin's theory.

Norton's Example 2

We will use the same circuit as that for the Thevenin's theory shown in Figure 3-14. Because we calculate the Norton's resistance, R_N, in the same way as we calculate the Thevenin's resistance, we can say $R_N = R_{THEV} = 3.53k\Omega$. This means we can calculate the Norton's current I_N. This is the current flowing through a short circuit placed across the terminals where the load resistance has been removed. As there are two sources in this circuit, this Norton's current will be due to both sources and we must calculate each source, independent from the other. Then we add the results together.

The Norton's Current Due to V1

The circuit to determine this current is shown in Figure 3-32.

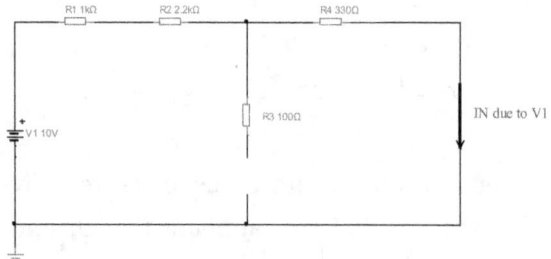

Figure 3-32. *The Circuit to Calculate I_N Due to V1*

We can see that R_3 plays no part in the circuit, as no current can flow through it. This means that the circuit is a simple series circuit made up of R_1, R_2, and R_4 all connected in series. We can use Ohm's Law to determine the current flowing, as follows:

122

$$I_{Ndue\ to\ V1} = \frac{V_1}{R_1 + R_2 + R_4} = \frac{10}{1E^3 + 2.2E^3 + 330} = 2.833mA$$

The Norton's Current Due to I$_{S1}$

We can use the circuit shown in Figure 3-33 to determine this current.

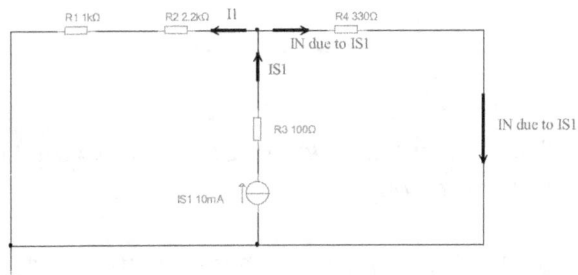

Figure 3-33. *The Circuit to Help Calculate I_N Due to the Current Source I_{S1}*

Note that the current I_{S1} will split when it gets to the junction of R_2, R_3, and R_4. We need to determine the current that will flow through R_4, as this will be the Norton's current due to this current source. We can use the current divider rule to determine the current I_N due to I_{S1} as follows:

$$I_{N\ Due\ to\ IS1} = \frac{I_{S1}(R_1 + R_2)}{R_1 + R_2 + R_4} = \frac{10E^{-3}(1E^3 + 2.2E^3)}{1E^3 + 2.2E^3 + 330} = 9.065mA$$

Note that the resistance R_3 plays no part in this calculation because the 10mA from the current source flows out at the top of R_3 and splits at the node to I_1 and I_N.

This means that the total Norton's current is:

$$I_N = I_{N\ Due\ to\ V1} + I_{N\ Due\ to\ IS1} = 2.833^3 + 9.065E^3 = 11.898mA$$

CHAPTER 3 FURTHER DC ANALYSIS

We can now create the Norton's equivalent circuit, which is shown in Figure 3-34.

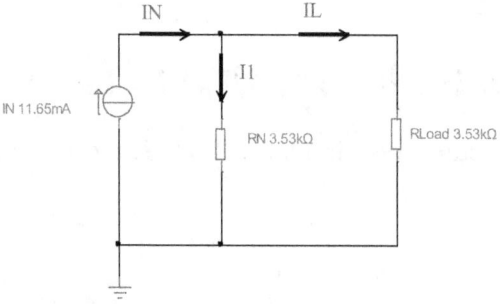

Figure 3-34. *The Norton's Equivalent Circuit, with the Load Set for Maximum Power in the Load*

We include the load resistance, which is set to the same value of the Norton's resistance R_N. This means that the load current will simply be half the value of the Norton's current. This means that I_L is:

$$I_L = \frac{I_N}{2} = \frac{11.898E^{-3}}{2} = 5.949 mA$$

This is the same value as that calculated using the Thevenin's theory approach.

Exercise 3.4

Create the Norton's equivalent circuit for the circuit shown in Figure 3-21 and the three circuits shown in Exercise 3.3.

Converting from Thevenin's to Norton's

There may be occasions when, having created a Thevenin's equivalent circuit, you might think it would be useful to have a Norton's equivalent circuit. In those cases, you can convert from a Thevenin's circuit to a

124

Norton's circuit. Of course, you might want to convert the other way around as well. To explain the process, we will convert the Thevenin's equivalent circuit in Figure 3-35 to a Norton's equivalent circuit.

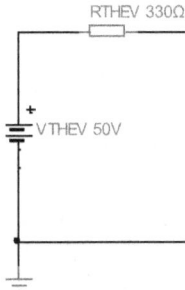

Figure 3-35. *The Thevenin's Equivalent Circuit*

The Norton's current is the short circuit current, that is., the current that would flow through a short circuit placed across the output terminals. With respect to the Thevenin's circuit shown in Figure 3-35, this would connect the bottom of the R_{THEV} resistance to the ground. This means that we can calculate the Norton's current as follows:

$$I_N = \frac{V_{THEV}}{R_{THEV}} = \frac{50}{330} = 151.151E^3 = 151.151mA$$

From our previous work, we know that the Norton's resistance will be the same as the Thevenin's resistance, R_{THEV}. This means that:

$$R_{NORT} = R_{THEV} = 330\Omega$$

We can now construct the Norton's equivalent circuit, as a shown in Figure 3-36.

CHAPTER 3 FURTHER DC ANALYSIS

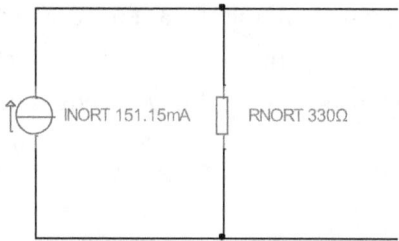

Figure 3-36. *The Norton's Equivalent Circuit*

We could convert this circuit back to a Thevenin's equivalent circuit using the following relationship:

$$R_{THEV} = R_{NORT}$$

$$V_{THEV} = I_{NORT} R_{NORT}$$

Exercise 3.5

Convert the equivalent circuits shown in Figure 3-37 to the opposite equivalent circuit.

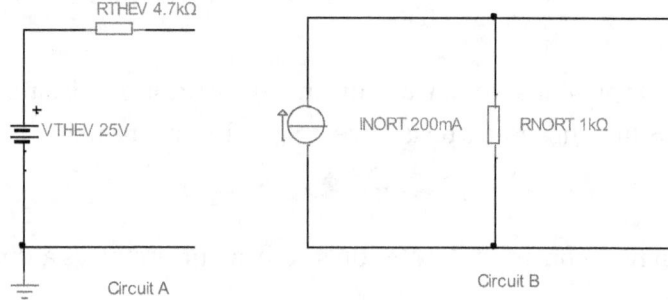

Figure 3-37. *The Circuits for Exercise 3.5*

CHAPTER 3   FURTHER DC ANALYSIS

Summary

This chapter explained a range of circuit analysis theories. We used the theories to calculate the currents and voltage drops in circuits with more than one source, including circuits with voltage and current sources. I hope you have found this chapter both interesting and informative.
In the next chapter, we start our investigation into DC transients. We will start with the series RL circuit to show how the current builds up and decays.

Answers to Exercise 3.2

Current	Circuit a	Circuit b
IR_1	2.146m	4.78m
IR_2	5.278m	-1.117m
IR_3	-3.132m	5.901m
VA	5.278V	-52514mV
WR_2	27.856mW	586.4µW

Answers to Exercise 3.3

	Circuit a	Circuit b	Circuit c
R_{THEV}	269.5	3.53k	1.259k
V_{THEV}	4.083	42	128.873
I_{Load}	7.575m	5.949m	51.191m

127

CHAPTER 3   FURTHER DC ANALYSIS

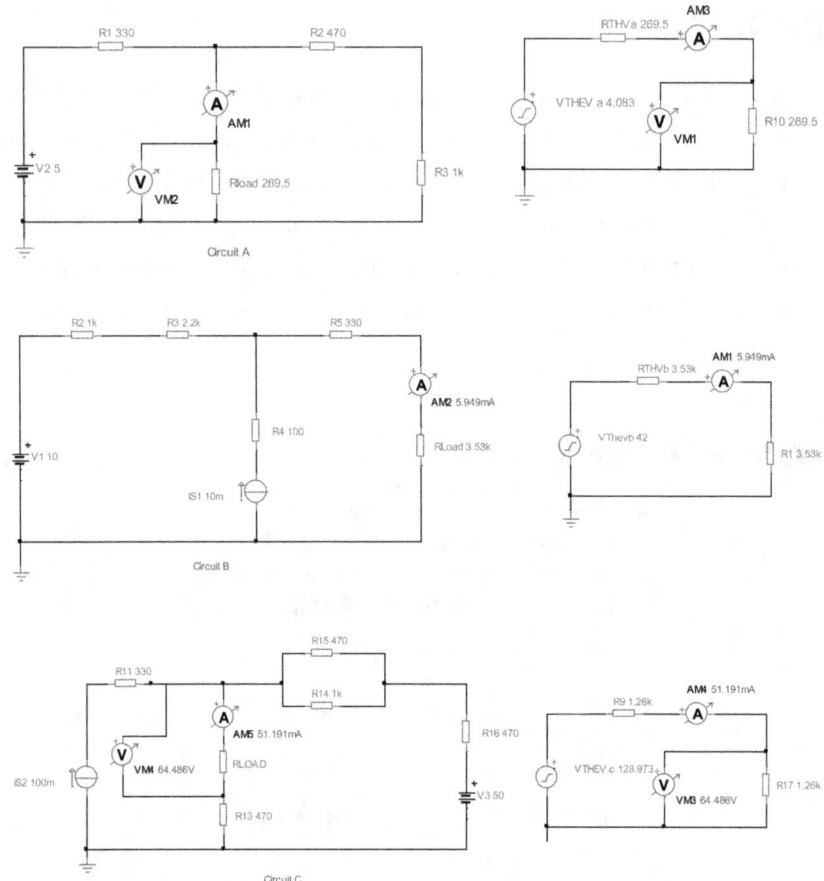

Answers to Exercise 3.4

Circuit	I_{NORT}	R_{NORT}
Figure 3-21	714.285mA	10.5
Circuit a	15.15mA	269.5
Circuit b	11.898mA	3.53k
Circuit c	102.36mA	1.26k

CHAPTER 3   FURTHER DC ANALYSIS

Answers to Exercise 3.5

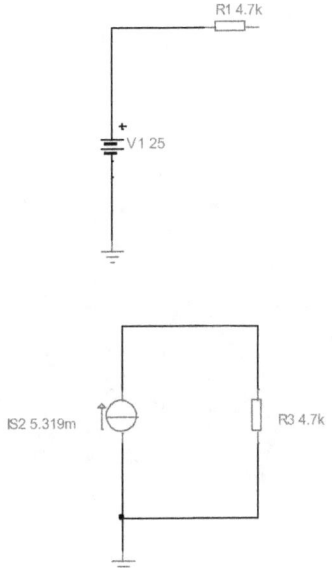
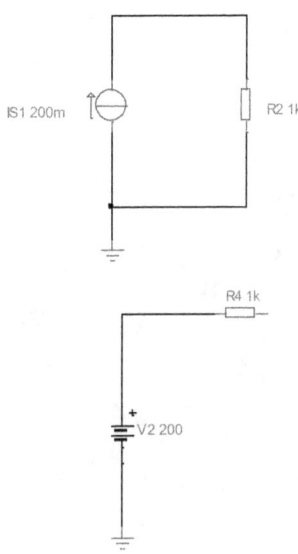

129

CHAPTER 4

DC Transients in LR Circuits

In this chapter, we discuss what transients are and how important they are to engineering. We then look at the transients for the DC LR circuit with zero initial conditions and then extend the analysis to look at how the circuit responds when it has some initial conditions. Finally, we briefly look at how the simple inductor can transform a 12V car battery into a large enough voltage to cause a spark to jump across the gap in a spark plug and ignite the fuel in a cylinder.

After reading this chapter, you will:

- Understand the importance of transients in electrical circuits.

- Have an appreciation of what the time constant *tau* is and how it relates to LR circuits.

- Be able to predict what will happen with DC transients over time in a LR circuit.

I feel I should warn you that there is quite a bit of mathematical work in proving some of the expressions and theories in this chapter. I don't think I should apologise too much, as I want to show you how important maths is to the engineer. Also, I want to show you that the maths is not as difficult as you might think. Of course, you can just skip the proofs, but I hope you don't, as the use of maths is a skill the would-be engineer should learn. If an ex-wagon driver can do it, then surely you can learn the skill as well.

Inductors

Because this chapter analyses circuits with inductors in them, we should first understand what an inductor is. Basically, an *inductor* is a length of wire wound around a former to create a coil. When a current is forced to flow through the coil, a magnetic field is set up around it. That magnetic field, if it is changing, can induce a voltage in a nearby length of wire, or coil. If the magnetic field around the coil does not change, but a nearby length of wire is moved through the magnetic field, then the inductor can induce a voltage across the length of wire. This is indeed one of the principal ways in which we generate the mains voltage. Therefore, I think inductors get their name from this ability to induce a voltage. We look at them more closely in Chapter 9 when looking at magnetic fields. The main purpose of this introduction is to give you an idea of what an inductor is and the units of inductance. The units are the Henry H and a $1H$ inductance, is a very high value not normally used. The typical value of inductance is the low mH or even µH. Inductance is given the symbol L, since I is used for current.

Inductors in a Series and in Parallel

Inductors combine in a series and in parallel the same way as resistors combine, which means in a series, the total inductance value, L_T, is simply the sum of the individual values. For example, if we have the following three inductances—L_1 = 20mH, L_2 = 25mH and L_3 = 15mH—then the total inductance value L_T would be:

$$L_T = L_1 + L_2 + L_3$$

Therefore, we have:

$$L_T = 20E^{-3} + 25E^{-3} + 15E^{-3} = 60mH$$

If the same three inductances are connected in parallel, we calculate their total inductance the same way that we calculate the total resistance of three resistors in parallel. This means:

$$L_T = \frac{1}{\dfrac{1}{L_1} + \dfrac{1}{L_2} + \dfrac{1}{L_3}}$$

$$L_T = \frac{1}{\dfrac{1}{20E^{-3}} + \dfrac{1}{25E^{-3}} + \dfrac{1}{15E^{-3}}} = \frac{1}{156.6667} = 6.383mH$$

Remember that the total inductance must be smaller than the lowest value, just the same as with resistors. That's basically all I want to say about inductors for now, so let's move on to the main subject of this chapter.

Transients and Transient Analysis

Whenever a system, be it an electrical circuit or a mechanical device, starts up, it is most at risk to damage. The shock of being forced to come out of a stable state and settle down into a new steady state of activity can be very disturbing at least, if not critically damaging. Just think about how difficult and annoying it can be for us to wake up and get to work. Whilst you are at work, you settle into your steady routine and usually work smoothly without damage. The same can be said about electrical circuits and most engineering systems. Your car engine makes the most noise, usually, when it starts up from being cold. However, when it gets to a warm cruising speed, it usually runs well. It is during the transition from one steady state

CHAPTER 4   DC TRANSIENTS IN LR CIRCUITS

to another that most systems damage themselves. Therefore, the study of what happens during these initial moments of transition is important and engineers need to understand it. In this chapter, we take our first look at these important transients.

Inductors and Capacitors

So far, we have concentrated on DC circuits with resistors. However, inductors and capacitors are reactive components and are mostly concerned with AC circuit analysis. Therefore, in this chapter I do not go into much detail about their characteristics except to discuss the effect they have on the current that is forced to flow through them when a voltage, in this case a DC voltage, is applied across them.

Current Lag in an Inductor

An inductor, in its simplest form, is a length of wire. If we can make current flow through this wire, then the length of wire must have been connected to one turn of a coil of wire, as it makes up the circular path the current flows around. To increase the inductive effect, we usually concentrate this length of wire into a coil of many turns and then close the circuit. This now coiled wire will have an inherent resistance, which is the resistance of the wire that makes up the coil. It will also have this new characteristic called inductance. The reason why we call it inductance is covered in more detail in Chapter 9.

When we force a current to flow through a length of wire, we set up a magnetic field around the wire. This ability to set up a magnetic field is increased when we coil the wire up to make an inductor. This magnetic field can then induce a voltage in another coil of wire.

CHAPTER 4 DC TRANSIENTS IN LR CIRCUITS

It is in creating this magnetic field that the inductor experiences a current lag. All materials, such as the copper that makes up the wire of the coil of an inductor, have within them a collection of magnetic domains, like little magnets. In their natural state, these domains all rest in random directions within the wire. In this random state the wire has no net magnetism because the domains cancel each other out. However, when we apply a voltage across the wire, or coil, we are trying to force a current to flow through the coil. The current flow initially struggles to flow through the coil, as the random alignment of these magnetic domains prevent the current from flowing easily. However, the current begins forcing the domains to align in one direction. As the domains start to align, the current starts to find it easier to flow through the coil. This then forces more domains to align up in the same direction, which in turns allows more current to flow easier through the coil. This effect continues until all the domains are aligned and the current can now flow at a maximum. This aligning of the domains takes time and so the current is said to lag behind the voltage in an inductor as it reaches its maximum value. This lag, or delay, can be interpreted as a phase difference or shift between the voltage being applied and the current reaching a maximum. This phase shift for a pure inductor is 90°.

One other important aspect of this phase shift is that eventually the ability of the inductor to impede the current flow falls to 0. However, we must realise that this is only for a DC voltage, as with an AC supply, we change the direction of current flowing through the coil in a repetitive cyclic action at the frequency of supply. This constant changing of the direction of the current flowing through the coil means, with an AC supply, we are constantly realigning the magnetic domains inside the inductor and changing the magnetic field around the inductor. You learn in Chapter 8 that inductive impedance, given the symbol X_L, can be calculated using this formula:

$$X_L = 2\pi f L$$

CHAPTER 4   DC TRANSIENTS IN LR CIRCUITS

For DC, the frequency *f* is 0Hz as we don't change the polarity of DC. Therefore, the inductive impedance X_L will equal 0Ω to a DC supply. This agrees with what we have discussed about the current lag in the inductor. However, that does not mean that the inductor acts as a short circuit across the supply. That is because there is this inherent resistance of the wire that is in all inductors, as it's the resistance of the wire that makes up the coil of the inductor. This inherent resistance will set the maximum current that will flow through the inductor when all the magnetic domains have been aligned into one direction. One more property of the inductor is that there is some inherent or stray capacitance between the turns of wire that make up the inductor. This capacitance is very small and for all intents and purposes it can be ignored. What it does mean is that an inductor can be viewed as an RLC circuit that has a resonant frequency. However, we don't normally concern ourselves with this characteristic of the inductor. Because this chapter is concerned with DC, we can ignore it for now.

The DC LR Circuit

Now that you have a good idea of what an inductor is and why, with a DC circuit, the current slowly rises from 0 to a maximum value, we will start our study of DC transients with a LR circuit. The first transient circuit we investigate is the DC LR circuit shown in Figure 4-1.

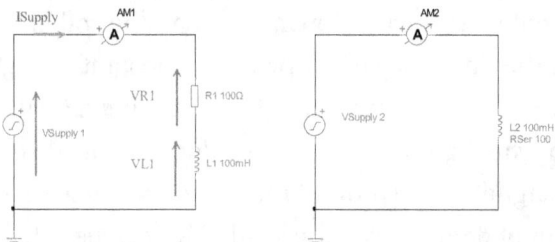

Figure 4-1. *The Test Circuit for the LR Transient Analysis*

CHAPTER 4   DC TRANSIENTS IN LR CIRCUITS

We have shown that to DC the inductor will eventually have no impedance to the current. This in turn suggests that to DC, the inductor will eventually act like a short circuit across the supply, but the internal resistance of the inductor prevents this. With the TINA ECAD software, we can represent this with a resistor in series with the inductor, as I did with the first of the two circuits shown in Figure 4-4. Alternatively, we can add some resistance into the component properties of the inductor using the Inductor properties window shown in Figure 4-2.

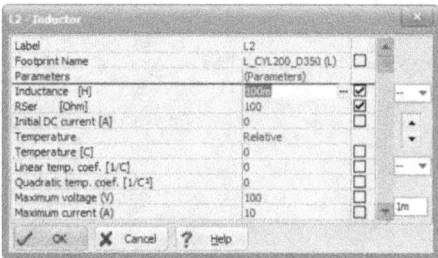

Figure 4-2. *The Component Properties Window for the Inductor L2 in the Test Circuit*

This is what I did for the second circuit shown in Figure 4-1. When we simulate the circuit, you will see that both circuits perform the same.

What we are trying to simulate is what will happen in the circuit during those first important seconds from when we first switch the circuit on until it settles down to its steady state conditions. We could try to use timed switches for this, but a better idea is to apply a square wave, which stays at the maximum for enough time for the circuit to settle down to its new steady state conditions. Then it returns to 0V for enough time for the circuit to return to its steady state zero conditions. The time the voltage is high represents when the circuit is switched on and the time the voltage is at 0V represents the time the circuit is switched off. This is what we are doing with the two V_{Supply} generators. Figures 4-3 and 4-4 show how we can use the generator to create this square wave voltage with. The generator symbol is the fourth icon on the current component bar.

137

CHAPTER 4   DC TRANSIENTS IN LR CIRCUITS

Figure 4-3. *The Voltage Generator Component in TINA*

If you double-click the generator icon, the VG1 Voltage Generator parameter window appears, as shown in Figure 4-4.

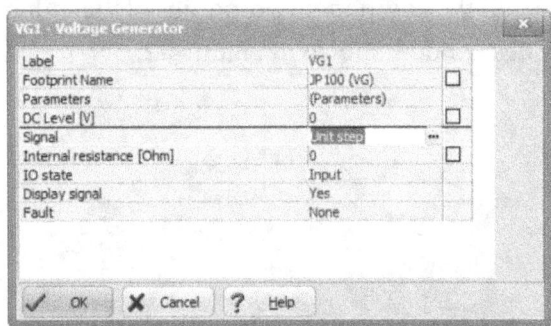

Figure 4-4. *The VG1 Voltage Generator parameter window*

If you click Unit Step, the phrase will turn blue, and three dots will appear. If you click the three dots, the Signal Editor window will appear. Select the general waveform, which is seventh waveform option, as I have done in Figure 4-5.

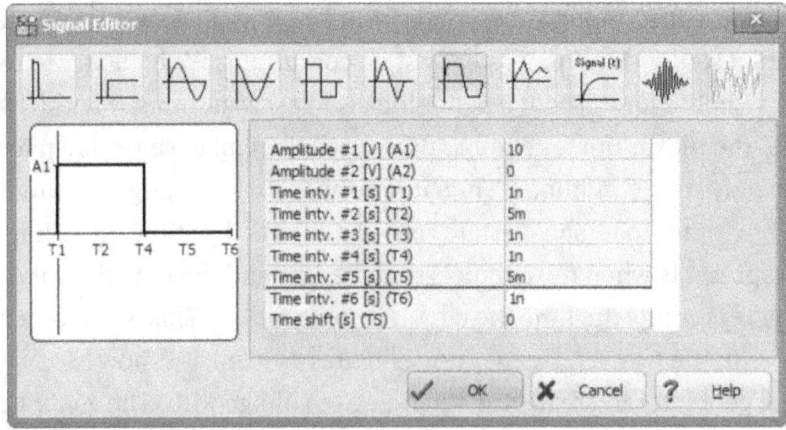

Figure 4-5. *The Signal Editor Window for the Voltage Generator*

We are trying to create a square wave that goes from 0 to 10V for 5ms and then goes to 0V for another 5ms. The editor requires the following settings:

- Amplitude 1, which is the peak volage: Set it to 10
- Amplitude 2, the second peak voltage: set it to 0
- T1, the first rise time: Set it to 1ns (nanosecond), which is a very fast rise time
- T2, the first pulse width: Set it to 5ms
- T3, the first fall time: Set it to 1ns
- T4, the second rise time: Set it to 1ns
- T5, the second pulse width: Set it to 5ms
- T6, the final fall time: Set it to 1ns
- TS, this is an option to give the waveform some delay in starting in seconds: Set this to 0

I used this general waveform instead of the square wave option number five, as we will want to vary the mark and space time with different simulations. Once you are happy with the settings, click the OK button. The editor will disappear, leaving you with the VG1 Voltage Generator parameter window still open. Here, you can change the label from VG1 to V_{Supply} if you want to, as I have. Once you are happy with your settings, simply click the OK button and the window will close, leaving you with the voltage generator reflecting your changes, but not the signal.

Now you need to add the resistor, inductor, ammeter, voltmeter, and arrows in the normal fashion, as described in Chapter 10. When you are ready to simulate the circuit, I will go through the process of creating the transient analysis simulation.

CHAPTER 4 DC TRANSIENTS IN LR CIRCUITS

The Time Constant (Tau) of the LR Circuit

We said we will keep the square wave voltage at its maximum for enough time. Indeed, we have set the pulse width to 5ms. This implies that we can determine what is "enough" time. With the inductor it will be the time it takes the current to align all the magnetic domains and reach a maximum. However, how do we determine how long that time will be? For that we can use some of the basic analysis tools we have already looked at. We will start by using Kirchhoff's Voltage Law. To do that we will look at the first circuit shown in Figure 4-1. Using KVL, we can say that at any time:

$$V_{Supply} = V_R + V_L$$

We will use this statement to derive an expression for the current in the circuit. The first step is to relate the two volt drops around the circuit to current flowing in the circuit. We can use Ohm's Law to show that:

$$V_R = iR$$

However, the expression for the volt drop across the inductor comes from an analysis of magnetism, which I have left until Chapter 9. For now, we will just state that:

$$V_L = L\frac{di}{dt}$$

This means we can say:

$$V_{Supply} = iR + L\frac{di}{dt}$$

We are using lowercase *i* even though this is a DC analysis. This is because over these initial transient periods, the current will be changing.

CHAPTER 4   DC TRANSIENTS IN LR CIRCUITS

The expression for V_{Supply} is now a differential equation, which will require some challenging maths to solve. There are two terms in the right side, but we cannot say that the current i is common to both terms, as one term is using the current i and the other is using the rate of change of the current (i.e., di by dt). We can convert the expression for KVL applied to the LR transient circuit into an algebraic equation by using the Laplace Transforms. This should then enable us to take out any common terms.

Using Laplace Transforms

Laplace transforms are a list of transforms created by the French mathematician Pierre Simon Laplace and extended by the British physicist Oliver Heaviside. Engineers use them to help solve differential equations. They basically enable us to create an algebraic equation out of the differential, or even integral, expressions we come across. The best way to explain how they can be used is to go through an example. We will use them to solve the differential equation we just derived from KVL. We will split the analysis into two time periods—the time the circuit is switched on and the time the circuit is switched off.

The Time the Circuit Is Switched On

This is when the supply to the circuit is switched to a high, which will set to V_{Supply} i.e. 10V in this case. To create the Laplace equation for this period, we will choose the appropriate Laplace transform for each term in the KVL expression.

Using KVL, we have already shown that:

$$V_{Supply} = iR + L\frac{di}{dt}$$

CHAPTER 4   DC TRANSIENTS IN LR CIRCUITS

The Laplace transforms are a table of standard transforms that transform a time-related term, such as a differential or integral, to a Laplace term and vice versa. This then enables us to manipulate the expressions as if they were simple algebraic equations. We use the Laplace transforms to go from the time domain to the S, or Laplace domain. This may seem like some sort of trick, but the tables are created by a mathematical process involving integration and have been proven by Laplace and Heaviside. We will use the tables to help us solve the differential equation. A list of the most common Laplace transformations is in the appendix.

We need to use the Laplace transform for each term one at a time.

The Applied Voltage V_{Supply}

If we do not know what type of voltage the V_{Supply} is, we can simply state the Laplace transform of an unknown by using the bar symbol above the variable. Therefore, we have:

$$L\{V_{Supply}\} = \bar{V}$$

Note that we use the symbology $L\{\}$ to denote we are moving into the S or Laplace domain. I am also placing a bar above the $\underline{V}$ as we have not yet defined what type of voltage it is. Therefore, it is a variable, so place the bar above it. Later we will define what type of voltage the supply is.

The Current i Used in iR

The current i is the unknown quantity we are trying to determine; therefore, it is given the general Laplace transform for an unknown by using the bar symbol above the variable, as follows:

$$L\{i\} = \bar{i}$$

CHAPTER 4   DC TRANSIENTS IN LR CIRCUITS

The Voltage Across the Resistor VR

This is simply R times the Laplace of i:

$$L\{iR\} = \bar{i}R$$

The Differential of the Current i

If we look at the Laplace tables, listed in the appendix, we can see that:

$$L\left\{\frac{dx}{dt}\right\} = S\bar{x} - x_0$$

With our differential, we are using i and t, which means we can say:

$$L\left\{\frac{di}{dt}\right\} = L\left(S\bar{i} - i_0\right)$$

The term $i_{(0)}$ is the initial current flowing in the circuit. If we assume the circuit has been left disconnected for some time, then the initial current will be 0. This means that we can say:

$$L\left\{\frac{di}{dt}\right\} = LS\bar{i}$$

We now have the Laplace transform for all the terms in the differential equation we created using KVL. This means that we can now say:

$$\bar{V} = \bar{i}R + LS\bar{i}$$

143

CHAPTER 4   DC TRANSIENTS IN LR CIRCUITS

If we now decide that the voltage will be a simple step input going from 0V to V_{Supply}, which is a constant DC value, then knowing the Laplace of a constant 1 is simply $\frac{1}{S}$, where 1 is the constant used in the Laplace tables. In this case, our constant is V_{Supply} so we can replace the Laplace 1 with this:

$$1 = V_{Supply}$$

Therefore, the Laplace transform will be:

$$L\{V_{Supply}\} = \frac{V_{Supply}}{S}$$

This means that the Laplace equation now becomes this:

$$\frac{V_{Supply}}{S} = \bar{i}R + LS\bar{i}$$

This is now an algebraic equation and the $\bar{i}$ term can be taken out as a common factor on the right side (RHS) of the equals sign. This gives:

$$\frac{V_{Supply}}{S} = \bar{i}(R + LS)$$

Which means we can say:

$$\bar{i} = \frac{V_{Supply}}{S(R + LS)}$$

It is normal to ensure the coefficient of S is 1 and with this expression the coefficient at present is L. Therefore, if we divide top and bottom of the fraction on the right by L, we get:

$$\bar{i} = \frac{\frac{V_{Supply}}{L}}{S\left(S + \frac{R}{L}\right)}$$

CHAPTER 4 DC TRANSIENTS IN LR CIRCUITS

Instead of dividing the top and bottom, i.e., the numerator and denominator of the fraction on the right side, we could simply multiply the top and bottom by $\dfrac{1}{L}$ as this achieves the same result. However, it is easier to see what happens. We do that to the numerator and the denominator to keep the fraction equal so we don't really change anything. However, doing that gives us this:

$$\bar{i} = \dfrac{V_{Supply} \times \dfrac{1}{L}}{S(R+LS) \times \dfrac{1}{L}} = \dfrac{\dfrac{V_{Supply}}{L}}{S\left(\dfrac{R}{L} + \dfrac{LS}{L}\right)}$$

$$i = \dfrac{\dfrac{V_{Supply}}{L}}{S\left(S + \dfrac{R}{L}\right)}$$

I hope you can follow the process, and I apologise if you know how to complete the process. Note that dividing V_{Supply} by 1 as we did here does not change anything. It hopefully made it easier to see how we multiplied V_{Supply} by $\dfrac{1}{L}$.

To change this equation into a time domain equation for i, we can try to use the Inverse Laplace transforms. The only problem is that the compound fraction on the right side does not have a standard inverse Laplace transform. Well, we can't just give up—we must try to see if we can manipulate the expression into one that fits the standard Laplace transforms.

CHAPTER 4　DC TRANSIENTS IN LR CIRCUITS

Partial Fractions

The fraction $\dfrac{\frac{V_{Supply}}{L}}{S\left(S+\frac{R}{L}\right)}$ is a compound fraction that is made up of a set of partial fractions. There is a set of transforms that show how a compound fraction can be split into its separate parts. Using this, we can show that the compound fraction can be made up from two parts:

$$\frac{\frac{V_{Supply}}{L}}{S\left(S+\frac{R}{L}\right)} \equiv \frac{A}{S} + \frac{B}{S+\frac{R}{L}}$$

This is because when adding the two fractions, as with the two on the right side, we create a common denominator by simply multiplying the two denominators of the fractions, which would give us the denominator on the left side. We are using the equate sign (the $\equiv$) and not the equals sign as we don't know the values of A and B. We have to determine the value of the constants A and B. The first thing we do is multiply both sides of the equate sign $\equiv$ by the denominator on the left. This will produce:

$$\frac{\frac{V_{Supply}}{L}}{S\left(S+\frac{R}{L}\right)} \times S\left(S+\frac{R}{L}\right) \equiv \frac{A}{S} \times S\left(S+\frac{R}{L}\right) + \frac{B}{S+\frac{R}{L}} \times S\left(S+\frac{R}{L}\right)$$

This will cancel down to:

$$\frac{V_{Supply}}{L} \equiv A\left(S+\frac{R}{L}\right) + BS$$

CHAPTER 4 DC TRANSIENTS IN LR CIRCUITS

This equation has two unknowns, and we can't easily solve it. However, if we let S = 0, we will get rid of the unknown B:

$$\frac{V_{Supply}}{L} \equiv A\left(0 + \frac{R}{L}\right) + B(0)$$

From which we can say the following:

$$\frac{V_{Supply}}{L} = A\left(\frac{R}{L}\right)$$

If we now multiply both sides by $\frac{L}{R}$, we get:

$$\frac{V_{Supply}}{L}\left(\frac{L}{R}\right) = A\left(\frac{R}{L}\right)\left(\frac{L}{R}\right)$$

When we cancel this down, we get:

$$A = \frac{V_{Supply}}{R}$$

If we now let $= -\frac{R}{L}$, which will make the term in the bracket multiplied by A go to 0, we get:

$$\frac{V_{Supply}}{L} \equiv A\left(-\frac{R}{L} + \frac{R}{L}\right) + B\left(-\frac{R}{L}\right)$$

This cancels down to:

$$\frac{V_{Supply}}{L} = -\left(\frac{R}{L}\right)B$$

If we now multiply both sides by $\frac{L}{R}$ we get:

$$-B = \frac{V_{Supply}}{R}$$

147

CHAPTER 4 DC TRANSIENTS IN LR CIRCUITS

Now multiplying both sides by -1 gives us this:

$$B = -\frac{V_{Supply}}{R}$$

We now have a value for both constants A and B, which means we can say:

$$\frac{\frac{V_{Supply}}{L}}{S\left(S+\frac{R}{L}\right)} = \frac{\frac{V_{Supply}}{R}}{S} - \frac{\frac{V_{Supply}}{R}}{S+\frac{R}{L}}$$

This then means that:

$$\bar{i} = \frac{\frac{V_{Supply}}{R}}{S} - \frac{\frac{V_{Supply}}{R}}{S+\frac{R}{L}}$$

We can now take the inverse Laplace of all three terms to move back into the time domain:

$$L^{-1}\{\bar{i}\} = i$$

$$L^{-1}\left\{\frac{\frac{V_{Supply}}{R}}{S}\right\} = \frac{V_{Supply}}{R}$$

Finally:

$$L^{-1}\left\{\frac{\frac{V_{Supply}}{R}}{S+\frac{R}{L}}\right\} = \frac{V_{Supply}}{R} e^{-\frac{R}{L}t}$$

CHAPTER 4 DC TRANSIENTS IN LR CIRCUITS

This means that the Laplace equation transforms back into this time equation:

$$i = \frac{V_{Supply}}{R} - \frac{V_{Supply}}{R} e^{-\frac{R}{L}t}$$

We can take the term $\frac{V_{Supply}}{R}$ out as a common factor, which gives us this expression:

$$i = \frac{V_{Supply}}{R}\left(1 - e^{-\frac{R}{L}t}\right)$$

This is the general expression for how the current builds up in a transient RL circuit, assuming the initial current was 0A. The exponential term inside the brackets is exponential decay, which means it will eventually go to 0. At that time the current ' will reach a maximum value equal to:

$$i = \frac{V_{Supply}}{R}$$

This means that the current will be limited only by the resistance R in the circuit. This will be when the magnetic domains inside the coil have all aligned and no longer impede the current.

We can test this expression out by simulating the circuit shown in Figure 4-6.

CHAPTER 4 DC TRANSIENTS IN LR CIRCUITS

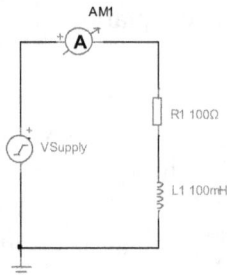

Figure 4-6. *The Test Circuit for the Current Build up in a Series RL Circuit*

The generator will provide the V_{Supply}. In this instance, it is set to a step input that rises from 0V to 10V the instant the circuit is turned on. This means that the V_{Supply} is a DC voltage of 10V. We can now put the values from the circuit into the expression. This gives us this:

$$i = \frac{10}{100}\left(1 - e^{-\frac{100t}{100E^{-3}}}\right)$$

This in turn gives:

$$i = 0.1\left(1 - e^{-1000t}\right)$$

The e^{-1000t} term is exponential decay, which will eventually reach a very small value, almost 0. It will never actually reach 0, but convention states that after five-time constants, the exponential term will be so close to 0 that we can accept it as being equal to 0. If we examine the general term for an exponential decay:

$$e^{-at}$$

CHAPTER 4 DC TRANSIENTS IN LR CIRCUITS

The term a is the inverse of the time constant for the exponential decay. With respect to the expression for the current in the RL circuit, we can see that the coefficient of t is $\dfrac{R}{L}$. This means that with respect to the series, the RL circuit is:

$$\frac{R}{L} = a$$

Because a is the inverse of the time constant, we can say:

$$Time\ constant\ '\tau' = \frac{L}{R}\ seconds$$

This seems to suggest that L divided by R produces units of time. How does Henry's H divided by Ω give us time t as the units? We need to use dimensional analysis to understand why the units for the time constant τ are in seconds. First, we can use the expression for the voltage across the inductor, which is:

$$V = L\frac{di}{dt}$$

This means a one Henry coil will induce 1V across it when the current changes by 1Amp in one second. This means that we can say:

$$1V = 1L\frac{1I}{1t}$$

As all the coefficients of the variables are equal to 1, we can omit them:

$$V = L\frac{I}{t}$$

151

CHAPTER 4 DC TRANSIENTS IN LR CIRCUITS

We can transpose this to L to show that:

$$L = \frac{Vt}{I}$$

We can also use Ohm's Law, which states:

$$1A = \frac{1V}{1R}$$

That means we can say:

$$I = \frac{V}{R}$$

From this, we can transpose for R to show that:

$$R = \frac{V}{I}$$

If we look at the expression for τ in the RL circuit, we know:

$$\tau = \frac{L}{R}$$

This shows that τ is L divided by R. We have just shown that:

$$L = \frac{Vt}{I} \text{ and } R = \frac{V}{I}$$

So, this means:

$$L \div R = \frac{Vt}{I} \div \frac{V}{I}$$

When we divide by a fraction, we simply invert and multiply, which gives:

CHAPTER 4   DC TRANSIENTS IN LR CIRCUITS

$$L \div R = \frac{Vt}{I} \times \frac{I}{V}$$

The two Vs and the two Is cancel out and we are left with time t, which has the units of seconds:

$$L \div R = t$$

The units cancel down to the units of time. A similar analysis can be applied to the CR time constant, which we will look at in Chapter 5.

The time constant τ is an important aspect of any system that follows and exponential function. Here, in our first investigation of the time constant, we are applying it to a series RL circuit. However, it can be applied to the CR circuit, which we investigate in Chapter 5. It can also be applied to the response of motors, generators, and many other engineering systems. That's why it is essential that a would-be engineer fully understand the application of a time constant. The idea of a time constant can even be applied to humans, as that is why, in general, doctors say that it takes four hours before the effect of most tablets has sufficiently worn off and it is safe for us to take a repeat dosage.

To that end, there are a few characteristics of a system that follow an exponential expression with a time constant τ you should know about. In the build-up or growth, it can be shown that after one time constant has passed, the system will have reached 63.2% of its maximum, assuming the system was initially at 0. Similarly, with an exponential decay, the system will have fallen to around 36.8% of the starting value.

We can show that this is the case with the current build-up with the RL circuits we are using for the test. For example, the time constant for that circuit is:

$$\tau = \frac{100E^{-3}}{100} = 1ms$$

CHAPTER 4 DC TRANSIENTS IN LR CIRCUITS

When we use this as the value for time t (i.e. $t = 1ms$), we get the following in the current build-up expression:

$$i = \frac{V_{Supply}}{R}\left(1 - e^{-\frac{Rt}{L}}\right)$$

Using the other values for the circuit, we get:

$$i = \frac{10}{100}\left(1 - e^{-\frac{100}{100E^{-3}} \times 1E^{-3}}\right)$$

$$i = 0.1\left(1 - e^{-1}\right)$$

$$i = 0.1(1 - 0.36788)$$

$$i = 0.1(0.6321) = 0.06321 = 63.21mA$$

The term 0.6321 in the bracket is equal to 63.21%, so this means that after one time constant, the current will reach the expected 63.21% of the maximum.

We will now let time t equal 5ms, which is five times the time constant τ. When we put this into the expression, we get:

$$i = \frac{10}{100}\left(1 - e^{-\frac{100}{100E^{-3}} \times 5E^{-3}}\right)$$

$$i = 0.1\left(1 - e^{-5}\right)$$

$$i = 0.1\left(1 - 6.7379E^{-3}\right)$$

$$i = 0.1(0.99326) = 99.326mA$$

CHAPTER 4   DC TRANSIENTS IN LR CIRCUITS

This shows that when time is equal to 5τ, the exponential term falls to $6.738E^{-3}$, which means the term in the bracket has risen to 99.33% of the maximum. This is close enough to the maximum for engineers to say it will take approximately five-time constants for the system to have reached a maximum. Applying this to our test circuit, which has a time constant of 1ms, we can say it will take approximately 5ms for the current in the circuit to reach a maximum:

$$i = 0.1(1-0) = 100mA$$

Transient Analysis in TINA

We have shown how we can create the square wave input voltage to simulate turning a circuit on and then off. In this section, we go through the process of performing the transient analysis using TINA. After creating the circuit, we need to set the transient analysis up. To do this, first select Analysis from the Main Menu bar. This will open the drop-down menu, from which we can select Transients from the options, as shown in Figure 4-7.

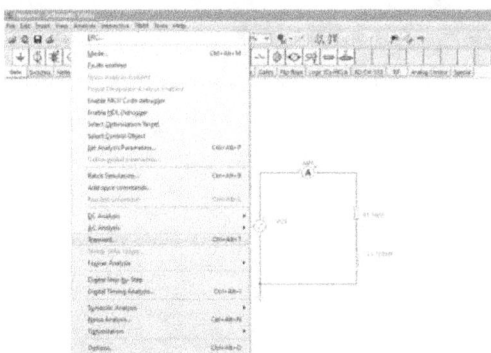

Figure 4-7. *The Analysis Drop-Down Menu*

155

CHAPTER 4   DC TRANSIENTS IN LR CIRCUITS

This will then open the Transient Analysis window, as shown in Figure 4-8.

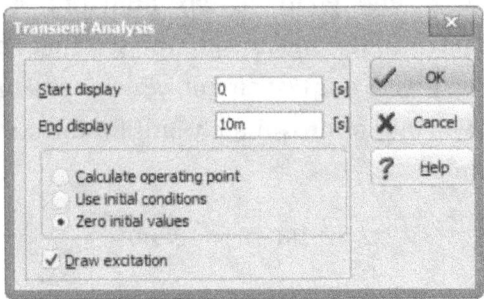

Figure 4-8. The Transient Analysis Window

We must set the Start Display time to 0 and the End Display time to 10ms. This time is equal to 10τ, which is enough time for the current to build up to a maximum and then decay back to 0A. We must also select the Zero Initial Values option to ensure that the initial current is 0. Finally, ensure that the Draw Excitation box is ticked. Once you are happy with the settings, click OK. The window will close, and the simulation will start. The test circuit waveforms we get are shown in Figure 4-9.

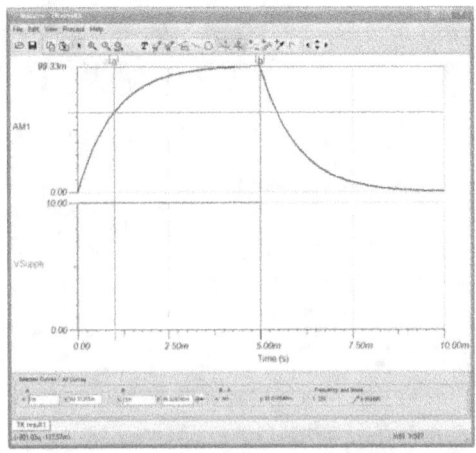

Figure 4-9. The Waveforms for the Test RL Transient Circuit

156

CHAPTER 4   DC TRANSIENTS IN LR CIRCUITS

The default display shows all curves on the same graph. To separate them, as they are shown in Figure 4-9, you need to select the View label from the menu bar. This will then open a drop-down menu from which you can select Separate Curves, as shown in Figure 4-10. When you select that option, the two curves are displayed separately, as shown in Figure 4-9. You can use the cursors a and b to highlight the important aspects of the curves. To move the cursor to a specific time, you can type the time in the x axis box once you have clicked the cursor onto the actual trace. After pressing the Enter button on your laptop, the cursor should then move to that time and the y axis box should display the current at that time.

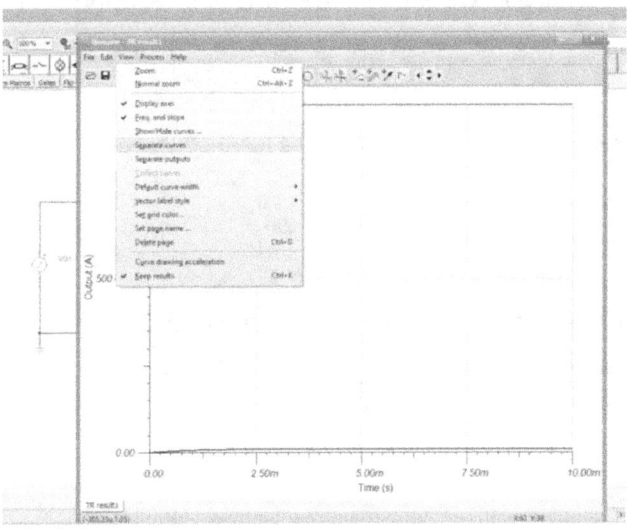

Figure 4-10. The TR Results Window

Using the displays in Figure 4-9, we can see that the current flowing in the circuit is shown as the AM1trace. You can see that it starts off at 0A even though the supply voltage has gone to 10V. Then, when the time has changed to 5ms, we see that the current has risen to 99.33mA, which is practically 100mA. This will be the maximum the current can rise to. If we

CHAPTER 4 DC TRANSIENTS IN LR CIRCUITS

examine cursor a we can see that after 1ms, which is one time constant, the current had reached 63.24mA, which is approximately 63.2% of the maximum current. Therefore, the simulation agrees with our analyses, which should give us some confidence in the work we have done so far.

The Decaying Current

We know that sometime after the supply voltage has been high at a maximum, the current will have risen to its maximum of $\frac{V_{Supply}}{R}$. Now we will see what happens when we switch the supply back to 0V. As we will be starting a new analysis, we will call this time 0. If we apply KVL, we can say:

$$0 = V_R + V_L$$

Therefore, relating the voltage drops to the current, we can say:

$$0 = iR + L\frac{di}{dt}$$

We will use a different analysis technique to derive the expression for the current during this period of decay. The expression we have is again what we call a *first order differential equation*, which complies with this format:

$$\frac{di}{dt} = f(i)$$

This means we have a differential of the variable *i* with respect to time *t* that equates to a function of *i*. We can use direct integration to solve this type of differential equation, but first we must separate the different variables (i.e., get the variable t on one side and the variable i on the other). This is done by rearranging it to this:

158

CHAPTER 4 DC TRANSIENTS IN LR CIRCUITS

$$dt = \frac{di}{f(i)}$$

If we rearrange the KVL equation, we get:

$$L\frac{di}{dt} = -iR$$

We can rewrite this as follows:

$$-iR = L\frac{di}{dt}$$

If we divide both sides by L, we get:

$$-\frac{iR}{L} = \frac{di}{dt}$$

We can separate the variables by first multiplying both sides by dt, which gives us this:

$$dt\left(-\frac{iR}{L}\right) = di$$

If we now multiply both sides by $-\frac{L}{iR}$, we get:

$$dt = -\frac{L}{iR} di$$

We have succeeded in separating the variables as required. Now we can use direct integrate on both sides:

$$\int 1\, dt = \int -\frac{L}{iR}\, di$$

159

CHAPTER 4   DC TRANSIENTS IN LR CIRCUITS

The 1 in the left integral is the invisible 1 that we write in front of the term dt, as 1dt = dt, as 1x = x. We don't normally write the 1 in front of the term, but it is always there. That is why I call it the *invisible* 1.

Taking the $-\dfrac{L}{R}$ constant out of the integral on the right side gives us:

$$\int 1\,dt = -\frac{L}{R}\int \frac{1}{i}\,di$$

When integrating, we should use limits of integration. With the left integral, which is with respect to time t, it is quite easy to choose some limits. This is because the lower limit cannot be less than 0, as we can't have negative time. Also, when we start our analysis, we will always reset the time to 0. The upper limit is some time t when we stop the analysis. This means the limits for that integral will be 0 and t. However, with the other integral on the right, it is not that straightforward to choose limits. In this instance, we will leave the limits out for that integral and use a constant of integration *k*. This means we can write the expression as follows:

$$\int_0^t 1\,dt = -\frac{L}{R}\int \frac{1}{i}\,di$$

Now carry out the integral.
On the left side, we get:

$$\int_0^t 1\,dt = (t)-(0) = t$$

On the right side, we get:

$$-\frac{L}{R}\int \frac{1}{i}\,di = -\frac{L}{R}\ln(i) + k$$

160

CHAPTER 4 DC TRANSIENTS IN LR CIRCUITS

This is using the standard integrals, a set of which is given in the appendix. Therefore, the complete integral is as follows:

$$t = -\frac{L}{R}\ln(i) + k$$

We need some boundary conditions to determine the value or expression for k. We know at time 0 there will be some initial current flowing in the circuit, which we will call i_0. In this case, because we know the current will have reached its maximum, because the circuit had been connected to the supply voltage for a time greater than 5τ, we can say:

$$i_0 = \frac{V_{Supply}}{R}$$

This means we can say when t = 0, $i = \frac{V_{Supply}}{R}$. Putting these values in, we get:

$$0 = -\frac{L}{R}\ln\left(\frac{V_{Supply}}{R}\right) + k$$

This means we can determine the value of the constant k as follows:

$$k = \frac{L}{R}\ln\left(\frac{V_{Supply}}{R}\right)$$

We can now substitute this in the equation for the complete integral, as follows:

$$t = -\frac{L}{R}\ln(i) + \frac{L}{R}\ln\left(\frac{V_{Supply}}{R}\right)$$

We can take $-\frac{L}{R}$ out as a common factor, which gives this:

$$t = -\frac{L}{R}\left(\ln(i) - \ln\left(\frac{V_{Supply}}{R}\right)\right)$$

161

CHAPTER 4 DC TRANSIENTS IN LR CIRCUITS

Nex, wet multiply both sides by $-\dfrac{R}{L}$, which gives:

$$-\frac{R}{L}t = (\ln(i)) - \ln\left(\frac{V_{Supply}}{R}\right)$$

Now we multiply both sides by -1, which gives:

$$\frac{R}{L}t = \ln\left(\frac{V_{Supply}}{R}\right) - \ln(i)$$

Subtracting the log of two terms is the same as the log of the division of the two terms. This means we can say:

$$\frac{R}{L}t = \ln\left(\frac{\frac{V_{Supply}}{R}}{i}\right)$$

Taking the antilog of both sides (note that we are using natural or Napierian or exponential logs) gives this:

$$e^{\frac{R}{L}t} = \frac{\frac{V_{Supply}}{R}}{i}$$

Calculators have two types of logs buttons. They are log to the base 10, as with the "log" button on your calculator and log to the base e, as with the "ln" button on your calculator. So, where is the antilog button? Well, if we appreciate that logs are simply the power, we raise the base number by to equal a number then you should, I hope, be able to appreciate that the antilog is the base number raised to that power. That is why, if you look at your calculator, you will find the antilog button is the second function of

CHAPTER 4   DC TRANSIENTS IN LR CIRCUITS

the log button. This means that the antilog to base 10 is 10^x, which is the second function of the log button. Also, the antilog to base e is the second function of the "ln" button (the e^x button). We will use this understanding in Chapter 5 when we look at the CR transient circuit.

The next step in our transposition is to multiply both sides by i:

$$ie^{\frac{R}{L}t} = \frac{V_{Supply}}{R}$$

Now divide by $e^{\frac{R}{L}t}$ to get the i on its own on the right side, which gives:

$$i = \frac{\frac{V_{Supply}}{R}}{e^{\frac{R}{L}t}}$$

This can be rewritten as follows:

$$i = \frac{V_{Supply}}{R} e^{-\frac{R}{L}t}$$

We now have an expression for i after the supply voltage has been switched to 0V assuming the current has reached a maximum value:

$$i = \frac{V_{Supply}}{R} e^{-\frac{R}{L}t}$$

This an exponential decay, which means the current will start at a value of $\frac{V_{Supply}}{R}$ and will eventually fall to zero amps. From our study before, we know it will take approximately five-time constants for the current to fall to 0. Using the values from the test circuit shown in Figure 4-6, we know that the time constant for the circuit is 1ms. This means that it will take approximately 5ms for the current to decay to 0. Also, we know that the maximum current will be 100mA. We can test this concept by applying

CHAPTER 4 DC TRANSIENTS IN LR CIRCUITS

a square wave voltage that will stay high at 10V for 5ms and then stay low at 0V for a further 5ms. When we do this, the waveforms obtained from the circuit are shown in Figure 4-11.

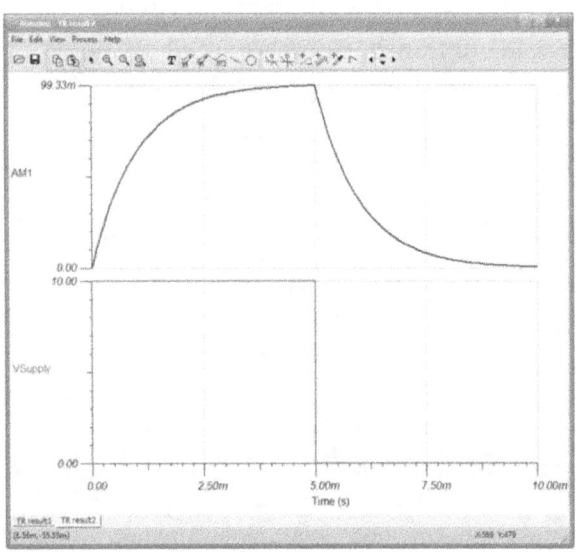

Figure 4-11. *The Current Build Up and Decay in the RL Test Circuit Shown in Figure 4-6*

As expected, we can see that the current takes 5ms to build up to the 99.33mA maximum. It then takes a further 5ms for the current to decay to almost zero amps. This agrees with the current expressions we have derived and so gives us some confidence in our work.

The RL Circuit with Some Initial Conditions

Now we will extend the analysis to see what difference there is if there is some initial current flowing in the circuit when we turn the supply back on. This situation could come about if we reapplied the supply before the current had fallen to 0. This is something we will do to test the expression we derive here.

CHAPTER 4   DC TRANSIENTS IN LR CIRCUITS

We will use calculus first, as we did before, and then use Laplace transforms. Using KVL, we have already shown that we can start with this expression:

$$V_{Supply} = iR + L\frac{di}{dt}$$

If we subtract iR from both sides, we get:

$$V_{Supply} - iR = L\frac{di}{dt}$$

We can now divide both sides by L and multiply by dt, which gives:

$$(V_{Supply} - iR)\frac{dt}{L} = di$$

If we divide both sides by the terms in the bracket we get:

$$\frac{1}{L}dt = \frac{1}{V_{Supply} - iR}di$$

We have separated the variables and can now integrate both sides with respect to their variables. As before, we need limits of integration and for time they will be 0 and t. With respect to the current, we can use $i_{(0)}$ and i, where $i_{(0)}$ is any initial current in the circuit and i is the current at the end of the analysis. That being the case, the integral is as follows:

$$\int_0^t \frac{1}{L}dt = \int_{i_0}^{i} \frac{1}{V_{Supply} - iR}di$$

The LHS integral goes to:

$$\left[\frac{t}{L}\right]_0^t = \left(\frac{t}{L}\right) - \left(\frac{0}{L}\right) = \frac{t}{L}$$

165

CHAPTER 4   DC TRANSIENTS IN LR CIRCUITS

I am using the notation of the square brackets [] to show that we have carried out the integration of the expression, the $\frac{1}{L}$ in this case, but we have not put the limits in. The next step is to use the normal brackets where we substitute the variable, in this case the t, with the limits, using the convention to subtract the lower limit from the upper limit. I will use this convention for all my integrals, as that is what I was taught during my degree back in 1987 to 1990. Old habits are hard to lose.

The right side has no standard integral so we must substitute the denominator of the fraction with another variable, such as u, as follows:

$$\text{Let } u = V_{Supply} - iR$$

If we now differentiate this expression for u with respect to i, knowing V_{Supply} is a constant, we can say:

$$\frac{du}{di} = -R$$

We need to remember that the differential of a constant is 0 and so the constant V_{Supply} goes to 0. This means that we can transpose this for di as follows:

$$di = -\frac{du}{R}$$

This means that we can now substitute the terms on the right side integral as follows:

$$\int_{i_0}^{i} \frac{1}{u} \left(-\frac{du}{R} \right)$$

Which simplifies to this:

$$\int_{i_0}^{i} -\frac{1}{Ru} du$$

CHAPTER 4 DC TRANSIENTS IN LR CIRCUITS

Therefore, taking the constant $\frac{1}{R}$ out of the integral gives this:

$$\frac{1}{R}\int_{i_0}^{i} -\frac{1}{u}du$$

This integrates to the following:

$$\frac{1}{R}\left[-ln(u)\right]_{i_0}^{i}$$

However, we know $u = V_{Supply} - iR$. Substituting this in means we don't have to change the limits of integration that were related to di to limits related to du.

$$\frac{1}{R}\left[-ln(V_{Supply} - iR)\right]_{i_0}^{i}$$

Putting the limits in gives the following:

$$\frac{1}{R}\left[\left(-ln(V_{Supply} - iR)\right) - \left(-ln(V_{Supply} - i_0R)\right)\right]$$

This simplifies to the following:

$$\frac{1}{R}\left[\left(ln(V_{Supply} - i_0R)\right) - \left(ln(V_{Supply} - iR)\right)\right]$$

Subtracting two logarithmic terms is the same as dividing them. This means we can say this:

$$\frac{1}{R}ln\left(\frac{V_{Supply} - i_0R}{V_{Supply} - iR}\right)$$

CHAPTER 4   DC TRANSIENTS IN LR CIRCUITS

This means that the complete integral becomes:

$$\frac{t}{L} = \frac{1}{R}\ln\left(\frac{V_{Supply} - i_0 R}{V_{Supply} - iR}\right)$$

If we multiply both sides by R, we get this:

$$\frac{R}{L}t = \ln\left(\frac{V_{Supply} - i_0 R}{V_{Supply} - iR}\right)$$

Now take the antilog of both terms, which gives this:

$$e^{\frac{R}{L}t} = \frac{V_{Supply} - i_0 R}{V_{Supply} - iR}$$

Now multiply both sides by $V_{Supply} - iR$ and divide both sides by $e^{\frac{R}{L}t}$:

$$V_{Supply} - iR = \frac{V_{Supply} - i_0 R}{e^{\frac{R}{L}t}}$$

Dividing by an exponential term raised to a power is the same as multiplying the numerator by the exponential raised to the negative power. This then gives us this:

$$V_{Supply} - iR = (V_{Supply} - i_0 R)e^{-\frac{R}{L}t}$$

We now subtract V_{Supply} from both sides, which gives:

$$-iR = (V_{Supply} - i_0 R)e^{-\frac{R}{L}t} - V_{Supply}$$

Now we expand the exponential term into the bracket, which gives:

CHAPTER 4 DC TRANSIENTS IN LR CIRCUITS

$$-iR = V_{Supply}e^{-\frac{R}{L}t} - i_0 Re^{-\frac{R}{L}t} - V_{Supply}$$

Now we multiply both sides by -1, which gives:

$$iR = V_{Supply} - V_{Supply}e^{-\frac{R}{L}t} + i_0 Re^{-\frac{R}{L}t}$$

Now we divide both sides by R, which gives:

$$i = \frac{V_{Supply}}{R} - \frac{V_{Supply}e^{-\frac{R}{L}t}}{R} + i_0 e^{-\frac{R}{L}t}$$

Finally, we take the term $\frac{V_{Supply}}{R}$ out as a common factor, which gives:

$$i = \frac{V_{Supply}}{R}\left(1 - e^{-\frac{R}{L}t}\right) + i_0 e^{-\frac{R}{L}t}$$

This is the expression that shows how the current in the RL circuit will change when there is an initial current flowing in the circuit.

We will now derive the same expression using Laplace transforms. It is always good practice to see if you can obtain the same results using a different approach. If the two results are the same, you have confidence that the results are correct.

From our previous work, we know that the Laplace of a first-order derivative is as follows:

$$L\left\{\frac{di}{dt}\right\} = L(S\bar{i} - i_0)$$

This time there will be some initial current flowing, so we can include it in the expression. This means that the Laplace of the derivative is as follows:

CHAPTER 4 DC TRANSIENTS IN LR CIRCUITS

$$L\left\{\frac{di}{dt}\right\} = L\left(S\bar{i} - i_0\right)$$

This means that expanding the L into the bracket, the Laplace equation for the RL transient with some initial conditions is as follows:

$$\frac{V_{Supply}}{S} = \bar{i}R + LS\bar{i} - Li_0$$

We can add the Li_0 term to both sides, which gives the following:

$$\frac{V_{Supply}}{S} + Li_0 = \bar{i}R + LS\bar{i}$$

We can now take the term $\bar{i}$' out as a common factor, which gives:

$$\frac{V_{Supply}}{S} + Li_0 = \bar{i}\left(R + LS\right)$$

Now we divide both sides by the term $(R + LS)$, which gives this:

$$\bar{i} = \frac{V_{Supply}}{S(R+LS)} + \frac{Li_0}{(R+LS)}$$

We should make the coefficient of S equal to 1, which means we need to divide the top and bottom of the two fractions by L. This gives us:

$$\bar{i} = \frac{\frac{V_{Supply}}{L}}{S\left(S+\frac{R}{L}\right)} + \frac{i_0}{\left(S+\frac{R}{L}\right)}$$

We have used partial fraction to split the compound fraction $\dfrac{\frac{V_{Supply}}{L}}{S\left(S+\frac{R}{L}\right)}$ into its two parts, which gives:

CHAPTER 4 DC TRANSIENTS IN LR CIRCUITS

$$\frac{\frac{V_{Supply}}{L}}{S\left(S+\frac{R}{L}\right)} = \frac{\frac{V_{Supply}}{R}}{S} - \frac{\frac{V_{Supply}}{R}}{S+\frac{R}{L}}$$

Therefore, we have:

$$\bar{i} = \frac{\frac{V_{Supply}}{R}}{S} - \frac{\frac{V_{Supply}}{R}}{S+\frac{R}{L}} + \frac{i_0}{\left(S+\frac{R}{L}\right)}$$

Using the inverse Laplace transforms, we get the following:

$$i = \frac{V_{Supply}}{R} - \frac{V_{Supply}}{R}e^{-\frac{R}{L}t} + i_0 e^{-\frac{R}{L}t}$$

Therefore, we have:

$$i = \frac{V_{Supply}}{R}\left(1 - e^{-\frac{R}{L}t}\right) + i_0 e^{-\frac{R}{L}t}$$

This is the same result as that obtained using calculus. We have gone through a lot of maths, but engineers need to be able to prove what they use is valid and mathematics is the most useful tool we have at our disposal. All you need is to be shown how you can use it and then practice it yourself. I hope this work shows you that you can do it.

The Simulation

Now we will test the expression using TINA to simulate the circuit. We will decide to have half of the maximum, as the initial current i_0 still flowing. We will use the values for the circuit shown in Figure 4-1. That means:

CHAPTER 4 DC TRANSIENTS IN LR CIRCUITS

- $V_{Supply} = 10V$
- $R = 100\Omega$ and $L = 100mH$
- The time constant τ is 1ms
- The maximum current = 100mA
- The initial current is therefore 50mA

We will use the expression for the current decay to determine how long we need to allow the circuit to discharge so that the current falls to 50mA. The decay expression is as follows:

$$i = \frac{V_{Supply}}{R} e^{-\frac{R}{L}t}$$

We need to rearrange this expression for time t. Whenever the required unknown is in the indices or power, we must use logs to transpose for it. Because there is the exponent e in the expression, it is easier to choose natural, or Napier, logs (i.e. logs to the base e). Therefore, taking the natural logs of both sides, we get:

$$Ln(i) = Ln\left(\frac{V_{Supply}}{R} e^{-\frac{R}{L}t}\right)$$

When we have the log of two terms multiplied together, we can rewrite this as the addition of the log of two terms (recall that logs follow the rules of indices). This gives us:

$$Ln(i) = Ln\left(\frac{V_{Supply}}{R}\right) + Ln\left(e^{-\frac{R}{L}t}\right)$$

CHAPTER 4 DC TRANSIENTS IN LR CIRCUITS

Using the third rule of logs the indices or power can be multiplied into the log. This gives:

$$Ln(i) = Ln\left(\frac{V_{Supply}}{R}\right) + -\frac{R}{L}t\ln(e)$$

We know that:

$$ln(e) = 1$$

Therefore, we have:

$$Ln(i) = Ln\left(\frac{V_{Supply}}{R}\right) - \frac{R}{L}t$$

If we add the term $\frac{R}{L}t$ to both sides, we get:

$$\frac{R}{L}t + Ln(i) = Ln\left(\frac{V_{Supply}}{R}\right)$$

Now we subtract the term $Ln(i)$ from both sides:

$$\frac{R}{L}t = Ln\left(\frac{V_{Supply}}{R}\right) - \ln(i)$$

We can rewrite the subtraction of two logs by the log of the division of the two terms, as again logs follow the rules of indices:

$$\frac{R}{L}t = Ln\left(\frac{\frac{V_{Supply}}{R}}{i}\right)$$

If we now multiply both sides by $\frac{L}{R}$, we get this:

CHAPTER 4 DC TRANSIENTS IN LR CIRCUITS

$$t = \frac{L}{R} Ln \left(\frac{V_{Supply}}{\frac{R}{i}} \right)$$

We can now calculate the time needed to allow the current to fall to half of its maximum (i.e., 50mA), by putting the values into the expression, which gives:

$$t = \frac{100E^{-3}}{100} Ln \left[\left(\frac{\frac{10}{100}}{50E^{-3}} \right) \right]$$

Therefore:

$$t = 693\,\mu s$$

This means that if we allow the RL circuit to discharge for 693μs, the current will fall to 50mA, assuming the current was starting from its maximum value. To confirm that the expression is correct, we can use this expression to determine the time the current had fallen to 25mA. This gives:

$$t = \frac{100E^{-3}}{100} Ln \left[\left(\frac{\frac{10}{100}}{25E^{-3}} \right) \right]$$

Therefore:

$$t = 1.386 ms$$

Note that these times are from when we switched the supply to 0V and so started to allow the current to decay.

CHAPTER 4   DC TRANSIENTS IN LR CIRCUITS

We can test this expression first by simulating the test circuit and use the cursor to display the time the current decayed to 50mA and 25mA. The results should agree with the times we calculated. However, this assumes we switched the circuit on for long enough, 5ms in this case, for the circuit to have reached a maximum. The waveforms are shown in Figure 4-12.

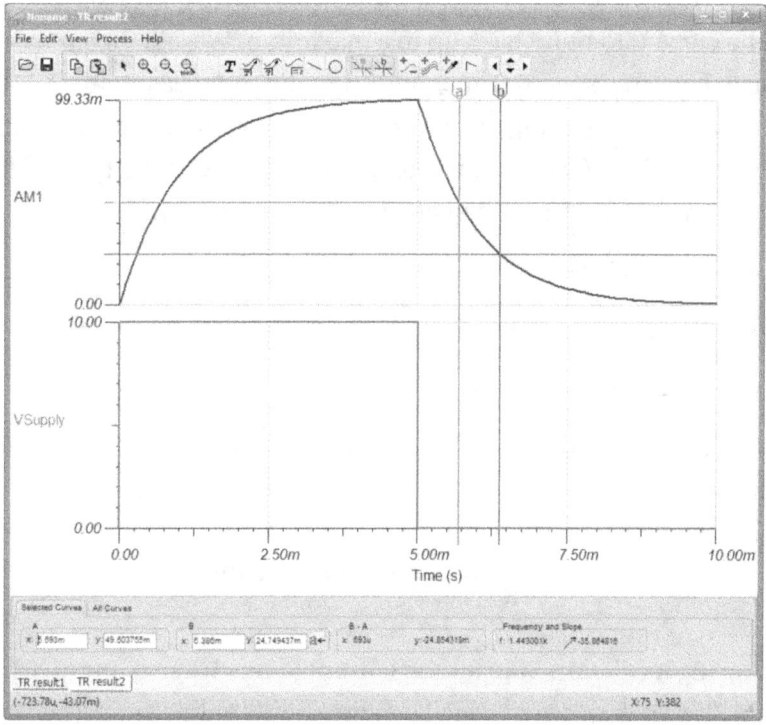

Figure 4-12. *The Waveforms to Confirm the Times of Decay*

Cursor a showed that the current had decayed to 49.6.03mA when time was 5.693ms and the current had decayed to 24.749mA when time was 6.386ms. We need to appreciate that in our calculations, time started again when we switched the voltage to 0V. This was when the real time was 5ms just after the current had grown to its maximum level. This means we need to add the 5ms to our calculated times to move into the time we switched

CHAPTER 4   DC TRANSIENTS IN LR CIRCUITS

the supply off to 0V. When we do that, we can see that the simulation confirms our calculations.

Now we will run a simulation to test our expression with some initial current. The idea behind this simulation is that we will let the current build up to a maximum and then let the current decay to 25% of the maximum. When the current decays to 25%, we will switch the supply back on and allow the current to build back up to a maximum. We will then measure the current at three specific times and compare the measurements with the calculated values using the current expression. To make this another example of the LR DC transients circuit, we will use different values for the circuit. The values for the circuit are as follows:

- $V_{Supply} = 15V$
- $R = 5\Omega$
- $L = 250mH$

Using the values for the circuit, we can calculate the time constant (tau) τ at:

$$\tau = \frac{L}{R} = \frac{250E^{-3}}{5} = 50E^{-3} = 50ms$$

Knowing it will take 5tau for the current to reach a maximum, which is 250ms. This means we need to keep the supply voltage high (i.e., the circuit turned on for 250ms). After that time, we can turn the circuit off by switching the supply voltage to 0V. We can calculate the maximum current at that time using this formula:

CHAPTER 4 DC TRANSIENTS IN LR CIRCUITS

$$i_{max} = \frac{V_{Supply}}{R} = \frac{15}{5} = 3A$$

This means that the 25% of maximum current is:

$$\frac{25}{100} \times 3 = 750mA$$

We can now calculate the time the current will fall to 750mA using:

$$t = \frac{L}{R} Ln\left(\frac{V_{Supply}}{R}\right)$$

Putting the values in, we get the following:

$$t = \frac{250E^{-3}}{5} Ln\left(\frac{\frac{15}{5}}{0.75}\right) = 69.315ms$$

We need to appreciate that with this calculation time starts when the circuit has just been switched from the V_{Supply} to 0V. This would be 250ms after the circuit had been initially switched on. Therefore, this calculated time of 69.315ms would be 319.315ms after the circuit had been switched on. This is the time highlighted by cursor a in Figure 4-13. The ammeter reading for AM1 at that point is around 756.03mA. This is very close to the expected 750mA. Also, we are using cursor b to measure the current at a time of 80ms after the V_{supply} voltage had been reapplied to the circuit. This would be a total of 399.315ms after the circuit had been first switched on. This is because the input voltage went back to 15V at a time of 319ms, as shown with the VG1 trace on Figure 4-16. At that time of 399.315ms,

177

CHAPTER 4   DC TRANSIENTS IN LR CIRCUITS

we can see that cursor b shows a reading of 2.55A. We will see if that reading is the same as our calculated current at t = 80ms after reapplying the supply later.

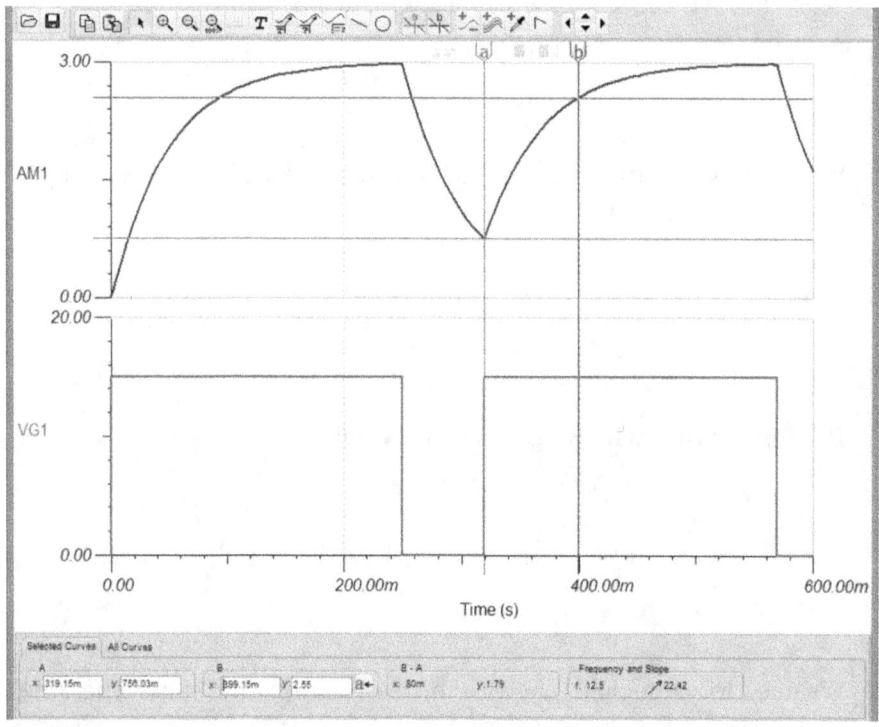

Figure 4-13. *The Waveforms for the Simulation of the New RL Circuit*

We can use the complete expression for the current buildup with some initial current to calculate the expected current 80ms after reapplying the supply voltage. The complete expression for the current is as follows:

$$i = \frac{V_{Supply}}{R}\left(1 - e^{-\frac{R}{L}t}\right) + \frac{V_{Supply}}{FR}e^{-\frac{R}{L}t}$$

178

CHAPTER 4 DC TRANSIENTS IN LR CIRCUITS

The term F represents the fraction of the maximum current that will be the initial current flowing when the supply is switched back on. As we want to turn the circuit back on with 25% of the maximum current flowing, we can set F to equal 4, which means we are setting the initial current to ¼ of the maximum. Putting in the values for the circuit and using the time of t = 80ms the calculated current is as follows. Note that time starts again at 0 when we reapply the 15V step input:

$$i = \frac{15}{5}\left(1 - e^{-\frac{5}{0.25} \times 80E^{-3}}\right) + \frac{15}{4 \times 5} e^{-\frac{5}{0.25} \times 80E^{-3}}$$

$$i = 3(1 - 0.201) + 0.75 \times 0.201 = 2.548 A$$

This agrees with the measured current shown with cursor b in Figure 4-13.

Just to confirm that the expression works, we can carry out the following two calculations.

T=20ms

$$i = \frac{15}{5}\left(1 - e^{-\frac{5}{0.25} \times 20E^{-3}}\right) + \frac{15}{4 \times 5} e^{-\frac{5}{0.25} \times 20E^{-3}}$$

$$i = 3(1 - 0.6703) + 0.75 \times 0.6703 = 1.492 A$$

T = 60ms

$$i = \frac{15}{5}\left(1 - e^{-\frac{5}{0.25} \times 60E^{-3}}\right) + 0.75 e^{-\frac{5}{0.25} \times 60E^{-3}}$$

$$i = 3(1 - 0.3012) + 0.75 \times 0.3012 = 2.322 A$$

CHAPTER 4 DC TRANSIENTS IN LR CIRCUITS

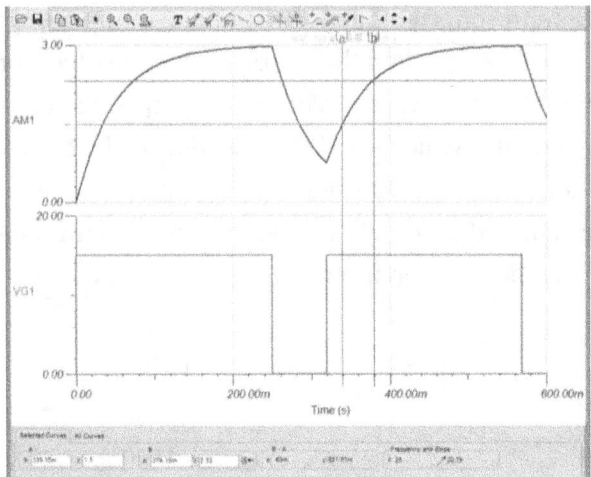

Figure 4-14. *The Measurements to Confirm the Two Extra Calculations*

We can use the cursors in Figure 4-14 to confirm these calculated results. The cursor a records a current of 1.5A at a time of 339.15ms, which is 20ms after the supply voltage had been switched back to 15V. Cursor b records a current of 2.33A at a time of 379.15ms, which is 60ms after switching the supply back on. Both these measurements confirm our calculations. In the second calculation, we used the current of 0.75A or 750mA for the value of the initial current. This is instead of describing it as a fraction of the maximum current.

If we knew how much initial current was flowing in the circuit before we turned the supply back on—in other words, if we knew the initial current i_0—the expression for the current build up could be written as follows:

$$i = \frac{V_{Supply}}{R}\left(1 - e^{-\frac{R}{L}t}\right) + i_0 e^{-\frac{R}{L}t}$$

CHAPTER 4 DC TRANSIENTS IN LR CIRCUITS

The Voltage Across the Resistor and the Inductor

We have spent some time developing the expressions for the current in the circuit but to complete the analysis we should consider how the voltage is divided within the circuit. We consider V_R, the voltage across the resistor first. We know that using Ohm's Law, the voltage across a resistor is simply the current flowing through it multiplied by the resistance value:

$$V_R = iR$$

If we assume that there is no initial current flowing through the circuit, then the current can be expressed as follows:

$$i = \frac{V_{Supply}}{R}\left(1 - e^{-\frac{R}{L}t}\right)$$

If we multiply this by R we get this:

$$V_R = V_{Supply}\left(1 - e^{-\frac{R}{L}t}\right)$$

When we consider the voltage across the inductor, we can apply KVL, which states that at any time:

$$V_{Supply} = V_R + V_L$$

This means that:

$$V_L = V_{Supply} - V_R$$

181

Therefore, using the expression for V_R, we get:

$$V_L = V_{Supply} - V_{Supply}\left(1 - e^{-\frac{R}{L}t}\right)$$

If we expand the brackets, we get:

$$V_L = V_{Supply} - V_{Supply} + V_{Supply}e^{-\frac{R}{L}t}$$

Which cancels down to:

$$V_L = V_{Supply}e^{-\frac{R}{L}t}$$

These are the voltage expressions during buildup, assuming that the initial current equals 0A.

The Voltage Expressions During Decay

We can again use Ohm's Law to calculate V_R. However, the expression for the current is as follows:

$$i = \frac{V_{Supply}}{R}e^{-\frac{R}{L}t}$$

This means that V_R is as follows:

$$V_R = V_{Supply}e^{-\frac{R}{L}t}$$

Again, we can use KVL to derive the expression for V_L. However, during the decay period, the voltage applied to the circuit is 0V. Therefore, we can say that:

$$0 = V_R + V_L$$

CHAPTER 4 DC TRANSIENTS IN LR CIRCUITS

This means that:

$$V_L = -V_R = -V_{Supply} e^{-\frac{R}{L}t}$$

$$V_L = -V_{Supply} e^{-\frac{R}{L}t}$$

To sum up the analysis, we can state the following expressions, assuming there is no initial current flowing in the circuit.

The period the circuit is turned on (connected to Vsupply):

$$i = \frac{V_{Supply}}{R}\left(1 - e^{-\frac{R}{L}t}\right) = \frac{V_{Supply}}{R}\left(1 - e^{-\frac{t}{\tau}}\right)$$

$$V_R = V_{Supply}\left(1 - e^{-\frac{R}{L}t}\right) = V_{Supply}\left(1 - e^{-\frac{t}{\tau}}\right)$$

$$V_L = V_{Supply} e^{-\frac{R}{L}t} = V_{Supply} e^{-\frac{t}{\tau}}$$

The period the circuit is turned off (connected to 0V):

$$i = \frac{V_{Supply}}{R} e^{-\frac{R}{L}t} = \frac{V_{Supply}}{R} e^{-\frac{t}{\tau}}$$

$$V_R = V_{Supply} e^{-\frac{R}{L}t} = V_{Supply} e^{-\frac{t}{\tau}}$$

$$V_L = -V_{Supply} e^{-\frac{R}{L}t} = -V_{Supply} e^{-\frac{t}{\tau}}$$

CHAPTER 4   DC TRANSIENTS IN LR CIRCUITS

These expressions can be confirmed with the waveforms shown in Figure 4-15.

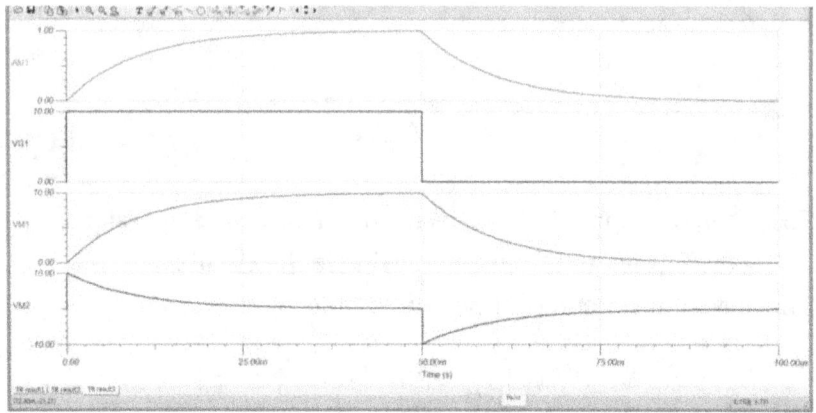

Figure 4-15. *The Growth and Decay Waveforms of a DC Transient RL Circuit*

The traces display the following:

- AM1 is the current flowing in the circuit.
- VG1 is the supply voltage applied to the circuit.
- VM1 is the voltage across the resistor.
- VM2 is the voltage across the inductor.

One thing that can be deduced from the waveforms is that the voltage across the inductor can be changed instantly, but the current flowing through the inductor takes time to change. This is why the inductor can be said to display some aspect of inertia, as it takes time to build up the current. However, once the current is flowing through the inductor, it does not like the current being forced to change. This is a very important and sometimes useful, but also sometimes annoying, aspect of inductors, in that an inductor will do all it possibly can to keep the current flowing through it once it has started to flow. Indeed, it is this very aspect of the

CHAPTER 4 DC TRANSIENTS IN LR CIRCUITS

inductor that allows the 12V of our car battery to become the kilovolts at the spark plug needed to ignite the fuel and make our cars move. It is also why we must take care that we don't burn out any switching device with inductive loads. The inductor really is a magical component.

Supplying the DC LR Circuit with an Irregular Supply

In this analysis, we use the previous component values:

- $V_{Supply} = 25V$
- $R = 10\Omega$
- $L = 150mH$

These are the component values used in the test circuit shown in Figure 4-16. However, the supply voltage will stay high for 30ms and then switch to low for 20ms. This means that during the first period of 30ms, the current flowing in the circuit will not have reached the maximum value. Also, during the 20ms period, the current will not have fallen to 0A. This means that during the second period of 30ms, the current will start to increase with some initial current flowing. We have to calculate the current over some different time periods.

We can calculate the time constant tau τ for the circuit using:

$$\tau = \frac{L}{R} = \frac{150E^{-3}}{10} = 15ms$$

First, we calculate the current flowing in the circuit 30ms after switching the circuit on, assuming the initial current was 0. We can use the following expression to calculate the value the current would build up to:

$$i = \frac{V_{Supply}}{R}\left(1 - e^{-\frac{t}{\tau}}\right)$$

CHAPTER 4   DC TRANSIENTS IN LR CIRCUITS

Putting the values in gives us:

$$i = \frac{25}{10}\left(1 - e^{-\frac{30E^{-3}}{15E^{-3}}}\right)$$

$$i = 2.5(1 - e^{-2}) = 2.162 A$$

During the next 20ms, the supply goes back to 0V, so the current will start to fall according to this expression:

$$i = i_0 e^{-\frac{t}{\tau}} = 2.162 e^{-\frac{20E^{-3}}{15E^{-3}}} = 569.9 mA$$

This means that during the next 30ms, the current will build up but with some initial current flowing. Therefore, we need to use the following expression to calculate the current at the end of this 30ms period:

$$i = \frac{V_{Supply}}{R}\left(1 - e^{-\frac{t}{\tau}}\right) + i_0 e^{-\frac{t}{\tau}}$$

Putting the values in, we get:

$$i = \frac{25}{10}\left(1 - e^{-\frac{30E^{-3}}{150E^{-3}} \times}\right) + i_0 e^{-\frac{30E^{-3}}{150E^{-3}}}$$

$$i = 2.5(1 - e^{-2}) + 569.9 E^{-3} e^{-2}$$

$$i = 2.1617 + 77.128 mA = 2.239 A$$

CHAPTER 4   DC TRANSIENTS IN LR CIRCUITS

We can now use this value of current as the initial current flowing when we turn the supply off again to determine how low the current will fall during the next 20ms. This means that over the next 20ms, we use this expression:

$$i = i_0 e^{-\frac{t}{\tau}} = 2.239 e^{-\frac{20E^{-3}}{15E^{-3}}} = 590.19 mA$$

This means that during the next 30ms (i.e., when we turn the supply back on for the third time), the current will build up but with this new initial current flowing. Therefore, we need to use the following expression to calculate the value of current at the end of this next 30ms period:

$$i = \frac{V_{Supply}}{R}\left(1 - e^{-\frac{t}{\tau}}\right) + i_0 e^{-\frac{t}{\tau}}$$

Putting the value in, we get:

$$i = \frac{25}{10}\left(1 - e^{-\frac{30E^{-3}}{150E^{-3}} \times}\right) + 590.19 E^{-3} e^{-\frac{30E^{-3}}{150E^{-3}}}$$

$$i = 2.5\left(1 - e^{-2}\right) + 590.19 E^{-3} e^{-2}$$

$$i = 2.1617 + 79.874 mA = 2.2416 A$$

We can confirm these calculations by simulating the circuit and completing a table of measurements to compare the calculated results with the measured results. The waveforms produced by the simulation are shown in Figure 4-17.

CHAPTER 4   DC TRANSIENTS IN LR CIRCUITS

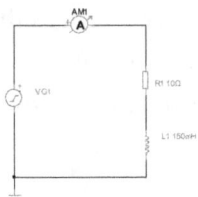

Figure 4-16. *The Test Circuit for the Irregular Supply*

The circuit shown in Figure 4-16 is the RL circuit used for the transient analysis. Figure 4-17 shows the supply voltage and current waveforms from the simulation.

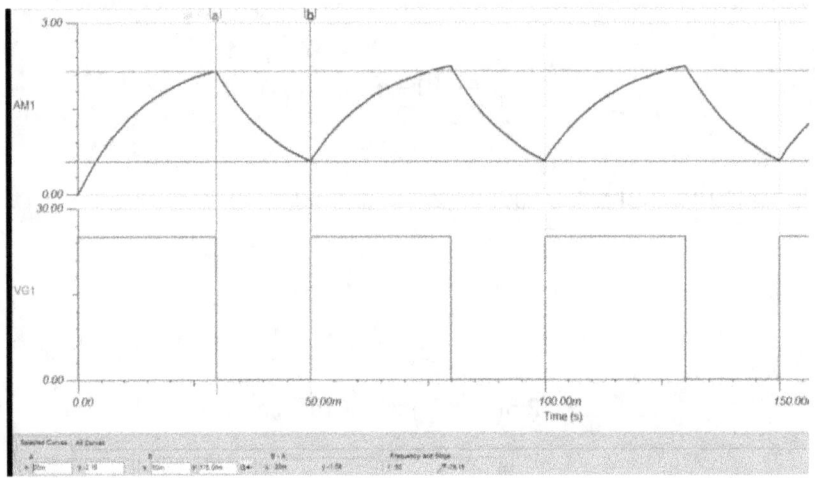

Figure 4-17. *The Waveforms to Show the Supply Voltage and Current for the Test circuit*

Cursor a shows what the current was after the first 30ms and cursor b shows the current after the first 50ms. Table 4-1 shows how the measured results compare to the calculated results.

188

CHAPTER 4 DC TRANSIENTS IN LR CIRCUITS

Table 4-1. *The Results for the Test Circuit Shown in Figure 4-16*

Time ms (Real Time) Time for Calculation	Calculated Result	Measured Result
(30) 30	2.162 A	2.16 A
(50) 20	569.9mA	576.06mA
(80) 30	2.239 A	2.23 A
(100) 20	590.19mA	584.8mA
(130) 30	2.2416 A	2.24 A

Table 4-1 shows that the measured results are very close to the calculated results. This shows that the theory is valid and the maths we used work. The values for the time in ms shown in the brackets are the times we must use in the calculations. The times written without brackets are the actual times we use when measuring the values from the displays shown in Figure 4-17.

This might be all well and good for the DC series RL circuit, but can the ideas be used elsewhere. Well of course they can—we will use the same concepts with the DC CR transient circuit in Chapter 5. More than that, we should appreciate that all systems have their own time constant. Motors, be they DC or AC, are basically RL circuits, and they will have their own time constants. Once we know the value of the time constant for any system, we can use the same maths to predict how the system will react to a sudden change. If we place a load onto a motor that is currently running, we can predict what the speed of the motor will reduce to and how long it will take to slow down to that speed. In general, doctors say we should wait around four hours before we take another does of the medicine. That is because the time constant of average person is 48 minutes and so it takes around 240 minutes (five-time constants) for the medicine to leave our system. I hope you can see that these simple DC transients have many applications.

The Power and Energy in an Inductor

The inductor does not dissipate any power, but it will expend some energy. It is difficult to comprehend that an inductor does not dissipate any power. The only component that truly dissipates power is the resistor. The inductor and capacitor only store power in the form of energy, which is given back in some form when they are finished. It is only the resistance of the wire that makes up the coil of wire of the inductor that gets hot and so dissipates power.

So, what about the energy? Well power can be defined as the rate in which we use energy. That means we can express power as follows:

$$P = \frac{dE}{dt}$$

Where P stands for Power and E stand for Energy. If we multiply both sides of the expression by dt, we get:

$$dE = Pdt$$

If we now integrate both sides, we can say:

$$\int 1 dE = \int P\, dt$$

There are some standard expressions for Power P and one we can use is:

$$P = vi$$

CHAPTER 4 DC TRANSIENTS IN LR CIRCUITS

When using inductors, we can say:

$$V = L\frac{di}{dt}$$

Therefore, with respect to an inductor, we can say:

$$P = L\frac{di}{dt}i = iL\frac{di}{dt}$$

This means we can also say:

$$\int 1 dE = \int iL\frac{di}{dt} dt$$

The two dt terms cancel out with the integral on the right, and so we are left with an integral with respect to current i, which means we can say:

$$\int_0^E 1 dE = \int_{i(0)}^I Li\, di$$

We are using the limits, which is the current when it has settled down, I, and the initial current $i_{(0)}$. With the integral of energy, we can use the limits of E and 0.

The constant L can be taken out of the integral, which gives us:

$$\int_0^E 1 dE = L\int_{i(0)}^I i\, di$$

If the circuit had been switched off for a long time, we know that when t = 0, $i_{(0)}$ = 0 and when t = 5τ i = I. When we integrate the expression for E, we get the following:

$$E = L\left[\left(\frac{I^2}{2}\right) - \left(\frac{0^2}{2}\right)\right]$$

CHAPTER 4 DC TRANSIENTS IN LR CIRCUITS

This means we can say that when an inductor has been forced to pass its maximum current, the energy used can be calculated using this expression:

$$E = \frac{1}{2}LI^2$$

The Car Ignition Circuit

One of the most common uses of a DC RL transient circuit is a car ignition system. The first system was patented by Charles Kettering in 1915. It allows the DC 12V battery to produce a 1.6kV at the spark plug and create a spark that ignites the fuel. It uses the energy that has been allowed to build up around the primary coil, called the *low-tension coil* or *low-tension circuit*, inside a transformer, known as *the ignition coil*, whilst the points are closed. Then, when the points are opened, by the cam on the rotor that rotates at the speed of the engine, the energy that was built up in the primary coil causes a high voltage pulse across the primary coil. This pulse is enlarged by the transformer action of the ignition coil to produce a high enough voltage that can cause a spark to jump across the gap in the spark plug in the engine cylinder. The following is a brief analysis of how this simple but remarkable circuit works.

The circuit has two distinct time periods over which it takes on two different characteristics. We look at the time the points are initially closed. The circuit that this creates is shown in Figure 4-18. The resistance R_1 is the actual resistance of the wire that makes up the inductor L_1. The inductor L_1 is the primary winding of a transformer made up of the low-tension circuit shown in Figure 4-18. The secondary winding is the high-tension circuit shown in Figure 4-18.

CHAPTER 4   DC TRANSIENTS IN LR CIRCUITS

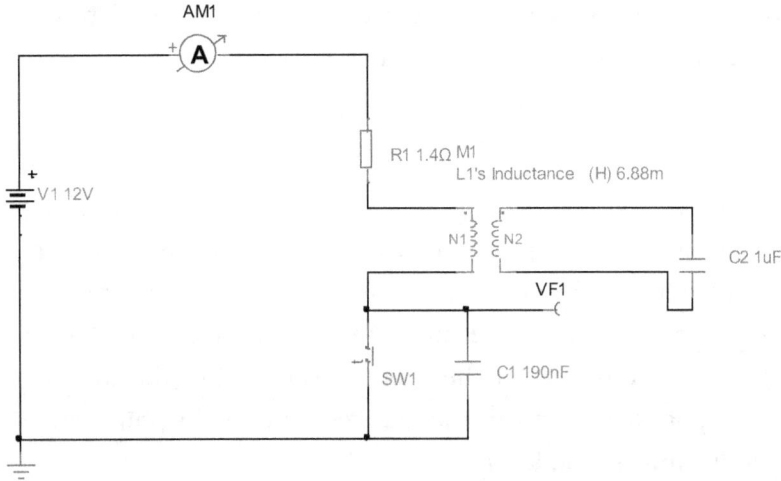

Figure 4-18. *The Test Circuit for the Car Ignition System*

The switch, SW1, is a simple representation of the points that open and close as the engine rotates. The capacitor C_1 is called the condenser, and it is used to control the voltage rise across the points to a level that they can cope with. The values for the components used in the circuit, and the timings used in the calculations, were taken from an actual ignition system. The values are listed for clarity here.

- R1 = 1.4Ω
- L1 = 6.88mH
- C1 = 190nF

We look at the operation with the engine running at idling speed of around 800rpm. If we divide this by 60, we get the frequency of rotation:

$$f_r = \frac{rpm}{60} = \frac{800}{60} = 13.33 Hz$$

193

CHAPTER 4   DC TRANSIENTS IN LR CIRCUITS

The points will open and close twice in one revolution of the engine, which means the frequency of the point f_p is as follows:

$$f_p = 2f_r = 2 \times 13.33 = 26.66 Hz$$

During each cycle, the points are closed for about 60% of the time; they are open for the remaining 40% of the time. When the points are closed, the current in the DC RL circuit builds up to a certain level. This level should be enough to create the energy required to create the spark at the spark plug. The points need to be open long enough for the current in the circuit to reduce to 0. Knowing that the frequency of the points is 26.66Hz, the periodic time is as follows:

$$T_p = \frac{1}{f_p} = \frac{1}{26.66} = 37.51 ms$$

This means that time the points are closed is as follows:

$$T_{closed} = \frac{60}{100} \times 37.51E^{-3} = 22.51 ms$$

The time the points are opened is:

$$T_{opened} = \frac{40}{100} \times 37.51E^{-3} = 15 ms$$

It is during the closed time that the current flowing through the low-tension circuit builds up. During this time the capacitor C_1 plays no part, as it is shorted out by the closed points. This means that the circuit is a simple DC RL transient circuit, and the current will build up according to this expression:

$$i_{closed} = \frac{V}{R}\left(1 - e^{-\frac{R}{L}t}\right)$$

CHAPTER 4   DC TRANSIENTS IN LR CIRCUITS

Putting the values in and using a time of 22.51ms (as this is when the points open and the circuit changes), we get:

$$i_{closed} = \frac{12}{1.4}\left(1 - e^{-\frac{1.4}{6.88E^{-3}} \times 22.51E^{-3}}\right) = 8.436A$$

We can calculate the energy that will have built up within the coil. This is:

$$E_{closed} = \frac{1}{2}L(i_{closed})^2$$

Putting the values in we get:

$$E_{closed} = \frac{1}{2} \times 6.88E^{-3} \times (8.436)^2 = 247.58mj$$

When the points open, this energy will be passed onto the capacitor C_1. We can use the expression for energy in a capacitor to determine what the voltage across the capacitor would rise to.

$$E = \frac{1}{2}CV^2$$

This means that voltage can be calculated using this:

$$V = \sqrt{\frac{2E}{C}}$$

Putting the values in, we get:

$$V = \sqrt{\frac{2 \times 247.58E^{-3}}{190E^{-9}}} = 1.614kV$$

195

CHAPTER 4   DC TRANSIENTS IN LR CIRCUITS

We can simulate the circuit shown in Figure 4-18 to compare the simulated results with the calculated results. The waveforms from the simulation are shown in Figure 4-19.

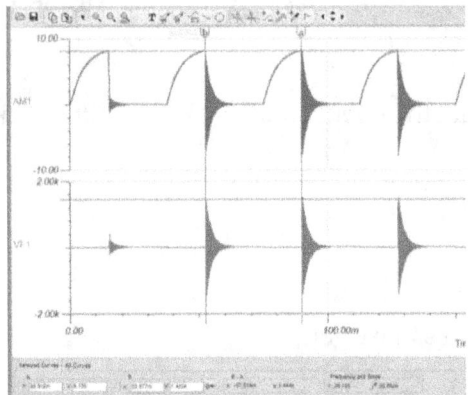

Figure 4-19. *The Current Flowing Through R1 and the Voltage Across C1*

Figure 4-19 is zoomed in around the time the points open and the circuit changes. We can see from the tracs AM1, the current has risen to 8.15Amps. Also, we can see from the trace VF1 that the voltage across the capacitor reaches 1.4kV. This difference between the calculated voltage and the simulated voltage is due to energy dissipation by the resistor R_1 as the current passes through it. However, the measured values confirm that our calculations are good. What is also more evident is the fact that the current and voltage start to oscillate during the time the points open— from 22.51m to 37.51ms. This is because, during that time, the circuit has now become a DC series RLC circuit, as shown in Figure 4-20.

CHAPTER 4   DC TRANSIENTS IN LR CIRCUITS

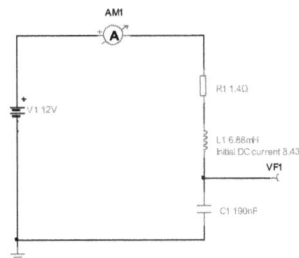

Figure 4-20. *The Low-Tension Circuit Once the Points Are Open*

We are just looking at the low-tension circuit in this analysis, so we are using a simple inductor instead of the transformer used in Figure 4-18. The circuit takes on the characteristics of a series RLC (Resistor, Inductor, and Capacitor) circuit. This circuit has two energy storage devices—one being the inductor, the other being the capacitor. This makes the circuit a second-order system whereas the RL circuit, from before, is a first-order system. When we look at AC analysis in Chapter 8, we investigate the series RLC circuit in more detail. However, the most important aspect of this circuit is that it will oscillate at its resonant frequency. This frequency can be calculated using this formula:

$$f_o = \frac{1}{2\pi\sqrt{LC}}$$

If we put the values from the circuit shown in Figure 4-20, we get the following:

$$f_o = \frac{1}{2\pi\sqrt{6.88E^{-3} \times 190E^{-9}}} = 4.402 kHz$$

If we simulate the circuit, we can display the waveforms as shown in Figure 4-21.

CHAPTER 4   DC TRANSIENTS IN LR CIRCUITS

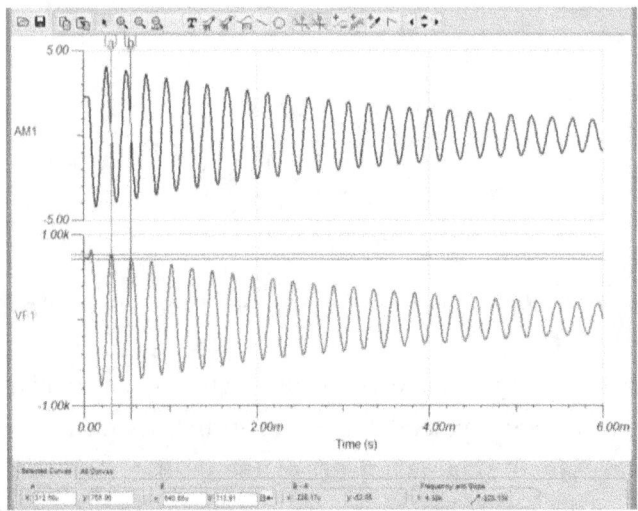

Figure 4-21. *The Waveforms from the Series RLC Circuit Shown in Figure 6-12*

If we look at the voltage across the capacitor as shown in trace VF1 in Figure 4-21, we can measure the periodic time for the oscillations, and it was 228.17µs. This agrees with the periodic time for a frequency of 4.402kHz. The oscillations will die away exponentially. This analysis is not complete, as we have not considered how the high-tension circuit loads the components of the low-tension circuit. That requires a more complex analysis that we look at in another book. However, the analysis does show that the simple inductor and capacitor can create some high-voltage oscillations—not bad for two so-called passive components.

Rearrange the Current Growth Expression for Time t

Earlier, we rearranged the decay expression for time t, so to complete the expressions we will transpose the current expression during growth for time t. The current expression is as follows:

$$i = \frac{V_{Supply}}{R}\left(1 - e^{-\frac{R}{L}t}\right)$$

As the variable t is in the power we need to use logs to complete this transposition. First, we multiply both sides by R. This gives:

$$iR = V_{Supply}\left(1 - e^{-\frac{R}{L}t}\right)$$

Now we expand the bracket, which gives:

$$iR = V_{Supply} - V_{Supply}e^{-\frac{R}{L}t}$$

Now we subtract V_{Supply} from both sides. This gives:

$$iR - V_{Supply} = -V_{Supply}e^{-\frac{R}{L}t}$$

Now we multiply both sides by -1, which gives.

$$V_{Supply} - iR = V_{Supply}e^{-\frac{R}{L}t}$$

Now we divide both sides by V_{Supply}, which gives.

$$\frac{V_{Supply} - iR}{V_{Supply}} = e^{-\frac{R}{L}t}$$

CHAPTER 4   DC TRANSIENTS IN LR CIRCUITS

Now we take the natural log of both sides. This gives us:

$$ln\left(\frac{V_{Supply} - iR}{V_{Supply}}\right) = ln\left(e^{-\frac{R}{L}t}\right)$$

Now we use the third rule of logs to bring the power down to multiply into the log. This gives us:

$$ln\left(\frac{V_{Supply} - iR}{V_{Supply}}\right) = -\frac{R}{L}t\,ln(e)$$

Knowing the log of the base number gives 1, we can say $ln(e) = 1$. This is why we use logs to the base e. This gives us:

$$ln\left(\frac{V_{Supply} - iR}{V_{Supply}}\right) = -\frac{R}{L}t$$

Now multiply both sides by $-\frac{L}{R}$ which gives us:

$$-\frac{L}{R}ln\left(\frac{V_{Supply} - iR}{V_{Supply}}\right) = t$$

Therefore, we can say:

$$t = -\frac{L}{R}ln\left(\frac{V_{Supply} - iR}{V_{Supply}}\right)$$

We can test this expression with the test circuit shown in Figure 4-22.

CHAPTER 4   DC TRANSIENTS IN LR CIRCUITS

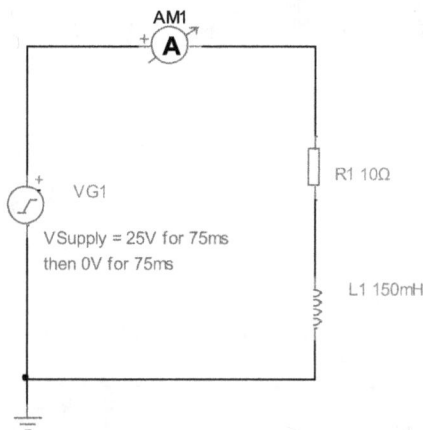

Figure 4-22. *The Test Circuit to Calculate the Time the Current Reaches 1A*

If we put the values into the expression, we can calculate the time the current reaches 1A:

$$t = -\frac{150E^{-3}}{10} \ln\left(\frac{25 - 1 \times 10}{25}\right)$$

Therefore:

$$t = -15E^{-3} \ln(0.6) = -15E^{-3} \times -0.5108$$

Therefore:

$$t = 7.662 \, mS$$

We can use the simulated waveforms shown in Figure 4-23 to confirm this result.

201

CHAPTER 4   DC TRANSIENTS IN LR CIRCUITS

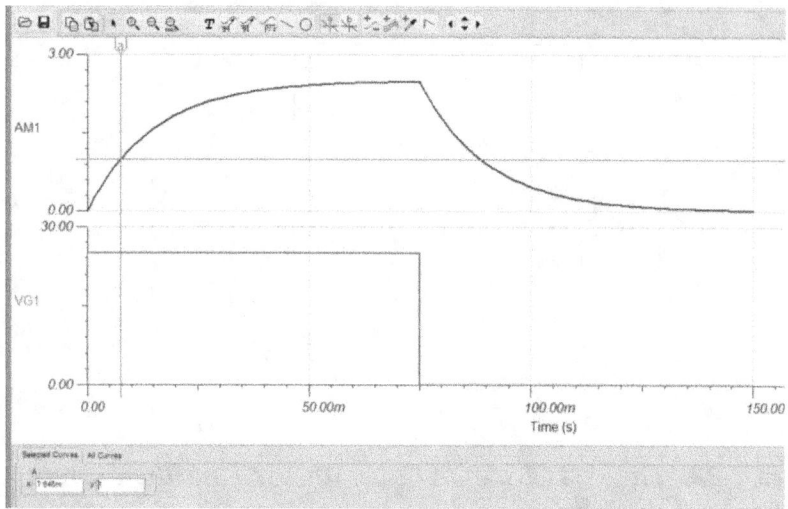

Figure 4-23. *The Current Waveform from the Test Circuit*

Using cursor a, we can see that after 7.646mA, the current reached 1Amp. This agrees very closely with the calculated time of 7.662 ms.

I hope the examples have shown you that with a bit of work we can develop expressions that allow you to predict what will happen in this simple DC circuit. However, as you read on through the book, you will learn how to use similar methods to predict the response of other circuits. In the meantime, practice what you have learnt by completing some exercises. The answers are listed after the summary at the end of this chapter.

Chapter 4 Exercises

The following exercises use the circuit shown in Figure 4-24.

CHAPTER 4 DC TRANSIENTS IN LR CIRCUITS

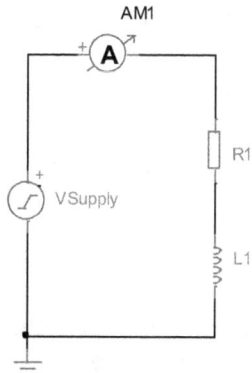

Figure 4-24. *The RL Circuit for the Exercises*

Exercise 4.1

The RL circuit was tested using the following two sets of values:

- V_{Supply} = 20V, R = 15Ω, L= 25mH

- V_{Supply} = 15V, R = 100Ω, L= 125mH

Calculate the following for both sets of values.

- The time constant τ

- The maximum current that will flow in the circuit; the current flowing in the circuit when time t = 1.25τ

- The voltage across the resistor and inductor when time t = 1.75τ

203

CHAPTER 4   DC TRANSIENTS IN LR CIRCUITS

Exercise 4.2

The following DC transient circuit was put together.

- $V_{Supply} = 25V$
- $R = 100\Omega$
- $L = 25mH$

The circuit has been switched on for a long time, greater than 5τ. The supply was then switched to 0V. The 25V supply was then reconnected, but before the current fell to 0A. If the current flowing through the circuit at the time the supply was taken back to 25V, which was 15% of the maximum, current calculate the following:

- The time between switching the supply down to 0V and reapplying the 25V DC supply.

- The current flowing through the circuit 250µs and 1ms after reapplying the voltage supply to the circuit

Exercise 4.3

The circuit in Figure 4-24 has an inductance value of 150mH. The supply voltage is 50V. Calculate the value of the resistor to change the time constant t to 1ms. Then determine the current flowing in the circuit 2ms and 2.5ms after the supply voltage had been reapplied, assuming a current of 50mA was still flowing when the supply voltage was reapplied.

Summary

In this chapter you learnt what transients are and used them to predict how the DC RL circuit will respond during its initial startup. The chapter explained some of the procedures for deriving the various expressions for the DC transient analysis.

CHAPTER 4   DC TRANSIENTS IN LR CIRCUITS

In the next chapter, we carry out some similar analysis on the DC CR transient circuit.

I hope you have found this chapter interesting and informative.

Answers to Exercise 4.1

	First Circuit	Second Circuit
Tau	1.667ms	1.25ms
I at t= 1.25Tau	951.33mA	107.02mA
VR at t = 1.75Tau	16.521V	12.393V

Answers to Exercise 4.2

Decay Time	I after 250us	I after 1ms
406us	171.83mA	246.107mA

Answers to Exercise 4.3

R= 150Ω

    I after 2ms = 295mA

    I after 2.5ms = 310mA

CHAPTER 5

DC Transients in CR Circuits

In Chapter 4, we looked at DC transients in LR circuits. In this chapter, we carry out a similar analysis but on the CR circuit. We will study the CR circuit when it has no initial voltage across the capacitor and then we will extend the analysis to include some initial voltage across the capacitor.

We will look at what a capacitor is and how we can use it to store a charge between the plates. We will look at capacitors in a series and in parallel.

After reading this chapter, you will:

- Understand the relationship between charge and voltage in a capacitor.

- Be able to determine the total capacitance of capacitors in a series and in parallel circuits.

- Understand the time constant for a simple DC CR circuit and be able to derive the expressions for the transients and use them to predict what will happen in the DC CR circuits.

- Understand how the time constant for the circuit can be used to predict when the voltage across the capacitor will reach a certain voltage.

CHAPTER 5   DC TRANSIENTS IN CR CIRCUITS

What Is a Capacitor?

A *capacitor* is basically two metal plates separated by some medium or substance. The medium that separates the plates can be these and other things:

- Air
- Paper
- Mica

A capacitive effect only needs two conductors separated by some medium to produce an effect. One of the most dramatic capacitive effects comes about when the clouds in the sky become positively charged by the electrostatic effect of them moving near each other. If the clouds gain sufficient charge, they will suck electrons from the ground and force them to neutralise the positive charge within the clouds. However, when this happens it leaves the ground below the clouds short of electrons. The ground sucks the electrons back down to the ground, which leaves the clouds with a positive charge, and the cycle repeats. This requires tremendous force which we see as lightening between the clouds and the ground. If we could slow lightening down, we would see that the force movement is lightening travelling up into the clouds. Nature is really quite something.

If a current is forced to pass into and through the plates of a capacitor, the electrons are forced off one plate and deposited on the other plate. This makes one plate positive and the other negative, which means that the capacitor has a voltage across it. The number of electrons that can be forced off the plates must be related to the area, A, of the plates. The ease that they can be forced off must be related to the distance d that the plates are apart. If capacitance is defined as the capacity of the component to store charge between its plates, or create this voltage across its plates, then capacitance must be related to area A and distance d. The bigger the area,

CHAPTER 5 DC TRANSIENTS IN CR CIRCUITS

the more electrons can be removed. The greater the distance, the harder it is to move them. Knowing this, we can relate capacitance C to area A and the distance d in that:

- C is directly proportional to A.
- C is inversely proportional to d.

Therefore, we can say that:

$$C \alpha \frac{A}{d}$$

To remove the sign of proportionality, α, we must have a constant of proportionality. This constant must be related to the makeup of the capacitor. If we look at the capacitor, we know we can alter the area of the plates and the distance between them but the medium between the plates will always be the same. If the medium is air, then it will always be air, if it's paper and air then it will always be paper and air. Therefore, the medium used between the plates will provide us with this constant of proportionality. For air, or more correctly "free space" the constant is:

$$8.8 \text{ E}^{-12}$$

This is called *the constant of permittivity*. The units are Farads per metre and this constant is given the symbol ε_o, the permittivity of free space. We can write a basic expression for Capacitance C such that:

$$C = \frac{\varepsilon_o A}{d}$$

$$C = \frac{8.8 \times 10^{-12} \times A}{d}$$

CHAPTER 5   DC TRANSIENTS IN CR CIRCUITS

As air is a primary medium, then all other mediums are related to air by a multiplier, which is a different for each material. This multiplier is called the *relative permittivity* and is given this symbol:

$$\varepsilon_r$$

Therefore, we can now write the complete expression for Capacitance C such that:

$$C = \frac{\epsilon_o \epsilon_r A}{d}$$

Example 5.1

If a capacitor was made from two plates, both measuring 50cm by 50cm, and were separated by air at 10mm, what would the value of the capacitance be?

We use this formula to solve this:

$$C = \frac{\epsilon_o A}{d}$$

$$C = \frac{8.8E^{-12} \times 50E^{-2} \times 50E^{-2}}{10E^{-3}} = 220E^{-12} = 220pF$$

This is a very small value. Repeat the calculations if the plates were 1m by 1m and the distance between them was still 10mm. You should get C=880pF.

This shows that the value of 1 Farad is a very large value. Indeed, the most common value for capacitors is in the range of microfarads, µF.

Even so if air was the medium used then we would need a very large plate area to create even a 1µF capacitor. To increase the value of capacitance without increasing the size of the plates, we must change the medium between the plates.

CHAPTER 5 DC TRANSIENTS IN CR CIRCUITS

Passing a current through a capacitor means passing a current through the medium. The easier it is to pass the current through the medium, the more charge will be transferred. If we put a medium other than air between the plates of the capacitor, we make it easier for the current to pass through the plates and therefore, we increase the charge transfer and increase the capacitance value.

The medium between the plates is termed *the dielectric* of the capacitor. This is why putting paper or mica in between the plates has the effect of multiplying the permittivity of the medium by ϵ_r, the relative permittivity.

Different materials have different values of ϵ_r. Table 5-1 lists the values for some typical dielectric materials.

Table 5-1. The Relative Permittivity of Some Materials

Dielectric	Relative Permittivity ϵ_r
Air	1.0005
Polyethylene	2.3
Paper	2 - 4
Glass	7
Mica	7

Consider the value of the capacitor in the first example. If paper was used for the dielectric, assuming the ϵ_r for paper to be 3:

$$A = 50cm \times 50cm$$

$$A = 0.25 \text{ m}^2 \text{ as } d = 10mm \text{ then } C = 660pF$$

Still not a lot more. There are some dielectrics that have a relative permittivity in the range of 70 to 20,000. But these are expensive.

The Parallel Plate Capacitor

Another way to increase the capacitance is to put a collection of capacitors in parallel with each other. This is because, unlike resistors, when capacitors are put in parallel, the total capacitance C_T is the sum of the individual capacitances.

Example 5.2

If three capacitors with values of $C_1=1\mu F$ $C_2=2\mu F$ $C_3=3\mu F$ are put in parallel, the total capacitance C_T would be:

$$C_T = C_1+C_2+C_3$$

$$C_T = 1 + 2 + 3$$

$$C_T = 6\mu F$$

Therefore, if many capacitors can be placed in parallel during manufacturing, a large value of capacitance can be made at one go. This is the concept of the *parallel plate capacitor.* This is basically how the electrolytic-type capacitor is made. There are many types of capacitors that are used for different applications. However, that is for a book more practical applications of electronics. This book is concerned with analysing electrical circuits.

Capacitors in Series

As we have seen how capacitors can be added in parallel, then to complete the picture we should see how capacitors add together when connected in series. Can you think of how they would add together? Yes, the same way that resistors add when connected in parallel. Therefore, to calculate the total capacitance of capacitors in series, we use this formula:

CHAPTER 5   DC TRANSIENTS IN CR CIRCUITS

$$C_T = \cfrac{1}{\cfrac{1}{C_1}+\cfrac{1}{C_2}+\cfrac{1}{C_3}\ldots+\cfrac{1}{C_n}}$$

However, if there are only two capacitors, C_1 and C_2, we can use the product over sum rule:

$$C_T = \frac{C_1 C_2}{C_1 + C_2}$$

Example 5.3

If two capacitors—C1=2µF and C2=4µF—were connected in series, the total capacitance would be calculated as follows.

$$C_T = \frac{C_1 C_2}{C_1 + C_2}$$

$$C_T = \frac{2\mu \times 4\mu}{2\mu + 4\mu} = \frac{2E^{-6} \times 4E^{-6}}{2E^{-6} + 4E^{-6}}$$

$$\therefore C_T = \frac{8E^{-12}}{6E^{-6}} = 1.33\mu F$$

Again, as with resistors and inductors in parallel, we can see that when capacitors are in series, the total capacitance will always be smaller than the lowest value capacitance.

Now we look at calculating the total capacitance of capacitors in series, parallel, and series parallel combinations.

Example 5.4

Determine the total capacitance of the three circuits shown in Figure 5-1.

213

CHAPTER 5   DC TRANSIENTS IN CR CIRCUITS

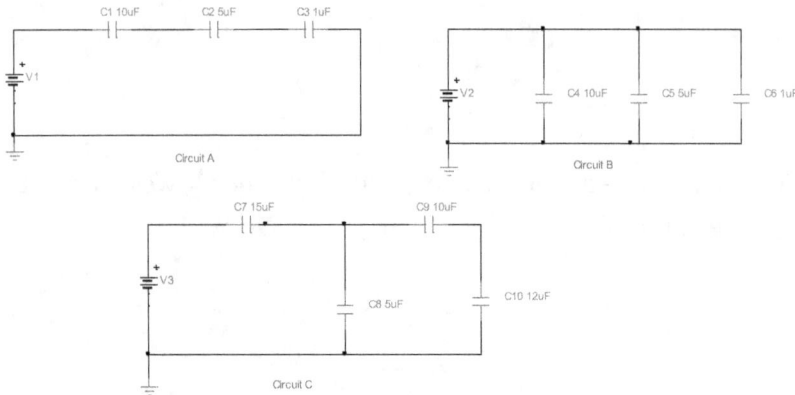

Figure 5-1. *The Three Circuits for Example 5.4*

We can calculate the total capacitance in circuit A using the following:

$$C_T = \frac{1}{\frac{1}{C1}+\frac{1}{C2}+\frac{1}{C3}} = \frac{1}{\frac{1}{10E^{-6}}+\frac{1}{5E^{-6}}+\frac{1}{1E^{-6}}} = 769.231E^{-9} = 769.231 nF$$

This is because the three capacitors are connected in series.

We can calculate the total capacitance in circuit B using the following:

$$C_T = C_4 + C_5 + C_6 = 10E^{-6} + 5E^{-6} + 1E^{-6} = 16E^{-6}$$

The circuit C is shown in Figure 5-2.

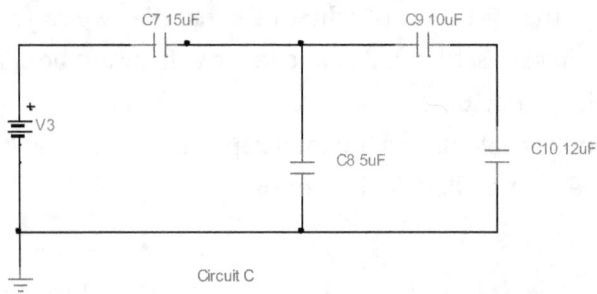

Figure 5-2. *Circuit C for Example 5.4*

214

Using the circuit shown in Figure 5-2, we see that we must first combine C9 and C10. As they are in series, we can combine them using the product over sum expression. This means that:

$$C_{COMB1} = \frac{C_9 C_{10}}{C_9 + C_{10}} = \frac{10E^{-6} 12E^{-6}}{10E^{-6} + 12E^{-6}} = 5.4545E^{-6}$$

We can also combine C_8 and C_{COMB1} as they are in parallel:

$$C_{COMB2} = C_8 + C_{COMB1} = 5E^{-6} + 5.4545E^{-6} = 10.4545E^{-6}$$

Finally, we can add C_7 to C_{COMB2} in series to calculate the total capacitance C_T as follows:

$$C_T = \frac{C_7 C_{COMB2}}{C_7 + C_{COMB2}} = \frac{15E^{-6} 10.4545E^{-6}}{15E^{-6} + 10.4545E^{-6}} = 6.161E^{-6} = 6.161 \mu F$$

The Charge on a Capacitor

We have said that we charge a capacitor by forcing a current to flow into it. This means that the charge, Q, must be related to the current being forced into the capacitor. We can carry out a simple experiment to look at the relationship between charge Q and current I. However, one problem is that we cannot easily measure the charge in a capacitor. We can measure the voltage across the capacitor, and that is what we will do with this experiment with TINA.

Note that this is not a practical experiment, as we would not be able to cope with the voltage we measured. This is a simulated experiment that allows us to examine the relationship between charge and current. The circuit for the experiment is shown in Figure 5-3. We will simply use a current source to force a constant current of 10mA to flow into a capacitor

CHAPTER 5   DC TRANSIENTS IN CR CIRCUITS

for 1 second. We will record the voltage across the capacitor at set time intervals. We will carry out the experiment with three different values of capacitance. The waveforms from the simulation are shown in Figure 5-4.

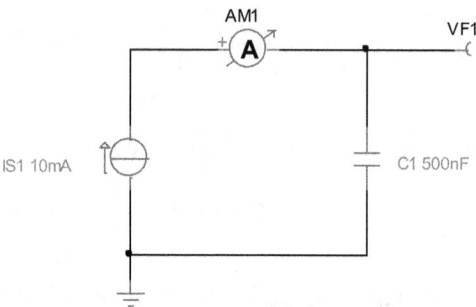

Figure 5-3. *The Circuit for the Charge Experiment*

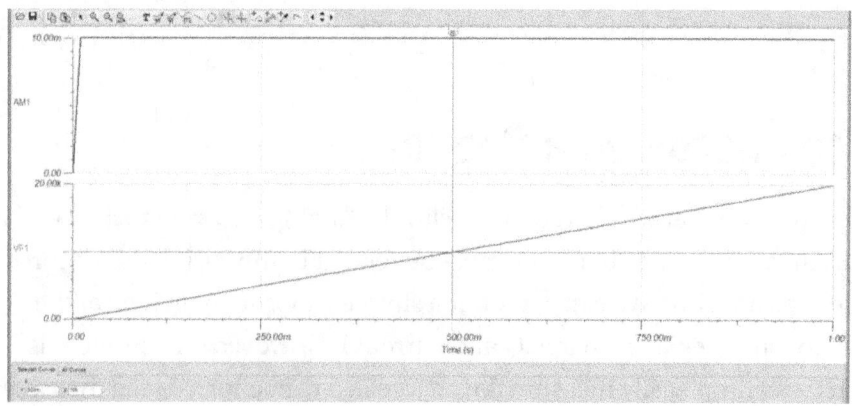

Figure 5-4. *The Current and Voltage Waveforms from the Experiment*

In Chapter 1, we stated that one of the expressions for charge in a capacitor was:

$$I = \frac{Q}{t}$$

CHAPTER 5 DC TRANSIENTS IN CR CIRCUITS

If this is correct, we can say the following:

$$Q = It$$

If we look at the waveforms in Figure 5-4, we can see that when time t was 500ms, the current was 10mA. Really at any time the current would be 10mA, as it was a constant current level set at 10mA. However, using those two reading and the expression for charge Q, we can say when t=500ms:

$$Q = 10E^{-3} \times 500E^{-3} = 5E^{-3} = 5mC$$

Using the waveforms from Figure 5-4, we can see that when time t was 500ms, the voltage across the capacitor was 10kV. In Table 5-2, you can for C equal to 500nF, the capacitor voltage when time is 500ms was the 10kV.

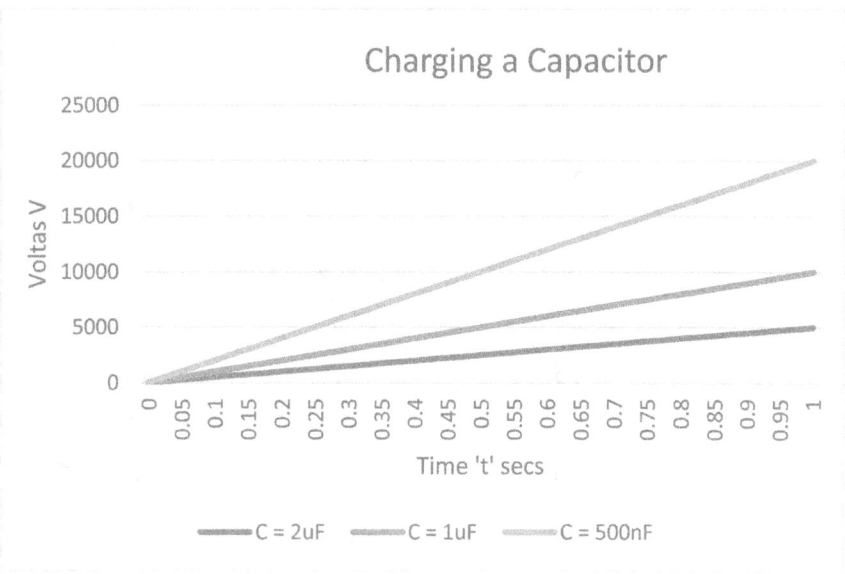

Figure 5-5. The Graph of the Three Simulated Experiments

The voltage measurements for the three experiments are recorded in Table 5-2.

CHAPTER 5   DC TRANSIENTS IN CR CIRCUITS

Table 5-2. *The Measurements for the Three Graphs*

Time t Seconds	Voltage V C=1uF	Voltage V C=10uF	Voltage V C=500nF
0	0	0	0
0.025	25	250	500
0.05	50	500	1000
0.075	75	750	1500
0.1	100	1000	2000
0.125	125	1250	2500
0.15	150	1500	3000
0.175	175	1750	3500
0.2	200	2000	4000
0.225	225	2250	4500
0.25	250	2500	5000
0.275	275	2750	5500
0.3	300	3000	6000
0.325	325	3250	6500
0.35	350	3500	7000
0.375	375	3750	7500
0.4	400	4000	8000
0.425	425	4250	8500
0.45	450	4500	9000
0.475	475	4750	9500
0.5	500	5000	10000

(*continued*)

Table 5-2. (*continued*)

Time t Seconds	Voltage V C=1uF	Voltage V C=10uF	Voltage V C=500nF
0.525	525	5250	10500
0.55	550	5500	11000
0.575	575	5750	11500
0.6	600	6000	12000
0.625	625	6250	12500
0.65	650	6500	13000
0.675	675	6750	13500
0.7	700	7000	14000
0.725	725	7250	14500
0.75	750	7500	15000
0.775	775	7750	15500
0.8	800	8000	16000
0.825	825	8250	16500
0.85	850	8500	17000
0.875	875	8750	17500
0.9	900	9000	18000
0.925	925	9250	18500
0.95	950	9500	19000
0.975	975	9750	19500
1	1000	10000	20000

CHAPTER 5   DC TRANSIENTS IN CR CIRCUITS

Now we will examine the graphs shown in Figure 5-5. We can see that they are all straight-line graphs so they must fit this general expression:

$$y = mx + C$$

The term y is the dependent variable that is plotted on the vertical axis. This means that for our graphs shown in Figure 5-5, y=V_C the voltage across the capacitor. The term x is the independent variable that goes on the horizontal axis. This means that for our graphs shown in Figure 5-5, x is time t. We can also see from the graphs that the constant C is zero (0V). This means the expressions for our three graphs is as follows:

$$V_C = mt$$

We need to determine the value for the term *m*, which is the gradient for the graphs. We can say that the three graphs show that the capacitor voltage is proportional to time t. This means we can say this:

$$V_C = \alpha t$$

The term α is the term for proportionality. We need to replace this term with the constant of proportionality. In all three experiments, the current was kept at a constant at 10mA. Also, for each individual constant the capacitor did not change. We only changed the capacitor value when we started a different experiment. We can see from the three graphs that, when we increased the capacitor value, the gradient decreased. This may suggest we can say that the gradient *m* is proportional to current *I* but inversely proportional to the capacitor value C. This means we can say:

$$V_C = \frac{I}{C} t$$

We can transpose this to say:

$$V_C C = It$$

CHAPTER 5   DC TRANSIENTS IN CR CIRCUITS

Using the expression from Chapter 1, we can say:

$$It = Q$$

This would suggest that we can say:

$$V_C C = Q$$

Where V_C is the voltage across the capacitor. This is one of the fundamental expressions that relates the charge within a capacitor to the voltage across it. We can check out the two expressions for Q by noting that when t=500ms, the current I was 10mA and the voltage across the capacitor was 10kV. This was when the capacitor was set at 500nF. Therefore, using these values to calculate the charge Q, we get:

$$Q = IT = 10E^{-3} \times 500E^{3} = 5mC$$

Using

$$Q = V_C C = 10E^{3} \times 500E^{-9} = 5mC$$

Confirms the two expressions. If we look at the expression $Q = IT$, knowing that this is when the current was a constant, it suggests that the relationship between charge Q and current I is:

$$Q = \int i \, dt$$

This works because if i was a constant at I then the integral would simply give:

$$Q = IT$$

The expression $Q = \int i \, dt$ is indeed the other fundamental expression for the charge in a capacitor.

CHAPTER 5 DC TRANSIENTS IN CR CIRCUITS

The Impedance of a Capacitor

We will look at this in more detail when we look at AC circuits in Chapters 8 and 9. For now, we use the expression for the impedance of a capacitor. Impedance is the AC equivalent of resistance and it explains how a capacitor will impede current flow. The symbol for capacitive impedance is X_C and the expression we use to calculate this is as follows:

$$X_C = \frac{1}{2\pi fC}$$

This shows that as the frequency f of the supply increases as the impedance decreases. This may explain why to DC a capacitor has an infinite impedance. The frequency of DC is 0, which means:

$$X_C = \frac{1}{2\pi \times 0 \times C} = \frac{1}{0} = \infty$$

Therefore, a capacitor can be said to block DC. However, as we will see in the next analysis, it does not block DC the instant the DC voltage is applied. Initially, the capacitor allows the current to flow, and it is only when the capacitor is fully charged that the capacitor will not allow any more DC current to flow into it.

The CR Transient with No Initial Voltage Across the Capacitor

We will now simulate an experiment to show how the current changes from a high level to 0 in the first few moments after switching a DC supply to a circuit containing a resistor and a capacitor. The resistor must be included. If it was not, the initial current would be too high, close to infinity, when we first turned the circuit on. Consider the circuit shown in Figure 5-6.

CHAPTER 5   DC TRANSIENTS IN CR CIRCUITS

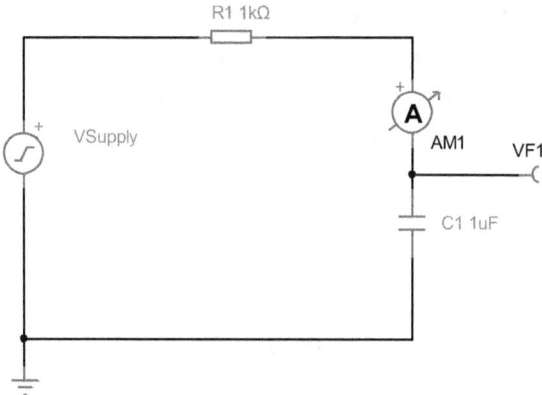

Figure 5-6. *The Test Circuit for the CR DC Transient*

We will simulate turning a supply voltage onto the circuit and then turning it off by creating a square wave that sends the supply voltage high to 10V for the first 5ms, which represents turning the circuit on. Then we send the supply voltage to 0V for another 5ms. This represents turning the circuit off. We will see later why we have set the two time periods to 5ms.

We are using the voltage pin VF1 to watch the voltage across the capacitor change over time. In a more practical situation, you would have to achieve this display using a storage scope. We will develop an expression for the voltage across the capacitor (i.e., V_C). We will use two approaches to derive this expression just as we did for the current in the LR circuit in Chapter 4.

We will start off by applying KVL, which states that we always have:

$$V_{Supply} = V_R + V_C$$

We can use Ohm's Law to show that:

$$V_R = iR$$

223

CHAPTER 5 DC TRANSIENTS IN CR CIRCUITS

However, we don't have a straightforward expression for V_C. We do know that by forcing a current to flow into the capacitor, we are charging the capacitor. There are two expressions we can use that relate charge Q to the capacitor, and they are:

$$Q = CV_C$$

And

$$Q = \int i\, dt$$

Because it is the same charge Q used in both expressions. the two expressions must be equal. This means we can say:

$$CV_C = \int i\, dt$$

If we differentiate both sides, because differentiation is the opposite of integration, we get the following:

$$C\frac{dV_C}{dt} = i$$

This is the same current that will flow through the resistor R, which means we can substitute this for i in the expression for V_R as follows:

$$V_R = C\frac{dV_C}{dt}R$$

This can be rewritten as follows:

$$V_R = CR\frac{dV_C}{dt}$$

This means, that using KVL, we can say this:

$$V_{Supply} = CR\frac{dV_C}{dt} + V_C$$

CHAPTER 5 DC TRANSIENTS IN CR CIRCUITS

This is a first-order differential equation, which we can solve by direct integration after separating the variables. This means putting all the terms associated with time t on one side and all terms associated with V_C on the other side of the expression. We start by subtracting V_C from both sides:

$$V_{Supply} - V_C = CR\frac{dV_C}{dt}$$

Now we divide both sides by CR, which gives:

$$\frac{V_{Supply} - V_C}{CR} = \frac{dV_C}{dt}$$

Now we multiply both sides by dt, which gives:

$$\frac{V_{Supply} - V_C}{CR} dt = dV_C$$

We can see that the numerator on the left contains variables associated with V_C. Therefore, if we multiply both sides by $\frac{1}{V_{Supply} - V_C}$ we get this:

$$\frac{1}{CR} dt = \frac{1}{V_{Supply} - V_C} dV_C$$

In this way we have all the variables associated with V_C on the right and the terms associated with time t on the left. We can now integrate both sides, but we need to include limits for the integration. With respect to time, we must start at time zero and end at some point in time t. With respect to the capacitor voltage, V_C, if we assume the circuit has been turned off for some time and the capacitor is fully discharged, then we can say we start with $V_C=0$ and end when V_C is charged with some voltage, which we call V_{END}. Therefore, the integral becomes:

$$\int_0^t \frac{1}{CR} dt = \int_0^{V_{END}} \frac{1}{V_{Supply} - V_C} dV_C$$

CHAPTER 5   DC TRANSIENTS IN CR CIRCUITS

The LHS integral goes to:

$$\left[\frac{t}{CR}\right]_0^t = \left(\frac{t}{CR}\right) - \left(\frac{0}{CR}\right) = \frac{t}{CR}$$

The RHS has no standard integral, so we must substitute the denominator of the fraction with another variable, such as u in this case, as follows:

$$Let\ u = V_{Supply} - V_C$$

If we now differentiate this expression for u with respect to V_C, then knowing V_{Supply} is a constant:

$$\frac{du}{dV_C} = -1$$

We need to remember that the differential of a constant is 0. This means that we can transpose this for dV_C as follows.

$$dV_C = -du$$

This means that we can now substitute the terms on the right-side integral as follows:

$$\int_0^{V_{END}} \frac{1}{V_{Supply} - V_C} dV_C \text{ is the same as } \int_0^{V_{END}} -\frac{1}{u} du$$

We don't need to change the limits of integration to limits with respect to u as we will substitute this again before we put the limits in.

Using the standard integrals, the integration becomes:

$$\left[-ln(u)\right]_0^{V_{END}}$$

226

CHAPTER 5 DC TRANSIENTS IN CR CIRCUITS

However, we know that:

$$u = V_{Supply} - V_C$$

So, substituting this back in gives:

$$\left[-ln\left(V_{Supply} - V_C\right)\right]_0^{V_{END}}$$

We can put the limits into the integral knowing we substitute the variable V_C with limits using upper limit V_{END} minus lower limit 0.

This gives us:

$$\left(-ln\left(V_{Supply} - V_{END}\right)\right) - \left(-ln\left(V_{Supply} - 0\right)\right)$$

Which simplifies to:

$$ln\left(V_{Supply}\right) - ln\left(V_{Supply} - V_{END}\right)$$

Therefore, the completed integral gives:

$$\frac{t}{CR} = ln\left(V_{Supply}\right) - ln\left(V_{Supply} - V_{END}\right)$$

The subtraction of two logs with the same base is the same as taking the log of the division of those two terms. This means that we can say:

$$\frac{t}{CR} = ln\left(\frac{V_{Supply}}{V_{Supply} - V_{END}}\right)$$

If we take the antilog of both terms to get rid of the ln, we get this:

$$e^{\frac{t}{CR}} = \frac{V_{Supply}}{V_{Supply} - V_{END}}$$

227

If we now invert both sides, we can say this:

$$\frac{1}{e^{\frac{t}{CR}}} = \frac{V_{Supply} - V_{END}}{V_{Supply}}$$

However, using the rules of indices, we can say:

$$\frac{1}{e^{\frac{t}{CR}}} \text{ can be rewritten as } e^{-\frac{t}{CR}}$$

Therefore, this means we can say:

$$\frac{V_{Supply} - V_{END}}{V_{Supply}} = e^{-\frac{t}{CR}}$$

Now we multiply both sides by V_{Supply}:

$$V_{Supply} - V_{END} = V_{Supply} e^{-\frac{t}{CR}}$$

Now we subtract V_{Supply} from both sides and get:

$$-V_{END} = V_{Supply} e^{-\frac{t}{CR}} - V_{Supply}$$

We multiply throughout by -1 to get:

$$V_{END} = V_{Supply} - V_{Supply} e^{-\frac{t}{CR}}$$

Finally, we take the term V_{Supply} out of the right side as a common factor to get:

$$V_{END} = V_{Supply} \left(1 - e^{-\frac{t}{CR}}\right)$$

CHAPTER 5   DC TRANSIENTS IN CR CIRCUITS

This is the standard expression for the growth of the voltage across the capacitor in a DC transient circuit. I know we have had to go through a lot of maths to derive this expression. When you see maths being used to derive these important expressions that you use in engineering, I hope it gives you the motivation to master this important skill. When you do, you'll have confidence that you can prove any theories you might want to use and solve any problems you come across in your career as an engineer. I believe that an engineer is more than a person who maintains systems; they design the systems that we will use in the future that will improve all our lives. That engineer needs all the skills that I want to show them and more.

If YOU look at the exponential $e^{-\frac{t}{CR}}$ term and compare it to the standard exponent, we can see:

$$e^{-\frac{t}{CR}} = e^{-\frac{t}{\tau}}$$

This shows that the term τ, which is Tau the time constant of the system, in this case the DC CR circuit, is:

$$\tau = CR$$

If we use the values from the circuit shown in Figure 5-1, we have this:

$$\tau = 1E^{-6} \times 1E^{3} = 1ms$$

From the theory of transients, we know that it will take approximately five-time constants τ for the circuit to reach its steady state conditions. The steady state conditions of the DC transient CR circuit are that the voltage across the capacitor will reach the supply voltage and the current in the circuit will have fallen to 0A. With respect to the circuit shown in Figure 5-1, the capacitor voltage will build up to a maximum of 10V and it will take approximately 5ms to do it. This also means it will take approximately 5m for the capacitor to fully discharge. That is why I chose the two 5ms time periods for the supply voltage.

CHAPTER 5   DC TRANSIENTS IN CR CIRCUITS

If we simulate the circuit, we will get the waveforms shown in Figure 5-7.

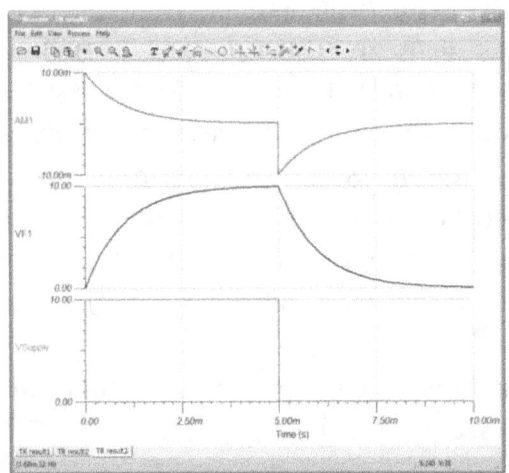

Figure 5-7. *The Waveforms from the DC Transient Circuit*

The V_{Supply} trace shows that we initially switch a 10V supply to the circuit for 5ms and then switch it back to 0V for a further 5ms. The VF1 trace shows how the voltage across the capacitor changes over time. It shows that the voltage reaches the maximum voltage of 10V after 5ms as expected. It also shows that it gradually falls back to 0v during the next 5ms.

The AM1 trace shows that the current starts at a maximum value of 10mA when time t=0. It then falls off to 0A when t=5ms. It also shows that the current changes instantly to $-10mA$, when the supply voltage changes to 0V. It then shows how the current reduces to 0A over the next 5ms. This means that the current has now changed direction and is flowing out of the capacitor, hence discharging the capacitor.

The waveforms show that we are charging the capacitor during the first 5ms as current has been flowing into the capacitor. Hence the current is positive. Then the capacitor is allowed to discharge as the current changes direction and flows out of the capacitor; hence the current is negative.

CHAPTER 5   DC TRANSIENTS IN CR CIRCUITS

This charging of the capacitor can be confirmed as the voltage across the capacitor builds up. Then we can see the capacitor is discharging as the voltage across it falls back to 0V.

Using the Charge Q in a Capacitor

Earlier I stated that $Q = \int i\, dt$. By differentiating both sides of this expression, we can say:

$$i = \frac{dQ}{dt}$$

Using KVL, we know:

$$V_{Supply} = iR + V_C$$

Therefore, we can say:

$$V_{Supply} = \frac{dQ}{dt}R + V_C$$

We also know that $Q = CV$, where V is V_C, the voltage across the capacitor. This means that we can also say $V_C = \frac{Q}{C}$. Putting this into the KVL expression, we get this:

$$V_{Supply} = \frac{dQ}{dt}R + \frac{Q}{C}$$

This expression is a differential equation that relates the KVL expression to charge, Q. If we move on to separate the variables, starting by subtracting $\frac{Q}{C}$ from both sides, we get this:

$$V_{Supply} - \frac{Q}{C} = \frac{dQ}{dt}R$$

231

CHAPTER 5 DC TRANSIENTS IN CR CIRCUITS

We should be able to derive the expression for the voltage across the capacitor assuming the initial voltage was 0V.

Exercise 5.1

Using the process of separating the variables and then using direct integration, see if you can derive the expression for the voltage across the capacitor. You should end up with the same final expression, which is as follows:

$$V_C = V_{Supply}\left(1 - e^{-\frac{t}{CR}}\right)$$

You might need to read through the similar derivation in Chapter 4. This agrees with our pervious expression for charging the capacitor. This approach confirms the relationship between current I, charge Q, and voltage V with a capacitor.

Example 5.5

We can evaluate the expression for V_C for different times and compare the results with the waveform VF1; see Figure 5-8.

CHAPTER 5 DC TRANSIENTS IN CR CIRCUITS

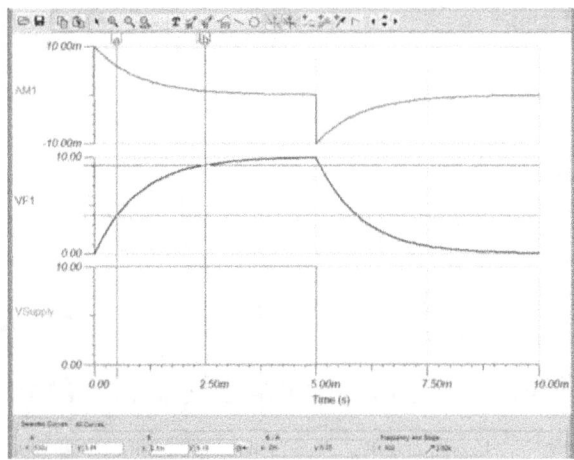

Figure 5-8. *The Voltage Across the Capacitor at Time=500µs and 2.5ms*

We will use a time of 500µs and then 2.5ms to calculate the voltage across the capacitor, using this expression:

$$V_C = V_{Supply}\left(1 - e^{-\frac{t}{CR}}\right)$$

When t=500µs:

$$V_C = 10\left(1 - e^{-\frac{500E^{-6}}{1E^{-3}}}\right)$$

$$V_C = 10(1 - 0.6065)$$

$$V_C = 3.934V$$

CHAPTER 5   DC TRANSIENTS IN CR CIRCUITS

When t=2.5ms:

$$V_C = 10\left(1 - e^{-\frac{2.5E^{-3}}{1E^{-3}}}\right)$$

$$V_C = 10(1 - 0.0821)$$

$$V_C = 9.18V$$

These calculations are close to the readings from the VF1 waveform shown in Figure 5-8.

The Current in the DC CR Transient Circuit

We need to develop the expression for the current flowing in the circuit. There are two approaches we can use—one uses Ohm's Law and the other uses Laplace transforms. First, we will use the Ohm's Law approach, as follows:

$$i = \frac{V_R}{R}$$

However, to use this, we need to develop an expression for the voltage V_R. To do this, we start by using KVL. This states:

$$V_{Supply} = V_R + V_C$$

Rearranging this for V_R gives the following:

$$V_R = V_{Supply} - V_C$$

CHAPTER 5   DC TRANSIENTS IN CR CIRCUITS

We have previously derived an expression for V_C as follows:

$$V_C = V_{Supply}\left(1 - e^{-\frac{t}{CR}}\right)$$

Now, we substitute this in the expression for V_R:

$$V_R = V_{Supply} - V_{Supply}\left(1 - e^{-\frac{t}{CR}}\right)$$

Expanding the bracket gives this:

$$V_R = V_{Supply} - V_{Supply} + V_{Supply}\, e^{-\frac{t}{CR}}$$

This cancels down to the following:

$$V_R = V_{Supply}\, e^{-\frac{t}{CR}}$$

We can now use Ohm's Law, which states:

$$i = \frac{V_R}{R}$$

Dividing the expression for V_R by R, we get:

$$i = \frac{V_{Supply}\, e^{-\frac{t}{CR}}}{R}$$

Example 5.6

The expression for the current i is an exponential decay and if we use values of t=0, t=500ms, t=2.5ms, and t=5ms, we get the following results. Knowing V_{Supply}=10V, R=1k, and C=1µF, we can carry out the calculations as follows.

235

CHAPTER 5 DC TRANSIENTS IN CR CIRCUITS

When t=0:

$$i = \frac{10e^{-\frac{0}{1E^{-6}1E^{3}}}}{1E^{3}} = \frac{10e^{0}}{1E^{3}}$$

Knowing $e^0 = 1$, we see that:

$$i = 10mA$$

When t=500μs:

$$i = \frac{10e^{-\frac{500E^{-6}}{1E^{-6}1E^{3}}}}{1E^{3}} = \frac{10e^{-0.5}}{1E^{3}}$$

$$i = \frac{10 \times 0.6065}{1E^{3}} = 6.065mA$$

When t=2.5ms:

$$i = \frac{10e^{-\frac{2.5E^{-3}}{1E^{-6}1E^{3}}}}{1E^{3}} = \frac{10e^{-2.5}}{1E^{3}}$$

$$i = \frac{10 \times 0.08208}{1E^{3}} = 0.8208mA$$

When t=5ms:

$$i = \frac{10e^{-\frac{5E^{-3}}{1E^{-6}1E^{3}}}}{1E^{3}} = \frac{10e^{-5}}{1E^{3}}$$

$$i = \frac{10 \times 6.738E^{-3}}{1E^{3}} = 67.394\mu A$$

CHAPTER 5   DC TRANSIENTS IN CR CIRCUITS

When we simulate the circuit and display the waveforms, as shown in Figure 5-9, we can compare these calculations with the measurements taken from the current waveform.

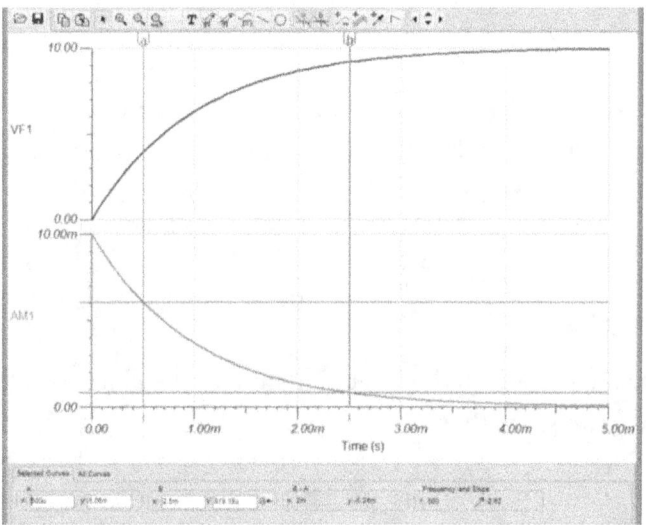

Figure 5-9. *The Current and Voltage Waveforms Over the first 5ms*

The measurements taken from Figure 5-9 agree with the current calculations. Also, when t=500µs, the current measured was 6.06mA and when t=2.5ms, the current was measured at 819.18µA. These measurements confirm the calculations and confirm the expressions for the current *i* are correct.

Using Laplace Transforms

We don't have to use Laplace transforms for this rather simple expression. However, as an engineer, you will come across more complex calculations and Laplace transforms can be one method of manipulating the expression. Therefore, it's good to practice using Laplace transforms by starting with some relatively simple examples. This CR transient is slightly

237

CHAPTER 5 DC TRANSIENTS IN CR CIRCUITS

more complex than the LR transient we looked at in Chapter 4. However, the approach is the same. We start by stating KVL, which shows the following:

$$V_{Supply} = V_R + V_C$$

We will use this KVL expression to derive the expression for the voltage across the capacitor and the current flowing through the capacitor. We can express both volt drops in terms of the current flowing through them as follows:

$$V_R = iR$$

However, when we used the relationship for the charge on the capacitor, we can show that:

$$i = C \frac{dV_C}{dt}$$

This is the same current that will flow through the resistor R. This means we can say:

$$V_R = CR \frac{dV_C}{dt}$$

This in turn means we can say:

$$V_{Supply} = CR \frac{dV_C}{dt} + V_C$$

This is a first-order differential equation, which we can solve using Laplace transforms by taking the Laplace transform of each of the terms, starting with the supply voltage V_{supply}. If we don't want to describe what type of supply we are applying to the circuit, we would identify this as a variable by place a bar above the term. Therefore, we would say:

CHAPTER 5   DC TRANSIENTS IN CR CIRCUITS

$$L\{V_{Supply}\} = \overline{V}_{Supply}$$

However, during the first 5ms of the analysis, we know the supply voltage is a constant of 10V. When we look at the standard Laplace transforms, we see that they express the constant simply as 1. Therefore, using those transforms, we can say that:

$$L\{1\} = \frac{1}{S}$$

Where 1 is the value of the constant. In this case, the constant is 10, so we replace the 1 with 10. Therefore, we can say that:

$$L\{V_{Supply}\} = L\{10\} = \frac{10}{S}$$

We now need the Laplace of the term:

$$CR\frac{dV_C}{dt}$$

This is a derivative multiplied by the term CR. Therefore, using the standard Laplace transforms, we can say:

$$L\left\{CR\frac{dV_C}{dt}\right\} = CR\left(S\overline{V}_C - V_{C0}\right)$$

The V_{C0} term represents the initial voltage across the capacitor. If we assume that the circuit has been disconnected for a long time and the capacitor is fully discharged, then we can say that $V_{C0} = 0$. This means that we can say:

$$L\left\{CR\frac{dV_C}{dt}\right\} = CRS\overline{V}_C$$

239

CHAPTER 5   DC TRANSIENTS IN CR CIRCUITS

Finally, we can take the Laplace of the last term V_C, which will be:

$$L\{V_C\} = \overline{V_C}$$

This is because the voltage V_C is the variable we are deriving the expression for. We now have the Laplace of all the terms, which means we can write the Laplace equation as follows:

$$\frac{10}{S} = CRS\overline{V_C} + \overline{V_C}$$

We can take the term $\overline{V_C}$ out as a common factor, as this is now an algebraic equation. It results in:

$$\frac{10}{S} = \overline{V_C}(CRS+1)$$

We can divide both sides by $CRS + 1$ or multiply both sides by $\frac{1}{CRS+1}$, which is mathematically the same. This gives the following:

$$\frac{10}{S} \times \frac{1}{1+CRS} = \overline{V_C}(1+CRS) \times \frac{1}{1+CRS}$$

I rewrote the term in the brackets to make it more readable; it means the same thing.

When we cancel out the terms on the right side and multiply the two fractions on the left side, we get:

$$\frac{10}{S(1+CRS)} = \overline{V_C}$$

It is more common the make the coefficient of S equal to 1. To do this, we need to divide top and bottom of the compound fraction on the left by CR. This gives the following:

$$\frac{\frac{10}{CR}}{S\left(\frac{1}{CR}+S\right)} = \overline{V_C}$$

There are no standard Laplace transforms for the compound fraction on the left side. This means that we need to convert the compound fraction into its two partial fractions. This can be done as follows:

$$\frac{\frac{10}{CR}}{S\left(\frac{1}{CR}+S\right)} \equiv \frac{A}{S} + \frac{B}{\frac{1}{CR}+S}$$

We need to determine the A and B constants. This is done as follows. First, we multiply both sides by the denominator on the left. This gives the following:

$$\frac{\frac{10}{CR}}{S\left(\frac{1}{CR}+S\right)}\left(S\left(\frac{1}{CR}+S\right)\right) \equiv \frac{A}{S}\left(S\left(\frac{1}{CR}+S\right)\right) + \frac{B}{\frac{1}{CR}+S}\left(S\left(\frac{1}{CR}+S\right)\right)$$

We can now cancel out the terms, which gives this:

$$\frac{10}{CR} = A\left(\frac{1}{CR}+S\right) + B(S)$$

We need to determine the A and B constants. If we let S=0, we will get rid of the constant B as follows:

$$\frac{10}{CR} = A\left(\frac{1}{CR}+0\right) + B(0)$$

CHAPTER 5 DC TRANSIENTS IN CR CIRCUITS

Which gives this:

$$\frac{10}{CR} = \frac{A}{CR}$$

If we multiply both sides by CR, we get:

$$A = 10$$

To get rid of constant A, we can let $S = -\frac{1}{CR}$:

$$\frac{10}{CR} = A\left(\frac{1}{CR} + -\frac{1}{CR}\right) + B\left(-\frac{1}{CR}\right)$$

This gives the following:

$$\frac{10}{CR} = -\frac{B}{CR}$$

If we multiply both sides by $-CR$, we get:

$$B = -10$$

Putting these constants into the partial fractions results in this:

$$\frac{\frac{10}{CR}}{S\left(\frac{1}{CR} + S\right)} = \frac{10}{S} - \frac{10}{\frac{1}{CR} + S}$$

We can confirm that this is correct by evaluating.

$$\frac{10}{S} - \frac{10}{\frac{1}{CR} + S}$$

CHAPTER 5   DC TRANSIENTS IN CR CIRCUITS

We create the common denominator by multiplying the two denominators. We also need to multiply the numerators by the opposite denominators. This gives us the following:

$$\frac{10}{S} - \frac{10}{\frac{1}{CR}+S} = \frac{10 \times \left(\frac{1}{CR}+S\right) - 10 \times S}{S\left(\frac{1}{CR}+S\right)} = \frac{\frac{10}{CR} + 10S - 10S}{S\left(\frac{1}{CR}+S\right)} = \frac{\frac{10}{CR}}{S\left(\frac{1}{CR}+S\right)}$$

This is the compound fraction we started with, which means the partial fractions we used are correct.

This means we can rewrite the Laplace equation as follows:

$$\overline{V_C} = \frac{10}{S} - \frac{10}{\frac{1}{CR}+S}$$

Now we can convert this back into a time equation by taking the inverse Laplace of all terms:

$$L^{-1}\{\overline{V_C}\} = V_C$$

$$L^{-1}\left\{\frac{10}{S}\right\} = 10$$

$$L^{-1}\left\{-\frac{10}{\frac{1}{CR}+S}\right\} = -10e^{-\frac{t}{CR}}$$

This means that the time equation for V_C becomes:

$$V_C = 10 - 10e^{-\frac{t}{CR}}$$

CHAPTER 5   DC TRANSIENTS IN CR CIRCUITS

Taking the 10 out as a common factor gives this:

$$V_C = 10\left(1 - e^{-\frac{t}{CR}}\right)$$

If we replace the 10v with the variable V_{Supply}, we get the general expression for V_C as follows:

$$V_C = V_{Supply}\left(1 - e^{-\frac{t}{CR}}\right)$$

This is the same expression as the one we derived using calculus.

We will now use Laplace transforms to derive the expression for the current i in the circuit. As before, we start with KVL, which states that:

$$V_{Supply} = V_R + V_C$$

We can express both volt drops in terms of the current flowing through them as follows:

$$V_R = iR$$

However, as before, we use the relationship for the charge on the capacitor to show that:

$$V_C = \frac{1}{C}\int i\, dt$$

Therefore, we can say:

$$V_{Supply} = iR + \frac{1}{C}\int i\, dt$$

We can't take the variable i out as a common factor, as one is algebraic, and the other is an integral. This is where Laplace transforms come in. We can create a Laplace equation that will be an algebraic equation. We start by taking the Laplace transform for each of the terms in the equation.

Now we determine the Laplace of the term iR. As i is the variable we are trying to create the expression for, we simply put a bar over the term i. As we are simply multiplying this by R, we can say that:

$$L\{iR\} = \bar{i}R$$

Lastly, we need to determine the Laplace of the term $\frac{1}{C}\int i\, dt$. As this is an integral multiplied by the term $\frac{1}{C}$, we simply multiply the Laplace of the integral by $\frac{1}{C}$. Using the standard Laplace transforms, as shown in the appendix, we can say:

$$L\{\int i\, dt\} = \frac{1}{S}\bar{i}$$

This means we write the Laplace equation as follows:

$$\frac{10}{S} = \bar{i}R + \frac{1}{C} \times \frac{1}{S}\bar{i}$$

$$\frac{10}{S} = \bar{i}R + \frac{1}{CS}\bar{i}$$

This is now an algebraic equation, and we can take the $\bar{i}$ out as a common factor. This gives us this:

$$\frac{10}{S} = \bar{i}\left(R + \frac{1}{CS}\right)$$

CHAPTER 5   DC TRANSIENTS IN CR CIRCUITS

We can add the two terms in the brackets, which gives us:

$$\frac{10}{S} = \bar{i}\left(\frac{RCS+1}{CS}\right)$$

We can now divide both sides by the term in the brackets, or multiply both sides by $\left(\frac{CS}{1+RCS}\right)$, which gives:

$$\frac{10}{S}\left(\frac{CS}{1+RCS}\right) = \bar{i}$$

This simplifies to the following:

$$\bar{i} = \frac{10C}{1+RCS}$$

If we divide the top and bottom of the fraction by RC, to get the coefficient of the S term in the denominator equal to 1, we get this:

$$\bar{i} = \frac{\frac{10C}{RC}}{\frac{1}{RC} + \frac{RCS}{RC}}$$

This simplifies to the following:

$$\bar{i} = \frac{\frac{10}{R}}{\frac{1}{CR} + S}$$

All that we need to do now is take the inverse Laplace of the terms in the equation. This gives us this:

$$L^{-1}\{\bar{i}\} = i$$

CHAPTER 5   DC TRANSIENTS IN CR CIRCUITS

$$L^{-1}\left\{\frac{\frac{10}{R}}{\frac{1}{CR}+S}\right\} = \frac{10}{R}e^{-\frac{t}{CR}}$$

This means that we can say:

$$i = \frac{10}{R}e^{-\frac{t}{CR}}$$

We can generalise it with this expression:

$$i = \frac{V_{Supply}}{R}e^{-\frac{t}{CR}}$$

This can be done only if the variable V_{Supply} is a constant DC voltage. This is the same expression as derived before using the Ohm's Law approach.

I hope by showing all the steps in deriving these equations—both by using calculus and by the Laplace transforms—you can see that each step is quite simple. If you take your time, you should be able to learn this very useful skill. It is a very powerful skill to learn, as you can use it to predict how circuits will work. One very useful example of this skill is the ECAD software that engineers use to test designs. The software does not have the actual components and equipment; it uses very powerful mathematical models that are only an extension of the skill we are practicing here. That's not to say that the models used by the ECAD software are simple; they are extremely complex and involve a lot of mathematics.

CHAPTER 5 DC TRANSIENTS IN CR CIRCUITS

Expressions for Periods of Growth

We now have the three expressions that we can use to determine how the three parameters—the voltage across the capacitor, the current i, and the voltage across the resistor—change over the period of growth. The three equations are as follows:

$$V_C = V_{Supply}\left(1 - e^{-\frac{t}{CR}}\right)$$

$$i = \frac{V_{Supply}}{R} e^{-\frac{t}{CR}}$$

$$V_R = V_{Supply} e^{-\frac{t}{CR}}$$

We can make some general statements about this CR DC transient circuit and they are discussed next.

The time constant Tau can be calculated using:

$$\tau = CR \text{ Seconds}$$

After one time constant has passed, the voltage builds up to 63.2% of the maximum. This can be proved by letting time t=CR seconds as follows.

$$V_C = V_{Supply}\left(1 - e^{-\frac{t}{CR}}\right)$$

$$V_C = V_{Supply}\left(1 - e^{-\frac{CR}{CR}}\right)$$

$$V_C = V_{Supply}\left(1 - e^{-1}\right)$$

CHAPTER 5   DC TRANSIENTS IN CR CIRCUITS

$$V_C = V_{Supply}(1 - 0.368)$$

$$V_C = V_{Supply}(0.6321)$$

This would be 63.21% of V_{Supply}.

After one time constant has passed, the current decays to 36.8% of its maximum. This can be shown by letting t=CR seconds, as follows:

$$i = \frac{V_{Supply}}{R} e^{-\frac{t}{CR}}$$

Therefore:

$$i = \frac{V_{Supply}}{R} e^{-\frac{CR}{CR}}$$

$$i = \frac{V_{Supply}}{R} e^{-1}$$

$$i = \frac{V_{Supply}}{R} \times 0.368$$

This would make the current equal to 36.8% of the maximum.

The voltage across the resistor uses the same equation except that it is not divided by R. This shows that the voltage across the resistor has fallen to 36.8% of the maximum after one time constant has passed. If we simulate the circuit shown in Figure 5-6 again and display the current and voltage across the resistor waveforms, we should be able to confirm these statements.

The simulated traces are shown in Figure 5-10. The trace AM1 is displaying the current in the circuit, and we can see, with cursor a that when t=1ms, which is equal to one time constant, the current has reduced to 3.68mA. This is equal to 36.8% of the maximum 10mA.

CHAPTER 5 DC TRANSIENTS IN CR CIRCUITS

Also, trace VM1 is displaying the voltage across the resistor. We can see when t=1ms, the voltage across the resistor falls to 3.68V. This is 36.8% of the maximum voltage of 10V.

We should also be able to see that if we add the voltage across the resistor, VM1, to the voltage across the capacitor, VF1, we will always get 10V, which shows that V_{Supply} will always equal to $V_R + V_C$, which obeys Kirchhoff's Voltage Law.

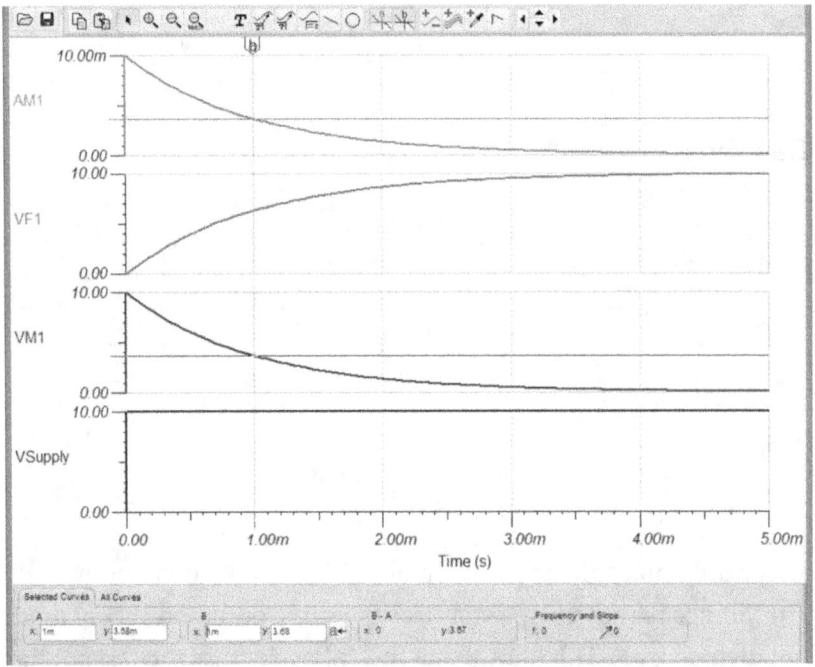

Figure 5-10. *The Voltage Across the Resistor and the Current Waveforms*

Discharging the Capacitor

During the next 5ms of the simulation of the test circuit shown in Figure 5-6, the voltage supplied to the circuit was switched to 0V. This means that the voltage across the capacitor, which had charged up to

CHAPTER 5 DC TRANSIENTS IN CR CIRCUITS

the supply voltage that was 10V during the first 5ms, would be more positive than V_{Supply}, which has just gone down to 0V. This would then allow a current to flow in the opposite direction (i.e., out of the capacitor) and allow it to discharge. We will now derive the expressions for the discharging circuit.

We can, as always, use KVL to show that:

$$V_{Supply} = V_R + V_C$$

Therefore, we can say:

$$V_{Supply} = CR\frac{dV_C}{dt} + V_C$$

As we are now discharging the capacitor, we know that the supply voltage V_{supply} will be 0. Therefore, we have:

$$0 = CR\frac{dV_C}{dt} + V_C$$

If we subtract V_C from both sides, we get:

$$-V_C = CR\frac{dV_C}{dt}$$

Multiplying by dt and dividing by V_C, we get:

$$-dt = CR\frac{dV_C}{V_C}$$

Dividing by CR gives this:

$$-\frac{1}{CR}dt = \frac{1}{V_C}dV_C$$

251

CHAPTER 5 DC TRANSIENTS IN CR CIRCUITS

If we now integrate both sides and use the appropriate limits, we get:

$$\int_0^t -\frac{1}{CR} dt = \int_{V_{Supply}}^{V_C} \frac{1}{V_C} dV_C$$

This integrates to:

$$\left[-\frac{t}{CR}\right]_0^t = \left[\ln V_C\right]_{V_{Supply}}^{V_C}$$

Which gives this:

$$-\frac{t}{CR} = \ln(V_C) - \ln(V_{Supply})$$

Using the laws of logs, we get this:

$$-\frac{t}{CR} = \ln\left(\frac{V_C}{V_{Supply}}\right)$$

taking the antilog of both sides gives this:

$$\frac{V_C}{V_{Supply}} = e^{-\frac{t}{CR}}$$

Multiplying both sides by V_{Supply}, we get this

$$V_C = V_{Supply} e^{-\frac{t}{CR}}$$

This means the capacitor voltage will start at the supply voltage and then decay exponentially until it reaches 0V, as the exponential term is a decay which will eventually go to 0.

CHAPTER 5 DC TRANSIENTS IN CR CIRCUITS

We can derive the same equation using Laplace transforms as follows. However, as an exercise see if you can use Laplace transforms to derive the same expression for V_C during the discharge period. Note that we will restart time at 0 when we switch the supply voltage back to 0V (i.e., when we switch the supply off). At that moment in time the initial voltage across the capacitor will be equal to V_{Supply}.

We can now derive the expression for the voltage across the resistor during this discharge period. We start by using KVL to show that.

$$V_{Supply} = V_R + V_C$$

We know $V_{Supply}=0$ and $V_C = V_{Supply} e^{-\frac{t}{CR}}$, so we can say.

$$0 = V_R + V_{Supply} e^{-\frac{t}{CR}}$$

Therefore, we can say:

$$V_R = -V_{Supply} e^{-\frac{t}{CR}}$$

We can use this to derive an expression for the current simply by dividing this expression by R. This gives us the following:

$$i = \frac{-V_{Supply} e^{-\frac{t}{CR}}}{R}$$

We now have the expressions for the discharge circuit. They are as follows:

$$V_C = V_{Supply} e^{-\frac{t}{CR}}$$

$$V_R = -V_{Supply} e^{-\frac{t}{CR}}$$

$$i = \frac{-V_{Supply} e^{-\frac{t}{CR}}}{R}$$

CHAPTER 5 DC TRANSIENTS IN CR CIRCUITS

Example 5.7

We will use the following parameters to evaluate the three expressions for the discharge circuit and then simulate a circuit with the same values to confirm the calculations.

V_{Supply}=20V when turned on and then 0V when turned off

R=500Ω

C=5µF

The times after turning the supply voltage back to 0V are Time=2ms and 3.5ms.

The Calculations

When time equals 2ms:

The voltage across the capacitor is defined as follows:

$$V_C = V_{Supply} e^{-\frac{t}{CR}}$$

$$V_C = 20 e^{-\frac{2E^{-3}}{5E^{-6} \times 500}}$$

$$V_C = 20 \times 0.4493 = 8.987$$

Here is the voltage across the resistor:

$$V_R = -V_{Supply} e^{-\frac{t}{CR}}$$

$$V_R = -20 e^{-\frac{2E^{-3}}{5E^{-6} \times 500}}$$

$$V_R = -20 \times 0.4493 = -8.987$$

CHAPTER 5 DC TRANSIENTS IN CR CIRCUITS

Here is the current flowing in the circuit:

$$i = \frac{-V_{Supply}}{R} e^{-\frac{t}{CR}}$$

$$i = \frac{-20}{500} e^{-\frac{2E^{-2}}{5E^{-6} \times 500}}$$

$$i = -40E^{-3} \times 0.4493 = -17.973 mA$$

When t=3.5ms.
Here is the voltage across the capacitor:

$$V_C = V_{Supply} e^{-\frac{t}{CR}}$$

$$V_C = 20 e^{-\frac{3.5E^{-3}}{5E^{-6} \times 500}}$$

$$V_C = 20 \times 0.2466 = 4.932V$$

Here is the voltage across the resistor:

$$V_R = -V_{Supply} e^{-\frac{t}{CR}}$$

$$V_R = -20 e^{-\frac{3.5E^{-2}}{5E^{-6} \times 500}}$$

$$V_R = -20 \times 0.2466 = -4.932V$$

Here is the current flowing in the circuit:

$$i = \frac{-V_{Supply}}{R} e^{-\frac{t}{CR}}$$

CHAPTER 5   DC TRANSIENTS IN CR CIRCUITS

$$i = \frac{-20}{500} e^{-\frac{3.5E^{-2}}{5E^{-6} \times 500}}$$

$$i = -40E^{-3} \times 0.2466 = -9.864 mA$$

Figure 5-11 shows the voltage across the capacitor and the supply voltage.

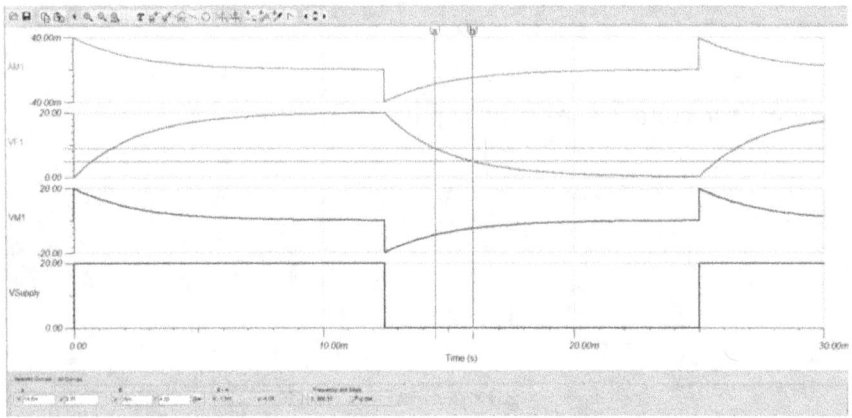

Figure 5-11. *The Displays of the Current AM1 Voltage Across the Capacitor VF1 and the Voltage Across the Resistor VM1*

The trace VF1 shows the voltage across the capacitor. Using the cursors, we can see that when t=14.5ms, cursor a shows that the voltage across the capacitor was 8.91V. When t=16ms, cursor b shows the voltage across the capacitor was 4.88V. These are very close to the calculated results. Note that we have to add 12.5ms to the time used in the calculations, as the circuit switched to the discharge period at t=12.5ms.

The voltage displays in Figure 5-11 that, during the first 12.5ms, if at any time we add the voltage across the resistor to the voltage across the capacitor we would get 10V. During the next 12.5ms, we would get 0V. These additions confirm KVL in that at any time, $V_{Supply} = V_R + V_C$.

CHAPTER 5 DC TRANSIENTS IN CR CIRCUITS

We can simulate the circuit again so that we can look at the current waveform. This will enable us to compare the calculated results to the simulated results. The waveforms from the simulation are shown in Figure 5-12.

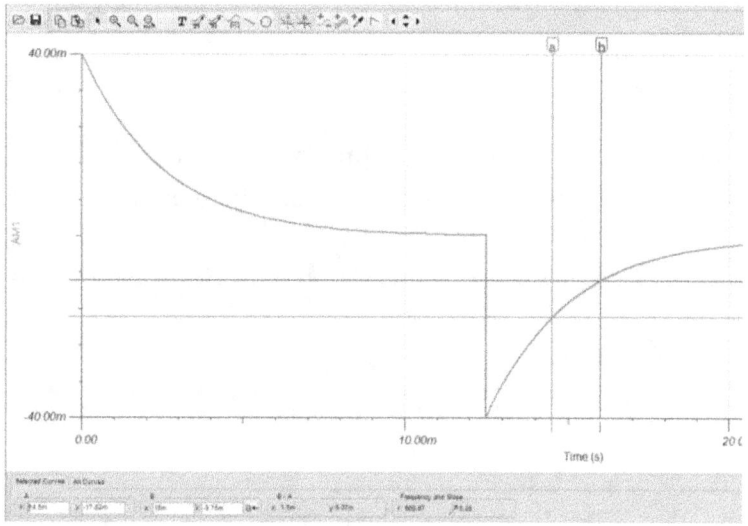

Figure 5-12. *The Current Flowing in the Circuit*

The trace AM1 shows the current flowing in the circuit. Using the cursors, we can see that when t=14.5ms, cursor a shows that the current was -17.82mA. When t=16ms, cursor b shows that the current was -9.75mA. These are very close to the calculated results. The current waveform shows that during the first 12.5ms, the current is positive (i.e., it is flowing into the capacitor and charging it). During the next 12.5ms, the current is negative (i.e., it is flowing out of the capacitor and discharging it).

These simulations show us that these expressions are valid.

CHAPTER 5   DC TRANSIENTS IN CR CIRCUITS

The CR Transient with Initial Conditions

We can now extend the analysis to create expressions for the voltages and currents in the circuit with some initial conditions during the charge-up period.

Exercise 5.2

Use any of the methods shown in the previous derivations to show that the expressions we will use for this analysis agree with these formulae:

$$V_C = V_{Supply}\left(1 - e^{-\frac{t}{CR}}\right) + V_{C0}e^{-\frac{t}{CR}}$$

$$V_R = \left(V_{Supply} - V_{C0}\right)e^{-\frac{t}{CR}}$$

$$i = \frac{\left(V_{Supply} - V_{C0}\right)e^{-\frac{t}{CR}}}{R}$$

As a hint, you should know that the capacitor voltage will not start from 0V; it will have some initial voltage, V_{C0}. Chapter 4 has some similar derivations that should help you.

Example 5.8

We can test these expressions by simulating the DC transient CR circuit with the following conditions.

- V_{Supply}=25V when turned on and 0V when turned off
- R=50Ω
- C=25μF
- V_{C0}=5V

CHAPTER 5 DC TRANSIENTS IN CR CIRCUITS

Start by calculating the time constant τ using this:

$$\tau = CR \text{ seconds}$$

Therefore:

$$\tau = 25E^{-6} \times 50 = 1.25ms$$

This means that it will take approximately 6.25ms (i.e., 5τ) for the circuit to settle down to its steady state conditions during the charge and discharge periods.

We will calculate the value of the parameters 5ms after the circuit has been switched on. Let's start with the voltage across the capacitor:

$$V_C = V_{Supply}\left(1 - e^{-\frac{t}{CR}}\right) + V_{C0} e^{-\frac{t}{CR}}$$

Putting the values in, we get the following:

$$V_C = 25\left(1 - e^{-\frac{5E^{-3}}{1.25E^{-3}}}\right) + 5e^{-\frac{5E^{-3}}{1.25E^{-3}}}$$

Therefore:

$$V_C = 25(1 - 0.01832) + 5 \times 0.01832$$

$$V_C = 25 \times 0.98168 + 0.0916$$

Therefore:

$$V_C = 24.663V$$

CHAPTER 5   DC TRANSIENTS IN CR CIRCUITS

Here is the voltage across the resistor:

$$V_R = (V_{Supply} - V_{C0})e^{-\frac{t}{CR}}$$

Putting the values in, we get the following:

$$V_R = (25-5)e^{-\frac{5E^{-3}}{1.25E^{-3}}}$$

Therefore, we have:

$$V_R = 20 \times 0.01832 = 0.3664V$$

We could use KVL to check these two voltage calculations, as we know $V_R + V_C$ must add up to the supply voltage, V_{Supply}. When we add them, we get this:

$$V_R + V_C = 0.3664 + 24.663 = 25.0294$$

This is close enough, as there will be some rounding errors.

The current flowing through the circuit can be calculated using the following:

$$i = \frac{(V_{Supply} - V_{C0})e^{-\frac{t}{CR}}}{R}$$

Putting in the calculated values from before, we have the following:

$$i = \frac{0.3664}{50} = 7.328 mA$$

After simulating the circuit, the waveforms shown in Figure 5-13 were obtained.

CHAPTER 5   DC TRANSIENTS IN CR CIRCUITS

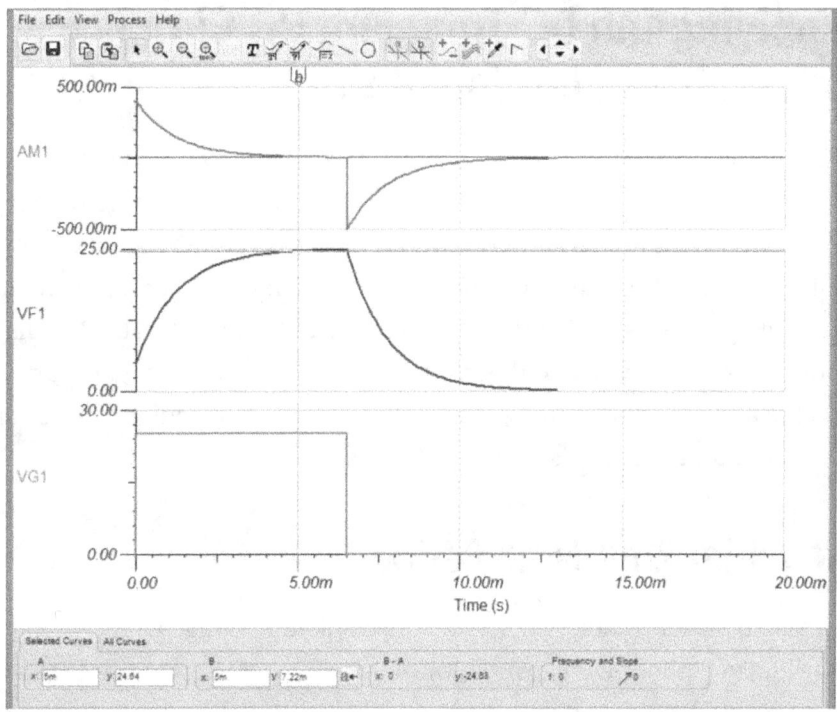

Figure 5-13. *The Waveforms from the Example Circuit with Initial Voltage*

Cursor a on trace VF1 shows that the voltage, after 5ms, has reached 24.64V. Cursor b on the AM1 trace shows that the current, after 5ms, has fallen to 7.22mA. These values are very close to our calculations.

When simulating the circuit in TINA, you can add some initial voltage to the capacitor; I explain how to do that in Chapter 10.

CHAPTER 5   DC TRANSIENTS IN CR CIRCUITS

Supplying the DC Transient CR Circuit with an Irregular Waveform

In this analysis, we will use the component values shown in the previous example, but with no initial voltage. However, the supply voltage will stay high for 2ms and then switch low for 1ms. These times mean that during the first period of 2ms, the capacitor will not reach the maximum voltage. Also, during the 1ms period the capacitor has not discharged to 0V. This means that during the second period of 2ms, the capacitor would start charging up with some initial voltage. We will have to calculate the voltage over different time periods.

The Initial 2ms Time Period

There is no initial voltage. Therefore, the capacitor voltage would rise according to the following expression:

$$V_C = V_{Supply}\left(1 - e^{-\frac{t}{CR}}\right)$$

We know that:

$$\tau = CR = 25E^{-6} \times 50 = 1.25 ms$$

We can test our calculations by choosing an appropriate time setting for the expression. We will choose time setting, which is 1.8ms for the charging period (i.e., close to the time the supply voltage is switched to the 25V supply). Then we choose 0.8ms for the discharge time, which is close to the time the supply is switched to 0V. I have chosen these time settings to stay away from the transition times—2ms and 1ms—as this is when the voltage is changing at a high rate, going from 25V to 0V in 1ns and from 0V to 25V in 1ns. These fast transitions make it difficult to measure the currents in the circuit from the simulations.

CHAPTER 5 DC TRANSIENTS IN CR CIRCUITS

The First Charge-Up Period

Putting a time of 1.8ms into the charging expression, we get the following:

$$V_C = 25\left(1 - e^{-\frac{1.8E^{-3}}{1.25E^{-3}}}\right)$$

$$V_C = 25(1 - 0.23693)$$

$$V_C = 25 \times 0.7631 = 19.0768V$$

To determine the current flowing in the circuit during the first charge-up period, we use the expression:

$$i = \frac{V_{Supply} e^{-\frac{t}{CR}}}{R}$$

Putting the values in, we get this:

$$i = \frac{25 e^{-\frac{1.8E^{-3}}{1.25E^{-3}}}}{50}$$

$$i = \frac{25 \times 0.23693}{50} = 0.118465A = 118.465mA$$

The First Discharge Period

The discharge of the voltage during the first 1ms of discharge time can be calculated using this expression:

$$V_C = V_{C0} e^{-\frac{t}{CR}}$$

263

CHAPTER 5   DC TRANSIENTS IN CR CIRCUITS

The voltage V_{CO} will be the voltage the capacitor has reached during the first 2ms. The voltage across the capacitor was calculated at 19.0768V when t=1.8ms. However, if we went to the full 2ms, then our calculations would have given the capacitor voltage at 19.953V.

Therefore, putting these values into the expression for the discharge, but with time t=0.8ms, we get this:

$$V_C = 19.953 e^{-\frac{0.8E^{-3}}{1.25E^{-3}}}$$

Which gives us this:

$$V_C = 19.953 \times 0.5273 = 10.521V$$

However, we will be calculating the capacitor voltage during the second charge-up period. This requires the capacitor voltage V_{CO}, that the capacitor has continued to discharge to until t=1ms. Using this value for time t to calculate the capacitor voltage during the first discharge, we get this:

$$V_C = 19.953 e^{-\frac{1E^{-3}}{1.25E^{-3}}} = 8.9655V$$

This is the value for V_{CO} we will use when calculating the capacitor voltage during the second 2ms charge-up period:

The Current Flowing During the First Discharge Period

We can use the general expression for the current during the discharge of the capacitor, which is:

$$i = \frac{-V_C}{R} e^{-\frac{t}{CR}}$$

CHAPTER 5 DC TRANSIENTS IN CR CIRCUITS

Where the voltage V_C is the voltage across the capacitor at the time of discharge. Using the previous calculations that determined when the circuit was switched on for the full 2ms, we know the capacitor voltage would be 19.953V. Therefore, using 0.8m for the time, we get:

$$i = \frac{-19.953}{50} e^{\frac{-0.8E^{-3}}{1.25E^{-3}}} = -210.421 mA$$

The Second Charge-Up Period

Now during the next 2ms, the capacitor will charge back up again toward the 25V, but with an initial voltage of 8.9655V. Therefore, to calculate the voltage across the capacitor, we must use:

$$V_C = V_{Supply}\left(1 - e^{-\frac{t}{CR}}\right) + V_{C0} e^{-\frac{t}{CR}}$$

Putting the value of t=1.8ms in, we get:

$$V_C = 25\left(1 - e^{-\frac{1.8E^{-3}}{1.25E^{-3}}}\right) + 8.9655 e^{-\frac{1.8E^{-3}}{1.25E^{-3}}}$$

This gives us the following:

$$V_C = 25(1 - 0.23693) + 8.9655 \times 0.23693$$

This gives us the following:

$$V_C = 25(0.7631) + 2.1242 = 21.202V$$

CHAPTER 5 DC TRANSIENTS IN CR CIRCUITS

The current flowing in the circuit during the second 1.8ms time can be calculated using this expression:

$$i = \frac{(V_{Supply} - V_{C0})e^{-\frac{t}{CR}}}{R}$$

Putting the values in, we get the following:

$$i = \frac{(25 - 8.9655)e^{-\frac{1.8E^{-3}}{1.25E^{-3}}}}{R50}$$

This gives.

$$i = \frac{16.0345 \times 0.2369}{50} = 75.98m$$

The Second Discharge Period

The voltage that the capacitor would discharge to over the next 0.8ms can be calculated using this formula:

$$V_C = V_{C0}e^{-\frac{t}{CR}}$$

Again V_{C0} will be the voltage the capacitor reached during this second 2ms. This will be 21.763V. Therefore, putting the values in, we get:

$$V_C = 21.763e^{-\frac{0.8E^{-3}}{1.25E^{-3}}}$$

Solving, we get:

$$V_C = 21.763 \times 0.5273 = 11.476V$$

CHAPTER 5 DC TRANSIENTS IN CR CIRCUITS

We can also calculate the current using this formula:

$$i = \frac{-21.763}{50} e^{\frac{-0.8E^{-3}}{1.25E^{-3}}} = -229.51 mA$$

We should now compare these calculations to the simulated results but remember that we must add the full 3ms to account for time through 3ms during the first charge period and discharge period for the capacitor. To compare the calculated results to the measured results from the circuit simulation, Table 5-3 shows the table of results. The time used in the calculations is shown in the brackets, and the real time is listed alongside those times.

Table 5-3. The Calculated and Measured Results

Time	Voltage Across the Capacitor		Current Flowing in the Circuit	
ms	Calculated Volts	Measured Volts	Calculated mA	Measured mA
(1.8) 1.8	19.076	19.075	118.465	118.493
(0.8) 2.8	10.521	10.525	-210.421	-210.53
(1.8) 4.8	21.202	21.225	75.98	75.499
(0.8) 5.8	11.476	11.411	-229.52	-228.22

We can see from Table 5-3 that the calculated results are very close to the measured results. This should help confirm that the methods we use are valid. Figure 5-14 shows the waveforms for the simulation for the circuit we just analysed. The value for the time in ms shown in the brackets are the times we must use in the calculations. The times written without brackets are the actual times used when measuring the values from the displays shown in Figure 5-14.

267

CHAPTER 5 DC TRANSIENTS IN CR CIRCUITS

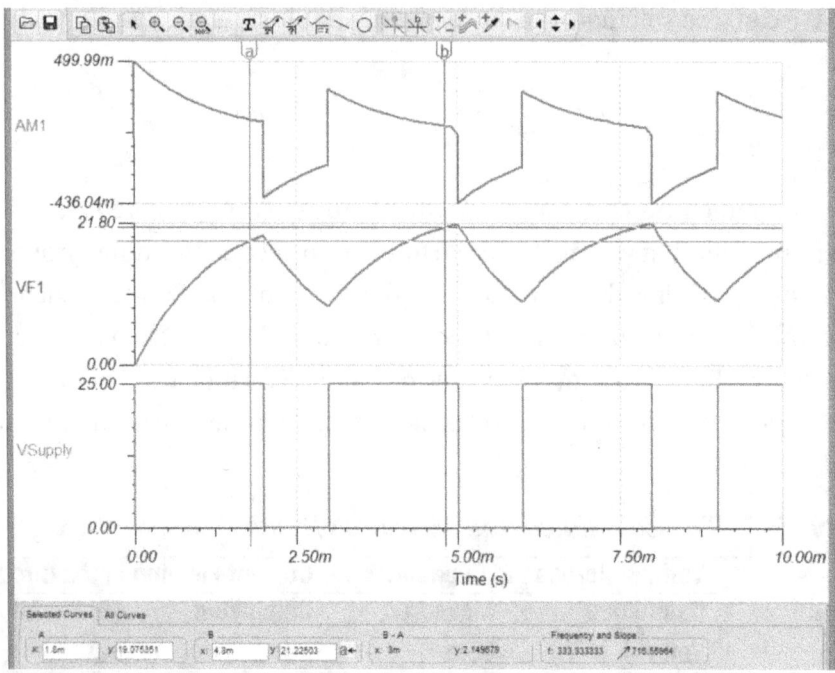

Figure 5-14. *The Voltage and Current Traces*

The traces shown in Figure 5-14 show some interesting results from the DC transient CR circuit. The two cursor readings confirm the results for the capacitor voltage recorded in Table 5-3. They also allow us to see some general characteristics of the CR circuit. The trace VF1 shows that we cannot change the voltage across the capacitor instantly. It takes time for the voltage to change. This characteristic can be seen in all the simulated waveforms of the capacitor voltage. The AM1 trace, which displays the current flowing in the circuit, shows that the direction of the current flow through the circuit and so the capacitor, can change instantaneously. Note, current flowing into the capacitor charges the capacitor up whilst current flowing out of the capacitor discharges the capacitor. We can make good use of the characteristic that shows we can't change the voltage across a capacitor instantly in various circuits, the multivibrator being one of them. However, that is for a book on analogue electronics.

CHAPTER 5   DC TRANSIENTS IN CR CIRCUITS

The maths we went through here work well, and they show you that with a bit of practice you can predict what will happen in some electrical circuits. Surely that is what engineers should be able to do.

Exercise 5.3

All these exercises relate to the DC CR transient circuit shown in Figure 5-15. The answers to this exercise are listed at the end of this chapter.

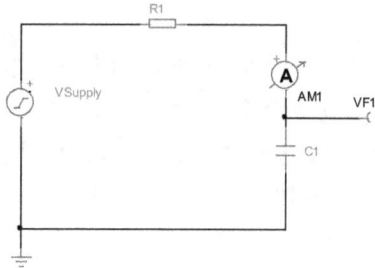

Figure 5-15. The Test Circuit for Exercise 5.4

Q1

If the capacitor value was 22µF, calculate the required value of resistance to give the circuit a time constant of 5ms.

Q2

With the capacitance given in Q1 and the resistance you have calculated in Q1, determine the following.

- The voltage across the capacitor
- The current flowing in the circuit
- The voltage across the resistor

269

CHAPTER 5   DC TRANSIENTS IN CR CIRCUITS

Ten milliseconds after applying a step input voltage of 10V, assume the capacitor was completely discharged before applying the step input voltage. Also calculate how long it would take for the voltage across the capacitor to reach 8.5V and 10V.

Q3

The components in the test circuit are as follows:

- R= 2.2k
- C=10µF

Determine what voltage waveform would be required to fully charge the capacitor to a charge of 150µC from 0 and then allow it to fully discharge before starting the sequence over again. Determine how long it would take for the capacitor to reach 63.2% of its maximum voltage. Then calculate the voltage across the capacitor 5ms after applying the supply, assuming the capacitor was fully discharged. Then calculate the voltage across the capacitor 5ms after the supply was switched to 0V.

Q4

The waveform shown in Figure 5-16 was applied to the test circuit.

CHAPTER 5   DC TRANSIENTS IN CR CIRCUITS

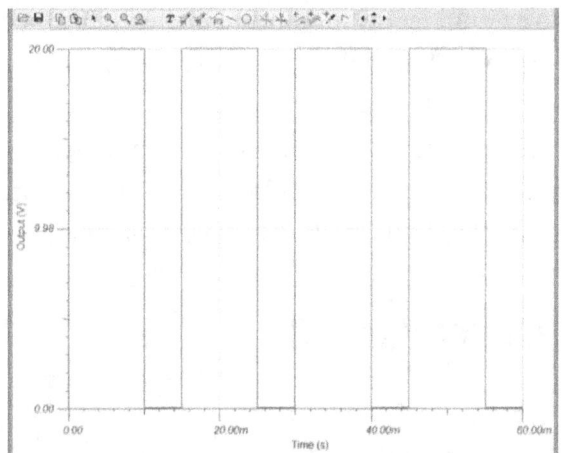

Figure 5-16. *On Time = 10ms, Off Time = 5ms*

If the resistance was 500Ω and the capacitance was 5μF, calculate the capacitor voltage, the current flowing in the circuit, and the voltage across the resistor at the following overall times.

- T=8ms
- T=13ms
- T=20m

Summary

In this chapter we studied the DC transients on a CR circuit. We learnt the importance of the time constant of a system. We also learnt how we can predict what will happen in a DC CR transient circuit.

We used some important mathematical processes to derive the expressions we used in the analysis of the circuits in this chapter. I hope you have learnt how useful this skill of manipulating and deriving

CHAPTER 5   DC TRANSIENTS IN CR CIRCUITS

expressions is to an engineer who wants to prove their concepts are correct. I hope you have found the work and the explanations interesting and useful.

In the next chapter, we look at some of the fundamentals of the three passive components in how we use colour coding to indicate their values and how we use standard set of values and wattage ratings.

Answers to Exercise 5.3

Q1

$$R = \frac{Tau}{C} = \frac{5E^{-3}}{22E^{-6}} = 227.273 \, \Omega$$

Q2

$$V_C = 10\left(1 - e^{-\frac{10E^{-6}}{5E^{-3}}}\right) = 10(1 - 0.1353) = 8.647 \, V$$

$$i = \frac{10}{227.273} e^{-\frac{10E^{-3}}{5E^{-3}}} = 44E^{-3} \times 0.1353 = 5.953 \, mA$$

$$V_R = V_{Supply} e^{-\frac{t}{CR}} = 10 e^{-\frac{10E^{-3}}{5E^{-3}}} = 10 \times 0.1353 = 1.353 \, V$$

$$t = CR \ln\left(\frac{V_{Supply}}{V_{Supply} - V_C}\right)$$

When VC=8.5V

$$t = 22E^{-6} \times 227.273 \times \ln\left(\frac{10}{10 - 8.5}\right) = 9.4856 \, mS$$

Q3

$$\tau = CR = 10E^{-6} \times 2.2E^{3} = 22ms.$$

$$Q = CV$$

Therefore:

$$V = \frac{Q}{C} = \frac{150E^{-6}}{10E^{-6}} = 15V$$

$$V_C = 15\left(1 - e^{-\frac{5E^{-3}}{22E^{-3}}}\right) = 3.049\,V$$

Then using:

$$V_C = V_{Supply} \times e^{-\frac{t}{CR}} = 15 \times e^{-\frac{5E^{-3}}{22E^{-3}}} = 11.95\,V$$

Q4

$$\tau = CR = 5E^{-6} \times 500 = 2.5ms.$$

When overall time is 8ms:

$$V_C = V_{Supply}\left(1 - e^{-\frac{t}{CR}}\right)$$

Therefore:

$$V_C = 20\left(1 - e^{-\frac{8E^{-3}}{2.5E^{-3}}}\right) = 19.185\,V$$

CHAPTER 5 DC TRANSIENTS IN CR CIRCUITS

When overall time is 13ms, we will be 3ms into the discharge time. We need to calculate the voltage across the capacitor when t=10ms.

Therefore:

$$V_C = 20\left(1 - e^{-\frac{10E^{-3}}{2.5E^{-3}}}\right) = 19.634\,V$$

The capacitor will now discharge from that voltage.
Using:

$$V_C = V_{Supply} \times e^{-\frac{t}{CR}} = 19.634 \times e^{-\frac{3E^{-3}}{2.5E^{-3}}} = 5.914\,V$$

The capacitor will continue to discharge until overall time is 15m. The voltage would reduce to:

$$V_C = V_{Supply} \times e^{-\frac{t}{CR}} = 19.634 \times e^{-\frac{5E^{-3}}{2.5E^{-3}}} = 2.657\,V$$

The capacitor will now start to charge back up but with this initial voltage across the capacitor. Therefore, we use:

$$V_C = 20\left(1 - e^{-\frac{5E^{-3}}{2.5E^{-3}}}\right) + 2.657 e^{-\frac{5E^{-3}}{2.5E^{-3}}}$$

Therefore, we get this:

$$V_C = 17.293 + 0.3596 = 17.653\,V$$

CHAPTER 6

The AC Voltage

This chapter starts our journey into the more useful application of electrical circuits. You learn how to create the AC supply in the UK, as well as worldwide, and why we need an AC supply. The chapter then moves on to the most common AC circuit, the series RL and RC circuits.

You will learn what complex numbers are and how you can use them to complete calculations on the AC RL and RC circuits.

After reading this chapter, you will:

- Understand why the AC supply to our homes is at a frequency of 50Hz.

- Appreciate what the argand or phasor diagram is.

- Know how to use complex numbers in the analysis of series AC circuits.

Generating the AC Voltage

I always think the term AC voltage is a bit of a quandary, as AC stands for alternating current, so why do we use the term to describe a voltage? But that is what we use. The other thing that I think is a contradiction is why we use the AC voltage at all, because most of the devices we use in the home can, and a lot do, run on a DC voltage. Indeed, a lot of the devices employ a rectifying circuit to change the AC into a much lower DC supply that then drives the device. When we look a bit further into the household supply, we will understand why we use the AC supply.

CHAPTER 6   THE AC VOLTAGE

If we tried to supply the home with DC over any distance, we would find it very inefficient. For example, consider the situation where the supplier had to send 12V DC to a series of homes that each wanted 12A (i.e., 144 Watts of power). If the resistance of the cables used to transmit this power was, say 10Ω, this would cause a problem. To help understand the problem, we can simulate a representation of the situation, as shown in Figure 6-1.

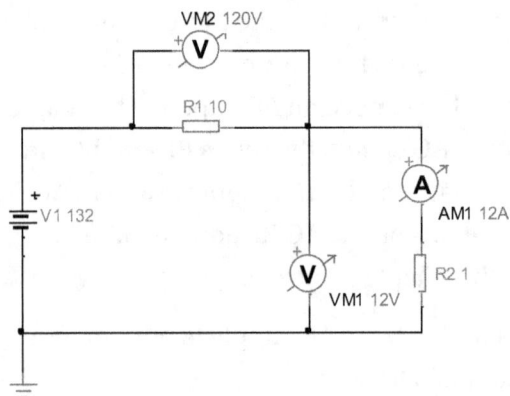

Figure 6-1. *Distributing 144W of Power DC Via Cable of 10Ω Resistance*

For a load to take 12A from a 12V source, the resistance of the load would have to be 1Ω, as shown in Figure 6-1. However, as the resistance of the cable was 10Ω and it has 12A passing through it, then there would be a volt drop of 120V across the cable, as shown by VM2. This means that to ensure the user received 12V at 12A, the generator would have to produce 132V at 12A, which is 1.584kW of power, using the formula *power = VI*. The actual cable being used to supply the power to the homes would dissipate 1.440kW of power, using the formula *power = I²R*. This is obviously very inefficient and not practical. An alternative had to be produced.

CHAPTER 6   THE AC VOLTAGE

The problem is the power that's dissipated by the cable. Power can be calculated using:

$$P = I^2 R$$

This is known as I^2R losses. It would be very difficult to reduce the resistance of the wire, but if we could reduce the current flowing through the cables, then we would reduce the I^2R losses in the cable. The problem is how to reduce the current flowing through the cables but then return it back to 12A at the load end? We need to ensure the user at the end of the cable still gets 144W of power with 12V at 12A of current. When we come to study transformers in my book *Mastering Advanced AC Analysis*, we will find that a transformer can be used to change the voltage and current across it.

The only problem is that a DC voltage will not pass across a transformer. It is mainly for that reason that we generate the UK mains voltage using an AC supply. The changing current of the AC supply, going positive and negative, creates the changing flux that allows the voltage across the primary to induce a voltage across the secondary. This means we can pass the power across a transformer using an AC supply. Transformers are close to 99% efficient, which means the power output from the transformer will be virtually the same as the power inputted to the transformer. This means that the VI product across the primary will be the same as the VI product across the secondary.

If we consider that we want the 144W across the secondary of a transformer (i.e., at the load end of the transmission line), we could get this power using the product of 12V at 12A across the secondary. However, across the primary coil of this transformer, we could get the same 144W of power using a VI product of 144V at 1A. The primary side of the transformer would be the fed from the cables of the transmission line. This would mean that the current flowing through the cables of the

CHAPTER 6   THE AC VOLTAGE

transmission line would now be 1A and so the voltage dropped across the cables would only be 10V. The actual power loss across the cables would be 10W using I^2R.

If we now look at the generator that feeds the transmission line, this will mean the generator would have to produce a voltage of 154V (i.e., the 144V at the primary of the load transformer plus the 10V dropped across the cables). This would mean the generator would have to produce 154W of power. This is already a big savings.

As we are not too concerned about I^2R losses at the generator, we could use a transformer at the generator end of the transmission line to allow the generator to produce a power of 154W using a VI product of 12V at 12.833A. So, the generator is now producing 12V at 12.833A, which is much closer to what the user needs. This is more efficient.

Figure 6-2 shows the two transformers; TR1 is a step-up transformer at the generator end of the transmission line. This will step up the voltage from the generator by a factor of 12. This means that the 12.833V, measured by VM3, at the generator is stepped up, using the transformer TR1, to 154V measured by VM1. At the same time, Tr1 steps the current down by a factor of 12, reducing the 12A, measured by AM3, at the generator, to the 1A as measured by AM1, in the transmission line. We must remember that we need to divide all meter readings by $\sqrt{2}$ to convert them from their peak values to their RMS values, as the meters in TINA display their peak values, not the RMS values.

CHAPTER 6   THE AC VOLTAGE

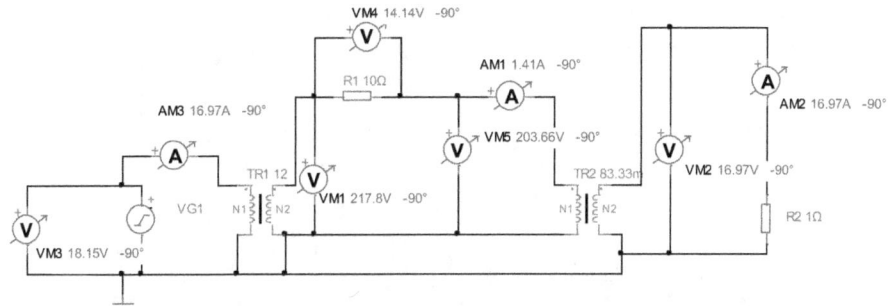

Figure 6-2. Using Transformers to Step Up and then Step Down the Supply

We can see that, at the load side of the transmission line, the transformer TR2 steps the voltage down by a factor of 12 and the current up by a factor of 12. The load voltage is now the required 12V and the load current is the required 12A, as measured by VM2 and AM2 respectively. This type of distribution system is much more efficient than the one shown in Figure 6-1.

I hope the example explains the essence of the problem of voltage dropped across the transmission line, and the principle of how using a transformer provides a solution to the problem of the I^2R losses. It also shows one reason we generate an AC type voltage in the UK, as well as worldwide, and that is because a DC voltage would not pass across a transformer. It may also help to explain why we transmit power around the country and the national grid at such high voltages—because the higher the voltage, the lower the current for the same power.

Generating AC Voltage

Now that you have seen why we need to generate an AC voltage, we will look at the main way we do that in the UK, as well as worldwide. We basically rotate a coil of wire inside a magnetic field. The principle is shown in Figure 6-3.

CHAPTER 6   THE AC VOLTAGE

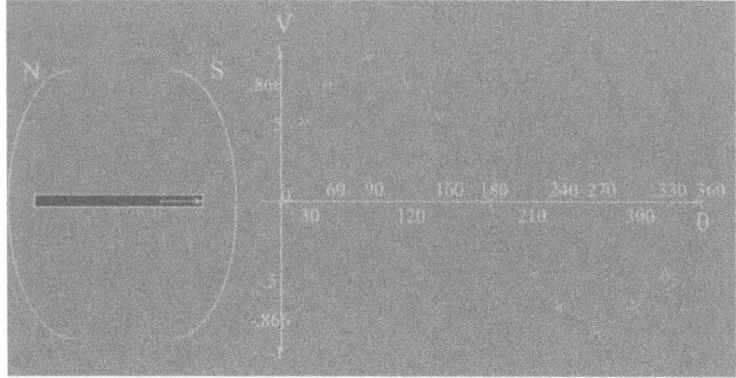

Figure 6-3. Rotating a Coil Inside a Magnetic Field

The coil is shown as being horizontal after completing one revolution. The lines of magnetic flux flow from the North to the South poles. This means that the coil is in line with the lines of the magnetic flux. This in turns means that the coil is not cutting or passing through any flux. That is why the voltage induced in the coil is at 0V, which corresponds to the coil having been turned through the maximum of 360° and now at an angle of 0°. If we assume that we start to turn the coil in an anticlockwise direction through some part of the revolution, say 30°, the coil starts to cut across some of the lines of flux. This corresponds to a voltage of 0.5V. As we progress to 60°, we reach a voltage of 0.866V. Then at 90°, the coil is perpendicular to the lines of flux and so the voltage induced is at a maximum of 1V.

As we continue to rotate the coil through the entire revolution, we can see that the voltage starts to reduce and reaches 0V at 180°. Then, as it progresses, the voltage starts to go negative and reaches -1V at 270°. The voltage then starts to decrease in a negative value until it returns to 0V at 360°.

We can relate the voltage induced to the number of degrees of rotation with the sin(θ) expression, where:

$$v = A\sin(\theta)$$

CHAPTER 6   THE AC VOLTAGE

A is the maximum and we assume A = 1, as we have so far with our description. If we then change the angle θ from 0 to 360, we can create Table 6-1, which shows the different voltages at each of the different angles.

Table 6-1. *The Generated Voltage v=Asin(θ)*

Angle (θ)	1 *Sin*(θ)
0	0
30	0.5
60	0.866
90	1
120	0.866
150	0.5
180	0
210	-0.5
240	-0.866
270	-1
300	-0.866
330	-0.5
360/0	0

Table 6-1 confirms that we can use the sine relationship to describe the induced voltage. However, in the UK, because of the number of coils on the rotor and the speed at which we rotate the generator, the peak voltage A is around 339v. I use this value because, when I took my degree in electrical and electronic engineering, the RMS voltage was 240v. However, now it

CHAPTER 6　THE AC VOLTAGE

can be closer to 220v RMS, which brings it closer to the voltage in Europe. Also, as the speed that the coil is rotated is 3000rpm, the frequency of the UK mains is 50Hz i.e. $f = \dfrac{3000}{60} = 50\text{Hz}$. In the United States, the frequency is 60Hz.

Figure 6-3 shows the horizontal axis of the voltage waveform as θ in degrees, and we know it will move the coil through 360° in one complete revolution. There are two other units we could use to describe the horizontal axis. We could use radians (rads) as the units for this axis. This works, as radians are related to the radius of the circle that the coil rotates through. We know that in one rotation the coil will travel through a distance equal to the circumference of a circle. We also know that the expression for the circumference of circle is as follows:

$$C = 2\pi r$$

Where r is the radius or one radian of the circle. Some people use the following expression for the circumference of a circle:

$$C = \pi D$$

Where D is the diameter of the circle. Whilst this is mathematically correct, engineers should not use this expression as there are no units of "diameters," but there are units of "radians." It is for that reason that I believe we should not use the second expression for the circumference. However, it is a free country and it does work the same mathematically.

The expression $C = 2\pi r$ means that if you could lay out the distance of one full circumference of any circle as one horizontal line, you would fit the length of the radius r into that line 2π times. This works because the term π is just a number. Indeed we can calculate π using:

$$\pi = \dfrac{22}{7} = 3.14286\ldots\ldots$$

CHAPTER 6   THE AC VOLTAGE

This means that we would fit the length of the radius some 6.286... times along the circumference of any circle. If we relate this concept to the degrees moved through in one complete revolution, we can say:

$$2\pi \ radians = 360 \ degrees$$

Therefore, we can say:

$$\pi \ radians = 180 \ degrees$$

From which we can say:

$$1 \ radian = \frac{180}{\pi} = 57.296^0$$

I hope you can now appreciate how we can use radians, instead of degrees, as the units for the horizontal axis on the graph of a sine wave voltage.

The third units we use have the units of time, t. This is because everything varies with time. We unfortunately get older in time, and everything changes with time, and so the mains voltage changes with time. So, how do we relate 360^0 or 2π rads to time? Well, the frequency of the supply relates to the number of cycles the waveform goes through in one second. Indeed, the units of frequency used to be called "cycles per second," a name that I think describes what frequency is. Therefore, a waveform with a frequency of 50 (i.e. 50Hz) goes through 50 cycles per second. We know that completing one cycle means we have gone through 360^0 or 2π rads. We have stated that we move through 360^0 in 2π radians. This means that we can express one degree as follows:

$$1^0 = \frac{2\pi}{360} \ radians$$

283

CHAPTER 6   THE AC VOLTAGE

This means that we will move through one degree in $1/360^{th}$ of 2π radians. Using this concept, we can say that we will move through 48° in:

$$48^\circ = \frac{2\pi}{360} \times 48 = 2\pi \times \frac{48}{360} = 2\pi \times \frac{4}{30} \; Radians$$

This means 48° is $4/30^{th}$ of 2π radians.

We can express moving through 270° as follows:

$$270^\circ = 2\pi \times \frac{270}{360} = 2\pi \times \frac{3}{4} \; Radians$$

This means 270° is $3/4$ of 2π radians.

Also, we can express moving through 450° as follows:

$$450^\circ = 2\pi \times \frac{450}{360} = 2\pi \times 1\frac{1}{4} \; Radians$$

Of course, this means we move through more than one complete revolution. We can show that the waveform moves through its cycle by multiplying the 2π radians by a fraction, even when that fraction that is greater than 1 (i.e., a vulgar fraction). To introduce the concept of time t we can use the periodic time T. This is the time it takes the waveform to go through one complete cycle or 2π radians. Therefore, we can say:

$$360^\circ = 2\pi \times \frac{t}{T} \; Radians$$

This is true when time t equals the periodic time T, and we can then say:

$$360^\circ = 2\pi \times \frac{T}{T} \; Radians$$

CHAPTER 6 THE AC VOLTAGE

Therefore, in general we can express the angle we move in t time as follows:

$$\theta = 2\pi \frac{t}{T} \text{ Radians}$$

This can be written as:

$$\theta = 2\pi \frac{1}{T} t \text{ Radians}$$

Knowing that, we can express the frequency f as follows:

$$f = \frac{1}{T}$$

Replacing $\frac{1}{T}$ with f in the expression for the angel θ, we can say this:

$$\theta = 2\pi f t \text{ Radians}$$

If we relate this to the UK mains with a frequency of 50Hz, we know T = 20ms. Therefore, if time t is 10ms, we have travelled through half the cycle and the angle θ would be 180° or π radians. We could write this as follows:

$$180 = 2\pi \frac{10E^{-3}}{20E^{-3}} = \pi \, Radians$$

The term *ft* describes the fraction that changes with time t; when t is the same as the periodic time T, then the fraction *ft* will equal 1. In this way, we can change the units of the horizontal axis to time t. This is shown in the Table 6-2, which was used to draw the graph shown in Figure 6-4.

CHAPTER 6   THE AC VOLTAGE

Table 6-2. *The Voltage of the UK Mains Related to Time t*

Time t in Seconds	Voltage v Volts	Square of the Voltages
0	0	0
0.001	104.7567611	10973.97899
0.002	199.2592005	39704.22899
0.003	274.2567611	75216.77101
0.004	322.408159	103947.021
0.005	339	114921
0.006	322.408159	103947.021
0.007	274.2567611	75216.77101
0.008	199.2592005	39704.22899
0.009	104.7567611	10973.97899
0.01	-2.5956E-13	6.73714E-26
0.011	-104.7567611	10973.97899
0.012	-199.2592005	39704.22899
0.013	-274.2567611	75216.77101
0.014	-322.408159	103947.021
0.015	-339	114921
0.016	-322.408159	103947.021
0.017	-274.2567611	75216.77101
0.018	-199.2592005	39704.22899
0.019	-104.7567611	10973.97899
0.02	1.1213E-12	0
Sum Ave	1.87448E-12	57460.5
Ave/ rms	8.9261E-14	239.7092

CHAPTER 6   THE AC VOLTAGE

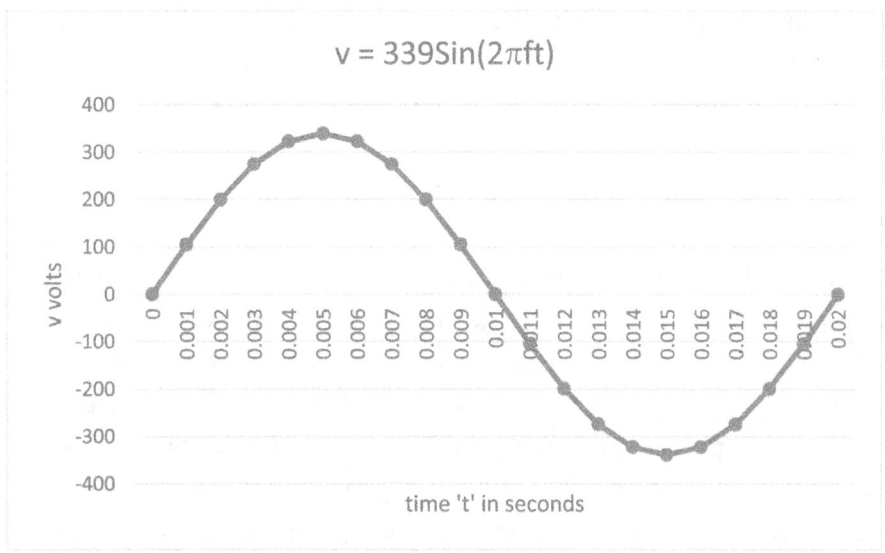

Figure 6-4. *The Graph of v = 339Sin(2πft)*

I hope you can see that because it takes 0.02s or 20ms to complete one cycle, this voltage waveform has a frequency of 50Hz. This is a graph of the voltage supply for the UK mains. This graph and Table 6-2 show that the term *ft* does describe what fraction of 2π radians the waveform has moved through as time moves on. This enables us to use time t as the units for the horizontal axis when describing a waveform that is cyclic.

One thing you might, or should be asking, is how does this the 240V become the voltage that we use to describe the UK mains voltage? That's not such an easy question to answer, but I will give you my best answer here.

The voltage in Figure 6-4 goes through an infinite number of values as it goes through one cycle. Therefore, if we were to choose one value to describe the voltage, which one would we choose? It is only 339V once in each cycle, as it is -339 180° later. It is 199.258V twice or any one voltage twice in the cycle. So, there is no obvious one value we could choose. So perhaps we could use the average. To do that we would need to add all the

287

CHAPTER 6 THE AC VOLTAGE

values the voltage goes through in one cycle. Then we would divide the result by the number of values. That is how we calculate the average, but the problem with that is the result of adding all the values up would be 0, as there is an equal number of positive and negative values.

We can use Excel, which is what I used to create the table and graph, to determine the average of the voltage values in Table 6-2. When we do, the sum of the voltage values is 1.87448E-12. Then, when we calculate the average of the voltage values, we get 8.926E-14, which is even closer to 0. This shows that trying to use the average to produce one voltage value that would describe the UK mains is useless. If we square the negative values, it will give us a positive result. So, we could try that, but to keep everything equal we should square the positive values as well. Doing that in Excel would give us the values shown in the third column of Table 6-2. We now can calculate the average. Again, using Excel, the average of the squared value was 57460.5. However, this is the average of set of squared values and so we should calculate the square root of this value to counter act the squaring in the first place. When we do that, the square root of the average values is 239.709V. This is the value that we use to give a value to the UK mains.

This must be a con though, as we have just come up with a way of getting a number that isn't equal to 0. Has this value of 240V any real meaning? As an engineer, that's what you should be asking. As you will see, the value of 240V does have meaning. It is called the RMS value of the mains because we take the *root of the mean of the square* of the voltages in the waveform.

It can be said that the RMS of an AC voltage is the same value as a DC voltage that would produce the same power in the load. That suggests that the 240V mains supply is the equivalent of having a 240V DC battery in your house. That's quite a mouthful to say, but there is a simple experiment we can simulate in TINA will prove this is true. If we simulate the circuit shown in Figure 6-5, we can measure the current flowing through the 1kΩ load.

CHAPTER 6 THE AC VOLTAGE

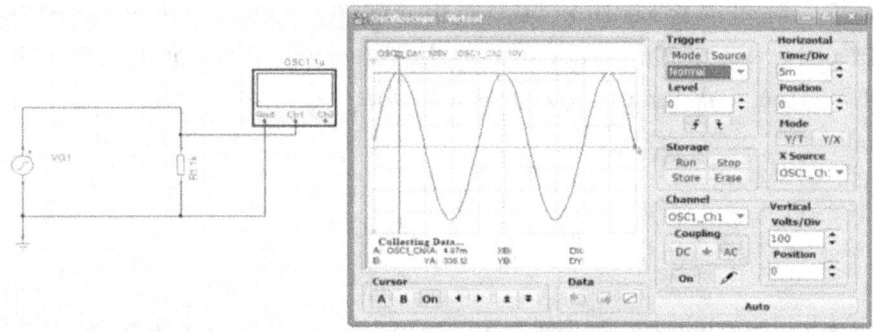

Figure 6-5. *The Test Simulation to Measure the Current Flowing Through R1*

An oscilloscope cannot measure current, it can only measure voltage and time. However, we can use those measurement to calculate the frequency of the waveforms measured and, as in this case, the current flowing through the resistor R_1. To calculate the frequency, we must use this expression:

$$f = \frac{1}{T}$$

The term f is for frequency and T is for the periodic time. This is the time the waveform takes to go through one complete cycle that covers all the values the waveform has. This waveform is a simple sinusoidal wave and from the oscilloscope, we can see it takes four divisions to complete one cycle. As each division is set to 5ms per division, we can see it takes 20ms to complete one cycle. Therefore, the value for T is 20ms. Now we can calculate the frequency as follows:

$$f = \frac{1}{20E^{-3}} = 50Hz$$

CHAPTER 6 THE AC VOLTAGE

To calculate the current flowing through R_1, we simply need to divide the peak voltage of the waveform by the value of the resistor. This would give us the peak value of the current flowing through the resistor as follows:

$$i = \frac{338.12}{1E^{-3}} = 338.12 mA$$

Knowing that the RMS of a sine wave can be calculated as follows:

$$rms = \frac{Peak}{\sqrt{2}}$$

Then the RMS current flowing through R_1 is:

$$i_{rms} = \frac{338.12 mA}{\sqrt{2}} = 239.07 mA$$

If a DC voltage of 240V was applied across a 1kΩ resistor, then the current flowing through the resistor can be calculated using Ohm's Law as follows:

$$I = \frac{V}{R} = \frac{240}{1E^3} = 240 E^{-3} = 240 mA$$

Power is related to current and both methods produce the same value of current, so we can say this confirms that the RMS of the AC voltage does represent the DC voltage required to get the same power in the load. Note that the power can be calculated using:

$$P = i^2 R = I^2 R = VI = \frac{V^2}{R}$$

CHAPTER 6   THE AC VOLTAGE

To be more correct when dealing with AC circuits, the expression for power becomes this:

$$P = viCos(\theta)$$

However, when looking at DC and purely resistive loads, we can ignore the Cos(θ) as θ = 0 and the Cos(0) = 1.

Calculating the RMS of a Waveform

We have stated that the RMS of a sine wave can be calculated using this formula:

$$rms = \frac{Peak}{\sqrt{2}}$$

As always, I like to show you how that expression can be derived. The values stated in Table 6-2 prove that the RMS of the UK mains is 240V but that is not the proof of the expression for the RMS of the UK mains. We will go through that now.

We start by stating how we can calculate the mean of the waveform. To calculate the mean of anything, we need to sum all the values. In maths, integration is a summing action, as it sums an infinite number of values that the expression for the waveform produces. I used to say that we indicate the summing action using this symbol:

- *sum of a set of values*

However, this is when we have a limited set of values. If we have an expression for the waveform, we can obtain an infinite number of values and so the summing symbol Σx becomes:

=the integral of the expression

CHAPTER 6   THE AC VOLTAGE

Well, that's my explanation for the integral sign.

This means the sum of the parts of the waveform can be obtained using:

$$Sum = \int f(t)\,dt$$

Where $f(t)$ is the expression that describes the waveform. The waveform is cyclic, which means it repeats itself every cycle, so we need to integrate over only one complete cycle. This means we can say the following:

$$Sum = \int_0^T f(t)\,dt$$

This means we should be summing all the possible values in one complete cycle, as T is the periodic time for the waveform and we are integrating with respect to time t. To change this to the mean, we simply need to divide this summing expression by all the values. We can do this using this formula:

$$Mean = \frac{1}{T}\int_0^T f(t)\,dt$$

We can use integration to obtain the mean of the function. However, we need to square all these values first, so that we can obtain the mean of the squared function. This can be done using the following:

$$Mean\ of\ f(t)^2 = \frac{1}{T}\int_0^T f(t)^2\,dt$$

CHAPTER 6   THE AC VOLTAGE

Great, we are almost there. All we need to do now is square root this expression. Therefore, the expression for the RMS of a waveform becomes:

$$rms = \sqrt{\frac{1}{T}\int_0^T f(t)^2 \, dt}$$

This can be rewritten as follows:

$$rms = \left(\frac{1}{T}\int_0^T f(t)^2 \, dt\right)^{\frac{1}{2}}$$

Either one will work, so we will use the first. This expression will produce the RMS of the function if we have an expression for the function.

The RMS of a Sine Wave

The expression for an AC voltage such as the UK mains can be expressed as follows:

$$v = V_M Sin(2\pi ft)$$

Where V_M is the maximum or peak voltage. This peak voltage is a constant for a particular waveform. Therefore, we can say:

$$rms = \sqrt{\frac{1}{T}\int_0^T \left(V_M Sin(2\pi ft)\right)^2 \, dt}$$

This can be written as follows:

$$rms = \sqrt{\frac{1}{T}\int_0^T \left(V_M^2\right)\left(Sin(2\pi ft)\right)^2 \, dt}$$

CHAPTER 6   THE AC VOLTAGE

($V_M{}^2$) is a constant for that waveform, so it can be taken out of the integral. This means that we can say the following:

$$rms = \sqrt{\frac{V_M{}^2}{T} \int_0^T \left(Sin(2\pi ft)\right)^2 dt}$$

The problem is that there is no standard integral for the function $(Sin(2\pi ft))^2$. However, we have trig identities to come to our rescue. Using trig identities, which can be used to show that certain trig expressions can be replaced with other trig expression that mean the same thing, we can say:

$$\left(sin(A)\right)^2 = sin^2(A)$$

Also, using this identity:

$$cos 2A = 1 - 2sin^2(A)$$

We can say this:

$$sin^2(A) = \frac{1 - cos 2A}{2}$$

We could rewrite this as follows:

$$sin^2(A) = \frac{1}{2}(1 - cos 2A)$$

Therefore, using these identities, we can say:

$$\left(Sin(2\pi ft)\right)^2 = \frac{1}{2}\left(1 - cos(4\pi ft)\right)$$

CHAPTER 6 THE AC VOLTAGE

This then means that the following is true:

$$rms = \sqrt{\frac{V_M^2}{T} \int_0^T \frac{1}{2}(1-\cos(4\pi ft))\,dt}$$

We can take the ½ out of the integral, so this becomes:

$$rms = \sqrt{\frac{V_M^2}{2T} \int_0^T (1-\cos(4\pi ft))\,dt}$$

When we carry out the integral as $\cos(4\pi ft)$ fits the standard set of integrals in that:

$$a\cos(nx) \text{ integrates to } \frac{a\sin(nx)}{n}$$

See the "Advanced Common Formula" in the appendix. In the expression, the $a = 1$ and $n = 4\pi f$. The variable x is $x = t$. This means that:

$$\cos(4\pi ft) \text{ intgrates to } \frac{\sin(4\pi ft)}{4\pi f}$$

Putting this into the expression for the RMS, we get:

$$rms = \sqrt{\frac{V_M^2}{2T}\left[t - \frac{\sin(4\pi ft)}{4\pi f}\right]_0^T}$$

If you use the standard integrals, you will see that the constant a integrates to a*t* so our constant 1 integrates to 1*t* or just t.

295

CHAPTER 6   THE AC VOLTAGE

Putting in the limits (i.e., replace the variable t with the upper and lower limits and subtract the lower limits from the upper limits), we have the following:

$$rms = \sqrt{\frac{V_M^2}{2T}\left[\left(T - \frac{\sin(4\pi fT)}{4\pi f}\right) - \left(0 - \frac{\sin(4\pi f0)}{4\pi f}\right)\right]}$$

We know that:

$$\sin(4\pi fT) = \sin\left(4\pi \frac{T}{T}\right) = \sin(4\pi) = 0 \text{ and } \sin(4\pi f0) = 0$$

Therefore, we get this:

$$rms = \sqrt{\frac{V_M^2}{2T} \times T}$$

The two Ts cancel out, which gives:

$$rms = \sqrt{\frac{V_M^2}{2}} = \frac{\sqrt{V_M^2}}{\sqrt{2}}$$

This then means that:

$$rms = \frac{V_M}{\sqrt{2}} = \frac{peak}{\sqrt{2}}$$

This is true for a sinusoidal waveform. We can also show that:

$$\frac{1}{\sqrt{2}} = 0.7071$$

296

So, we can also say that the Rms of a sine wave is as follows:

$$rms = 0.7071 \times peak\ value$$

I prefer to use this:

$$rms = \frac{peak}{\sqrt{2}}$$

I hope you have found this derivation a useful exercise in using some mathematical processes to prove the expression for the RMS of a sine wave. At the very least, it has shown that you can only use the previous expression if the waveform is a sine wave.

Impedance

Now we are ready to start our investigation into impedance. I start off by saying that impedance is the AC equivalent of resistance. Just as resistance is the ability of a resistor to resist current flow in a circuit, impedance is the ability of an inductor or capacitor to resist or impede current flow in a circuit. Chapter 4 explained that because the act of changing direction of current flow realigns the magnetic domains inside the inductor, the impedance of an inductor, X_L, can be calculated using:

$$X_L = 2\pi fL$$

In Chapter 5, you learnt that because you can change the direction of current flow through the capacitor quickly, if not instantly, you can calculate the impedance of a capacitor, X_C, using the following:

$$X_C = \frac{1}{2\pi fC}$$

CHAPTER 6   THE AC VOLTAGE

Now we will look at the simple series RL circuit, shown in Figure 6-6.

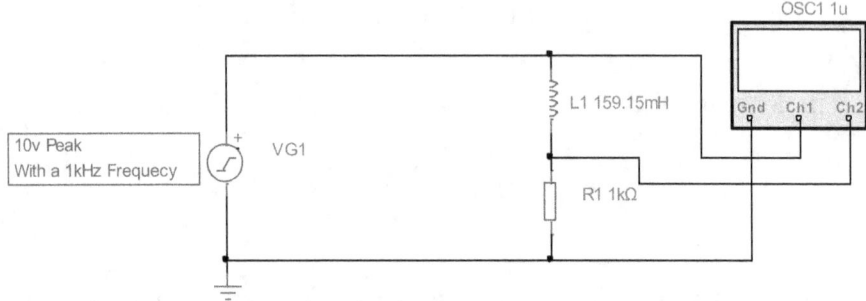

Figure 6-6. *The Series RL Circuit*

Figure 6-6 shows the test circuit for the series RL circuit. We are using the oscilloscope to display the supply voltage using Channel 1 of the oscilloscope, and the voltage across the resistor using Channel 2. In this way we can display the supply voltage, which will be the reference for the circuit and the current flowing in the circuit. We can use the voltage across the resistor to show the current flowing through the circuit by simply dividing the voltage measurements by the value of the resistor. This will give us the magnitude of the current. We are using the voltage across the resistor as the resistor is a non-reactive component, which means the current flowing through the resistor is in phase with the voltage across it. The displays from the oscilloscope are shown in Figure 6-7.

CHAPTER 6 THE AC VOLTAGE

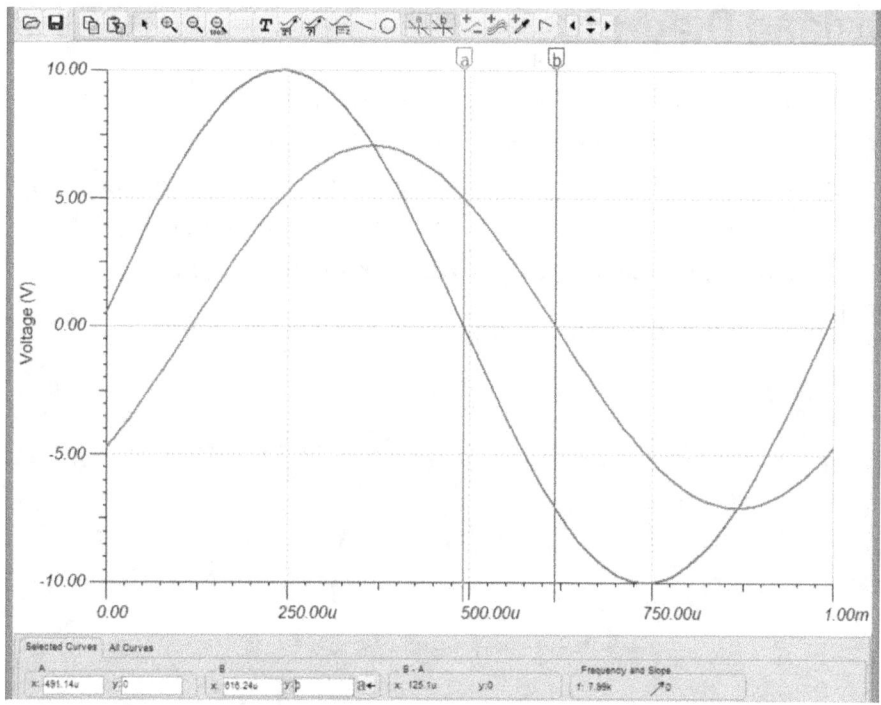

Figure 6-7. *The Oscilloscope Display for the Series RL*

We can use the two cursors on the display to show the time difference between the supply voltage (the green display from channel1) and the voltage across the resistor, which we can use to determine the current flowing in the circuit (the brown display from channel 2). The reason we want to do this is because the current is a phasor quantity, as are all electrical quantities, even resistance R. Therefore, before we go any further, it's important to look at phasor quantities on an *argand diagram,* which is just a posh word for a phasor diagram.

CHAPTER 6   THE AC VOLTAGE

Argand Diagrams

Argand diagrams are graphs on which we can draw phasor diagrams to represent all types of electrical quantities. We will use our first argand diagram to draw the graphs of the two impedances and the total impedance of the test circuit shown in Figure 6-6. The actual argand or phasor diagram for the impedance of the circuit from Figure 6-6 is shown in Figure 6-8.

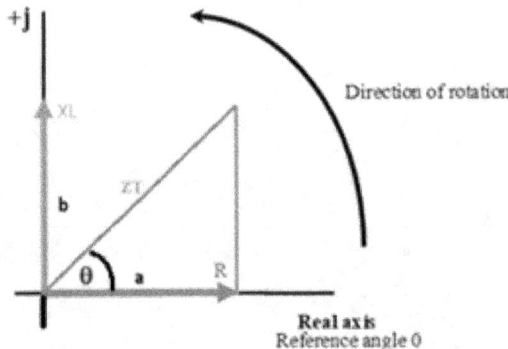

Figure 6-8. *The Phasor Diagram for the RL Circuit Shown in Figure 6-6*

I explain the diagram as we go along. The first thing to do is calculate the two impedances. The resistor R_1 has a constant resistance of 1kΩ. However, the impedance of the inductor changes with frequency and we can calculate it using the following:

$$X_L = 2\pi fL$$

Putting the values in, we get:

$$X_L = 2\pi \times 1E^3 \times 159.15E^{-3} = 1k\Omega$$

CHAPTER 6   THE AC VOLTAGE

We now need to draw these two phasor quantities on the phasor diagram. I call it a phasor diagram from now on as we are drawing phasor quantities on it. As these two impedances are phasor quantities, they both have a magnitude, which is the value you would measure with your meters, and a direction, which is the angle associated with the quantities. This is sometimes called the *argument*. With the resistor the angle is $0°$, which is why we sometimes ignore the angle when discussing resistance. The angle is $0°$ because the resistor is a non-reactive component, which means that when a current is forced, by a voltage across the resistor, to flow through the resistor, the current has no reaction. This really means that the current is in phase with the voltage. The resistance on the phasor diagram is drawn in the positive horizontal axis, with a phase of $0°$, in phase with reference, which is the voltage. Some people try to use the current as the reference in a series circuit. This is because the current is constant in a series circuit. That is true, however, it is more correct to always use the voltage as the reference as you will come across circuits that are a mixture of series and parallel connections. Also, there can be no current without a voltage, so you should always use the supply voltage as the reference.

Just as the resistor is a non-reactive component, both inductance and capacitance are reactive components. This is because they cause a reaction with the current, when it is forced to flow through them by a voltage source. In the pure inductor and capacitor, the current will be $90°$ out of phase with the voltage across it. In this phasor diagram, the voltage is the reference and is at $0°$. This means that both pure inductive impedances and capacitive impedances, which are $90°$ out of phase with the reference, should be drawn on the vertical axis. However, note that inductive and capacitive impedances are $180°$ out of phase with each other. This places them on either the +j or -j axis. In Chapter 4 you learned that the current in an inductor lags behind the voltage by $90°$. Well, because of the maths, which I will show later in this chapter, to make the current in a pure inductor lag the voltage by $90°$, the impedance X_L must lead the reference by $90°$. This means it must go on the +j axis as shown in Figure 6-8. Note

301

CHAPTER 6   THE AC VOLTAGE

that all phasors rotate around the phasor diagram in an anticlockwise direction. As X_L and R both have a magnitude of 1k then both phasors have the same length, as shown in Figure 6-8.

Now, we have explained why the two phasors are drawn on the phasor diagram we must explain the rest of the diagram and how it can be used to determine the total impedance Z_T. As this is a simple series circuit then the total impedance Z_T is simply the sum of the two impedances. However, is not just a simple scalar sum, it is a phasor sum. We know that the impedance of the resistor is 1kΩ and the impedance of the inductor is also 1kΩ. The total impedance is not as simple as 1k + 1k = 2kΩ. We can complete the phasor sum graphically by adding the X_L phasor to the resistance phasor. The way we do this is walk the length of one phasor; in this case we walk the length of the resistance phasor. Then stop and turn to face in the direction of the other phasor; in this case, the X_L phasor. This would mean turning anticlockwise through 90°. Now we walk the distance of the X_L phasor. This is shown as the thinner pale blue line going vertically upwards from the end of the resistor phasor in Figure 6-8. When we get to the end of this added phasor, there are no more phasors to add, and we are exhausted by all this walking, so we must take the shortest route back to the origin at the crossing of the two axes. This is shown by the brown phasor labelled Z_T in Figure 6-8. The length of the resultant phasor will equate to the total impedance in the circuit.

This is the magnitude of the total impedance in the circuit. However, being a phasor, this is only half the story. All phasors will have an angle associated with them. We need to include this angle in the description of the total impedance Z_T. This is the angle θ shown in Figure 6-8. We can simply measure the angle with a protractor, and it should be 45°, as this is the diagonal of a square. We now need to determine if the angle is positive or negative. This is where the direction of rotation of the phasor comes in. In Figure 6-8, the direction of rotation is anticlockwise. This gives the

CHAPTER 6   THE AC VOLTAGE

angle a positive value. Indeed, that is why the vertical axis is labelled +j. This means that we can express the total impedance of the circuit shown in Figure 6-6 as follows:

$$Z_T = length\ of\ ZT\ at\ an\ angle\ of\ 45^0$$

Of course, we would relate the length to impedance and state this as an actual value.

Calculating Z_T Using Trigonometry

Drawing graphs is all well and good but it takes a very long time, and it is difficult to be accurate. A quicker and more accurate method is to use trigonometry. If we look at Figure 6-8, we can see that as we add the X_L phasor to the resistor phasor, we are creating a right-angled triangle. This is because there are only two phasors, and they are 90° apart. This means that the resultant of adding these two phasors (i.e., the Z_T phasor) is the hypotenuse of the right-angled triangle. This means that we can use Pythagoras theorem to calculate the length or magnitude of the total impedance Z_T. Therefore, we can calculate Z_T using:

$$Z_T = \sqrt{R^2 + X_L^2}$$

Putting the values in, we get:

$$Z_T = \sqrt{(1E^3)^2 + (1E^3)^2} = 1.414 k\Omega$$

Now we need to calculate the angle θ. Again, using trigonometry we can use Tan to calculate the angle. This is because this is true:

$$Tan(\theta) = \frac{opposite}{adjucant}$$

303

CHAPTER 6   THE AC VOLTAGE

You can use this short sentence as a memory aid about trigonometry:
Some Old Horses Canter Across Hedges To Overcome Age
You can use this to remember:

$$\text{Some} = \frac{\text{Old}}{\text{Horses}} \text{ therefore } \sin(\theta) = \frac{\text{Opposite}}{\text{Hypotenuse}}$$

$$\text{Canter} \frac{\text{Across}}{\text{Hedges}} \text{ therefore } \cos(\theta) = \frac{\text{Adjacent}}{\text{Hypotenuse}}$$

$$\text{To} = \frac{\text{Overcome}}{\text{Age}} \text{ therefore } \tan(\theta) = \frac{\text{Opposite}}{\text{Adjacent}}$$

This was something I was told when I was 12 and I have never forgotten it.

Using Figure 6-8, we can see that the phasor X_L, the thinner light blue phasor that we added to the resistor phasor, is the length that is opposite to the angle θ. We can also see that the phasor R is the length adjacent to (next to) the angle θ. This means we can say:

$$\tan(\theta) = \frac{\text{Opposite}}{\text{Adjacent}} = \frac{X_L}{R}$$

As we want to calculate the angle θ we need to take the inverse Tan of both sides. This gives:

$$\theta = \tan^{-1}\left(\frac{X_L}{R}\right)$$

CHAPTER 6   THE AC VOLTAGE

Putting the values in, we get the following:

$$\theta = Tan^{-1}\left(\frac{1E^3}{1E^3}\right) = 45^O$$

If we look at Figure 6-8, we should be able to appreciate that the phasor Z_T passes through the diagonal of a square made up of sides X_L and R. This would suggest that the angle θ is 45º, which agrees with our calculations. We now need to link the magnitude of Z_T and the angle θ together. This can be stated as follows:

$$Z_T = \sqrt{R^2 + X_L^2} \left\langle Tan^{-1}\left(\frac{X_L}{R}\right)\right\rangle$$

In the test circuit shown in Figure 6-8, we can say the following:

$$Z_T = 1.414E^3 \left\langle 45^O \right\rangle \Omega$$

Calculating the Current and Volt Drops in the Circuit

We should be able to confirm that our method of using trigonometry is valid by simulating the circuit and taking some measurements to confirm the following calculations. We have already calculated the total impedance in the circuit in both magnitude and angle. The total impedance is as follows:

$$Z_T = 1.414E^3 \left\langle 45^O \right\rangle \Omega$$

CHAPTER 6 THE AC VOLTAGE

This is the way we express the phasor quantity (i.e., as a magnitude with its associated angle). We will look at this in more detail later in this chapter. For now, we move on to calculate the current using Ohm's Law. It states that:

$$i = \frac{v}{Z_T}$$

It is normal practice to use the RMS values when carrying out these calculations. Figure 6-6 shows that the supply voltage has a peak or maximum value of 10v. From our work earlier in this chapter, we know that:

$$V_{rms} = \frac{V_M}{\sqrt{2}} = \frac{10}{\sqrt{2}} = 7.071v$$

This is the magnitude of the supply voltage v_{Supply}, but we need the angle associated with this as well. Well, because the supply voltage is the reference, as without a voltage we have nothing, then the angle associated with v_{Supply} is 0. This means that we can state that the V_{Supply} is as follows:

$$v_{Supply} = 7.071 \langle 0° \rangle v$$

This means that we can say:

$$i = \frac{7.071 \langle 0° \rangle}{1.414E^3 \langle 45° \rangle} \; Amps$$

This is a special kind of division, and we will look at it in more detail later in the chapter. For now, I explain that with this type of division we divide the two magnitudes and subtract the angles. This means that:

$$i = \frac{7.071}{1.414E^3} \langle 0° - 45° \rangle = 5E^{-3} \langle -45O \rangle$$

CHAPTER 6   THE AC VOLTAGE

Therefore, we can say that:

$$i = 5mA \langle -45^\circ \rangle$$

When we simulated the circuit shown in Figure 6-6, the waveforms obtained were as shown in Figure 6-7. The Channel 2 trace displays the voltage across the resistor R. The peak voltage was measured at 7.07v. We can use that display to measure the current flowing in the circuit by simply dividing the voltage by the value of the resistor, which in this case was 1kΩ. This means that the peak current in the circuit was 7.07mA. If we now divide that by $\sqrt{2}$ we get a current of 5mA. This agrees with our calculations. We can also use the two traces shown in Figure 6-7 to determine the phase angle associated with the current. This is done by taking a reading of the time differences between the two waveforms and using it as follows to calculate the phase difference:

$$Phase\ Diff = time\ Diff \times freq \times 360$$

Putting the values in, we get:

$$Phase\ Diff = 125e^{-6} \times 1E^3 \times 360 = 45^\circ$$

When we examine the two waveforms, we can see that the supply voltage, the Channel 1 trace, reaches the 0v point before the current, the Channel 2 trace, reaches it. This means that the current is lagging the voltage so we give it a negative value.

Therefore, we can express the current as follows:

$$i = 5mA \langle -45^\circ \rangle$$

Whoopee, this agrees with our calculations. Also, the negative angle shows that the current is lagging the voltage, which is true with inductors. However, the angle is less than -90° because of the effect of the series resistance, R.

CHAPTER 6   THE AC VOLTAGE

Using Complex Numbers to Represent Phasor Quantities

Now we will get to the crux of the matter and that is learning how to use complex numbers. The word "complex" might suggest that these numbers are very complicated. Well, I am here to tell you that they are not complex at all, and their use makes the complete analysis of AC circuits much easier.

So, what are complex numbers? In their simplest use, they are a way to express phasor quantities in a mathematical format. In their more complex use, they are how we can determine the square root of a negative number. We start with their more complex use, and after looking at them I hope you will agree that they are not that complex.

The Value of j

The term j is sometimes referred to as i. We have put j on the vertical axis in Figure 6-8. Some mathematicians label this axis as i for imaginary. That's because i is sometimes referred to as the imaginary answer to what is $\sqrt{-1}$. Engineers use j, quite possibly because we use i for current and therefore, using i could cause confusion. I always say that j can be interpreted in two ways—the first is with determining the square root of a negative number which I try to explain now. You can calculate the square root of 4 as follows:

$$\sqrt{4} = 2$$

Let's try to look at in a different way. We know:

$$2 \times 2 = 4$$

CHAPTER 6   THE AC VOLTAGE

To be more correct, we should say:

$$\sqrt{4} = -2 \ or + 2 \ as - 2 \times -2 \ also = 4$$

Therefore, we should say:

$$\pm\sqrt{N}$$

However, we mostly use the positive results in engineering. When dealing with square roots, we could say:

$$\sqrt{2} \times \sqrt{2} = \sqrt{4} = 2$$

We know we can say:

$$\sqrt{2} = 1.414214....$$

Therefore, we can also say:

$$1.414214 \times 1.414214 = 2 \ which \ is \ correct.$$

Let's try the same with this:

$$\sqrt{9} = 3$$

This could be expressed as follows:

$$\sqrt{3} \times \sqrt{3} = \sqrt{9} = 3$$

We know this:

$$\sqrt{3} = 1.73205$$

$$1.73205 \times 1.73205 = 2.99999....$$

309

So that seems to work. This would suggest that:

$$\sqrt{2\times 2} = \sqrt{4} = \sqrt{2}\times\sqrt{2} = 2$$

Or

$$\sqrt{3\times 3} = \sqrt{9} = \sqrt{3}\times\sqrt{3} = 3$$

You could try this with more examples, but in essence it should show us that:

$$\sqrt{N\times M} = \sqrt{N}\times\sqrt{M}$$

When we look at negative numbers, we can express:

$$-4 \text{ as } -1\times 4$$

Therefore, we can say that:

$$\sqrt{-4} = \sqrt{-1\times 4} = \sqrt{-1}\times\sqrt{4} = \sqrt{-1}\times 2$$

But we still have the problem of what this is:

$$\sqrt{-1}$$

Yes, in true mathematical form, we just made up a symbol to represent $\sqrt{-1}$. We invented the term j or i:

$$j = \sqrt{-1} \text{ and } j^2 = -1$$

This means we could say:

$$\sqrt{-4} = j2$$

CHAPTER 6   THE AC VOLTAGE

Well, what rubbish, I hear you say. Maybe or maybe not, but better mathematicians than you and me have I come up with this, so let's see what happens later. Also, you can appreciate why they would have called $\sqrt{-1}$ is the imaginary i.

j Means Moving Through 90⁰

I started this journey by saying that j can be interpreted in two ways. The way I prefer to interpret j is that it indicates moving a phasor through 90⁰. Consider the phasor diagram shown in Figure 6-9.

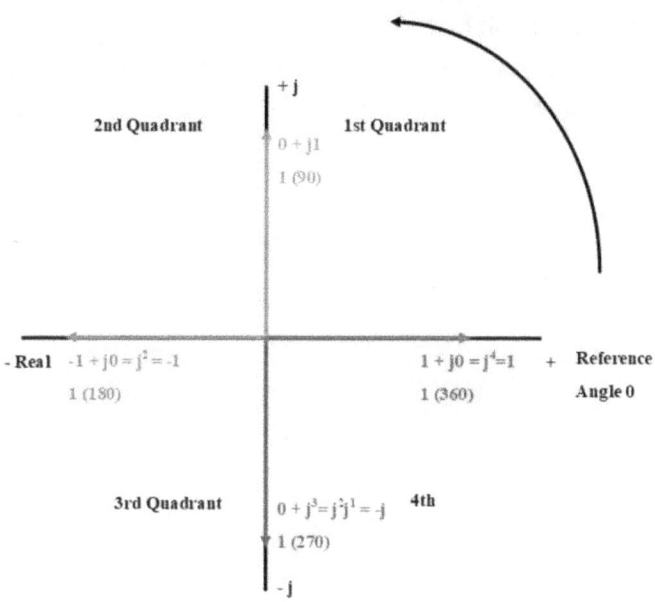

Figure 6-9. *The Phasor Diagram of a Phasor of Magnitude 1*

Figure 6-9 tries to show how the representation of a phasor alters as it rotates around the phasor diagram. It is the same phasor, but its representation changes as it moves through 90⁰ four times from its starting or its initial position on the + real axis. This point on the axis is the

311

CHAPTER 6   THE AC VOLTAGE

reference point and it has the angle of 0°. The first move takes the phasor through 90°, and we can see that it ends up on the +j axis with a magnitude of 1. This is one move through j. We can now label the phasor with the term +j.

Now if we move the phasor through another 90° we can see that it ends up on the negative real axis. This is an initial move through j plus a second move through j, i.e., j², after which we have ended up at -1 and we can label the phasor with the term -1. This would agree with the concept that $j^2 = -1$.

The next move through 90° brings the phasor down to the -j point. This is a move through j, then j, then j, i.e., j³, again ending up on the -j point. Here we can label the phasor as -j.

One final move through 90° brings us back to the +real point. We have moved through 360° to end back up at 0°. Finally, we can again label the phasor as +1.

I hope this interpretation shows you why I say j means moving through 90°. Let's see if it helps with the concept that j is the square root of −1. If that is so, then surely, we can say:

$$if \sqrt{-1} = j \text{ then } j^2 = -1$$

If we now look at the phasor diagram in Figure 6-9, then if we move through j then j i.e., j², again, we get to -1 on the phasor diagram. This could suggest that:

$$j \times j = j^2 = -1$$

Figure 6-9 shows that another move through j brings us to -j. This could suggest that:

$$j \times j \times j = j^3 = j^2 j^1 = -1 \times j = -j$$

312

CHAPTER 6   THE AC VOLTAGE

Finally, the last move through j takes us back to the origin (i.e., on the +1 real point). This could suggest that:

$$j \times j \times j \times j = j^4 = (-1) \times (-1) = 1$$

I am sure there is a more mathematical proof that $j = \sqrt{-1}$ and $j^2 = -1$ but I am quite happy to explain it this way. I hope you can follow what I am trying to say but it's not the easiest thing to explain. Using the term j in this way, we can say:

$$\sqrt{-4} = j2 \text{ and } \sqrt{-9} = j3$$

Indeed, we can say:

$$\sqrt{-n} = jn$$

Complex Numbers

The term j is used when we use complex numbers to describe a phasor quantity. If we look at the resultant of adding the two phasors X_L added to R in Figure 6-6, we can create an expression for the very end of the phasor Z_T from the origin at 0. We can see that to get the very end of the phasor, we could have walked along the real axis the length R then turned in the direction of the +j axis and walked the length X_L. This means that we could write the coordinates in some form of directions as follows:

$$\text{End of } Z_T = R + jX_L$$

Although this is indicating where the very end of the phasor is it is more normal to just say:

$$Z_T = R + jX_L$$

CHAPTER 6   THE AC VOLTAGE

This means that in this case:

$$Z_T = 1000 + j1000$$

In this way we are using complex numbers, as we are using the term j, to describe the phasor Z_T. However, this format, although useful, does not tell us much about the phasor except where the very end of it is on the phasor diagram. We need to know the magnitude and angle of the phasor. We have already determined the magnitude and angle of the phasor Z_T using trigonometry. We have shown that:

$$Z_T = 1.414k \langle 45° \rangle$$

Both expressions represent the same phasor—it's just that they are the two ways we can represent a phasor quantity using complex numbers. The two ways are called:

- Rectangular or coordinate format
- Polar format

There is a third method of representing complex numbers and that is in exponential format. However, we don't normally use that format in engineering, so I will leave that for my book on mathematics. What I will say is that because we can use the exponential format, we multiply the associated angles by adding and divide the angles by subtracting. This is because the angles follow the rules of indices.

If we look at the phasor diagram in Figure 6-8, we can see that we are also using the letter *a* to represent movement along the real axis and the letter *b* to represent movement along the j axis. Using those two letters, we could say:

$$Z_T = a + jb$$

CHAPTER 6   THE AC VOLTAGE

The expression $a + jb$ is the general expression for any phasor written in rectangular or coordinate format. When it comes to the general expression for any phasor written in polar format, we use:

$$r\langle \theta^\circ \rangle$$

Where r is the magnitude of the phasor and θ is the angle associated with it. If we use our example shown in Figure 6-8, the r = 1.414E³ and θ = 45°.

To explain the process, we will change the resistance in the circuit shown in Figure 6-7 and see how it affects the performance of the circuit. We will change the resistance value to 100Ω. We could redraw the phasor diagram but the idea of using complex numbers means we don't need to do that. Using complex numbers, we can say:

$$Z_T = R + jX_L$$

We know R = 100 and XL = 1000. Therefore, we can say:

$$Z_T = 100 + j1000$$

We could use this to draw the phasor as we know where the very end of the phasor would be on the phasor diagram, but we don't want to do that. We can use the values of R and X_L to create the polar format of the phasor. Using the trig from before, we can say:

$$r = \sqrt{R^2 + X_L^2} = \sqrt{100^2 + 1000^2} = 1004.99 \Omega$$

We can also calculate the angle θ using this:

$$\theta = Tan^{-1}\left(\frac{X_L}{R}\right)$$

315

CHAPTER 6   THE AC VOLTAGE

Therefore, we have:

$$\theta = Tan^{-1}\left(\frac{1000}{100}\right) = 84.29°$$

We can write these two terms out in one expression to show that:

$$Z_T = 1004.99 \langle 84.29 \rangle \Omega$$

We can use this polar format expression to calculate the current flowing as follows:

$$i = \frac{v_{Supply}}{Z_T} = \frac{7.071\langle 0° \rangle}{1004.99\langle 84.29° \rangle} = \frac{7.071}{1004.99}\langle 0° - 84.29° \rangle = 7.036\langle -84.29° \rangle mA$$

From experience, you can write this as follows:

$$i = 7.036E^{-3}\langle -84.29° \rangle A$$

As you could easily forget that it is really milliAmps not Amps.

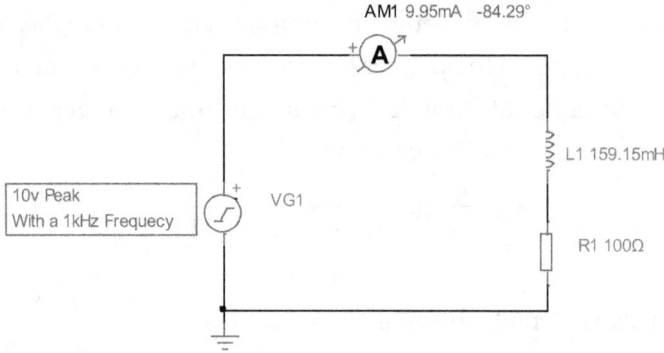

Figure 6-10. *The Simulation with R = 100Ω*

316

CHAPTER 6   THE AC VOLTAGE

Figure 6-10 shows the simulation of the circuit when the resistor has been changed to 100Ω. We are using an ammeter to measure the current flowing in the circuit; however, this is my one major issues with TINA. The software always displays the peak value, not the RMS value. This means that we need to divide the reading of the ammeter by $\sqrt{2}$ to get this:

$$i = 7.036E^{-3} \left\langle -84.29^{o} \right\rangle A$$

This agrees with the value we calculated.

We will change the circuit again and repeat the calculation. This time we will keep the resistance at 100Ω and the inductance at 159.15mH and change the frequency to 500Hz. This means that the value of X_L will change as follows:

$$X_L = 2\pi fL = 2\pi \times 500 \times 159.15E^{-3} = 500$$

We can now calculate the total impedance Z_T as follows:

$$Z_T = \sqrt{R^2 + X_L^2} \left\langle Tan^{-1} \left(\frac{X_L}{R} \right) \right\rangle$$

Note that we are using polar format and combining the two parts, magnitude and angle, as one expression. Putting the values in, we get this:

$$Z_T = \sqrt{100^2 + 500^2} \left\langle Tan^{-1} \left(\frac{500}{100} \right) \right\rangle$$

Which gives us this:

$$Z_T = 509.87 \left\langle 78.69^{o} \right\rangle \Omega$$

317

CHAPTER 6   THE AC VOLTAGE

We can use this value of Z_T to calculate the current, as follows:

$$i = \frac{7.071\langle 0^o \rangle}{509.87\langle 78.69^o \rangle} = 13.868E^{-3}\langle -78.69^o \rangle A$$

When we simulate the changed circuit, we get this:

$$13.866E^{-3}\langle -78.69^o \rangle A$$

After dividing the ammeter reading by $\sqrt{2}$.

I hope these examples confirm that you can use complex numbers to represent phasors in this way.

The Resistor Capacitor Circuit

Consider the circuit shown in Figure 6-11.

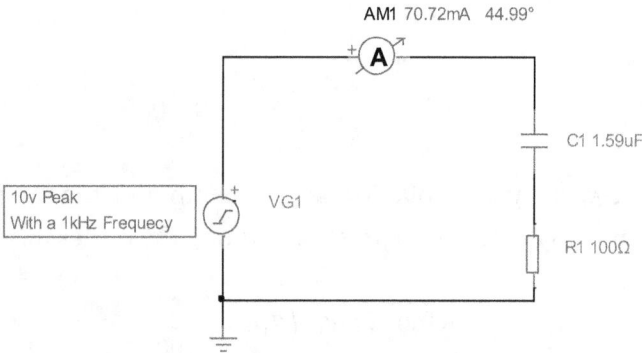

Figure 6-11. *The Resistor Capacitor Series Circuit*

As with all electrical circuits, we must calculate the current flowing in the circuit, as this can cause the most damage. We can always use Ohm's Law to calculate the flowing current, which states:

$$i = \frac{v_{Supply}}{Z_T}$$

318

CHAPTER 6   THE AC VOLTAGE

As this is a series circuit, we can calculate the value of Z_T by summing the impedances in the circuit. There are just two impedances—R and X_C—but we know that this would be a phasor sum. Therefore, to calculate Z_T we must use this:

$$Z_T = R - jX_C$$

We are using the rectangular format to show that this is a phasor sum and we use the -j because the impedance X_C is 180° out of phase with X_L. Therefore, this must go on the -j axis of the phasor diagram. We need to calculate the impedance X_C. This can be calculated using:

$$X_C = \frac{1}{2\pi fC} = \frac{1}{2\pi \times 1E^3 \times 1.59E^{-6}} = 100\,\Omega$$

This means that we can express Z_T as follows:

$$Z_T = 100 - j100$$

In polar format, we can say this:

$$Z_T = \sqrt{R^2 + (-X_C)^2} \left\langle Tan^{-1}\left(\frac{-X_C}{R}\right) \right\rangle$$

Putting the values in, we can say:

$$Z_T = \sqrt{100^2 + (-100)^2} \left\langle Tan^{-1}\left(\frac{-100}{100}\right) \right\rangle$$

$$Z_T = 141.421 \left\langle -45°\right\rangle \Omega$$

CHAPTER 6 THE AC VOLTAGE

We can now calculate the current flowing in the circuit as follows:

$$i = \frac{7.071\langle 0^o \rangle}{141.421\langle -45^o \rangle} = 50E^{-3}\langle 45^o \rangle A$$

If we divide the ammeter reading shown in Figure 6-11 by $\sqrt{2}$ we get the same result. The calculations show that the current is leading the voltage, which is what we expect with a more capacitive circuit.

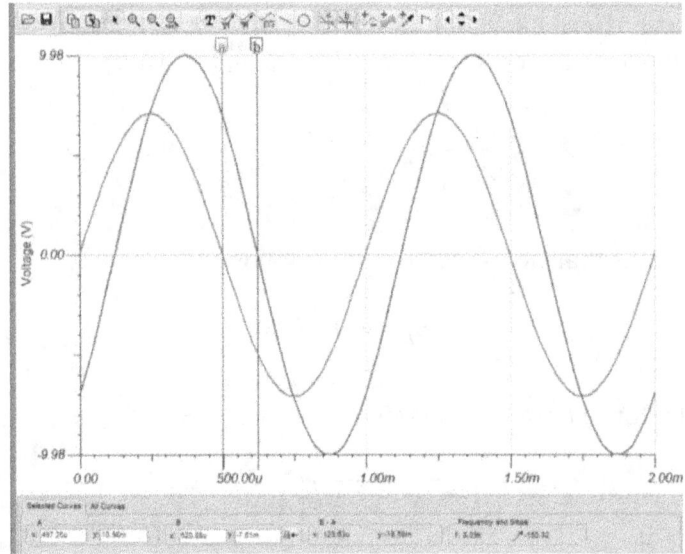

Figure 6-12. *The Oscilloscope Traces from the Circuit Shown in Figure 6-11*

If we use the voltage and current traces shown in Figure 6-12, we can calculate the peak current and the phase difference between the supply voltage and the current. The voltage across the resistor is the brown waveform and its peak value was measured at 7.07v. If we divide this by 100, the resistance value, we get a value for the peak current:

$$i_{Peak} = \frac{v_{Peak}}{R} = \frac{7.07}{100} = 70.0E^{-3} \; Amps$$

CHAPTER 6   THE AC VOLTAGE

Converting this to the RMS gives:

$$rms\ i_{magnitude} = \frac{70.0E^{-3}}{\sqrt{2}} = 50E^{-3}\ Amps = 50mA$$

In Figure 6-12, we can see that the time difference between the two waveforms is 123.63µS. We can use this time difference to calculate the phase difference using:

$$Phase\ Diff = time\ Diff \times freq \times 360$$

Putting the values in, we get:

$$Phase\ Diff = 123.63E^{-6} \times 1E^{3} \times 360 = 44.51^{o}$$

From Figure 6-12 we can see that the brown trace, which represents the current flowing in the circuit, gets to 0, coming from positive to negative, before the voltage trace gets to 0 in the same direction. This means that the current is leading the supply voltage, which is what we expect.

Converting Rectangular to Polar and Polar to Rectangular Formats

Before we go too far with these electrical examples, it's important to know how to convert from one format to the other with complex numbers. If we use the general terms, we can say the rectangular format is as follows:

$$a + jb$$

This converts to polar format using:

$$polar = \sqrt{a^2 + b^2} \left\langle Tan^{-1}\left(\frac{b}{a}\right)\right\rangle$$

CHAPTER 6   THE AC VOLTAGE

Polar format is as follows:

$$r\langle\theta\rangle$$

The angle θ can have the units of degrees or radians so we need to know what units we are working in. Normally, we will be using degrees in the book so we need to ensure, unless stated otherwise, we have the calculated set to degrees.

If we use the phasor diagram shown in Figure 6-6, we can see that the length a is the length along the real axis. The length b, which is the length up the +j axis, can be projected to be the length opposite the angle θ. Lastly, the length Z_T is the magnitude of the resultant, and it is related to the length r. They are the hypotenuse of the right-angled triangle. If we now consider the angle θ, we can express the cos (θ) using:

$$\cos(\theta) = \frac{a}{r}$$

Therefore, we can say:

$$a = r\cos(\theta)$$

Where a is the real term as it is on the real axis. Similarly, we can say:

$$\sin(\theta) = \frac{b}{r}$$

Therefore, we have:

$$b = r\sin(\theta)$$

Where b is the j term as it is on the j axis:

CHAPTER 6 THE AC VOLTAGE

Therefore, to convert from polar to rectangular, we use:

$$a + jb = r\cos(\theta) + jr\sin(\theta)$$

Example 6.1

Convert.

$$3 + j4$$

To polar:

$$r\langle\theta\rangle = \sqrt{3^2 + 4^2} \left\langle Tan^{-1}\left(\frac{4}{1}\right)\right\rangle$$

$$r\langle\theta\rangle = 5\langle 53.13^o\rangle$$

Convert

$$r\langle\theta\rangle = 5\langle 53.13^o\rangle$$

To rectangular:

$$a + jb = 5\cos(53.13^o) + j5\sin(53.13^o)$$

Therefore:

$$5\langle 53.13^o\rangle = 3 + j4$$

This is expected.

Now that you can use complex numbers to calculate impedances, currents, and voltages in electrical circuits, we will go through some more examples.

323

CHAPTER 6   THE AC VOLTAGE

Example 6.2

Calculate the current flowing through the circuit shown in Figure 6-13 and the voltage across the resistor and inductor. Use KVL to confirm your calculations of the volt drops.

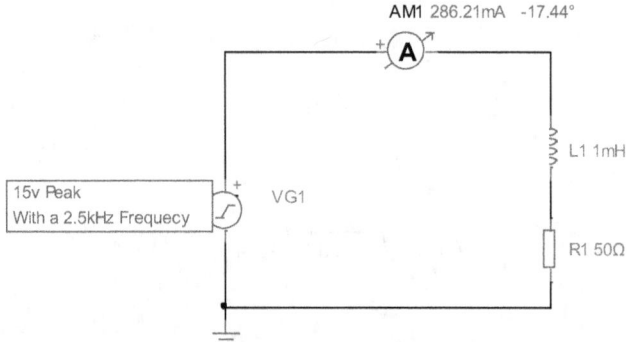

Figure 6-13. The Circuit for Example 6.2

Start by using Ohm's Law, which says:

$$i = \frac{v_{Supply}}{Z_T}$$

Express v_{Supply} with the RMS value using:

$$v_{Supply} = \frac{v_{Peak}}{\sqrt{2}} = \frac{15}{\sqrt{2}} = 10.607v$$

We need to determine the impedance X_L, which we can do using this:

$$X_L = 2\pi fL = 2\pi \times 2.5E^3 \times 1E^{-3} = 15.708\Omega$$

324

CHAPTER 6   THE AC VOLTAGE

We will need to include the angle associated with the impedance X_L. From the phasor diagram shown in Figure 6-6, we can see that X_L sits on the +j axis. As j means moving through 90° then the angle associated with X_L is 90°. This means that X_L is as follows

$$X_L = 15.708 \langle 90^o \rangle$$

If we relate this position of X_L to the general rectangular format of a + jb we can say that a = 0 and b = X_L. This means that in rectangular format we can say:

$$X_L = 0 + jX_L = 0 + j15.708 = j15.708$$

We can do the same for the resistor phasor R. Because it sits on the horizontal axis in rectangular format, we can say:

$$R = R + j0 = 50 + j0$$

This is in rectangular format, but in polar format the magnitude is 50, the length of the phasor and as it is on the horizontal axis, as shown in Figure 6-6. The angle is 0°. Therefore, in polar format:

$$R = 50 \langle 0^o \rangle$$

The rectangular format for the two impedances may seem a bit obvious, but if we can express the two phasors in rectangular format, we can add them to calculate Z_T as follows:

$$Z_T = (R + j0) + (0 + jX_L)$$

CHAPTER 6   THE AC VOLTAGE

When adding complex numbers, something we can only do in rectangular format, we add all the real terms (i.e., the a terms) together, and then add all the imaginary terms (the j terms) together. This would give us the following:

$$Z_T = (R+0) + j(0+X_L) = R + jX_L$$

Now we can calculate the total impedance in both rectangular and polar formats as follows:

$$Z_T = R + jX_L$$

Therefore:

$$Z_T = 50 + j15.707 \, \Omega$$

In polar format, we have:

$$Z_T = \sqrt{50^2 + 15.707^2} \left\langle Tan^{-1}\left(\frac{15.707}{50}\right) \right\rangle$$

Therefore:

$$Z_T = 53.409 \langle 17.44^o \rangle \, \Omega$$

We can now calculate the current flowing in the circuit as follows:

$$i = \frac{10.607 \langle 0^o \rangle}{53.409 \langle 17.44^o \rangle} = 198.599 E^{-3} \langle -17.44^o \rangle \, A$$

Now we can calculate the volt drop across the inductor using this:

$$v_L = i \times X_L$$

CHAPTER 6   THE AC VOLTAGE

Therefore, we have this:

$$v_L = \left(198.599E^{-3}\langle-17.44°\rangle\right) \times \left(15.708\langle 90°\rangle\right)$$

With complex multiplication, we simply multiply the two magnitudes and add the two angles. This gives us this:

$$v_L = 198.599E^{-3} \times 15.708\langle-17.44+90\rangle$$

This in turn gives this:

$$v_L = 3.12\langle 72.56°\rangle v$$

To calculate the volt drop across the resistor, we use:

$$v_R = i \times R$$

Therefore, we get this:

$$v_R = \left(198.599E^{-3}\langle-17.44°\rangle\right) \times \left(50\langle 0°\rangle\right)$$

Note the angle associated with the resistance is 0, as its phasor lies on the + real axis, which is the reference; see Figure 6-6.

This gives:

$$v_R = 9.93v\langle-17.44°\rangle v$$

These two voltage calculations confirm the theory that the current flowing through the resistor is in phase with the voltage across the resistor, as the angle for the voltage across the resistor is the same as the angle for the current. This is because resistance is a non-reactive component. Conversely, the current flowing through the inductor is 90° behind the voltage across the inductor. Hence the inductor is a reactive component.

CHAPTER 6   THE AC VOLTAGE

We can now use KVL to confirm that:

$$v_{Supply} = v_R + v_L$$

However, we can see that we can't simply add the two magnitudes, as 3.12 + 9.93 would give us 13.05V, which is too much. That is because this is a phasor sum. We could draw the two phasors out on a phasor diagram, and this is shown in Figure 6-14. However, this takes too long, and it is difficult to be very accurate. Instead, we will add the two volt drops using complex numbers.

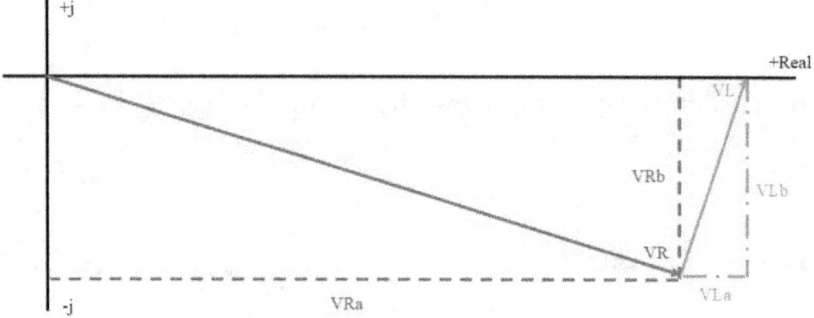

Figure 6-14. *The Phasor Diagram for VR + VL*

Figure 6-14 shows how the phasors of V_R, in solid red and V_L, in solid blue, added together. The process is to walk the length of the V_R phasor. Then turn in the direction of the V_L phasor and walk its length. Then we walk the shortest path back to get to the origin. This would be the resultant of adding the two phasors together. If we could measure the length of this resultant phasor, it would equal the 10.607v of the supply. This would then agree with KVL.

Adding the Two Volt Drops

The addition of complex numbers is only done in rectangular format. This means that we need to convert the polar format to rectangular format. This can be done as follows:

$$a + jb = r\cos(\theta) + jr\sin(\theta)$$

Putting the values for r and θ, in we get:

$$v_R = 9.93v \angle (-17.44^o) = 9.93\cos(-17.44^o) + j9.93\sin(-17.44^o)$$

This gives us:

$$v_R = 9.474 - j2.976\, v$$

If you look at the v_R phasor in Figure 6-14, you should be able to see that you get to the very end of the v_R phasor by walking 9.474 along the real axis. This is the length red dashed line VRa in Figure 6-14. Then turn 90° to be parallel to the -j axis and walk down the 2.976, the length of the red dashed line VRb in Figure 6-14. We would then arrive at the very end of the V_R phasor. I hope this helps you to appreciate why I say that the rectangular or coordinate format pinpoints the very end of the phasor.

Now we need to convert the v_L phasor from polar to rectangular. This is done as follows:

$$v_L = 3.12 \angle (72.56^o) = 3.12\cos(72.56^o) + j3.12\sin(72.56^o)\, v$$

This gives.

$$v_L = 0.935 + j2.9766\, v$$

CHAPTER 6   THE AC VOLTAGE

We now need to add the V_L phasor to the end of the V_R phasor. It is a bit more difficult to explain how we get to the very end of the v_L phasor that we add to V_R. This is because we must move the origin of where we start adding this v_L phasor to the very end of the v_R phasor. From that point, we move the short distance of 0.935 in a horizontal direction away from the end of the v_R phasor. This is the length of the blue dashed line VLa, as shown in Figure 6-14. Now we turn in the direction vertically upwards, in parallel with the j axis. Then we walk the distance 2.9766 vertically up. This is the length of the blue dashed line VLb. This would end perfectly on the horizontal + real axis at $0°$. That is why the j term for v_L is the same as the -j term component of the v_R phasor but positive. This means that the shortest path back to the origin would take us back along the real axis at a length that would be equal to the 10.607v of the supply voltage. The angle would be 0 degrees, as it is along the real axis.

I hope you can see how we could add the two phasors graphically, but it would take too long, and it would be difficult to be accurate. However, now we have both volt drops expressed in rectangular format we can now add them as two complex numbers to show that KVL still applies to AC circuits as it does to DC circuit. We can add the two volt drops as follows:

$$v_{Supply} = (9.474 - j2.976) + (0.935 + j2.9766)$$

To add these two complex numbers, as we do with all complex numbers, we simply add all real terms together and the add all j terms together. This leads to:

$$v_{Supply} = (9.474 + 0.935) + j(-2.976 + 29766)$$

This gives:

$$v_{Supply} = 10.409 + j0006 \, v$$

CHAPTER 6   THE AC VOLTAGE

The small differences are due to rounding errors in our calculations. However, I hope this example helps confirm that you can use complex numbers in this way. I hope you also see that complex numbers are not very complex at all. There is one process that uses the complex conjugate that is a bit more involved.

Example 6.3

Consider the CR circuit shown in Figure 6-15.

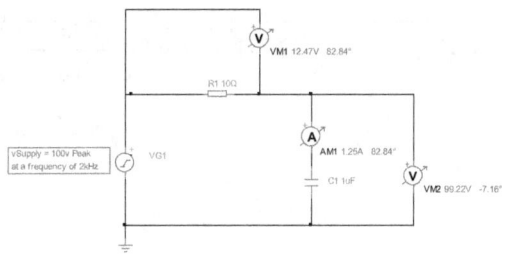

Figure 6-15. *The CR AC Circuit for Example 8.5*

We will use complex numbers to confirm the measurements from the meters shown in Figure 6-15. However, we must remember that the measurements shown are peak values. First, we must calculate the impedance of the capacitor. This can be calculated as follows:

$$X_C = \frac{1}{2\pi fC} = \frac{1}{2\pi \times 2E^3 \times 1E^{-6}} = 79.5775\,\Omega$$

The angle associated with X_C is -90, as X_C goes on the –j axis. This means that in polar format:

$$X_C = 79.5775 \langle -90 \rangle\,\Omega$$

331

CHAPTER 6   THE AC VOLTAGE

In rectangular format, X_C is:

$$X_C = 0 - j79.57753 \, \Omega$$

Now we can determine the total impedance Z_T as follows:

$$Z_T = R - jX_C = 10 - j79.5775 \, \Omega$$

We need to convert this into polar so that we can divide it. Therefore, we get:

$$Z_T = \sqrt{(10)^2 + (79.5775)^2} \left\langle Tan^{-1}\left(\frac{-79.577}{10}\right) \right\rangle$$

This gives:

$$Z_T = 80.2033 \langle -82.84 \rangle \, \Omega$$

Now we can calculate the current flowing in the circuit as follows:

$$i = \frac{v_{Supply}}{Z_T} = \frac{70.71 \langle 0 \rangle}{80.2033 \langle -82.84 \rangle} = 881.643 E^{-3} \langle 82.84 \rangle$$

We can calculate the volt drop across the resistor as follows:

$$v_R = i \times R = \left(881.643 E^{-3} \langle 82.84 \rangle\right) \times \left(10 \langle 0 \rangle\right)$$

Therefore, we can say that:

$$v_R = 8.81643 \langle 82.84 \rangle \, v$$

Similarly, we can calculate v_C as follows:

$$v_C = \left(881.643 E^{-3} \langle 82.84 \rangle\right) \times \left(79.5775 \langle -90 \rangle\right)$$

This gives us:

$$v_C = 70.159 \angle -7.16 \; v$$

We need to convert these to rectangular so that we can add them together and then use KVL to confirm our work:

Converting v_R gives the following:

$$8.81643 \angle 82.84 = 8.81643\cos(82.84) + j8.81643\sin(82.84) \; v$$

This gives:

$$v_R = 1.0989 + j8.74768 \; v$$

Converting v_C gives:

$$70.159 \angle -7.16 = 70.159\cos(-7.16) + j70.159\sin(-7.16)$$

This gives:

$$v_C = 69.9881 - j8.7447 \; v$$

We can now add these together, which gives:

$$v_C = (1.0989 + j8.74768) + (69.6229 - j8.7447) \; v$$

This gives:

$$v_{Supply} = 70.722 + j0.003$$

This is close enough.

CHAPTER 6   THE AC VOLTAGE

Using the Complex Conjugate

There is a lot of work in changing from rectangular to polar and back again. This is quite awkward and can lead to rounding errors. If we use the complex conjugate, we can do all the calculations in just rectangular format, which might reduce the rounding errors. I won't say this method is any easier, as there are some awkward bits you need to be aware of, but I will take you through the process and let you decide which method you think is best. First, however, I explain what the complex conjugate is. The complex conjugate may have some deep inner meaning, but I explain it this way. Given the complex number:

$$a + jb$$

The complex conjugate is the same number except that the sign of the j term has been changed. Therefore, the complex conjugate of

$$a + jb$$

is

$$a - jb$$

The following examples help you understand what the complex conjugate is.

Example 6.4

Consider the complex conjugate of the following numbers:

$$3 + j4 \text{ is } 3 - j4$$
$$2 - j5 \text{ is } 2 + j5$$

Only the sign of the j or imaginary term is changed.

CHAPTER 6 THE AC VOLTAGE

The best way to explain how to use the complex conjugate is to go through an example.

Example 6.5

Let's divide the following two complex numbers:

$$\frac{3+j4}{2+j3}$$

The first thing we do is multiply the division by 1. This should not change anything.

$$\frac{3+j4}{2+j3} \times 1 = \frac{3+j4}{2+j3}$$

However, let's consider the following divisions:

$$\frac{10}{10} = 1$$

$$\frac{223.55}{233.55} = 1$$

$$\frac{\sin(30)}{\sin(30)} = 1$$

$$\frac{2a+6b}{2a+6b} = 1$$

Anything divided by itself equals 1, so we will now multiply the same complex division by 1, but expressed in a special way:

$$\frac{3+j4}{2+j3} \times \frac{2-j3}{2-j3}$$

335

CHAPTER 6   THE AC VOLTAGE

This is still multiplying the original division by 1, as follows:

$$\frac{2-j3}{2-j3} = 1$$

I hope you can see that the second division of complex numbers is made up of numbers that are the complex conjugate of the denominator in the original division. Now we must carry out the multiplication, which is best rewritten as follows:

$$\frac{(3+j4)\times(2-j3)}{(2+j3)\times(2-j3)}$$

This is done in the same way as expanding any two brackets (i.e., we multiply everything in the second bracket by the first bracket). We will do the two multiplications separately, starting with the two numerators. This is as follows:

$$(3+j4)\times(2-j3)$$

This gives:

$$(3\times2)+(3\times(-j3))+((j4)\times2)+((j4)\times(-j3))$$

This gives:

$$(6)+(-j9)+(j8)+(-j^2 12)$$

Before we collect the like terms, we must remember that:

$$j^2 = -1 \text{ and so} \left(-j^2\right) = (-\times -1) = +1$$

Therefore, the four terms are really

$$(6)+(-j9)+(j8)+(12)$$

This then gives us the following:

$$18-j1$$

Now we can multiply the denominator:

$$(2+j3)\times(2-j3)$$

This gives us the following:

$$(2\times2)+(2\times(-j3))+((j3)\times2)+((j3)\times(-j3))$$

This gives us the following:

$$(4)+(-j6)+(j6)+(-j^2 9)$$

Again, we know that:

$$-j^2 = +1$$

Therefore, we have this:

$$(4)+(-j6)+(j6)+(9)$$

Which gives us this:

$$13+j0=13.$$

CHAPTER 6   THE AC VOLTAGE

This shows that, by multiplying a complex number by its complex conjugate, we end up with a wholly real number. This is sometimes called *rationalizing* a complex number.

However, if we go back to our original division, we get this:

$$\frac{3+j4}{2+j3} = \frac{(3+j4)\times(2-j3)}{(2+j3)\times(2-j3)} = \frac{18-j1}{13} = \frac{18}{13} - \frac{j1}{13} = 1.3846 - j0.07692$$

Therefore, when we use the complex conjugate, we can divide complex numbers in rectangular format. We will repeat the calculations in Example 6.3 but this time we will not covert back and forth from rectangular to polar.

Therefore, we know that:

$$v_{Supply} = 70.71 + j0$$

And:

$$Z_T = 10 - j79.5775 \, \Omega$$

This means that to calculate the current i, we can use:

$$i = \frac{(70.71+j0)\times(10+j79.5775)}{(10-j79.5776)\times(10+j79.5775)}$$

This is using the complex conjugate of the denominator Z_T. The next step involves a lot of multiplication; however, if we consider the general complex number multiplied by its conjugate, we might discover a short cut.

$$(a+jb)\times(a-jb) = (a\times a) + (a\times(-jb)) + (jb\times a) + ((jb)\times(-jb))$$

CHAPTER 6 THE AC VOLTAGE

This gives:

$$(a^2)+(-jab)+(jab)+((-j)^2 b^2)$$

$$(a^2)+(b^2)$$

This will happen every time we multiply a complex number by its complex conjugate; we end up with a real term that is the sum of the coefficients squared (i.e., a²+b²). This means that with this calculation:

$$i = \frac{(70.71+j0)\times(10+j79.5775)}{(10-j79.5776)\times(10+j79.5775)}$$

We can rewrite it as follows:

$$i = \frac{(70.71+j0)\times(10+j79.5775)}{10^2+79.5775^2} = \frac{(70.71+j0)\times(10+j79.5775)}{6432.5785}$$

We need only multiply the numerator. This gives us the following:

$$(70.71+j0)\times(10+j79.5775)$$

$$=(70.71\times 10)+(70.71\times j79.5775)+(j0\times 10)+(j0\times j79.5775)$$

$$=707.1+j5626.925$$

This gives us this:

$$i = \frac{707.1+j5626.925}{6432.5785} = \frac{707.1}{6432.5785}+\frac{j5626.925}{6432.5785} = 0.10992+j0.87475\ A$$

339

CHAPTER 6 THE AC VOLTAGE

If we multiply this by R, we should get the volt drop across the resistor (i.e., v_R) as follows:

$$v_R = (0.10992 + j0.87475) \times (10 + j0)$$

$$v_R = 1.0992 + j0.87475 \, v$$

This is very close to the rectangular value we got for v_R in the original calculation. We can calculate v_C in the same way:

$$v_C = (0.10992 + j0.87475) \times (0 - j79.57753)$$

This gives.

$$v_C = (0.10992 \times -j79.57753) + ((-j79.57753) \times (j0.87475))$$

This gives.

$$v_C = 69.60965 - j8.74716 \, v$$

This is close to the same value we calculated before. This shows that using the complex conjugate works just as well as using polar format. It is up to you, as to which method you use. However, there are some advantages in keeping everything in rectangular format.

Exercise 6.1

Now it's time for you to carry out some calculations. There are two circuit to analyse, and each circuit has three sets of values. Calculate the following for each circuit using each of the values:

- The impedance of the reactive component.
- The total impedance, ZT.
- The current flowing in the circuit.

CHAPTER 6 THE AC VOLTAGE

- The volt drop across the resistor.
- The volt drop across the reactive component.
- Use KVL to confirm your calculations.

The circuits for Exercise 6.1 are shown in Figures 6-16 and 6-17. The solutions are shown in the appendix.

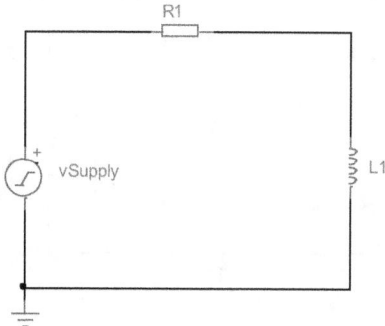

Figure 6-16. *The RL Circuit for Exercise 6.1*

The set of values for the circuit.

Set a:

- The v_{Supply} is 20v peak at 2kHz.
- Resistor R_1 is 25Ω.
- The inductor value L_1 is 7.958mH.

Set b:

- The v_{Supply} is 120v peak at 8kHz.
- Resistor R_1 is 15Ω.
- The inductor value L_1 is 596.831µH.

CHAPTER 6   THE AC VOLTAGE

Set c:

- The v_{Supply} is 100v peak at 5kHz.
- Resistor R_1 is 20Ω.
- The inductor value L_1 is 3.1831mH.

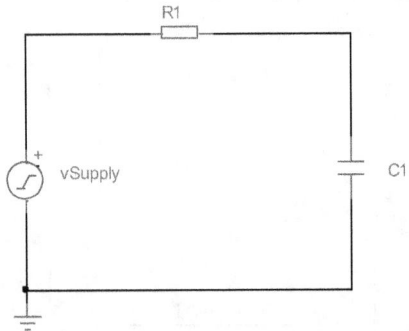

Figure 6-17. *The RC Circuit for Exercise 6.1*

The set of values for the circuit.

Set a:

- The v_{Supply} is 20v peak at 2kHz.
- Resistor R_1 is 25Ω.
- The inductor value C_1 is 1.061μF.

Set b:

- The v_{Supply} is 120v peak at 8kHz.
- Resistor R_1 is 15Ω.
- The inductor value C_1 is 159.155nF.

CHAPTER 6   THE AC VOLTAGE

Set c:

- The v_{Supply} is 100v peak at 5kHz.
- Resistor R_1 is 20Ω.
- The inductor value C_1 is 3.1831μf.

Exercise 6.2

Draw the phasor diagram for the impedances in set a for both circuits.

Exercise 6.3

Draw the voltage phasor diagrams for set a for both circuits.

Rectification

At the start of this chapter, I explained why we generate an AC voltage at the generating stations. If you look at most of the domestic appliances in your home, you might find that most of them work on DC. This means that we must convert the AC voltage that arrives at our home to DC for most of our equipment. It is probably only the washing machine, dryer, and heaters that run on AC. The act of converting an AC voltage to a DC voltage is called *rectification*, perhaps because it is rectifying the problem that came about when we changed from supplying our homes with DC to supplying our homes with AC. Considering a basic AC voltage shown in Figure 6-18, to convert this to DC we simply need to stop the negative part from being passed onto the load. We could stop the positive part but it is easier to stop the negative part from being applied to the load—in this case the resistor R1.

343

CHAPTER 6   THE AC VOLTAGE

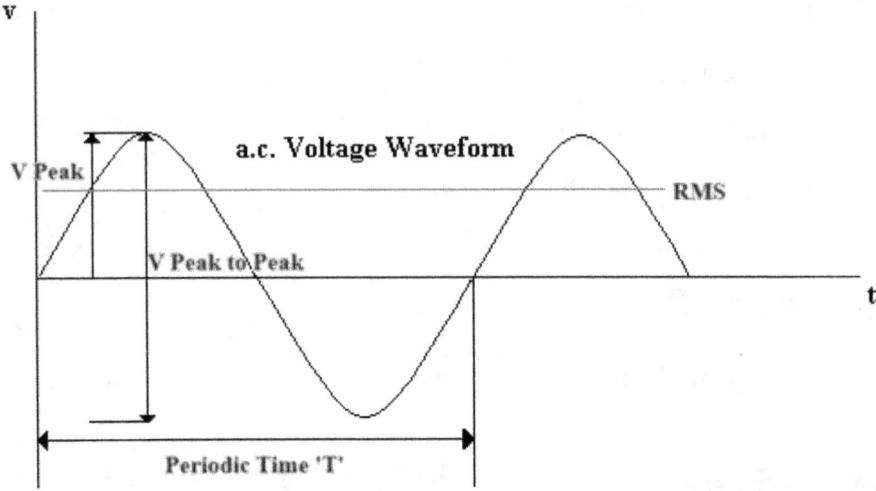

Figure 6-18. *A Basic AC Voltage Waveform*

If we relate the AC voltage shown in Figure 6-18 to the UK mains, we can make the following statements:

- The frequency is 50Hz, and the periodic time, which can be calculated using $T = \dfrac{1}{F} = \dfrac{1}{50} = 20ms \text{ or } 0.02sec$.
- The V Peak is approximately 339v.
- The RMS is approximately 240v.
- The V peak to peak is simply twice that of the V peak voltage.

To stop the negative half from being passed onto the load, we could try putting a switch between the voltage source, VG1, and the load R1, so that we could turn off the source every time the voltage went negative. This would be impossible to do manually. However, engineers came up with an electronic switch in the form of a diode. These diodes were originally made from an anode and cathode encased in a glass tube in which a vacuum was created. Nowadays, we use didoes that are made from a

CHAPTER 6   THE AC VOLTAGE

semiconductor material such as silicon or germanium. The modern diode acts like a switch in that it automatically closes and allows current to flow through it when the voltage at the anode becomes approximately 0.7V greater than the voltage at the cathode. If we look at the waveform shown in Figure 6-18, we see that this will happen during the positive half of the AC voltage input. When the voltage at the anode falls below 0.7V greater than the cathode voltage, the switch will open, and the diode will prevent current from flowing through it. This will happen during the negative half of the input voltage. In this way, we can see that we could prevent the negative half-cycle of the input voltage from being passed onto the load. This is shown in Figure 6-19.

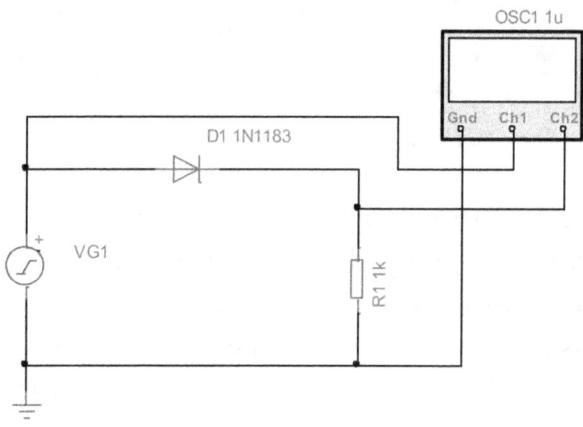

Figure 6-19. The Simple Diode Used as an Electronic Switch to Remove the Negative Half-Cycle

Figure 6-19 shows a simple circuit we can use in TINA to test the operation of a diode and remove the negative half-cycle of the AC voltage source. The oscilloscope displays, shown in Figure 6-20, show the input voltage source and the voltage after the diode (i.e., the voltage across the load R1).

CHAPTER 6   THE AC VOLTAGE

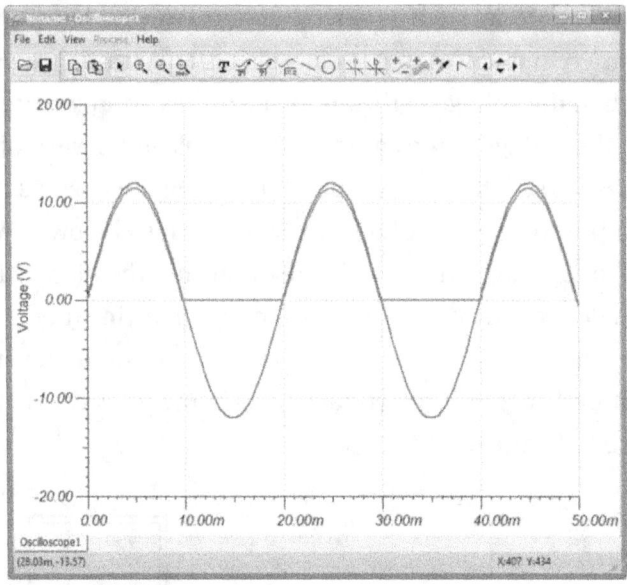

Figure 6-20. *The Oscilloscope Traces*

Using Figure 6-20 we can just make out that one trace is slightly lower in peak voltage than the other. This is the voltage across R1 (i.e., the voltage after the diode.) The slight difference is due to the volt drop across the diode, which is approximately 0.7V. The peak voltage of the AC input has been kept at 12V so that we can see the voltage difference between the two traces. If I had set the peak voltage at 339V, you would not be able to see the difference. Also, the 1N1183 diode would have a problem coping with that voltage level.

CHAPTER 6   THE AC VOLTAGE

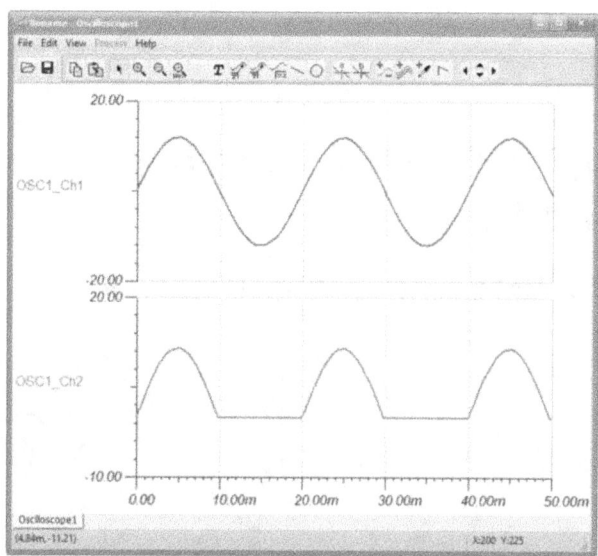

Figure 6-21. The Traces of the Oscilloscope, Separated

Figure 6-21 shows more clearly that the diode has prevented the negative half of the input from being passed onto the output. This type of rectification is called *half-wave rectification*, as only half of the input is used. The equipment will respond to the average voltage of the waveform.

Full-Wave Rectification

An improvement to half-wave rectification is a circuit that uses both the positive and negative halves of the mains input voltage. This is termed full-wave rectification and one of the early solutions was to use a split transformer. This is a transformer that had two sets of coils on the secondary. However, this has two major drawbacks:

- The maximum voltage is half of what could be achieved from using the complete secondary output.

- The manufacture of a true centre tapped transformer is very difficult.

347

CHAPTER 6   THE AC VOLTAGE

An easier and better alternative is to use a bridge rectifier, discussed next.

Full-Wave Rectification Using the Bridge Rectifier

The circuit for the bridge rectifier is shown in Figure 6-22.

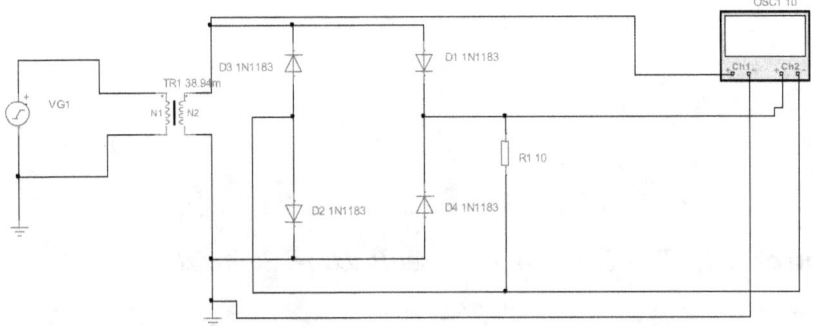

Figure 6-22. *The Typical Bridge Rectifier Circuit*

Figure 6-22 shows a full-wave bridge rectifier without smoothing. The waveforms obtained from this circuit are shown in Figure 6-23.

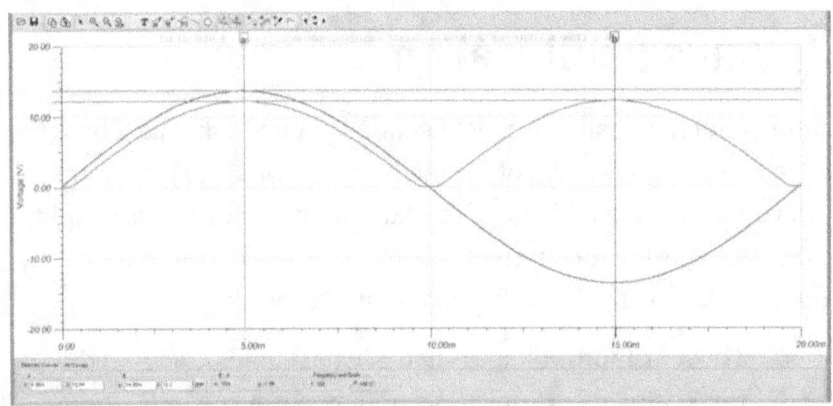

Figure 6-23. *The Voltage Waveforms for the Full-Wave Rectifier*

CHAPTER 6   THE AC VOLTAGE

We can use the cursors to show the difference between the peak of the secondary voltage and the peak of the voltage across the load. The green waveform is the voltage across the secondary of the transformer and cursor a shows the peak at 13.64v. The brown waveform is the voltage across the load resistor R1 and cursor b shows the peak is 12.2v. The difference of 1.4v is because there are two diodes in series across the load output. Each will drop around 0.7V to keep the diodes turned on. We can also see that the voltage across the load is DC, as it has two positive pulses, whereas the voltage across the secondary is AC, as it goes positive and negative.

Smoothing

The output of the half-wave and full-wave rectifier could be improved by adding a capacitor across the output. This would act like a temporary source, storing some charge whilst the main source is switched off from the load by the diode. Figure 6-24 shows the effect of adding a smoothing capacitor across the output of a half-wave rectifier circuit.

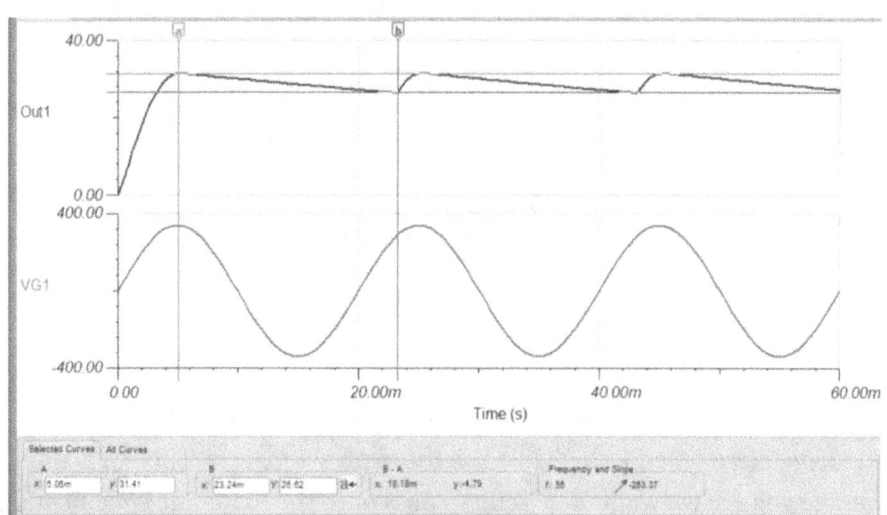

Figure 6-24. *The Output of a Half-Wave Rectifier with Smoothing Capacitor*

349

CHAPTER 6   THE AC VOLTAGE

The trace Out1 shows that the output voltage is not as lumpy. This is because the capacitor is acting as a temporary battery to supply the load when the diode is turned off.

Now that we have studied what rectification, is it would be useful if we could decide how to select the components for the rectification circuit. We will just look at a simple half-wave rectifier and a simple full-wave rectifier.

To fully explain how to design power supply units (i.e. a PSU) would take a full book on its own. We will start by specifying what we want from our rectification circuit. The input would be the UK mains. In this example, the output would be 12V with an allowable ripple voltage of 1V at a maximum current of 250mA. We know the basic circuit would be that as shown in Figure 6-19. However, the first thing we need to determine is the *turns ratio* of the transformer. To calculate the turns ratio of the transformer, we need to the peak secondary voltage. This can be related to the required average voltage of the PSU using the following.

For the half-wave, we have:

$$Vave = Vmax - \frac{Vripple}{2}$$

But

$$Vmax = Vsecpk - 0.7$$

$$\therefore Vave = (Vsecpk - 0.7) - \frac{Vripple}{2}$$

$$\therefore Vave + \frac{Vripple}{2} = Vsecpk - 0.7$$

$$\therefore Vsecpk = Vave + \frac{Vripple}{2} + 0.7$$

The derivation of this expression is explained in my book *Mastering Analogue Electronics*; we will just use the expression here. The V_{ave} is the average voltage we want the circuit to pass onto the load. The specification has set this to 12V. The term V_{secpk} is the peak voltage across the secondary

CHAPTER 6 THE AC VOLTAGE

of the transformer. The V_{ripple} is the amount of voltage drop the customer will allow at the output when the load is taking the maximum current. This has been set to 1V ripple at 250mA. Therefore, the V_{ripple} is 1V. The 0.7 relates the voltage dropped across the diode when it is conducting. Using these values, we can calculate the secondary peak voltage of the transformer as follows:

$$V_{secpk} = 12 + \frac{1}{2} + 0.7 = 13.2V$$

This will be the peak voltage across the secondary of the transformer. We know that the peak voltage, the V_{pripk}, of the transformer primary coil will be the peak voltage of the UK mains—339V. This means that we can now calculate the turns ratio of the transformer using this formula:

$$Turns\ Ratio = \frac{Vpripk}{Vsecpk} = \frac{339}{13.2} = 25.682$$

We will simulate the circuit in TINA to confirm that it works as expected. However, one issue I have with TINA is that it calculates the turns ratio using the inversion of this expression. Therefore, the turns ratio for TINA is as follows:

$$Turns\ Ratio = \frac{V_{secpk}}{V_{pripk}} = \frac{13.2}{339} = 38.94m$$

To choose which diode to use, we need to consider the maximum voltage and the current it would have to cope with. The maximum voltage is termed the *peak inverse voltage* for the diode and this should be greater than the peak-to-peak voltage we would expect across the secondary of the transformer. This would simply be twice the peak voltage across the secondary (i.e., twice 13.2V, or 26.4V). The peak current would be 250mA as specified for the load; however, there will be some extra current required to charge the capacitor.

CHAPTER 6 THE AC VOLTAGE

To determine the value of the smoothing capacitor, we can use the following expression:

$$C = i\frac{dt}{dV_C}$$

The derivation of this expression is in my other book. The current is the maximum load current of 250mA. The dt is approximately 16ms for the half-wave circuit and the dV_C is simply the allowable ripple voltage. Putting these values into the expression, the value of the capacitor would be as follows:

$$C = 250E^{-3}\frac{16E^{-3}}{1} = 4E^{-3} = 4mF$$

We need to calculate the value of the load resistance that draws the maximum current from the circuit. This can be calculated as follows:

$$R = \frac{V}{I} = \frac{12}{250E^{-3}} = 48$$

The circuit can now be simulated, as shown in Figure 6-25:

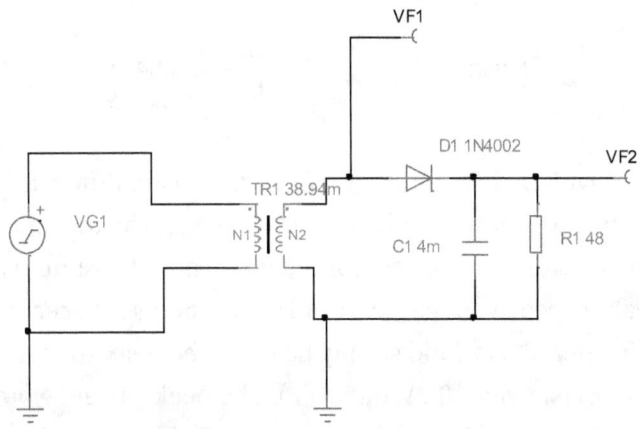

Figure 6-25. *The Half-Wave Rectifier with Smoothing Capacitor*

CHAPTER 6   THE AC VOLTAGE

The output voltage of the half-wave rectifier with smoothing is shown in Figure 6-26.

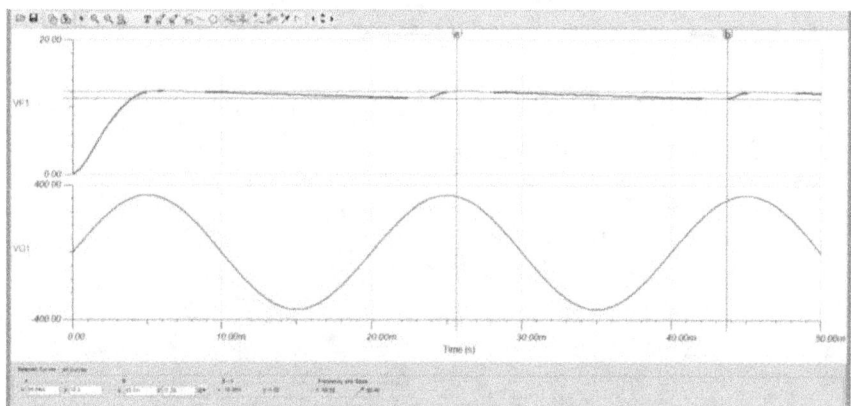

Figure 6-26. *The Voltage Waveforms for the Half-Wave Rectifier with Smoothing*

The two cursors are used to measure the ripple voltage across the output. We can see that is 1.02V, which is the maximum ripple we specified for the output.

A Full-Wave Rectifier Power Supply

We will briefly look at designing a full-wave rectifier that will produce a 10V output at 1A with an allowable ripple of 1V. To calculate the turns ratio of the transformer, we need to determine the peak voltage of the secondary output from the transformer. We can calculate this using:

$$Vsecpk = Vave + \frac{Vripple}{2} + 1.4$$

CHAPTER 6 THE AC VOLTAGE

Therefore:

$$Vsecpk = 10 + \frac{1}{2} + 1.4 = 11.9$$

Knowing the primary voltage will be the UK mains (the V_{pripk} = 339). Therefore, the turns ratio can be calculated as follows:

$$Turns\ Ratio = \frac{Vpripk}{Vsecpk} = \frac{339}{11.9} = 28.49$$

Using TINA, we have:

$$Turns\ Ratio = \frac{Vsecpk}{Vpripk} = \frac{11.9}{339} = 35.1m$$

We can calculate the value of the smoothing capacitor using the following:

$$C = i\frac{dt}{dV_C}$$

As this is full-wave rectification, the dt time will be approximately 8ms. Therefore, knowing that the dV_C is the allowable ripple voltage of 1V and the current I is 1A, we can calculate the value of the smoothing capacitor as follows:

$$C = 1 \times \frac{8m}{1} = 8mF$$

This is a large capacitor, but we are taking a lot of current from the power supply. The capacitor of this size would be an electrolytic type. The circuit for the full-wave rectifier with the smoothing capacitor is shown in Figure 6-27.

CHAPTER 6   THE AC VOLTAGE

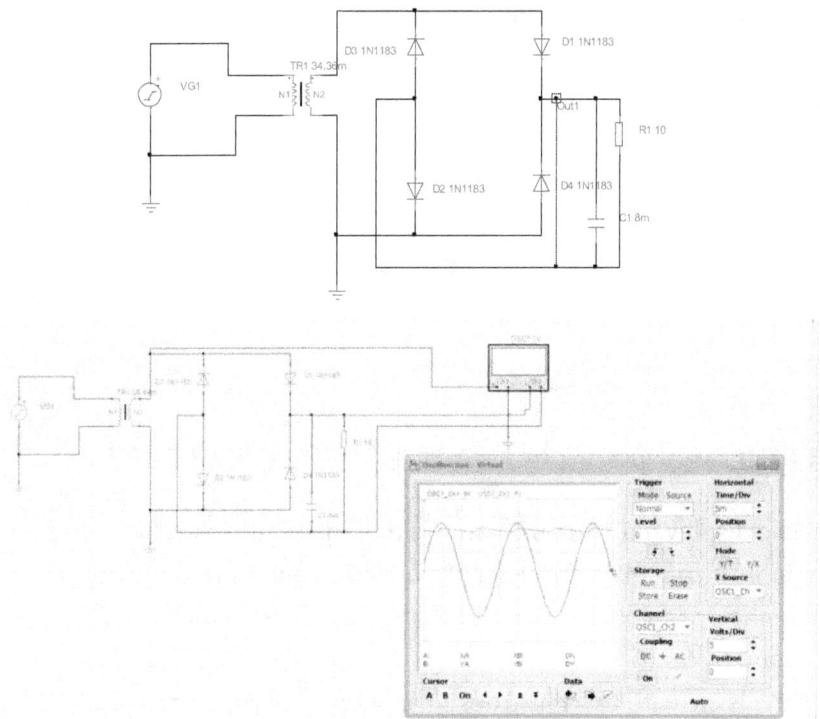

Figure 6-27. *The Full-Wave Rectifier with Smoothing Capacitor*

We are using the oscilloscope in TINA to measure the output voltage; this display is shown in Figure 6-28. The resistor value for R_1 has been calculated using Ohm's Law as follows, knowing the voltage was the 10V average and the current was the maximum of 1Amp:

$$I = \frac{V}{R} \therefore R = \frac{V}{I} = \frac{10}{1} = 10\Omega$$

355

CHAPTER 6   THE AC VOLTAGE

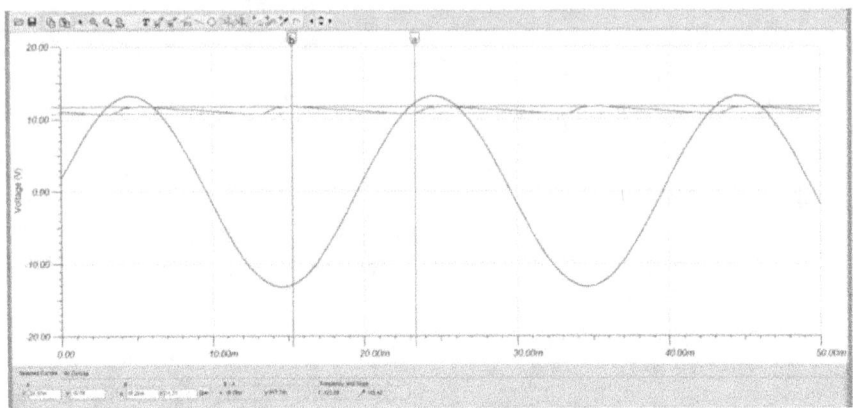

Figure 6-28. The Output Voltage of the Rectifier Circuit

The display in Figure 6-28 shows that the dt time is 8.08ms and that the ripple is 917.7mV. These results are close enough to confirm that the method of calculations we have used for these parameters is fairly accurate.

One issue with this basic design of a PSU is that, for high-power circuits, if the frequency is low at 50Hz, then the physical size of the transformer is quite large. It has been found that if we can rectify at higher frequencies for the same power level, the physical size of the transformer can be reduced. To accommodate this phenomenon, engineers rectify the mains directly at the peak of 339V. They then use chopper circuits to chop this rectified DC up at high frequencies, typically at 35kHz. This means that they can use small transformers to step down this chopped quasi-AC voltage to DC again with a second rectifier circuit. This is in essence how we get away with very small AC adapters to power mobile phones and other smart electrical equipment. This is a very specialised subject called SWMPS—*Switch Mode Powe Supplies*—and is definitely a book on its own.

Exercise 6.4

Design a full-wave rectifier circuit to meet the following specifications:

- The average voltage is 9V.
- The allowable ripple voltage is 100mV.
- The maximum current that can be taken from the supply is 100mA.

Summary

This chapter looked at why and how we generate the UK mains voltage. We studied what phasor diagrams are with respect to impedances and how to use complex numbers to represent phasors. We learnt what complex numbers are and how to represent them in rectangular and polar formats. We learnt how to multiply and divide complex numbers. We studied how to use complex numbers to represent the impedance of RL and RC circuits.

We then went on to look at rectification, studying why we do it and how the two basic forms of half-wave and full-wave rectification are achieved.

In the next chapter, we use complex numbers to represent RLC circuits. You learn what the RLC circuit is and why it is one of the most important circuits in audio electronics.

I hope you have found this chapter informative and useful and you are happy to move on to Chapter 7.

Answers to Exercise 6.1

The RL Circuit

CHAPTER 6 THE AC VOLTAGE

Set	X_L	Z_T	i	v_R	v_L
A	100⟨90⟩	103.08⟨75.96⟩	137.19E^{-3}⟨−75.96⟩	3.43⟨−75.96⟩	13.72⟨14.06⟩
B	30⟨90⟩	33.541⟨63.435⟩	2.53⟨−63.435⟩	37.95⟨−63.435⟩	75.89⟨26.57⟩
C	100⟨90⟩	101.98⟨78.69⟩	693.38E^{-3}⟨−78.69⟩	13.87⟨−78.69⟩	69.34⟨11.31⟩

The RC Circuit

Set	X_C	Z_T	i	v_R	v_C
A	75⟨−90⟩	79.059⟨−71.57⟩	178.8E^{-3}⟨71.57⟩	4.47⟨71.57⟩	13.416⟨−18.43⟩
B	125⟨−90⟩	125.897⟨−83.16⟩	673.99E^{-3}⟨83.16⟩	10.11⟨83.16⟩	84.25⟨−6.84⟩
C	10⟨−90⟩	22.36⟨−26.57⟩	3.16⟨26.56⟩	63.24⟨26.56⟩	31.62⟨−63.43⟩

Answers to Exercise 6.2

The Impedance Phasor Diagrams

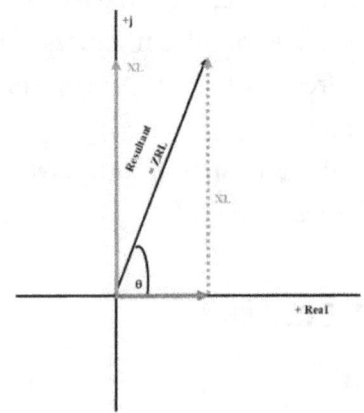

CHAPTER 6   THE AC VOLTAGE

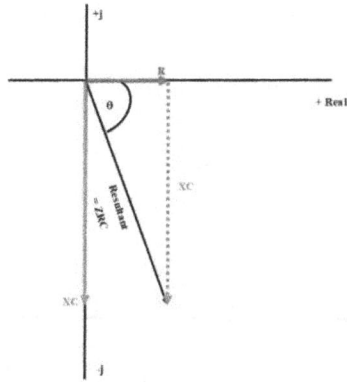

Answers to Exercise 6.3

The Voltage Phasor Diagrams

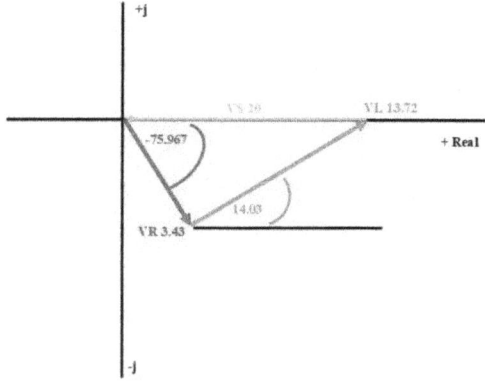

359

CHAPTER 6   THE AC VOLTAGE

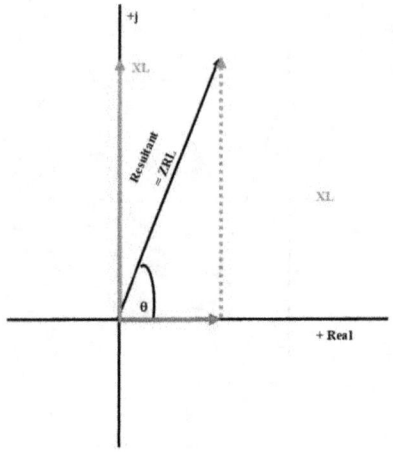

CHAPTER 7

The Series RLC Circuit

In this chapter, we are going to move on from the series RL and series RC circuits we looked at in Chapter 6, to look at the series RLC circuit. We will explain why this circuit is one of the most important audio circuits. We will learn about resonance, selectivity, Q, and bandwidth.

After reading this chapter, you will be able to design a series RLC circuit to tune to different radio frequencies.

The First Circuit in an Audio System

An audio system, be it a simple radio or a video system, that gets its information through radio waves needs a circuit at the front end of the system. That circuit must be able to tune into the particular signal that it wants from all the signals that find their way to the input of the system (i.e., the ariel, or antenna, of the system). A circuit that could be used at the front end of a radio could be some sort of series RLC circuit attached to the input. As you will see later in the chapter, the series RLC circuit can be very selective and can magnify the voltage at its input. A typical series RLC circuit is shown in Figure 7-1.

CHAPTER 7 THE SERIES RLC CIRCUIT

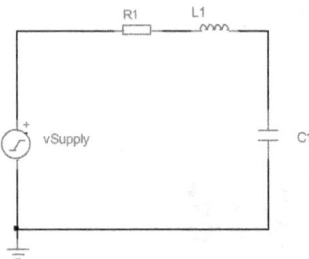

Figure 7-1. *A Typical Series RLC Circuit*

The supply voltage would normally be the induced signal at the ariel. The idea of the series RLC circuit is that it can select the one frequency the system wants from the many that arrive at the ariel. The circuit then operates at a maximum efficiency and increases the small voltage it receives at the ariel to be a more useful voltage at the output of the circuit with needing any power from a power supply. In most cases, the output is taken from across the capacitor.

The Resonant Frequency of the Series RLC Circuit

The RL and RC circuits we looked at in Chapter 6 were first-order circuits as they only have one energy storage device. With the RL, that was the inductor which stored the energy in the form of a magnetic field around the inductor. With the RC circuit, it was the capacitor that stored the energy on the form of a charge between its plates. However, with the RLC circuit, we have both energy storage devices, so this is a second-order system. The two energy storage devices swap the energy between themselves by one device taking all the energy then getting rid of it by passing the energy back to the other device. This passing of the energy between the two devices means that the current is flowing in alternating directions through the resistor. Every time the current passes through the resistor some energy

CHAPTER 7 THE SERIES RLC CIRCUIT

is lost. However, at the correct frequency, the resonant frequency of the circuit, enough energy is placed back into the circuit from the input to keep the circuit oscillating (i.e., passing this energy between the inductor and capacitor forever). We will investigate what happens if the resistance in the circuit was very low, ideally zero, later in this chapter.

We have stated that it is at the resonant frequency that the circuit is most efficient, so we need to know how to calculate this frequency of resonance. The energy that flows around the circuit is proportional to the current flowing in the circuit. This current will be a maximum when the total impedance of the circuit is at a minimum. The total impedance will be the phasor sum of the three impedances. That means we can say:

$$Z_T = (R + j0) + (0 + jX_L) + (0 - jX_C)$$

$$Z_T = R + jXL - jXC$$

In Chapter 6 we said the expression for X_L and X_C were:

$$X_L = j2\pi fL \text{ and } X_C = -j\frac{1}{2\pi fC}$$

In this chapter, we introduce the term ω. It is a shorthand way of writing $2\pi f$:

$$\omega = 2\pi f$$

This means we can express X_L and as follows:

$$X_L = j\omega L$$

Also, we can say this:

$$X_C = -j\frac{1}{\omega C}$$

CHAPTER 7   THE SERIES RLC CIRCUIT

Therefore, we can write the expression for Z_T as follows:

$$Z_T = R + j\omega L - j\frac{1}{\omega C}$$

Therefore, we can say:

$$Z_T = R + j\left(\omega L - \frac{1}{\omega C}\right)$$

The impedances X_L and X_C vary with frequency, but resistance R is a constant that does not change with frequency. We have said that the current will be a maximum when the impedance reaches a minimum. We can see from the expression for X_L and X_C that X_L increases from 0 to infinity as frequency varies from 0 to infinity, but X_C decreases from infinity to 0. This means that there will be one frequency when X_L must equal XC. This will be the resonant frequency, sometimes called the frequency of oscillation. At that frequency we can say the following:

$$\omega L - \frac{1}{\omega C} = 0$$

This means that the total impedance at that frequency will be equal to R, as X_L will be cancelled out by X_C.

Therefore, knowing that at the resonant frequency, we can say this:

$$\omega L = \frac{1}{\omega C}$$

If we divide both sides by ωL we can say this:

$$1 = \frac{1}{\omega L \times \omega C} = \frac{1}{\omega^2 LC}$$

CHAPTER 7 THE SERIES RLC CIRCUIT

Knowing $\omega = 2\pi f$ we can say this:

$$1 = \frac{1}{(2\pi f)^2 LC} = \frac{1}{4\pi^2 f_o^2 LC}$$

This means we can say this:

$$f_o^2 = \frac{1}{4\pi^2 LC}$$

Taking the square root of both sides, we can say this:

$$f_o = \frac{1}{2\pi\sqrt{LC}}$$

The term f_o is the frequency of oscillations. At this frequency X_L will equal X_C and the total impedance Z_T will be equal to the value of the resistance R.

Example 7.1

We will carry out an analysis of a series RLC circuit with the following values:

- V_{Supply} is 20V peak at a frequency of 1.5kHz.
- The value of the resistor is 15Ω.
- The value of inductance L_1 is 3.1831mH.
- The value of capacitance C_1 is 3.5368μF.

We will use these values to calculate the impedance of the reactive components and so draw the phasor diagram of the three impedances. We will then calculate the total impedance of the circuit, then the current flowing in the circuit, and then the voltages across each component.

CHAPTER 7 THE SERIES RLC CIRCUIT

First, the impedance of the inductor and the capacitor:

$$X_L = \omega L = 2\pi fL = 2\pi \times 1.5E^3 \times 3.1831E^{-3} = 30\,\Omega$$

$$X_C = \frac{1}{\omega C} = \frac{1}{2\pi fC} = \frac{1}{2\pi \times 1.5E^3 \times 3.5368E^{-6}} = 30\,\Omega$$

We can express each impedance in complex form so that we can draw them on the phasor diagram.

The resistance phasor can be expressed as follows:

$$R = R + j0 = 15 + j0\,\Omega$$

The inductance impedance phasor can be expressed as follows:

$$X_L = 0 + j\omega L = 0 + j30\,\Omega$$

The capacitance impedance phasor can be expressed as follows:

$$X_C = 0 - j\frac{1}{\omega C} = 0 - j30\,\Omega$$

Now we can construct the impedance phasor diagram, starting with the resistance. This has a real part of 15 but no j part. This means that the phasor sits on the + real axis only, at a length of 15. The inductive impedance has no real part and only a +j part of 30. This means that the phasor goes vertically up the +j axis a length of 30. The capacitive impedance also has no real part and only a -j part of 30. This means that it goes vertically down the -j axis a length of 30. The phasor diagram is shown in Figure 7-2.

CHAPTER 7   THE SERIES RLC CIRCUIT

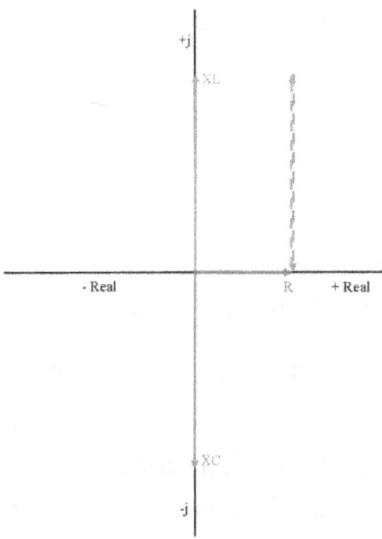

Figure 7-2. *The Impedance Phasor diagram*

The three phasors are shown in Figure 7-2. The phasor diagram also shows what happens when we add the three phasors together. First, we walk the length of the resistance phasor. Then we turn through 90° to get ready to walk vertically upward the length of the inductive impedance phasor. Next, we turn through 180° as X_C is 180° out of phase with the X_L phasor. Now we walk the length of the capacitive impedance phasor. As the X_L and X_C phasors are both the same length we end up back at the very end of the resistance phasor. All that is left to do in adding the three phasors together is to walk directly back to the origin. This would take us back directly the length of the resistance phasor. This means that the resultant of the phasor addition is the length of the resistance phasor. This means at this particular frequency, the total impedance is just the value of the resistor, which in this case is 15Ω. Also, the phase associated with the total impedance is 0°.

CHAPTER 7   THE SERIES RLC CIRCUIT

This result can be confirmed by using complex numbers to calculate the total impedance of the circuit at this frequency of 1.5kHz. This can be done as follows:

$$Z_T = R + j\left(\omega L - \frac{1}{\omega C}\right)$$

Putting the values is gives the following:

$$Z_T = 15 + j(30-30) = 15 + j0 \, \Omega$$

This agrees with the phasor addition shown in Figure 7-2. Also, when we convert the expression for the total impedance from rectangular to polar, we get:

$$15 + j0 = \sqrt{15^2 + 0^2} \left\langle Tan^{-1}\left(\frac{0}{15}\right)\right\rangle = 15\langle 0°\rangle \, \Omega$$

This also agrees with the position of the resistance phasor in Figure 7-2. This means that the frequency of 1.5kHz must be the resonant frequency, as the impedance can go no lower than just the resistance value. We can check this by calculating the frequency of oscillation, or resonance, using the following:

$$f_o = \frac{1}{2\pi\sqrt{LC}}$$

Putting the values in gives this:

$$f_o = \frac{1}{2\pi\sqrt{3.1831E^{-3} \times 3.5368E^{-6}}} = 1.5kHz$$

CHAPTER 7   THE SERIES RLC CIRCUIT

This confirms that the circuit is at resonance. We can now calculate the current flowing through the circuit. This can be done using the following:

$$i = \frac{v_{Supply}}{Z_T} = \frac{14.142\langle 0°\rangle}{15\langle 0°\rangle} = 942.809E^{-3}\langle 0°\rangle \text{ Amps}$$

Note that we are using the RMS value of the v_{Supply} as you should always use the RMS in most of your calculations. Now we can calculate the voltages across the three components.

The voltage across the resistor can be calculated using the following:

$$v_R = ir = \left(942.809E^{-3}\langle 0°\rangle\right) \times \left(15\langle 0°\rangle\right) = 14.142\langle 0°\rangle v$$

The voltage across the inductor can be calculated using:

$$v_L = iX_L = \left(942.809E^{-3}\langle 0°\rangle\right) \times \left(30\langle 90°\rangle\right) = 28.284\langle 90°\rangle v$$

The voltage across the capacitor can be calculated using the following:

$$v_C = iX_C = \left(942.809E^{-3}\langle 0°\rangle\right) \times \left(30\langle -90°\rangle\right) = 28.284\langle -90°\rangle v$$

This seems impossible as the volt drops around the circuit are more than the voltage applied to the circuit. We will see later that this is the Q or quality factor of the series circuit. Before that, we will use KVL to show that these calculations are correct. We know that, using KVL, we can say:

$$v_{Supply} = v_R + v_L + v_C$$

However, this is a phasor sum. Therefore, as we can only add complex numbers in their rectangular format, it might have been better to calculate the voltage using rectangular format. We will do that now. The voltage across the resistor is as follows:

$$v_R = \left(942.809E^{-3} + j0\right)\left(15 + j0\right)v$$

369

CHAPTER 7   THE SERIES RLC CIRCUIT

This gives us the following:

$$v_R = (942.809E^{-3} \times 15) + (942.809E^{-3} \times j0) + (j0 \times 15) + (j0 \times j0)$$

This gives us the following:

$$v_R = 14.142 + j0\, v$$

The voltage across the inductor is as follows:

$$v_L = (942.809E^{-3} + j0)(0 + j30)$$

This gives us the following:

$$v_L = (942.809E^{-3} \times 0) + (942.809E^{-3} \times j30) + (j0 \times 0) + (j0 \times j30)$$

This gives us the following:

$$v_L = 0 + j28.284\, v$$

The voltage across the capacitor is as follows:

$$v_C = (942.809E^{-3} + j0)(0 - j30)$$

This gives us the following:

$$v_L = (942.809E^{-3} \times 0) + (942.809E^{-3} \times -j30) + (j0 \times 0) + (j0 \times -j30)$$

This gives us the following:

$$v_C = 0 - j28.284\, v$$

Now we can add the three phasors together and use KVL to confirm the calculations. This is done as follows:

$$14.142 + j0 = (14.142 + j0) + (0 + j28.284) + (0 - j28.284)$$

This gives us the following:

$$14.142 + j0 = (14.142 + 0 + 0) + j(0 + 28.284 - 28.284) = 14.142 + j0 \, v$$

This confirms our calculations. For further confirmation, you can simulate the circuit shown in Figure 7-3.

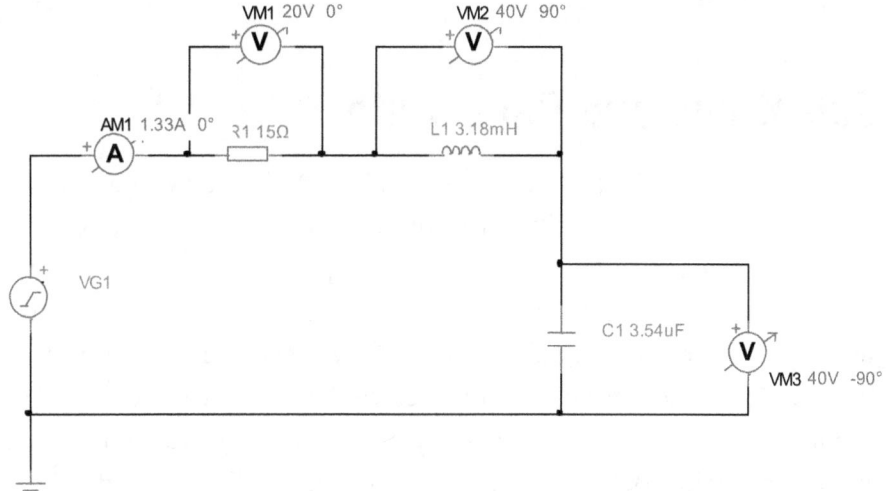

Figure 7-3. *The Simulation of the Series RLC Circuit for Example 1*

You must remember that the meters display the peak values, not the RMS. However, after dividing the magnitude of the meter reading by $\sqrt{2}$, we get the same results as the values we calculated.

We can now make some statements about the resonance of the series RLC circuit:

- When at resonance, the impedance reduces to a minimum at the value of the resistance R.

CHAPTER 7   THE SERIES RLC CIRCUIT

- The current will be at a maximum and it will be in phase with the supply voltage.

- The magnitude of the impedance of X_L will equal the magnitude of the impedance of X_C.

- The voltage across the capacitor or inductor will be greater than the supply voltage.

- This is the voltage magnification or Q factor of the series RLC circuit.

Selectivity and Bandwidth

The main use of this series RLC circuit is to select the wanted frequency from the many frequencies that are present at the ariel. The means we need to understand how to control which frequencies the circuit selects. We have shown that the circuit would be most efficient when it receives signals at its resonant frequency or frequency of oscillation. However, it is impossible to design a circuit that receives just the one frequency. The circuit will also respond to some of another, if not all the frequencies, that are present at the ariel. However, it is the degree of efficiency that defines how the circuit responds to the resonant frequency and all the other frequencies. This concept can be investigated by sweeping the circuit with a large range of frequencies and measuring its response to this sweep of frequencies. TINA give us an AC Analysis option that we can use to sweep the circuit with a range of frequencies and display how the various voltages and currents change with frequency. Figure 7-4 shows us how we can select the AC Transfer Characteristics from the AC Analysis drop-down option from the Analysis tab on the main menu bar. We will use this option to show how the circuit responds over a range of frequencies.

CHAPTER 7   THE SERIES RLC CIRCUIT

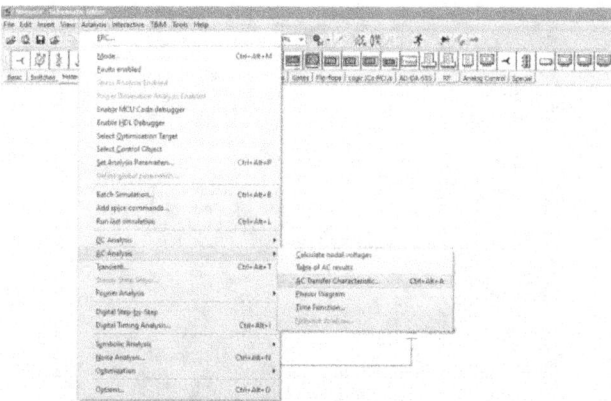

Figure 7-4. The AC Transfer Characteristics Option from the AC Analysis

To use the AC Transfer Characteristics, we must add the voltage or current meters to measure the response of interest. We will use the analysis to show how the current taken from the supply varies with frequency. This means we need to set up the circuit as shown in Figure 7-5.

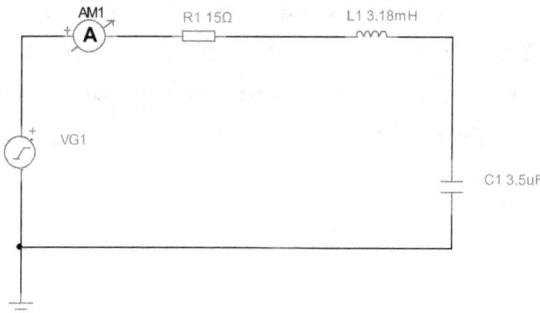

Figure 7-5. The RLC Test Circuit for the Signal Analyser

Now that we have set up the circuit, we must select the AC Transfer Characteristics, as shown in Figure 7-4. When we do that, we get the AC Transfer Characteristics window, as shown in Figure 7-6.

373

CHAPTER 7   THE SERIES RLC CIRCUIT

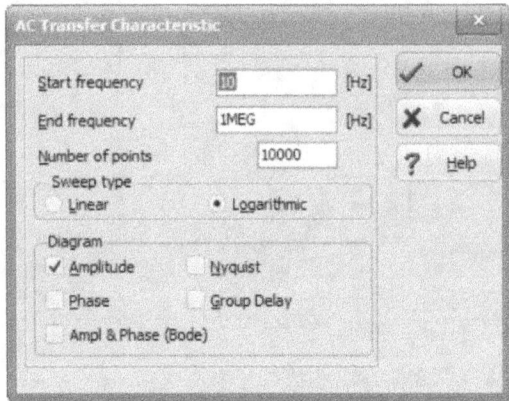

Figure 7-6. *The AC Transfer Characteristics Window*

I changed the number of points from the default 100 to 10000. This is to ensure that we get an accurate response from the simulation and don't miss the important frequencies. We are only really interested in amplitude or actual value of the measurement, so I selected that option here. We can leave the start and end frequency at their default settings and the sweep type to logarithmic. Once you are happy with the settings, click OK to start the simulation. You don't need to set up a particular input voltage for VG1, as this simulation sets up its own AC input voltage with a peak value of 1V. It then applies this input voltage whilst changing the frequency from 10Hz to 1MHz. When the simulation is finished, you will be presented with a display as shown in Figure 7-7.

CHAPTER 7   THE SERIES RLC CIRCUIT

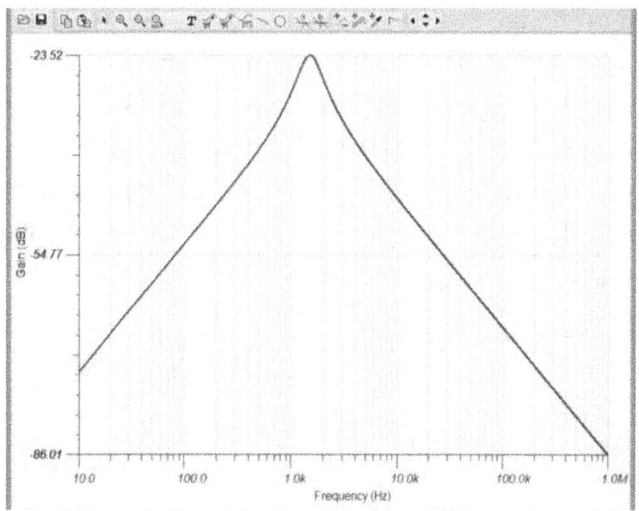

Figure 7-7. *The Default Display from the AC Transfer Simulation*

The default display is not what we want for this analysis. We need to change the vertical axis. To do that, double click the Gain (dB) option on the display. When you do that, you'll get the Set Axis window, as shown in Figure 7-8.

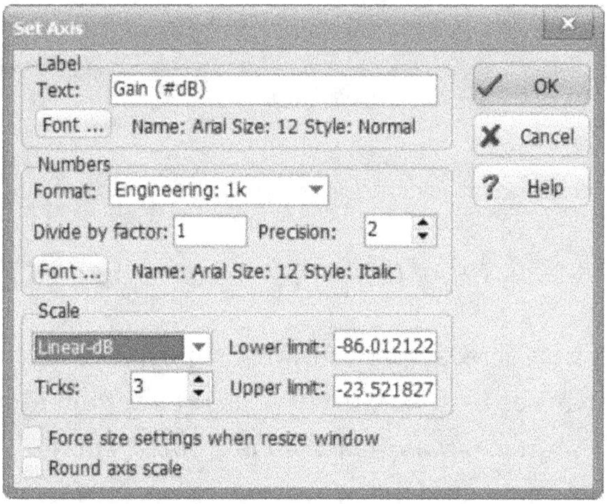

Figure 7-8. *The Set Axis Window*

375

CHAPTER 7   THE SERIES RLC CIRCUIT

We need to change the Scale option from the default setting of Linear-dB to just Linear. Do clicking the small down arrow next to the window. Then select Linear from the options that appear. Make sure the two boxes labelled Force Size Setting When Resize Window and Round Axis Scale remain unticked. We can change the Label text from the default Gain (#dB) to Current Amps. Then click OK; the display should change to what's shown in Figure 7-9.

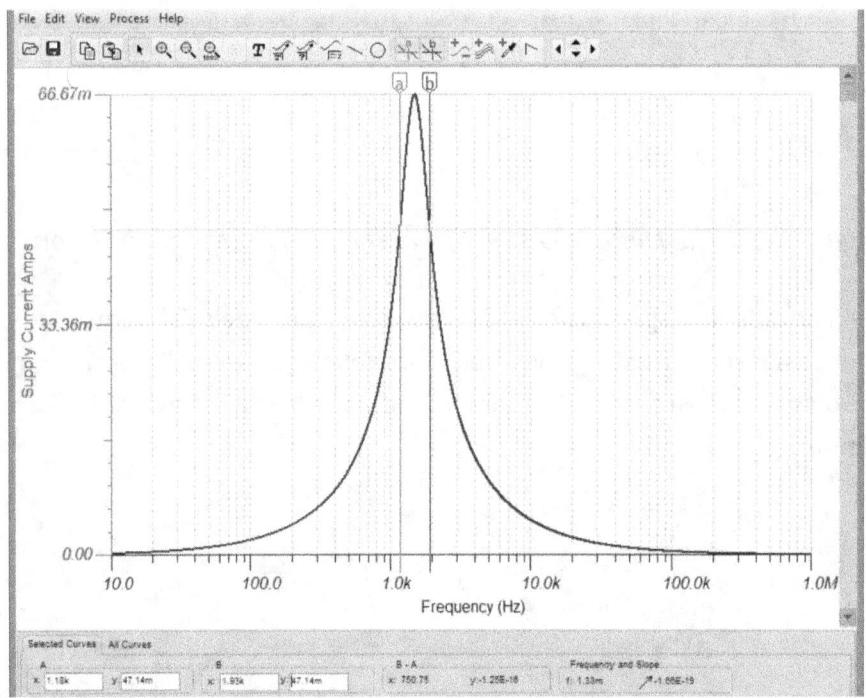

***Figure 7-9.** The Display of the Supply Current Against Frequency*

The display now shows clearly how the supply current changes with frequency. We can see that the current peaks at a certain frequency. Using the cursor, this frequency was measured at 1.5kHz. This is the resonant frequency for the circuit and the measured frequency was the same as the calculated value. However, in the display in Figure 7-9, we are using the two cursors to measure the bandwidth of the circuit.

376

CHAPTER 7   THE SERIES RLC CIRCUIT

The Bandwidth and Selectivity of the Series RLC Circuit

I have stated that it is impossible to design a circuit that will select just one frequency from all those that are captured by the ariel. However, the signal that is captured by the aerial must be of sufficient strength to be of use to the rest of the circuit. That begs the question what *sufficient* strength is. The industry uses the benchmark of half power point to define what a sufficient strength is. If we use dBs as with gain, then the half power point would be when the gain had fallen by 3dBs from the maximum gain. This is generally referred to as the -3dB point. When we use current or voltage to define the half power point, it would be when the current or voltage had fallen to 0.7071 of the maximum value. As the current rises and falls, there will be two frequencies at which the current has fallen to 0.7071 of the maximum value. The maximum value of the current would be when the impedance of the circuit has fallen to its minimum value of just R. This would be at the resonant frequency. In this case that would be when $Z_T = 15\Omega$. Therefore, the value of the maximum current would be:

$$i_{peak} = \frac{1}{15} = 66.667E^{-3} = 66.667mA$$

This agrees with the peak of the display shown in Figure 7-9. Therefore, the two half power points would be at the frequency when the current had fallen to this:

$$half\ power\ point\ current = 0.7071 \times 66.667E^{-3} = 47.14mA$$

I placed cursor a at the low frequency when the current reaches this value and cursor b at the high frequency. The difference between the high and low frequency is what is termed the *bandwidth* of the circuit. This is shown in the display of Figure 7-9 as B-A = 750.75 Hz. The actual range of frequency at which the circuit receives enough power is from 1.18kHz to

377

CHAPTER 7   THE SERIES RLC CIRCUIT

1.93kHz. This means that this series RLC circuit will be able to hear any signal that has a frequency within that range. This range of frequencies is what is termed the *bandwidth of the circuit."* The effect of this bandwidth can be explained by the following example.

Assume Radio 1 transmits at 1.5kHz (this is only an example it's not the actual frequency for Radio 1). This RLC circuit would be able to respond to that station. Now, let's assume that Radio 4 transmits at 1.7kHz. That would cause a problem, as 1.7kHz is within the band of frequencies that this RLC circuit can respond to. We either have to reduce the bandwidth of this circuit or ensure that no other station can transmit at a frequency between 1.18kHz to 1.93kHz.

We can try reducing the resistance in the circuit, as this would not affect the resonant frequency of the circuit, but it might reduce the bandwidth. When we did that and simulated the circuit, the AC display of the current is shown in Figure 7-10.

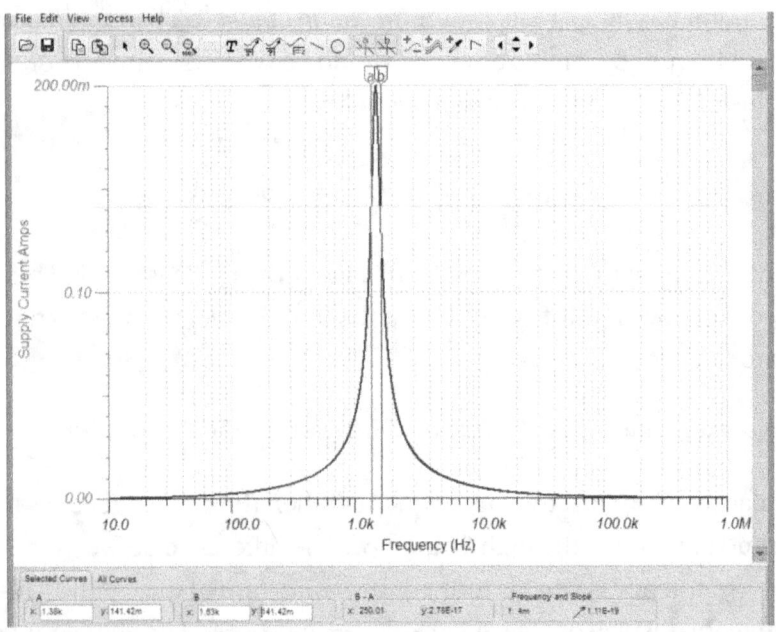

Figure 7-10. *The Resistance Reduced to 5Ω*

CHAPTER 7 THE SERIES RLC CIRCUIT

The maximum current was now increased to:

$$i_{Peak} = \frac{1}{5} = 200mA$$

The two half power points were when:

$$i_{half\ power} = 0.7071 \times 200mA = 141.42mA$$

The bandwidth has now been reduced to:

$$BW = 1.63E^3 - 1.38E^3 = 250.01Hz$$

I hope you can see that as the bandwidth has been reduced, then the selectivity of the circuit (i.e., the ability to select just a few frequencies) has been improved. Indeed, the circuit would now receive only Radio 1, as Radio 4 is outside the band of frequencies at which the circuit gets at least half the maximum power. I hope this explains the importance of bandwidth and selectivity of this type of circuit.

The Quality Factor Q in a Series RLC Circuit

The voltage levels that arrive at the ariel of a radio receiver would be very low, in the order of millivolts. That means that we would want to increase the voltage before passing it onto the rest of the circuit. Normally, that would involve some sort of amplification, but that would take power from the supply so that it could add it to the signal. That would be an extra power requirement and not the most efficient solution.

The series RLC circuit has a magical quality termed the *Q factor*. In the series circuit, this would produce some voltage magnification across one of the reactive components. The output is normally taken from across the capacitor, so we will use the AC Analysis option to look at how the voltage across the capacitor changes with frequency. The circuit we will use for

CHAPTER 7   THE SERIES RLC CIRCUIT

this simulation is shown in Figure 7-5, but with the ammeter removed. The AC Analysis supplies the circuit with a 1V source but sweeps the frequency over a range of frequencies set by you. The display from the AC Transfer Characteristics is shown in Figure 7-11.

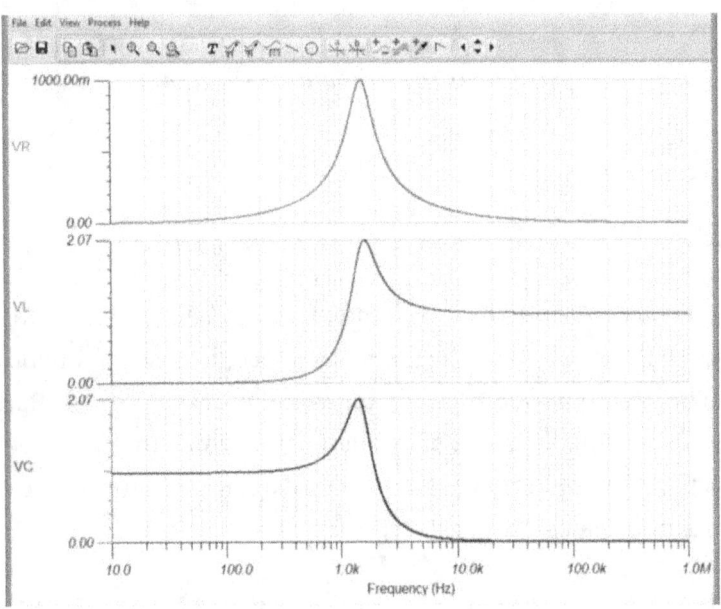

Figure 7-11. The Three Volt Drops

The waveforms in Figure 7-11 show that, at the low frequencies, all the supply voltage is dropped across the capacitor at 1V until we get to about 200Hz. This is because at the low frequencies, the capacitor has the highest impedance. In fact, at DC, which has a frequency of 0, the impedance of the capacitor is at infinity. As the frequency increases, the impedance of the capacitor reduces. We can see that at the high frequencies above around 4kHz, the inductor is taking all the supply voltage. This is because at the higher frequencies, the inductor has the highest impedance. Between the frequencies of around 200Hz to 4kHz, we can see that the voltage across the resistor steadily increases until at the resonant frequency all the 1V from the supply is dropped across the resistor.

CHAPTER 7 THE SERIES RLC CIRCUIT

However, we can see that at the resonant frequency, the voltage across the capacitor equals the voltage across the inductor at 2V. This would suggest that we have 5V in total, which according to KVL is not possible. However, the voltage across the capacitor is in total anti-phase with the voltage across the inductor and so has a phasor quantity, which is what they are—they cancel out and so we are left with the 1V across the resistor. However, at the resonant frequency, the circuit has now provided us with 2V across the capacitor or the inductor. This means we have magnified the supply voltage of 1v by a factor of 2. All this is done without taking power from the supply. This is the voltage magnification of the series RLC circuit, and it comes about because of the phase difference in the two reactive components. This is the Q factor of the series RLC circuit.

We will see if changing the resistor affects the Q. Note that we can't change either L or C as we don't want to change the resonant frequency. Reducing the resistance to 5Ω gives the display shown in Figure 7-12.

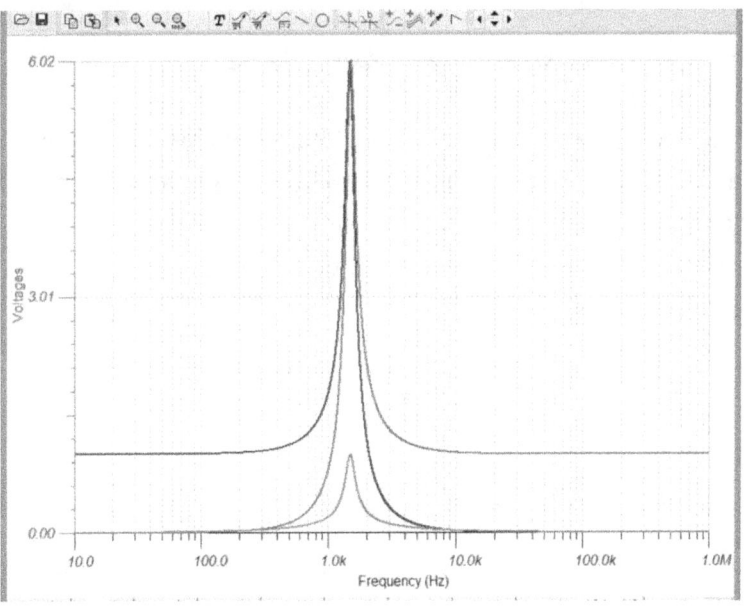

Figure 7-12. *The Resistance Reduced to 5Ω*

CHAPTER 7   THE SERIES RLC CIRCUIT

We can see that the voltage across the capacitor and inductor have increased to 6V and the resonant frequency has not changed. This would suggest that the Q has increased. If we now increase the value of resistance to 45Ω, we get the waveforms shown in Figure 7-13.

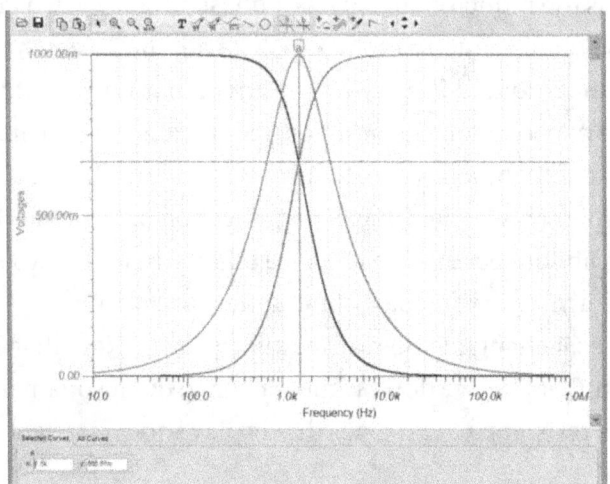

Figure 7-13. *The Resistance Increased to 45Ω*

Figure 7-13 shows that when R was 45Ω, the voltage across the capacitor and inductor was around 666.67mv, an actual attenuation. This means that the quality factor Q is inversely proportional to resistance. Knowing that Q is the voltage magnification in the series RLC circuit, we can say the following:

$$Q = \frac{v_C}{v_{in}} = \frac{v_L}{v_{in}}$$

At resonance, we can say the following:

$$v_{in} = v_R = iR$$

We can express V_L as follows:

$$v_L = i\omega L$$

This means that we can say the following:

$$Q = \frac{i\omega L}{iR} = \frac{\omega L}{R}$$

Using the values in Example 7.1, we know that:

$$\omega L = 30 \text{ therefore } Q = \frac{30}{15} = 2$$

When R was reduced to 5Ω we have the following:

$$Q = \frac{30}{5} = 6$$

When R was increased to 45Ω we have the following:

$$Q = \frac{30}{45} = 0.66667$$

The values agree with the simulated results.

We have already shown that the bandwidth is related to the resistance of the circuit in a similar way to Q. Also, the selectivity of the circuit is related to the Q. The relationship between them is:

- When Q increases, the bandwidth reduces and the selectivity increases.
- When Q decreases, the bandwidth increases and the selectivity reduces.

CHAPTER 7 THE SERIES RLC CIRCUIT

The bandwidth is the range of frequencies centred on the resonant frequency f_o. By varying Q, as we have just done, we have shown that Bandwidth BW is inversely proportional to Q. We can express this as follows:

$$BW \propto \frac{1}{Q}$$

The constant that can be associated with BW is the resonant frequency given the symbol f_o frequency of oscillation. Therefore, if we replace the proportional sign with this constant of proportionality, we can say this:

$$BW = \frac{f_o}{Q} = \frac{f_o}{\frac{\omega L}{R}} = \frac{f_o}{1} \div \frac{\omega L}{R} = \frac{f_o}{1} \times \frac{R}{\omega L}$$

We are only really concerned with the Q and BW at resonance, which means:

$$\omega L = 2\pi f_o L$$

Therefore, we can say the following:

$$BW = \frac{f_o}{1} \times \frac{R}{2\pi f_o L}$$

This then gives us an expression for bandwidth as follows:

$$BW = \frac{R}{2\pi L}$$

When R is 15Ω, then BW is follows:

$$BW = \frac{15}{2\pi \times 3.1831 E^{-3}} = 750 \; correct$$

When R is reduced to 5Ω:

$$BW = \frac{5}{2\pi \times 3.1831E^{-3}} = 250 \text{ correct}$$

When R is increased to 45Ω:

$$BW = \frac{45}{2\pi \times 3.1831E^{-3}} = 2.25k \text{ correct}$$

In all these calculations the values of inductance L and capacitance C are unchanged and so the resonant frequency does not change. Also, the supply voltage was kept at 14.142V.

Example 7.2

In this next example we analyse the series RLC circuit when the frequency of supply is different from the resonant frequency. The circuit for this analysis is shown in Figure 7-14.

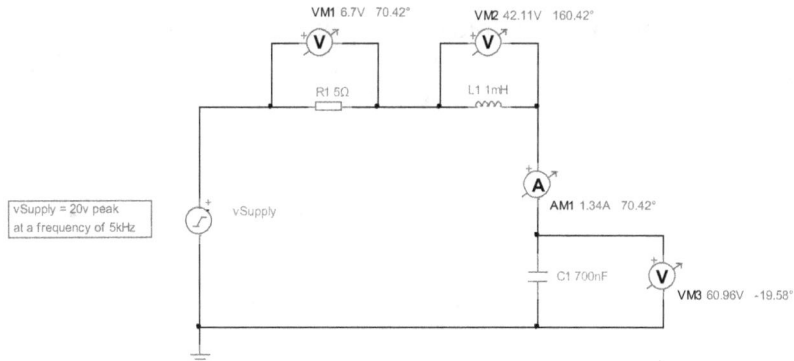

Figure 7-14. *The Circuit for Example 7.2*

CHAPTER 7   THE SERIES RLC CIRCUIT

We will confirm all the meter readings by calculations and draw the impedance phasor and voltage phasor diagrams. The impedance of the inductor and capacitor is as follows:

$$X_L = 2\pi fL = 2\pi \times 5E^3 \times 1E^{-3} = 31.4159 \, \Omega$$

$$X_C = \frac{1}{2\pi fC} = \frac{1}{2\pi \times 5E^3 \times 700E^{-9}} = 45.4728 \, \Omega$$

We can now calculate the total impedance using the following:

$$Z_T = R + j(X_L - X_C) = 5 + j(31.4159 - 45.4728) = 5 - j14.0569$$

Convert this to polar so it's ready to calculate the current:

$$Z_T = \sqrt{5^2 + (-14.0569^2)} \left\langle Tan^{-1}\left(\frac{-14.0569}{5}\right)\right\rangle$$

Therefore:

$$Z_T = 14.9197 \langle -70.4197 \rangle \, \Omega$$

We need to calculate the RMS supply voltage:

$$v_{Supply} = \frac{20}{\sqrt{2}} 14.142 \langle 0 \rangle v$$

Now we can calculate the current using the following formula:

$$i = \frac{v_{Supply}}{Z_T} = \frac{14.142 \langle 0^o \rangle}{14.9197 \langle -70.4197^o \rangle} = 947.8743E^{-3} \langle 70.4197^o \rangle \, Amps$$

The voltage across the resistor is.

$$v_R = i \times R = \left(947.8743E^{-3} \langle 70.4197^o \rangle\right)\left(5\langle 0^o \rangle\right) = 4.7394 \langle 70.4197^o \rangle v$$

CHAPTER 7 THE SERIES RLC CIRCUIT

The voltage across the inductor is as follows:

$$v_L = i \times X_L = \left(947.8743E^{-3} \langle 70.4197° \rangle\right)\left(31.4159 \langle 90° \rangle\right) = 29.7783 \langle 160.4197° \rangle v$$

The voltage across the capacitor is as follows:

$$v_C = i \times X_C = \left(947.8743E^{-3} \langle 70.4197° \rangle\right)\left(45.4728 \langle -90° \rangle\right)$$
$$= 43.1025 \langle -19.5803° \rangle v$$

If we convert these voltages to rectangular, we can add them to confirm the calculations using KVL.

Convert the voltage across the resistor:

$$v_R = 4.7394 \langle 70.4197° \rangle = 4.7394 \cos(70.4197°) + j4.734 \sin(70.4197°)$$

Therefore:

$$v_R = 1.5883 + j4.4653 \, v$$

Convert the voltage across the inductor:

$$v_L = 29.7783 \langle 160.4197 \rangle = 29.7783 \cos(160.4197) + j29.7783 \sin(160.4197)$$

Therefore:

$$v_L = -28.056 + j9.979 \, v$$

Convert the voltage across the capacitor:

$$v_C = 43.1025 \langle -19.5803° \rangle = 43.1025 \cos(-19.5803°)$$
$$+ j43.1025 \sin(-19.5803°)$$

Therefore:

$$v_C = 40.61 - j14.4448 \, v$$

CHAPTER 7   THE SERIES RLC CIRCUIT

We can now add these together to confirm what KVL says:

$$v_{Supply} = (1.5883 + j4.4653) + (-28.056 + j9.98869) + (40.61 - j14.4448)$$

This gives us the following:

$$v_{Supply} = 14.142 + j3.147E^{-5} \; v$$

This is very close to the 14.142+j0V it should be.

Now we can draw the phasor diagrams. The impedance phasor diagram is shown in Figure 7-15.

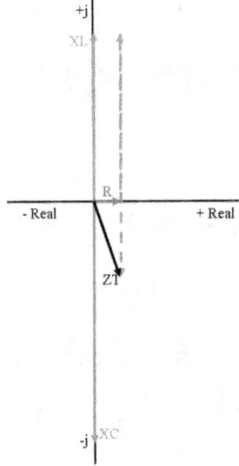

Figure 7-15. *The Impedance Phasor*

Figure 7-15 shows that because the X_C phasor is greater than the X_L phasor, we end up below the horizontal and the resultant phasor is longer than the resistance phasor. Also, we can see that its angle is negative with respect to the reference + real axis. This does seem to agree with the complex polar representation for Z_T, which stated.

$$Z_T = 14.9197 \, \angle -70.4197 \, \Omega$$

CHAPTER 7 THE SERIES RLC CIRCUIT

The voltage phasor diagram is shown in Figure 7-16.

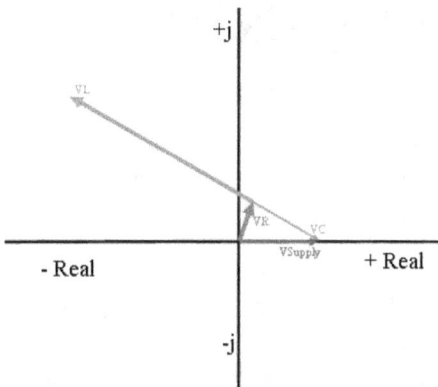

Figure 7-16. *The Voltage Phasor Diagram*

Figure 7-16 shows the result of adding the three voltage phasors together. We start by going the length of the v_R phasor. We then turn in the direction of the v_L phasor. This turns us through 90° with respect to the position of the v_R phasor. We then walk the length of the v_L phasor. Then we turn in the direction of the v_C phasor. This will mean we turn through 180° with respect to the position of the v_L phasor. When we get to the end of the v_C phasor, we end up on the horizontal + real axis. The shortest route back to the origin will now represent the v_{Supply} phasor. This confirms that KVL still applies to AC circuits when we add the voltage phasors on a phasor diagram. However, I am sure you can see that it is quicker and easier to use complex numbers to add the three voltages together and confirm KVL still applies to the AC series RLC circuit. I hope you are now happy to use complex numbers to represent phasor quantities and that when you get used to using them, you will agree that they are not all that complex. However, saying you can work with complex numbers sounds very clever, doesn't it.

CHAPTER 7   THE SERIES RLC CIRCUIT

The Parallel Circuit at Resonance and Dynamic Impedance

Example 7.3

We can now move onto the parallel RLC circuit. The circuit we will look at is shown in Figure 7-17.

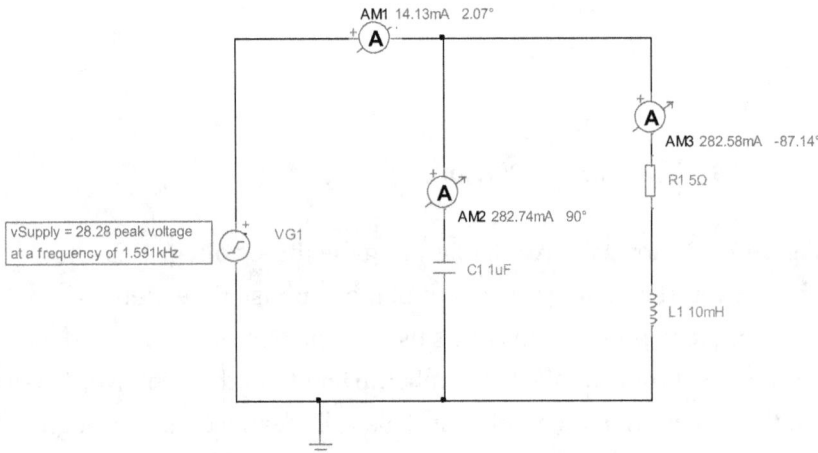

Figure 7-17. *The Parallel RLC Circuit*

To understand what resonance is and the impedance of the parallel RLC circuit, termed dynamic impedance Z_D is, we need to look at the phasor diagram for the three currents in the circuit. The three currents are:

- The supply current, i_{Supply}
- The current through the capacitor, i_C
- The current through the R and L path, i_{RL}

A phasor diagram, or argand diagram, needs a reference and the reference is the supply voltage v_{Supply}.

CHAPTER 7   THE SERIES RLC CIRCUIT

As the capacitor through which i_C flows is ideal, then at all frequencies i_C will lead v_{Supply} by 90°. This means that i_C will always be vertically up on the phasor diagram.

The current i_{RL} would, were it not for the resistor, be flowing through a pure inductor and so it would lag the supply voltage by 90. This would mean that it would go down the vertical axis on the phasor diagram. However, the resistor prevents this from happening. If i_{RL} was to flow through a resistor without the inductor, then the current would be in phase with v_{Supply}. However, the resistor and inductor combine their effects on the phase of the current, depending upon the ratio of their impedances. When the resistor is more dominant i_{RL} is more in phase with v_{Supply}. When the inductor is more dominant i_{RL} tends to lag v_{Supply} more closely to 90°. The impedance of the inductor, X_L, is frequency dependant. At low frequencies X_L is small and so the resistor dominates. At high frequencies X_L is high and so it dominates. This effect is shown in the current phasor diagrams shown in Figures 7-18 and 7-19.

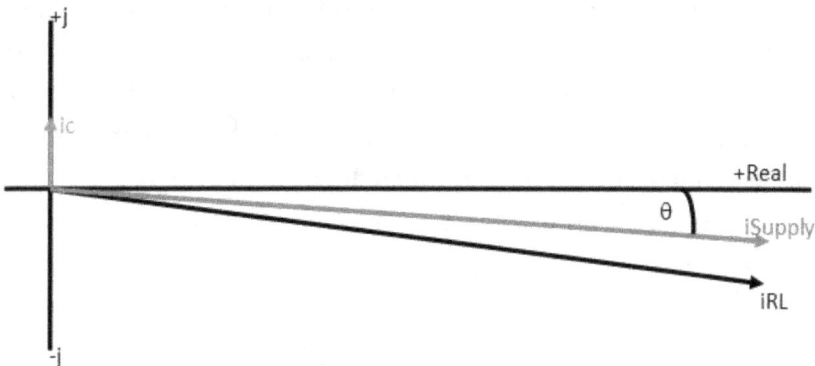

Figure 7-18. *The Current Phasors at Low Frequencies*

Figure 7-18 is the phasor diagram at low frequency and Figure 7-19 is the phasor diagram at high frequency.

CHAPTER 7   THE SERIES RLC CIRCUIT

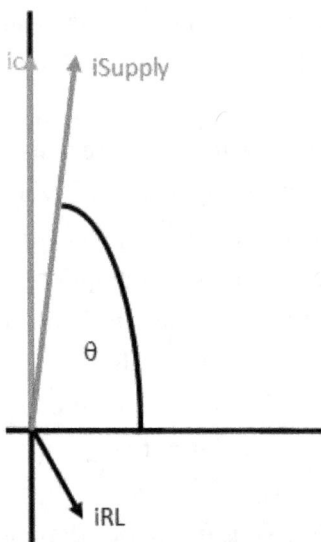

Figure 7-19. *The Current Phasors at High Frequencies*

Figures 7-18 and 7-19 show that the phasor for the supply current goes from lagging the supply voltage at the low frequencies to leading the supply at the high frequencies. This is because at the low frequencies the impedance of the capacitor is high and so very little current flows through the capacitor. Yet at these low frequencies the impedance of the inductor is low and so a lot of current flows through the I_{RL} branch of the circuit. At the high frequencies, the opposite is true. The fact that the supply current goes from lagging to leading means that at some frequency the supply current will be in phase with the supply voltage. This will be when the circuit is said to be at *resonance*, that is, when the supply current is in phase with the supply voltage. This agrees with the definition of resonance for the series RLC circuit.

The more interesting phasor diagram is shown in Figure 7-20. This is when the circuit is at resonance. Note that, although the quantities in all the phasor diagrams are not to scale, the diagram in Figure 7-20 shows that the supply current has fallen to its lowest level. Also, the supply current

CHAPTER 7 THE SERIES RLC CIRCUIT

is in phase with the supply voltage, which is the condition for resonance. The current i_{RL}, is still not purely inductive because of the resistance of the wire in the inductor. The other interesting fact is that both i_{RL} and i_C are larger than the supply current i_{Supply}. This is due to the Q factor or current magnification of the parallel circuit. The angle β, in Figure 7-20, by which i_{RL} lags the supply voltage, is because the resistor and inductor make up a series RL circuit.

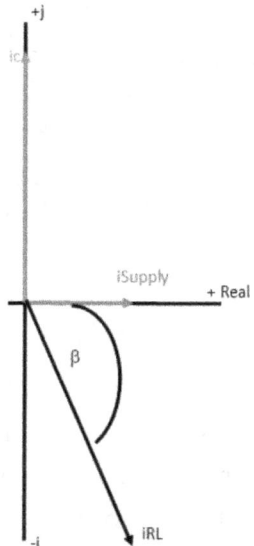

Figure 7-20. *The Current Phasors When the Circuit Is at Resonance*

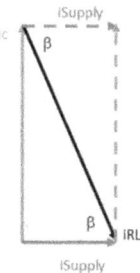

Figure 7-21. *The Series RL Circuit Phasor Diagram*

393

CHAPTER 7   THE SERIES RLC CIRCUIT

You learned in Chapter 6 that in the series RL circuit the angle associated with the impedance of that series RL circuit is the ratio $\beta = \tan^{-1}\dfrac{XL}{R}$. I use the word *ratio* as all the angles created in a right-angled triangle are simply the ratio of two sides of the triangle. To make this phasor easier, appreciate in this way we can rearrange the current phasors into the triangle shown in Figure 7-21. Using the triangle shown in Figure 7-21, we can use trigonometry to show the following points:

$$Sin(\beta) \text{ is the ratio of } \dfrac{i_C}{i_{RL}}$$

$$Cos(\beta) \text{ is the ratio of } \dfrac{i_{Supply}}{i_{RL}}$$

$$Tan(\beta) \text{ is the ratio of } \dfrac{i_C}{i_{Supply}}$$

The next interesting factor we can determine from the three phasor diagrams is that at the resonant frequency the supply current has fallen to a minimum. This is opposite to the response of the series circuit and shows that, again as an opposite to the series circuit, the impedance of the parallel circuit must have risen to a maximum. This maximum impedance at resonance is called the dynamic impedance Z_D of the parallel circuit.

The following maybe a lengthy bit of maths to derive the expression for the dynamic impedance and resonant frequency of the parallel RLC circuit. You may want to skip this and just go to Example 7.4. However, I do think the derivation is a good use of your understanding of trigonometry and you might find it useful. It is entirely up to you, but thanks for reading what you do want to read.

CHAPTER 7   THE SERIES RLC CIRCUIT

We will use what we know of these phasor diagrams to derive an expression for the dynamic impedance and the resonant frequency. When we use the ratios of the trig relationships we can show, using the Tan ratio for *Tan(β)*, that:

$$i_C = i_{Supply} Tan(\beta) \quad \text{Equation 1}$$

If we use Ohm's Law, we can relate the two currents to the supply voltage and impedances, as follows:

$$i_C = \frac{v_{Supply}}{X_C} \quad \text{and} \quad i_{Supply} = \frac{V_{Supply}}{Z_D}$$

We are using the term Z_D, not Z_T, as we are looking at the parallel circuit when it is a resonance.

We have already said that $\tan(\beta) = \frac{XL}{R}$ which means we can substitute the terms in Equation 1 with terms that relate them to supply voltage and impedances, as follows:

$$i_C = i_{Supply} Tan(\beta)$$

$$\frac{V_{Supply}}{X_C} = \frac{V_{Supply}}{Z_D} \times \frac{X_L}{R}$$

This can be rewritten as follows:

$$\frac{V_{Supply}}{X_C} = \frac{V_{Supply} X_L}{Z_D R}$$

CHAPTER 7 THE SERIES RLC CIRCUIT

If we multiply both sides by Z_D, we get this:

$$\frac{Z_D V_{Supply}}{X_C} = \frac{V_{Supply} X_L}{R}$$

Now if we multiply both sides by $\dfrac{X_C}{V_{Supply}}$ we get:

$$Z_D = \frac{V_{Supply} X_L}{R} \times \frac{X_C}{V_{Supply}}$$

This then simplifies to:

$$Z_D = \frac{X_L X_C}{R}$$

If we substitute the following relationships for X_L and X_C into the expression for Z_D, we get:

$$X_L = \omega L \text{ and } X_C = \frac{1}{\omega C}$$

The expression for Z_D becomes:

$$Z_D = \frac{\omega L \times \dfrac{1}{\omega C}}{R} = \frac{\dfrac{L}{C}}{R}$$

$$\therefore Z_D = \frac{L}{CR}$$

Note this is only when the circuit is at resonance and, as the supply current is in phase with the supply voltage, then Z_D is purely resistive even though it depends on the value of C and L. We will continue with this bit of maths to derive an expression for the resonant frequency for the parallel RLC circuit.

CHAPTER 7   THE SERIES RLC CIRCUIT

If we now look at the ratio of sin (β), which states that:

$$\sin(\beta) = \frac{i_C}{i_{RL}}$$

We can rearrange this to show that:

$$i_C = i_{RL}\sin(\beta) \qquad \text{Equation 2}$$

As the current i_{RL} flows through the series RL path of the parallel circuit, and the voltage across that series RL path is simply the supply voltage, then we can say the following:

$$|i_{RL}| = \frac{v_{Supply}}{\sqrt{R^2 + (X_L)^2}}$$

We are placing the term i_{RL} inside two parallel lines to indicate we are talking about the magnitude of i_{RL}.

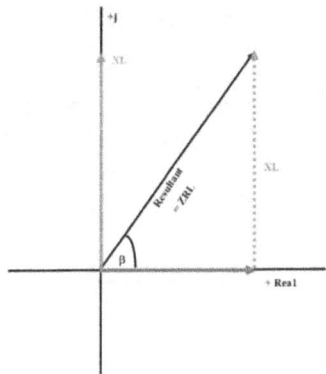

Figure 7-22. *The Impedance Phasor of the Series RL Path*

CHAPTER 7 THE SERIES RLC CIRCUIT

If we consider the impedance phasor of the series RL path of the circuit, as shown in Figure 7-22, we can say that:

$$sin(\beta) = \frac{X_L}{Z_{RL}}$$

This is the same β angle as the one shown in Figure 7-21. Then, knowing this:

$$|Z_{RL}| = \sqrt{R^2 + (X_L)^2}$$

We can say the following:

$$sin(\beta) = \frac{X_L}{\sqrt{R^2 + (X_L)^2}}$$

If we now substitute these impedances into the terms in Equation 2, we get this:

$$i_C = i_{RL} \, sin(\beta)$$

$$\frac{v_{Supply}}{X_C} = \frac{v_{Supply}}{\sqrt{R^2 + (X_L)^2}} \times \frac{X_L}{\sqrt{R^2 + (X_L)^2}}$$

This can be rearranged as follows:

$$\frac{v_{Supply}}{X_C} = \frac{v_{Supply} X_L}{\left(\sqrt{R^2 + (X_L)^2}\right)^2}$$

The square root on the right side is cancelled out by the square, so this simplifies to the following:

$$\frac{v_{Supply}}{X_C} = \frac{v_{Supply} X_L}{R^2 + (X_L)^2}$$

CHAPTER 7 THE SERIES RLC CIRCUIT

If we multiply both sides by $\dfrac{1}{v_{Supply}}$ we get this:

$$\frac{v_{Supply}}{X_C} \times \frac{1}{v_{Supply}} = \frac{v_{Supply} X_L}{R^2 + (X_L)^2} \times \frac{1}{v_{Supply}}$$

This simplifies to the following:

$$\frac{1}{X_C} = \frac{X_L}{R^2 + (X_L)^2}$$

We can, using a few more procedures, simply invert both sides, which gives us the following:

$$X_C = \frac{R^2 + (X_L)^2}{X_L}$$

If we now multiply both sides by X_L we get this:

$$X_C X_L = R^2 + (X_L)^2$$

We need to introduce the variable f into the equation, as we are trying to develop an express for the resonant frequency. Therefore, if we substitute the following relationships for X_L and X_C we get the following:

$$\frac{1}{\omega C} \omega L = R^2 + (\omega L)^2$$

This simplifies to this:

$$\frac{L}{C} = R^2 + (\omega L)^2$$

CHAPTER 7   THE SERIES RLC CIRCUIT

If we now subtract R² from both sides we get the following:

$$\frac{L}{C} - R^2 = (\omega L)^2$$

This can be rewritten as follows:

$$\frac{L}{C} - R^2 = \omega^2 L^2$$

If we now multiply both sides by $\frac{1}{L^2}$ we get this:

$$\left(\frac{L}{C} - R^2\right)\frac{1}{L^2} = (\omega^2 L^2)\frac{1}{L^2}$$

This simplifies to.

$$\frac{1}{LC} - \frac{R^2}{L^2} = \omega^2$$

If we substitute ω with 2πf we get this:

$$(2\pi f)^2 = \frac{1}{LC} - \frac{R^2}{L^2}$$

Moving the square into the terms in the bracket gives us the following:

$$4\pi^2 f^2 = \frac{1}{LC} - \frac{R^2}{L^2}$$

Now dividing both sides by $4\pi^2$ or multiplying both sides by $\frac{1}{4\pi^2}$, we get this:

$$\frac{4\pi^2 f^2}{4\pi^2} = \left(\frac{1}{LC} - \frac{R^2}{L^2}\right)\frac{1}{4\pi^2}$$

CHAPTER 7 THE SERIES RLC CIRCUIT

This simplifies to the following:

$$f^2 = \frac{1}{4\pi^2}\left(\frac{1}{LC} - \frac{R^2}{L^2}\right)$$

If we now square root both sides, we get this:

$$\sqrt{f^2} = \sqrt{\frac{1}{4\pi^2}}\sqrt{\left(\frac{1}{LC} - \frac{R^2}{L^2}\right)}$$

This simplified to this:

$$f = \frac{1}{2\pi}\sqrt{\frac{1}{LC} - \frac{R^2}{L^2}}$$

This is the complete expression for the resonant frequency, termed the frequency of oscillation f_o. However, if the term $\frac{R^2}{L^2}$ is very small compared to the term $\frac{1}{LC}$ then it can be ignored and we can use this:

$$f = \frac{1}{2\pi\sqrt{LC}}$$

However, for the parallel RLC circuit, I prefer to use the complete expression, which is:

$$f_O = \frac{1}{2\pi}\sqrt{\frac{1}{LC} - \frac{R^2}{L^2}}$$

We have gone through quite a bit of maths to derive these expressions, but the point is to show that the expressions you used are correct. Of course, we don't need to prove these expressions, as they are the standard expressions used in the parallel RLC circuit. It is entirely up to you.

CHAPTER 7   THE SERIES RLC CIRCUIT

The Currents Flowing in the Parallel Circuit
Example 7.4

We will calculate all three currents in the circuit when the frequency is set to the resonant frequency and the RMS voltage is 20V. We use the simplified expression for f_O and the complete expression to see if there is a difference.

Before we can determine the value of the supply current, we need to calculate the total impedance, Z_T. The circuit can be described as two impedances in parallel with each other, as shown in Figure 7-23.

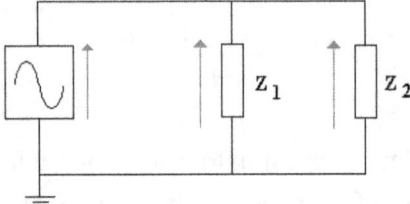

Figure 7-23. The Two Impedances in Parallel

To determine Z_T, we can use the product over sum rule, as the two impedances are in parallel with each other. Therefore, Z_T can be expressed as follows:

$$Z_T = \frac{Z_1 Z_2}{Z_1 + Z_2}$$

This shows us that we need to determine Z_1 and Z_2 first, before we can determine Z_T.

CHAPTER 7   THE SERIES RLC CIRCUIT

The Impedance Z_1

Z_1 is the capacitor, and it can be expressed as a complex number as:

$$Z_1 = 0 - j\frac{1}{\omega C}$$

Note that ω is the same as $2\pi f$, and $\frac{1}{2\pi fC} = X_C$ therefore:

$$Z_1 = 0 - jX_C$$

This means we need to know the frequency before we can continue with the calculations. We will do all the calculations at so-called resonance frequency, which we will calculate using the same expression that was used for the series circuit:

$$f_0 = \frac{1}{2\pi\sqrt{LC}}$$

Therefore, the resonant frequency, f_O, which is the frequency we will use for all the calculations, is:

$$f_0 = \frac{1}{2\pi\sqrt{10E^{-3} \times 1E^{-6}}}$$
$$\therefore f_O = 1.591 kHz$$

If we use the more correct or complete expression for f_O, we get:

$$f_O = \frac{1}{2\pi}\sqrt{\frac{1}{LC} - \frac{R^2}{L^2}}$$

Putting the values in, we get:

$$f_O = \frac{1}{2\pi}\sqrt{\frac{1}{LC} - \frac{R^2}{L^2}}$$

403

CHAPTER 7   THE SERIES RLC CIRCUIT

Therefore:

$$f_o = \frac{1}{2\pi}\sqrt{100E^6 - 250E^3} = \frac{1}{2\pi}\sqrt{99750000}$$

$$f_o = 1589.56 \text{ Hz}$$

This is very close to the 1.591khz from before but $\frac{R^2}{L^2}$ is quite small in comparison to $\frac{1}{LC}$.

PUTTING this value into f_o, using $f_o = 1.591$kHz, for the expression for X_C we have:

$$X_C = \frac{1}{2\pi \, 1.591E^3 \, x1E^{-6}}$$

$$\therefore X_C = 100.03 \, \Omega$$

Putting this value into the expression for Z_1, we have:

$$Z_1 = 0 - j100.03 \, \Omega.$$

These calculations involve phasor quantities which we are representing using complex numbers, so it would be useful to state Z_1 in polar format, $r\langle\theta$, as well. We use the following expression to convert from rectangular to polar:

$$r\langle\theta = \sqrt{a^2 + b^2} \, \langle \tan^{-1}\frac{b}{a}$$

From the expression for Z_1 a = 0 and b = -100.03, therefore putting the values into the expression, we have:

$$Z_1 = \sqrt{0^2 + (-100.03)^2} \, \langle \tan^{-1}\frac{-100.03}{0}$$

$$\therefore Z_1 = \sqrt{0 + 10006.9} \, \langle \tan^{-1} -\infty$$

CHAPTER 7   THE SERIES RLC CIRCUIT

$$\therefore Z_1 = 100.03 \langle -90^\circ \rangle$$

Note that $\dfrac{1}{0} = \infty$ and $\dfrac{1}{\infty} = 0$ also $Tan^{-1}(-\infty) = -90^\circ$ and $Tan^{-1}(\infty) = +90^\circ$.

The Impedance Z_2

A similar process can be gone through for the impedance Z_2. However, Z_2 is made up of a resistor R and an inductor with an impedance X_L in series with each other. Therefore, immediately we can see that:

$$Z_2 = R + jX_L$$

R is simply 5Ω and this is constant for all frequencies.
To determine X_L we must use this:

$$X_L = \omega L = 2\pi fL$$
$$\therefore X_L = 2\pi \times 1.591E^3 \times 10E^{-3}$$
$$\therefore X_L = 99.965 \, \Omega$$

Note the value for X_L is very nearly the same as the value for X_C but then this is the resonant frequency.

We can now express Z_2 in rectangular format and then convert it to polar format.

$$Z_2 = 5 + j99.965 \, \Omega$$

Z_2 converts to polar in the following manner, knowing that here a = 75 and b = 99.965.

$$Z_2 = \sqrt{5^2 + 99.965^2} \left\langle tan^{-1} \frac{99.965}{5} \right.$$

$$\therefore Z_2 = \sqrt{25 + 9993} \left\langle tan^{-1} 19.933 \right.$$

405

CHAPTER 7 THE SERIES RLC CIRCUIT

$$\therefore Z_2 = 100.09 \angle 87.14 \, \Omega$$

To sum up then:

$$Z_1 = 0 - j100.03$$

$$Z_1 = 100.03 \angle -90$$

$$Z_2 = 5 + j99.965$$

$$Z_2 = 100.09 \angle 87.14 \, \Omega$$

We can now put these values into the expression for Z_T as follows:

$$Z_T = \frac{Z_1 Z_2}{Z_1 + Z_2}$$

$$Z_T = \frac{(100.03 \angle -90)(100.09 \angle 87.14)}{(0 - j100.03) + (5 + j99.965)}$$

$$Z_T = \frac{10012.003 \angle -2.86}{5 - j0.065}$$

We need to convert 5 - j0.065 to polar:

$$5 - j0.065 = \sqrt{5^2 + (-0.065)^2} \angle \left(Tan^{-1} \left(\frac{-0.065}{5} \right) \right) = 5 \angle -0.745$$

Therefore, we have:

$$Z_T = \frac{10012.003 \angle -2.86°}{5 \angle -0.745°}$$

$$Z_T = 2002.4006 \angle -2.115° \, \Omega$$

CHAPTER 7 THE SERIES RLC CIRCUIT

If we now calculate the total impedance using the correct value for f_o, i.e., $f_o = 1589.56 \ Hz$, we can compare the two sets of results:

$$Z_1 = 0 - j\frac{1}{2\pi \times 1589.56 \times 1E^{-6}} = 0 - j100.125 \ \Omega$$

In polar format:

$$Z_1 = 100.125 \langle -90 \rangle \ \Omega$$

$$Z_2 = 5 + j2\pi \times 1589.56 \times 10E^{-3} = 5 + j99.875 \ \Omega$$

In polar format:

$$Z_2 = \sqrt{5^2 + 99.875^2} \left\langle Tan^{-1}\left(\frac{99.875}{5}\right)\right\rangle = 100 \langle 87.134 \rangle \ \Omega$$

We can now calculate Z_T as follows.

$$Z_T = \frac{(100.125\langle -90^o \rangle)(100\langle 87.134^o \rangle)}{(0 - j100.125) + (5 + j99.875)} = \frac{10{,}012.5\langle -2.866^o \rangle}{5 - j0.25}$$

$$Z_T = \frac{10{,}012.5\langle -2.866^o \rangle}{5.006\langle -2.862^o \rangle} = 2000.1\langle -0.004^o \rangle \ \Omega$$

This is very close to the value we got using the simplified expression for f_o. However, I do think we should use the correct expression as the angle should be 0 as it is almost zero with the correct expression for f_o.

If we put the values for the circuit into the expression for Z_D we have:

$$Z_D = \frac{10E^{-3}}{1E^{-6} \times 5} = 2k\Omega$$

CHAPTER 7   THE SERIES RLC CIRCUIT

As this should be purely resistive then the angle should be 0. This means:

$$Z_D = 2000 \langle 0 \rangle \, \Omega$$

This is very close to the value for Z_T calculated using $f_o = 1589.56 \, Hz$. Also using that value for f_o, the angle for Z_T is virtually 0. This means that the angle for the current would also be 0, which confirms that the circuit would be at resonance. This shows that the complete expression for the frequency of resonance, or oscillation, is the correct expression to use.

We can now use this value for Z_T to determine the value of the supply current using:

$$i_{Supply} = \frac{v_{Supply}}{Z_T}$$

$$i_{Supply} = \frac{20 \langle 0^o \rangle}{2000.1 \langle -0.004^o \rangle}$$

$$i_{Supply} = 9.9995E^{-3} \langle 0.004^o \rangle \, A$$

$$or \ i_{Supply} = 9.9995 \langle 0.004^o \rangle \, mA$$

We can also calculate the value of the currents flowing through the capacitor and the series RL circuit.

The Current Through the Capacitor (i_C)

The expression for this current can be stated from Ohm's Law to be:

$$i_C = \frac{v_{Supply}}{Z_1}$$

CHAPTER 7 THE SERIES RLC CIRCUIT

Note that we use the supply voltage v_{Supply} as this is the voltage across the capacitor. Therefore, putting in the values, we have:

$$i_C = \frac{20\langle 0°\rangle}{100.03\langle -90°\rangle}$$

$$i_C = 199.94E^{-3}\langle 90°\rangle\, A$$

As we need to add the currents, to confirm Kirchhoff's Current Law, we need to express this current, and all the currents, in rectangular format (i.e., a +jb). Therefore, we must convert the polar format complex number to rectangular format and to do that we must use the expressions:

$$a = rCos(\theta°)$$

$$b = rSin(\theta°)$$

$$\therefore rectangular = rCos(\theta°) + jrSin(\theta°)$$

Therefore:

$$\therefore i_C = 199.94E^{-3}Cos(90°) + j199.94E^{-3}Sin(90°)$$

$$\therefore i_C = 0 + j199.94E^{-3}\, A$$

The Current i₁

This current flows through the impedance Z_2, therefore:

$$i_{Z2} = \frac{20\langle 0°\rangle}{100\langle 87.134\rangle}$$

$$i_{Z2} = 200E^{-3}\langle -87.134°\rangle\, A$$

CHAPTER 7   THE SERIES RLC CIRCUIT

In rectangular format, we have:

$$\therefore i_{Z2} = 200E^{-3} \cos(-87.14^o) + j200E^{-3} \sin(-87.14^o)$$

$$\therefore i_{Z2} = 9.9791E^{-3} - j199.751E^{-3} \ A$$

We can now add these two currents together to confirm the value for i_{Supply} as follows:

$$\therefore i_{Supply} = (0 + j199.94E^{-3}) + (9.9791E^{-3} - j199.751E^{-3}) \ A$$

$$\therefore i_{Supply} = 9.9791E^{-3} + j189E^{-6} \ A$$

If we convert this to polar format, we have:

$$i_{Supply} = 9.981E^{-3} \langle 1.085^o \rangle \ A$$

This agrees very closely with the previous calculation for i_{Supply}, and therefore it confirms Kirchhoff's Current Law.

We can use the AC analysis to confirm this value for supply current at f = 1.591kHz, as shown in Figure 7-17. The results of the simulation are shown in Figure 7-17. We need to divide the readings by $\sqrt{2}$ to convert them to RMS readings. Table 7-1 shows the comparison between the calculated and the simulated results.

Table 7-1. *The Calculated Results versus the Simulated Results*

Calculated		Simulated	
i_{Supply}	9.981$E^{-3}\langle 1.085^o\rangle$	i_{Supply}	9.9914$E^{-3}\langle 2.07\rangle$
i_C	199.94$E^{-3}\langle 90\ A$	i_C	199.93$E^{-3}\langle 90\ A$
i_{RL}	200$\langle -87.134\ mA$	i_{RL}	199.81$\langle -87.14\ mA$

CHAPTER 7   THE SERIES RLC CIRCUIT

The table shows that the two sets of results are very close to each other. This suggests that the method is valid.

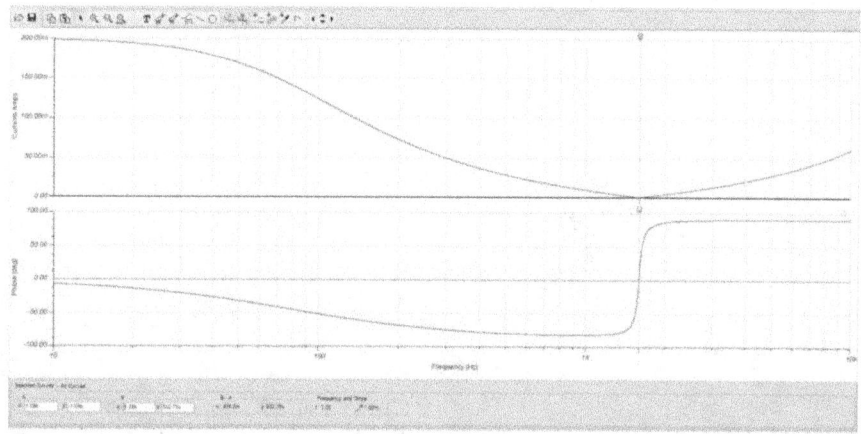

Figure 7-24. *The Supply Current Frequency Response in Magnitude and Phase*

Figure 7-24 shows that the supply current falls close to a minimum at a frequency of 1.59kHz and the phase is close to 0° at the same frequency.

Exercise 7.1

With respect to the circuit shown in Figure 7-17, with the value for R1 still at 5Ω, calculate the currents i_{Supply}, i_C, and i_1 when the frequency of the supply is:

- 500Hz
- 2000 Hz

Then confirm your answers using KCL.

411

CHAPTER 7   THE SERIES RLC CIRCUIT

Now we will change the value of resistance from 5Ω to 50Ω and see how this confirms the expression for the frequency of oscillation in a parallel circuit.

$$f_o = \frac{1}{2\pi}\sqrt{\frac{1}{LC} - \frac{R^2}{L^2}}$$

If we use the other expression for f_o, then the frequency of oscillation will not change. Therefore:

$$f_o = \frac{1}{2\pi\sqrt{10E^{-3} \times 1E^{-6}}}$$

$$\therefore f_o = 1.591 kHz$$

As the impedance Z_1 is not affected by the resistance, this would not change. Therefore:

$$Z_1 = 0 - j100.03$$

$$Z_1 = 100.03 \langle -90° \rangle \Omega$$

However, Z_2 would be affected by the change in resistance, as Z_2 is the series combination of R and X_L. Therefore:

$$Z_2 = 50 + j99.965 = 111.772 \langle 63.427° \rangle \Omega$$

Therefore:

$$Z_T = \frac{(100.03\langle -90°\rangle)(111.772\langle 63.427°\rangle)}{(0-j100.03)+(50+j99.965)} = \frac{11,180.553\langle -26.573°\rangle}{50 - j0.065}$$

$$Z_T = \frac{11,180.553\langle -26.573°\rangle}{50\langle -0.074°\rangle} = 223.611\langle -26.499°\rangle \Omega$$

CHAPTER 7 THE SERIES RLC CIRCUIT

We can now calculate the supply current as follows:

$$i_{Supply} = \frac{v_{Supply}}{Z_T}$$

$$i_{Supply} = \frac{20\langle 0°\rangle}{223.611\langle -26.499°\rangle}$$

$$i_{Supply} = 89.44E^{-3}\langle 26.499°\rangle\ A$$

$$or\ i_{Supply} = 89.44\langle 26.499°\rangle\ mA$$

This shows that the circuit is no longer at resonance, as the angle associated with the supply current is 26.499°, not 0° as it should be if the circuit was at resonance. The calculation for the supply current can be confirmed with the simulated circuit shown in Figure 7-25.

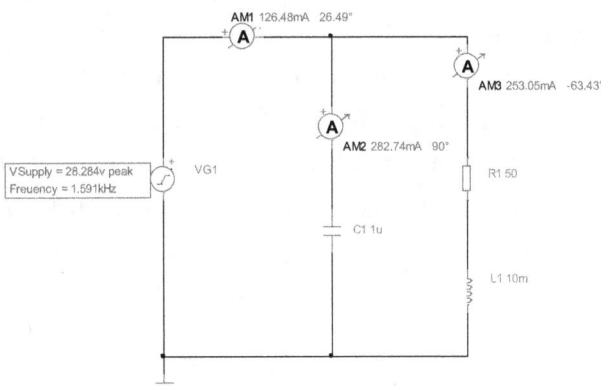

Figure 7-25. *The Simulated Circuit with R Changed to 50Ω*

413

CHAPTER 7   THE SERIES RLC CIRCUIT

Exercise 7.2

Use the complete expression for f_o to calculate the resonant frequency. Then calculate Z_T using the product over sum rule. Then calculate the supply current and confirm if the circuit is now at resonance. Finally calculate the dynamic impedance Z_D.

The Quality Factor (Q) of the Parallel RLC Circuit

In Chapter 5, you learned that the Q factor of the series circuit is its ability to magnify the supply voltage. When we look at the Q factor of the parallel RLC circuit, we will see something different. Just as with the series circuit, the parallel circuit is most efficient at resonance. If we look at the circuit shown in Figure 7-17, which is a simulation with the circuit operating close to resonance, we can see that the current taken from the supply (i.e., the supply current) is close to 10mA. However, the current flowing through the RL path of the circuit is around 200mA. This is an increase in the order of 20 times. This is the Q factor, or the *quality factor* of the parallel circuit. It is current magnification instead of voltage magnification. It shows that the circuit can take little current from the supply (i.e., use low power from the supply), yet it can have a high amount of current circulating through the RLC loop.

We can calculate the Q factor of the parallel circuit using practical measurements, knowing that we can express Q as follows:

$$Q = \frac{i_C}{i_{Supply}}$$

414

CHAPTER 7 THE SERIES RLC CIRCUIT

Using the measurements from the simulation shown in Figure 7-17, we get this:

$$Q = \frac{199.93E^{-3}}{9.9914E^{-3}} = 20.01$$

Note that we use only the magnitudes as Q is a scalar quantity and there are no units as amps/amps cancel out.

We can calculate Q using the following:

$$Q = \frac{\omega L}{R}$$

This is because Q is the ratio of the power stored in a circuit to the power dissipated in a circuit. We have already stated that the resistor is the only component that dissipated power. We can calculate the power the resistor dissipates using the following:

$$P = i^2 R$$

We have also stated that the inductor or the capacitor store power. If we consider the inductor which stores the power in the form of a magnetic field around it. We can relate this power to the current flowing through the inductor using the following:

$$P = i^2 \omega L$$

This means the ratio of power stored to power dissipated is:

$$\frac{Power\ Stored}{Power\ Dissipated} = \frac{i^2 \omega L}{i^2 R}$$

As the two currents are the same then we get this:

CHAPTER 7   THE SERIES RLC CIRCUIT

$$\frac{Power\ Stored}{Power\ Dissipated} = Q = \frac{\omega L}{R}$$

If we put the values in from the circuit shown in Figure 7-17, we get this:

$$Q = \frac{2\pi \times 1.591E^{-3} \times 10E^{-3}}{5} = 19.993$$

The Tuned Amplifier

In the early days of radio, we used AM, *amplitude modulation,* to transmit the radio signal. This led to the design of the superheterodyne receiver. This used tuned amplifiers to amplify the intermediate signal. These amplifiers used a parallel RLC circuit in the load to create transformer coupling between stages. This was an efficient method of amplifying the signal, as the parallel RLC circuit would take very low levels of current from the energy source, usually a DC battery, yet it could produce much higher circulating currents to induce a voltage in the secondary coil of the next amplifier. Indeed, I think, but I may be a little off, that the same principle is involved with the newish form of inductive charging for portable devices.

This concept works because of the Q, or the current magnification of the parallel RLC circuit. However, this requires that the resistance in the circuit is kept low. The problem is in deciding what a low value of resistance is.

An Alternative Expression for Z_T

We have shown already that the total impedance, Z_T, can be calculated using the following:

$$Z_T = \frac{Z_1 Z_2}{Z_1 + Z_2}$$

This is where:

$$Z_1 = -j\frac{1}{\omega C} \text{ and } Z_2 = R + j\omega L$$

If we use these terms, we might be able to derive an expression that is easier to use. We can see that the denominator can be expressed as follows:

$$Z_1 + Z_2 = \left(-j\frac{1}{\omega C}\right) + (R + j\omega L) = R + j\omega L - j\frac{1}{\omega C} = R + j\left(\omega L - \frac{1}{\omega C}\right)$$

If we now look at the numerator, we have:

$$Z_1 Z_2 = \left(-j\frac{1}{\omega C}\right)(R + j\omega L) = -j\frac{R}{\omega C} - j^2\frac{\omega L}{\omega C}$$

From our work with complex numbers, we know that $-j^2 = 1$. This means that the numerator now becomes:

$$Z_1 Z_2 = \frac{L}{C} - j\frac{R}{\omega C}$$

CHAPTER 7   THE SERIES RLC CIRCUIT

This then means that the expression for the total impedance becomes:

$$Z_T = \frac{\dfrac{L}{C} - j\dfrac{R}{\omega C}}{R + j\left(\omega L - \dfrac{1}{\omega C}\right)}$$

This is only true for circuits that have a parallel combination, as shown in Figure 7-17. It may look more awkward than the first expression but it can be completed with less converting of complex numbers. It is down to individual preference which approach you choose.

To sum up, we can say the following about the parallel RLC circuit:

1. To have an efficient circuit, we must keep the resistance low. If we do that, we can say the following.

   a. The resonant frequency can be calculated using:

   $$f_o = \frac{1}{2\pi}\sqrt{\frac{1}{LC} - \frac{R^2}{L^2}}$$

   b. If the term $\dfrac{R^2}{L^2}$ is much smaller than $\dfrac{1}{LC}$ we can use this expression:

   $$f_o = \frac{1}{2\pi\sqrt{LC}}$$

   c. However, it begs the question what is much smaller. I use the first expression as my preference.

2. The circuit is most efficient when the supply current is the lowest and the Q is the highest. This is when the dynamic impedance is at its highest.

CHAPTER 7   THE SERIES RLC CIRCUIT

a. We can calculate the dynamic impedance using the following: $Z_D = \dfrac{L}{RC}$

b. The quality factor Q is the current magnification, and it can be calculated using the following: $Q = \dfrac{i_C}{i_{Supply}}$ or $Q = \dfrac{\omega L}{R}$

c. We can calculate the total impedance Z_T using the following:

$$Z_T = \dfrac{Z_1 Z_2}{Z_1 + Z_2}$$

or

$$Z_T = \dfrac{\dfrac{L}{C} - j\dfrac{R}{\omega C}}{R + j\left(\omega L - \dfrac{1}{\omega C}\right)}$$

Example 7.5

Calculate the following for a parallel RLC circuit that has R = 5Ω, L = 200mH, and C = 25μF. The supply voltage is 30V RMS.

- The resonant frequency
- The dynamic impedance
- The supply current at resonance
- The capacitive current at resonance
- The current flowing through the RL branch at resonance
- The Q of the circuit at resonance

CHAPTER 7   THE SERIES RLC CIRCUIT

Solution

The resonant frequency is determined as follows:

$$f_o = \frac{1}{2\pi}\sqrt{\frac{1}{LC} - \frac{R^2}{L^2}}$$

$$f_o = \frac{1}{2\pi}\sqrt{\frac{1}{200E^{-3} \, 25E^{-6}} - \frac{5^2}{200E^{-3\,2}}}$$

$$f_o = \frac{1}{2\pi}\sqrt{200E^3 - 625}$$

$$f_o = \frac{1}{2\pi}\sqrt{199.365E^3} = 71.065 Hz$$

The dynamic impedance is determined as follows:

$$Z_D = \frac{L}{RC} = \frac{200E^{-3}}{5 \times 25E^{-6}} = 1600 \, \Omega$$

The supply current at resonance is determined as follows:

$$i_{Supply} = \frac{v_{Supply}}{Z_D} = \frac{30}{1600} = 18.75 mA$$

Alternatively, we can use this:

$$i_{Supply} = \frac{v_{Supply}}{Z_T}$$

CHAPTER 7 THE SERIES RLC CIRCUIT

We can calculate the total impedance Z_T using the following:

$$Z_T = \frac{\dfrac{L}{C} - j\dfrac{R}{\omega C}}{R + j\left(\omega L - \dfrac{1}{\omega C}\right)}$$

Putting the values in, we get:

$$Z_T = \frac{\dfrac{200E^{-3}}{25E^{-6}} - j\dfrac{5}{2\pi \times 71.065 \times 25E^{-6}}}{5 + j\left(2\pi \times 71.065 \times 200E^{-3} - \dfrac{1}{2\pi \times 71.065 \times 25E^{-6}}\right)}$$

$$Z_T = \frac{8000 - j447.914}{5 + j(89.3029 - 89.5827)} = \frac{8000 - j447.914}{5 - j0.2798} = \frac{8012.5294 \langle -3.205 \rangle}{5.008 \langle -3.2029 \rangle}$$

$$Z_T = 1602.506 \langle -0.0021° \rangle \,\Omega$$

This value for Z_T is close to the value for Z_D. The angle is close to 0° as the circuit is at resonance. We can now use this value for Z_T to calculate the supply current, as follows:

$$i_{Supply} = \frac{30 \langle 0° \rangle}{1602.506 \langle -0.0021° \rangle} = 18.721E^{-3} \langle 0.0021° \rangle \; Amps$$

The angle for the supply current is very close to 0° when the supply current is in phase with the supply voltage. This confirms the circuit is at resonance.

We can calculate the current flowing through the capacitor as follows:

$$i_C = \frac{v_{Supply}}{X_L} = \frac{30 \langle 0° \rangle}{\dfrac{1}{2\pi \times 71.065 \times 25E^{-6}} \langle -90° \rangle} = 334.886E^{-3} \langle 90° \rangle \; Amps$$

421

CHAPTER 7   THE SERIES RLC CIRCUIT

We can also calculate the current flowing through the RL branch as follows:

$$i_{RL} = \frac{v_{Supply}}{Z_{RL}} = \frac{30\langle 0^o \rangle}{89.44278\langle 86.7954^o \rangle} = 335.41E^{-3}\langle -86.7954^o \rangle \, Amps$$

We can now use Kirchhoff's Current Law to confirm our calculations. We need to convert the currents into rectangular format first. To convert from polar to rectangular we use this:

$$r\langle \theta \rangle = r\cos(\theta) + jr\sin(\theta)$$

The capacitor current i_C converts as follows:

$$i_C = 334.886E^{-3} \cos(90^o) + j334.886E^{-3} \sin(90^o) = 0 + j334.886E^{-3} \, Amps$$

The iRL current converts as follows:

$$i_{RL} = 335.41E^{-3} \cos(-86.7954^o) + j335.41E^{-3} \sin(-86.7954^o)$$

$$i_{RL} = 18.75E^{-3} - j334.886E^{-3} \, Amps$$

We can now add the two currents together which gives us the following:

$$i_{Supply} = i_C + i_{RL}$$

$$i_{Supply} = (0 + j334.886E^{-3}) + (18.75E^{-3} - j334.886E^{-3}) = 18.75E^{-3} + j0 \, Amps$$

CHAPTER 7 THE SERIES RLC CIRCUIT

All these results are the same.

The Q or quality factor at resonance is determined as follows:

$$Q = \frac{i_C}{i_{Supply}} = \frac{334.886E^{-3} \langle 0^o \rangle}{18.75E^{-3} \langle 0^o \rangle} = 17.889$$

However, using the following:

$$Q = \frac{\omega L}{R} = \frac{2\pi \times 71.065 \times 200 E^{-3}}{5} = 17.86$$

These are close enough to each other.

The simulation of the circuit is shown in Figure 7-26.

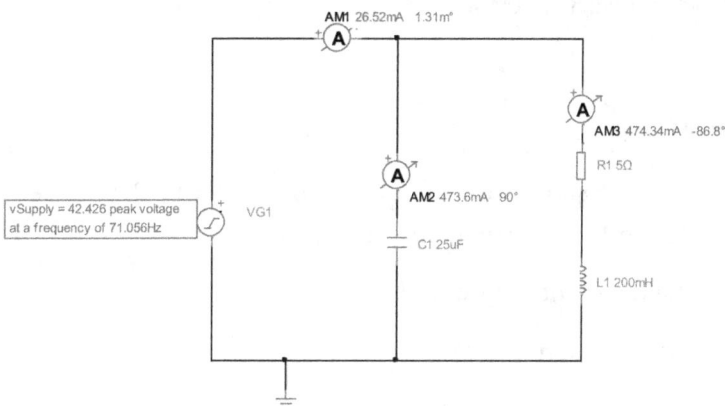

Figure 7-26. *The Simulation for Example 7.5*

Exercise 7.3

If a parallel RLC circuit has the component values shown in set A and set B, calculate the following:

- The resonant frequency
- The dynamic impedance

423

CHAPTER 7 THE SERIES RLC CIRCUIT

- The supply current at resonance
- The capacitive current at resonance
- The current flowing through the RL branch at resonance
- The Q of the circuit at resonance

Set A:

R = 10Ω, L = 250mH, and C = 5µF. The supply voltage is 10V RMS.

Set B:

R = 15Ω, L = 300mH, and C = 250nF. The supply voltage is 35V RMS.

Exercise 7.4

With respect to the series RLC circuit shown in Figure 7-27 that has values stated in set A and Set B, calculate the following:

- The resonant frequency
- The impedance at resonance
- The supply current at resonance
- The Q of the circuit at resonance

Set A:

R = 20Ω, L = 25mH, and C = 15µF. The supply voltage is 10V RMS.

CHAPTER 7   THE SERIES RLC CIRCUIT

Set B:

R = 5Ω, L = 350mH, and C = 250nF. The supply voltage is 35V RMS.

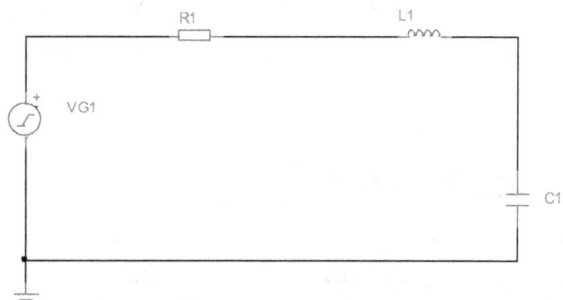

Figure 7-27. The Series RLC Circuit for Exercise 7.4

Summary

In this chapter we looked at resonance in the series and parallel RLC circuit. We saw that the series RLC circuit is a simple second-order system that can be used to select a small range of frequencies centred around its resonant frequency. At this frequency, the series circuit can be used to magnify the small input voltage to a more useful voltage across one of the reactive components, usually the capacitor. This makes the series RLC a useful circuit at the front end of any signal receiver device.

We also saw how the parallel circuit is slightly more involved than the series circuit and that it can be used to magnify the input current to a more useful value, circulating the reactive branches of the circuit.

CHAPTER 7 THE SERIES RLC CIRCUIT

Answers to Exercise 7.3

Set	f_0	Z_D	iSupply	iC	iRL	Q
A	142.21	$5k\langle 0\rangle$	$0.002\langle 0\rangle$	$0.0447\langle 90\rangle$	$0.0447\langle -87.44\rangle$	22.338
B	581.1	$8k\langle 0\rangle$	$4E^{-3}\langle 0\rangle$	$31.9E^{-3}\langle 90\rangle$	$32E^{-3}\langle -89.22\rangle$	73.023

Answers to Exercise 7.4

Set	f_0	Z_T	iSupply	VR	VL	VC
A	259.89	$20\langle 0\rangle$	$0.5\langle 0\rangle$	$10\langle 0\rangle$	$20\langle 90\rangle$	$20\langle -90\rangle$
B	538.042	$5\langle 0\rangle$	$7\langle 0\rangle$	$35\langle 0\rangle$	$8.28\langle 90\rangle k$	$8.28\langle -90\rangle k$

CHAPTER 8

AC Analysis

In Chapter 3, we used the Thevenin's, Norton's, and Superposition theorems to analyse DC circuits. In this chapter, we use the same theorems to analyse AC circuits.

Example 8.1

We start with a straightforward circuit, which is shown in Figure 8-1.

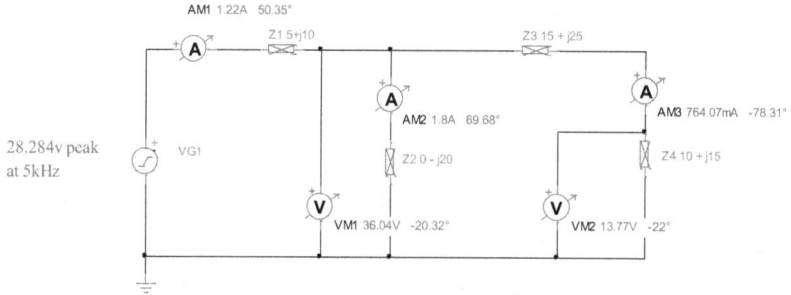

Figure 8-1. The Circuit for Example 8.1

In this example, we are using complex numbers to describe the sources and impedances. This fine because complex numbers can be used to represent phasors and all electrical quantities are phasor quantities. The sources and the impedances are as follows:

- $V1pk = 28.284 + j0 \ v$
- $V1rms = 20 + j0 \ v$

CHAPTER 8 AC ANALYSIS

- $Z_1 = 5 + j10 \ \Omega$
- $Z_2 = 0 - j20 \ \Omega$
- $Z_3 = 15 + j25 \ \Omega$
- $Z_4 = 10 + j15 \ \Omega$

With respect to the impedances, the real term is the actual value of the resistance that is in series with the j term. The j term is the reactive component of the impedance. If it is positive, the reactive component is an inductor. If it is negative, the reactive component is a capacitor.

We should represent these complex numbers in their polar format as well. As an exercise, see if you can convert the rectangular complex numbers to the following polar format:

- $V_{1rms} = 20 \langle 0 \rangle \ v$
- $Z_1 = 11.18 \langle 63.435 \rangle \ \Omega$
- $Z_2 = 20 \langle -90 \rangle \ \Omega$
- $Z_3 = 29.155 \langle 59.04 \rangle \ \Omega$
- $Z_4 = 18.028 \langle 56.31 \rangle \ \Omega$

Later in this chapter, we will look at how to determine the actual component values from impedances expressed in rectangular format.

We will use Thevenin's theory, which we used in Chapter 3, to determine the current flowing through the Z_4 impedance. This means we are calling Z_4 as the load impedance. The first thing to do is determine the Thevenin's impedance, which we will call Z_{THEV}. This means we should determine the impedance seen looking back into the circuit with the load removed and all sources replaced with their ideal internal impedance. To help, we will use the circuit as redrawn in Figure 8-2.

CHAPTER 8   AC ANALYSIS

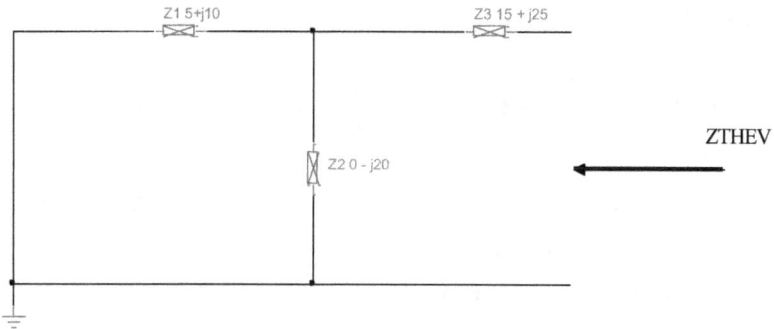

Figure 8-2. *The Circuit to Determine Z_{THEV}*

We need to combine Z_1 and Z_2 in parallel and then add the result to the impedance Z_3 to determine Z_{THEV}. This means we can say that, for this circuit:

$$Z_{THEV} = Z_3 + \frac{Z_1 Z_2}{Z_1 + Z_2}$$

$$\frac{Z_1 Z_2}{Z_1 + Z_2} = \frac{(11.18 \langle 63.435^o \rangle)(20 \langle -90^o \rangle)}{(5+j10)+(0-j20)} = \frac{223.6 \langle -26.565^o \rangle}{5 - j10}$$

$$\frac{Z_1 Z_2}{Z_1 + Z_2} = \frac{223.6 \langle -26.565^o \rangle}{11.1803 \langle -63.435^o \rangle} = 20 \langle 36.87^o \rangle \Omega$$

We need to convert this to rectangular format so that we can add it to Z_3. Therefore. We have this:

$$\frac{Z_1 Z_2}{Z_1 + Z_2} = 20 Cos(36.87^o) + j20 Sin(36.87^o) = 16 + j12 \, \Omega$$

Therefore, we can now determine Z_{THEV} as follows:

$$Z_{THEV} = (15 + j25) + (16 + j12) = 31 + j37 \, \Omega$$

CHAPTER 8 AC ANALYSIS

In polar format, we have the following:

$$Z_{THEV} = \sqrt{31^2 + 37^2} \left\langle Tan^{-1}\left(\frac{37}{31}\right)\right\rangle = 48.27 \langle 50.042 \rangle \, \Omega$$

Now we will calculate the Thevenin's voltage v_{THEV}. This is the voltage that would appear across the terminals where the load impedance had been removed. We will use the circuit shown in Figure 8-3.

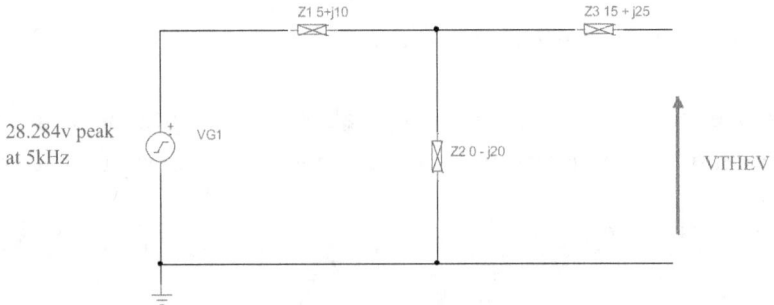

Figure 8-3. *The Circuit to Calculate V_{THEV}*

No current can flow through Z_3 so it plays no part in this calculation. This means that v_{THEV} will be the same as the voltage dropped across Z_2. Therefore, we can calculate v_{THEV} as follows:

$$v_{THEV} = \frac{V_1 Z_2}{Z_1 + Z_2}$$

Where v_1 is the RMS voltage from the supply, which is $v_1 = \frac{28.284}{\sqrt{2}} = 20v$. As the supply voltage is the reference, then the angle will be $0°$. Therefore:

$$v_{THEV} = \frac{(20\langle 0°\rangle)(20\langle -90°\rangle)}{(5+j10)+(0-j20)} = \frac{400\langle -90°\rangle}{5-j10} v$$

430

CHAPTER 8   AC ANALYSIS

Converting the denominator to polar, we have this:

$$v_{THEV} = \frac{400\langle-90°\rangle}{11.18\langle-63.435°\rangle} = 35.778\langle-26.565°\rangle v$$

This means we can now construct Thevenin's equivalent circuit, as shown in Figure 8-4.

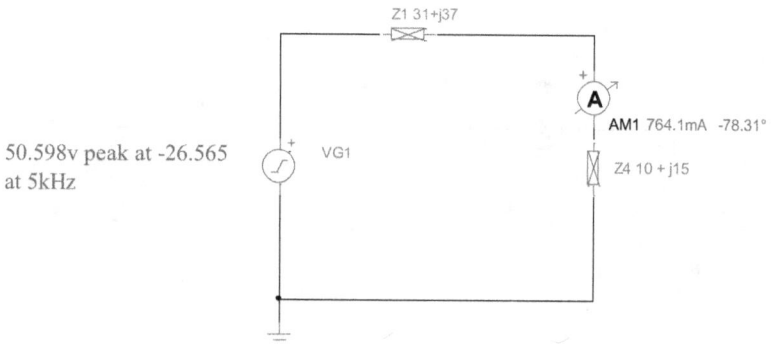

Figure 8-4. *Thevenin's Equivalent Circuit for Example 8.1*

Figure 8-4 shows the circuit with the load impedance back in place. The circuit has been simulated to show that the current flowing through Z_4 is $540.3E^{-3} \langle-78.31°\rangle$ A.

We will use the circuit shown in Figure 8-4 to calculate the current flowing through Z_4 as follows:

$$i_{Z4} = \frac{v_{THEV}}{(Z_{THEV})+(Z_4)} = \frac{35.778\langle-26.565°\rangle}{(31+j37)+(10+j15)} = \frac{35.778\langle-26.565°\rangle}{41+j52}$$

Converting the denominator to polar so that we can complete the division, we get:

$$i_{Z4} = \frac{35.778\langle-26.565°\rangle}{66.219\langle51.746°\rangle} = 540.298E^{-3}\langle-78.31°\rangle A$$

This agrees with the simulated results.

CHAPTER 8   AC ANALYSIS

Thevenin's Equivalent Circuit for a Circuit with Multiple Sources

Example 8.2

We now use Thevenin's theory to determine current flowing through a circuit with more than one source. The circuit we use for this example is shown in Figure 8-5.

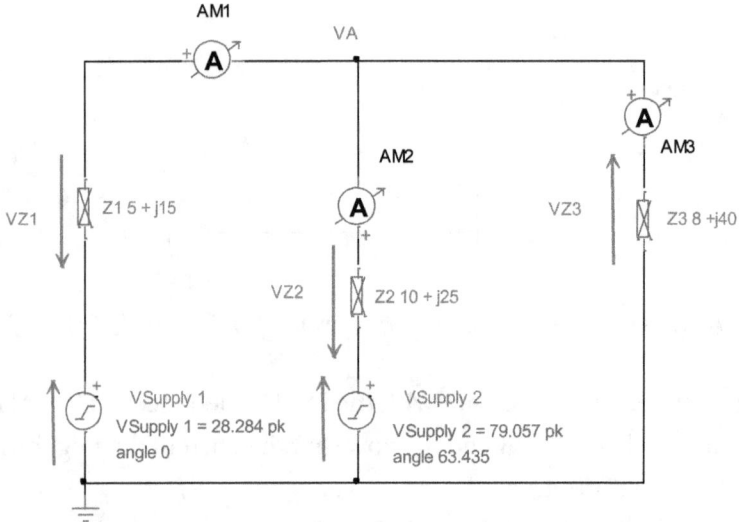

Figure 8-5. *The Circuit for Example 8.2*

We list all the impedances and sources in both rectangular and polar format.

The impedance:

- $Z_1 = 5 + j15 = 15.8114 \:\langle 71.565^\circ \rangle \: \Omega$
- $Z_2 = 10 + j25 = 26.926 \:\langle 68.196^\circ \rangle \: \Omega$
- $Z_1 = 8 + j40 = 40.792 \:\langle 78.69^\circ \rangle \: \Omega$

The sources:

- $v_{Supply\,1} = 20 + j0 = 20 \langle 0^\circ \rangle\ v$
- $v_{Supply\,2} = 25 + j50 = 55.902 \langle 63.435^\circ \rangle\ v$

Note that the polar format of the voltage sources uses the RMS values for the magnitude, because we always use RMS values in our AC calculations.

We are calculating all the currents in the circuit so we can choose any of the three impedances to call the load impedance. In this case, we will choose Z_3 as the load. The first thing we will do is remove the impedance Z_3. After replacing both voltage sources with a short circuit, we can calculate Thevenin's impedance (Z_{THEV}), as shown in Figure 8-6.

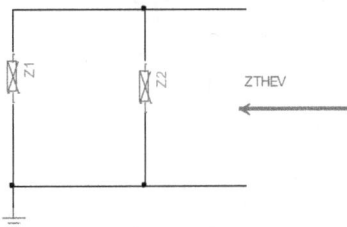

Figure 8-6. *The Circuit to Calculate Z_{THEV}*

We can see from Figure 8-6 that Z_{THEV} will simply be the parallel combination of Z_1 and Z_2. Therefore, we can say this:

$$Z_{THEV} = \frac{Z_1 Z_2}{Z_1 + Z_2}$$

Therefore:

$$Z_{THEV} = \frac{\left(15.8114 \langle 71.565^\circ \rangle\right)\left(26.926 \langle 68.196^\circ \rangle\right)}{(5+j15)+(10+j25)} = \frac{425.7378 \langle 139.761^\circ \rangle}{15+j40}$$

CHAPTER 8 AC ANALYSIS

Therefore:

$$Z_{THEV} = \frac{425.7378\langle 139.761°\rangle}{42.72\langle 69.444°\rangle} = 9.966\langle 70.317°\rangle \, \Omega$$

In rectangular format:

$$Z_{THEV} = 3.357 + j9.384 \, \Omega$$

Thevenin's Voltage V_{THEV}

As there are two voltage sources, we have to use the Superposition theory. We start by calculating v_{THEV} due to $v_{Supply\,1}$. We will use the circuit shown in Figure 8-7.

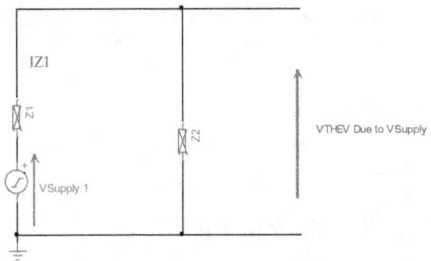

Figure 8-7. *The Circuit to Calculate V_{THEV} Due to $V_{Supply\,1}$*

Using Figure 8-7, we can use the voltage divider rule to calculate the voltage as follows:

$$v_{THEV\,Due\,to\,VSupply1} = \frac{v_{Supply1} Z_2}{Z_1 + Z_2}$$

Therefore:

$$v_{THEV\,Due\,to\,VSupply1} = \frac{(20\langle 0°\rangle)(26.926\langle 68.196°\rangle)}{(5+j15)+(10+j25)} = \frac{538.52\langle 68.196°\rangle}{15+j40}$$

434

Therefore:

$$v_{THEV\ Due\ to\ VSupply1} = \frac{538.52\langle 68.196°\rangle}{42.72\langle 69.444°\rangle} = 12.606\langle -1.248°\rangle v$$

We can now use the circuit shown in Figure 8-8 to calculate v_{THEV} due to $V_{SUPPLY2}$.

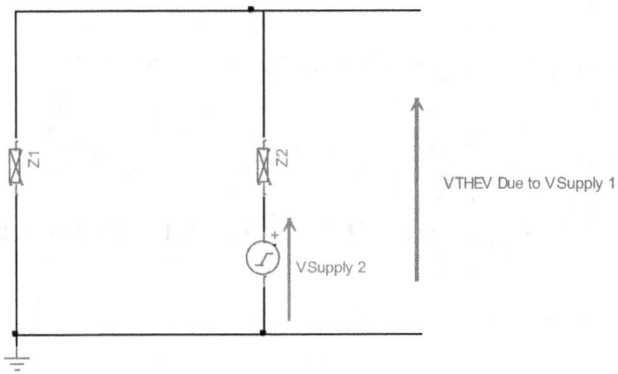

Figure 8-8. *The Circuit to Calculate V_{THEV} Due to $V_{Supply\ 2}$*

We can use the voltage divider rule again as follows:

$$V_{THEV\ Due\ to\ VSupply2} = \frac{V_{Supply2} Z_2}{Z_1 + Z_2}$$

Therefore:

$$V_{THEV\ Due\ to\ VSupply2} = \frac{(55.902\langle 63.435°\rangle)(15.8114\langle 71.565°\rangle)}{(5+j15)+(10+j25)} = \frac{883.89\langle 135°\rangle}{15+j40}$$

Therefore:

$$V_{THEV\ Due\ to\ VSupply2} = \frac{883.89\langle 135°\rangle}{42.72\langle 69.444°\rangle} = 20.69\langle 65.556°\rangle v$$

CHAPTER 8 AC ANALYSIS

We can now add the two results to determine V_{THEV} as follows:

$$V_{THEV} = V_{THEV\ Due\ to\ VSupply1} + V_{THEV\ Due\ to\ VSupply2}$$

However, we need to convert these to rectangular format before we can add them. Therefore:

$$V_{THEV\ Due\ to\ VSupply1} = 12.606\langle -1.248^o\rangle = 12.603 - j0.275\ v$$

$$V_{THEV\ Due\ to\ VSupply2} = 20.69\langle 65.556^o\rangle = 8.561 + j18.835\ v$$

Therefore:

$$V_{THEV} = (12.603 - j0.275) + (8.561 + j18.835) = 21.164 + j18.56\ v$$

In polar format, we have the following:

$$V_{THEV} = 28.149\langle 41.249^o\rangle\ v$$

We can now create Thevenin's equivalent circuit that would feed Z_3. This is shown in Figure 8-9.

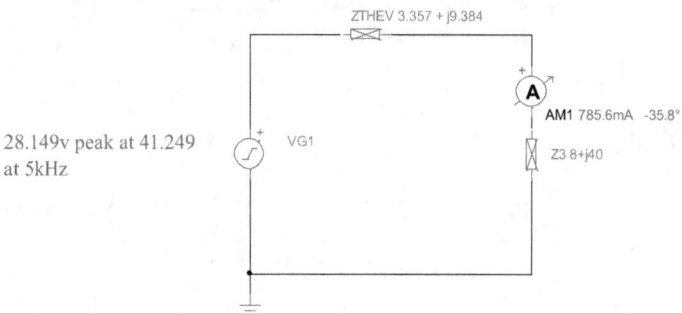

Figure 8-9. *Thevenin's Equivalent Circuit for Example 8.2*

We can calculate the current flowing through Z_3 as follows:

436

$$I_{Z3} = \frac{V_{THEV}}{Z_{THEV} + Z_3}$$

$$I_{Z3} = \frac{28.149 \langle 41.249^o \rangle}{(3.357 + j9.384) + (8 + j40)} = \frac{28.149 \langle 41.249^o \rangle}{11.357 + j49.384}$$

$$I_{Z3} = \frac{28.149 \langle 41.249^o \rangle}{50.673 \langle 77.049^o \rangle} = 555.503 E^{-3} \langle -35.8^o \rangle \, A$$

This agrees with the simulated result shown in Figure 8-9.

Example 8.3

We can confirm the calculations for Example 8.2 by creating Norton's equivalent circuit for the circuit shown in Figure 8-5.

We calculate Norton's impedance the same way we calculated Thevenin's impedance. Therefore, we can say that:

$$Z_{NORT} = Z_{THEV} = 9.966 \langle 70.317 \rangle \, \Omega = 3.357 + j9.384 \, \Omega$$

We now have to calculate the current that would flow through a short circuit placed across where the load Z_3 was. Figure 8-10 should help with this calculation.

CHAPTER 8   AC ANALYSIS

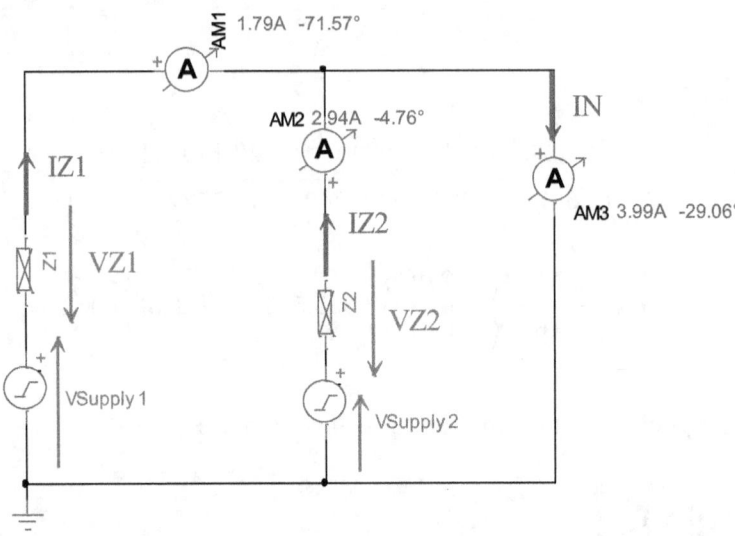

Figure 8-10. *The Load Z3 Replaced with a Short Circuit*

We can see in Figure 8-11 that using KCL, we can say:

$$i_N = i_{Z1} + i_{Z2}$$

Placing the short circuit across the output connects the top of both impedances Z_1 and Z_2 to ground. This means that we can calculate the two currents using:

$$i_{Z1} = \frac{v_{Supply1}}{Z_1} = \frac{20\langle 0°\rangle}{15.811\langle 71.565°\rangle} = 1.265\langle -71.565°\rangle \text{ Amps}$$

Similarly, we can say that.

$$i_{Z2} = \frac{v_{Supply2}}{Z_2} = \frac{55.902\langle 63.435°\rangle}{26.926\langle 68.199°\rangle} = 2.076\langle -4.764°\rangle \text{ Amps}$$

438

CHAPTER 8   AC ANALYSIS

We need to add the two currents together, so we need to convert them to rectangular format. Therefore:

$$i_{Z1} = 0.4 - j1.2 \; Amps$$

$$i_{Z2} = 2.069 - j172.415E^{-3} \; Amps$$

Therefore, we can say:

$$i_N = (0.4 - j1.2) + (2.069 - j172.415E^{-3}) = 2.469 - j1.3724 \; Amps$$

In polar format, we have:

$$i_N = 2.825 \langle -29.068° \rangle \; Amps$$

The ammeter readings in Figure 13-28 confirm these calculations as the RMS values of the current measured by the three ammeters give the same results.

We can now use Norton's equivalent circuit to determine the current flowing through the load Z_3. The circuit in Figure 8-11 shows Norton's equivalent circuit with the load placed across the output. Norton's equivalent circuit is the current source with Norton's impedance Z_N placed in parallel across the current source.

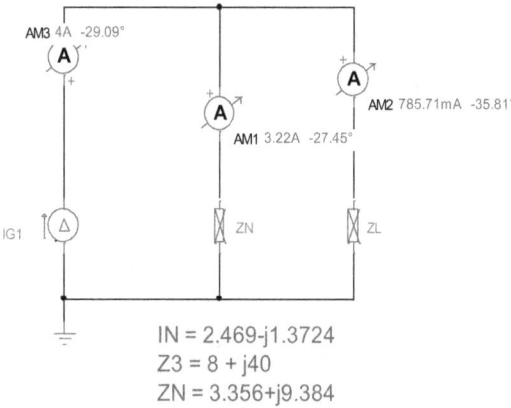

Figure 8-11. *Norton's Equivalent Circuit with the Load Connected*

CHAPTER 8   AC ANALYSIS

We can use the current divider rule to calculate the current flowing through the load as follows:

$$i_L = \frac{i_N Z_N}{Z_N + Z_L} = \frac{(2.825\langle-29.068°\rangle)(9.966\langle70.32°\rangle)}{(3.356+j9.384)+(8+j40)} = \frac{28.154\langle41.252°\rangle}{11.356+j49.384}$$

$$i_L = \frac{28.154\langle41.252°\rangle}{50.673\langle77.05°\rangle} = 555.602E^{-3}\langle-35.798°\rangle \, Amps$$

These currents agree with the Thevenin's results and the simulated meter readings in Figure 8-11.

The Maximum Power in the Load

In Chapter 3, you learned that one reason for using Thevenin's theory is that it can help determine the value of the load for which you achieve the maximum power in the load. Therefore, it seems reasonable that we should see how we can do the same with AC circuits.

Example 8.4

With respect to the circuit in Figure 8-12, we will use Thevenin's theory to determine the value of the load impedance for maximum power in the load.

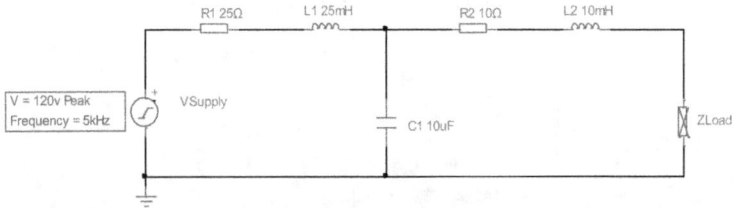

Figure 8-12. The Circuit for Example 8.4

440

CHAPTER 8   AC ANALYSIS

The approach is the same as with the DC circuit—the only difference is that the circuit has impedances instead of resistors and therefore complex numbers must be used.

Thevenin's Impedance Z_{THEV}

We will start by determining Thevenin's impedance, Z_{THEV}. To do this, we redraw the circuit with the load removed and the voltage source replaced by its ideal internal impedance, a short circuit. This is shown in Figure 8-13.

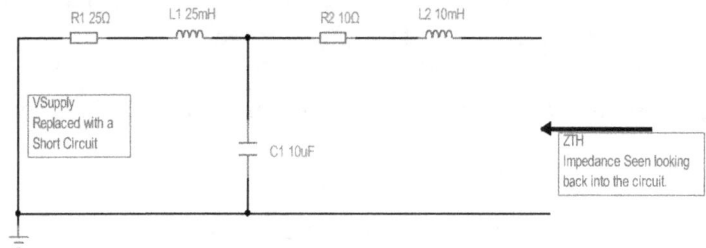

Figure 8-13. *The Redrawn Circuit to Help Calculate ZTH*

We can describe the circuit as three impedances, as shown in Figure 8-14.

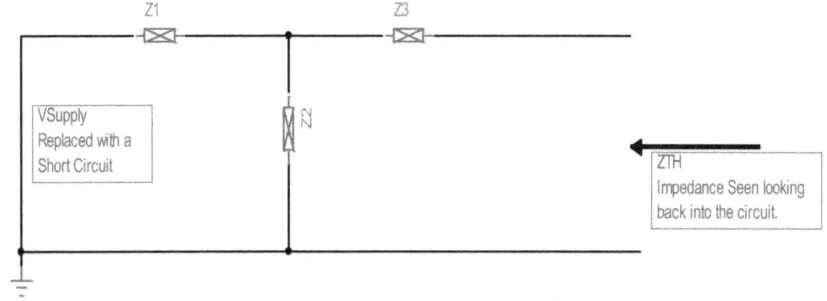

Figure 8-14. *The Circuit as Three Impedances*

441

CHAPTER 8 AC ANALYSIS

The first thing to do is calculate the three impedances—Z_1, Z_2, and Z_3—as follows:

$$Z_1 = R_1 + j\omega L_1$$

$$Z_2 = 0 - j\frac{1}{\omega C1}$$

$$Z_3 = R_2 + j\omega L_2$$

Calculate the value of ω first, using this:

$$\omega = 2\pi f$$

$$\therefore \omega = 2\pi \times 5E^3$$

$$\therefore \omega = 31415.926 \text{ Rads/sec}$$

Using this value for ω, the impedances can be calculated as follows:

$$Z_1 = R_1 + j\omega L_1$$

$$\therefore Z_1 = 25 + j31415.926 \times 25E^{-3}$$

$$\therefore Z_1 = 25 + j785.398 \, \Omega$$

In polar format, they are:

$$Z_1 = 785.796 \langle 88.177 \rangle \, \Omega$$

$$Z_2 = 0 - j\frac{1}{\omega C_1}$$

$$\therefore Z_2 = 0 - j\frac{1}{\left(31415.926 \times 10E^{-6}\right)}$$

$$\therefore Z_2 = 0 - j3.183 \, \Omega$$

442

In polar format, they are:

$$Z_2 = 3.183 \langle -90° \rangle \, \Omega$$

$$Z_3 = R_2 + j\omega L_2$$

$$\therefore Z_3 = 10 + j31415.926 \times 10E^{-3}$$

$$\therefore Z_3 = 10 + j314.159 \, \Omega$$

In polar format, they are:

$$Z_3 = 314.318 \langle 88.162° \rangle \, \Omega$$

When we look back into the circuit, we can see that Z_3 is in series with the parallel combination of Z_1 and Z_2. As there is no other circuitry behind the parallel combination of Z_1 and Z_2, we can start by calculating that parallel impedance. We combine Z_1 and Z_2 in parallel to make Z_{COMB1} as follows:

$$Z_{COMB1} = \frac{Z_1 Z_2}{Z_1 + Z_2}$$

$$Z_{Comb1} = \frac{(785.796 \langle 88.177° \rangle)(3.183 \langle -90° \rangle)}{(25 + j785.398) + (0 - j3.183)} = \frac{(2501.189 \langle -1.823° \rangle)}{25 + j782.215} = \frac{2501.189 \langle -1.823° \rangle}{782.514 \langle 88.169° \rangle} = 3.196 \langle -90° \rangle \, \Omega$$

In rectangular format:

$$Z_{Comb1} = 0 - j3.196 \, \Omega$$

Just to show how we could use the complex conjugate, I have calculated Z_{Comb1} using that approach here. It is up to you, which method you use, because they have the same result, which is what we should expect.

$$\therefore Z_{COMB1} = \frac{(25 + j785.398)(0 - j3.183)}{(25 + j785.398) + (0 - j3.183)}$$

CHAPTER 8 AC ANALYSIS

Using:

$$\therefore Z_{COMB1} = \frac{(25 \times 0) + (25 \times -j3.183) + (j785.398 \times 0) + (j785.398 \times -j3.183)}{25 + j782.215}$$

$$\therefore Z_{COMB1} = \frac{0 - j79.575 + j0 - j^2 2499.922}{25 + j782.215}$$

It should be remembered at this point that:

$$-j^2 = +1$$

Therefore we have:

$$Z_{COMB1} = \frac{2499.922 - j79.575}{25 + j782.215}$$

We will use the complex conjugate of the denominator to complete this division in rectangular format as follows:

$$Z_{COMB1} = \frac{(2499.922 - j79.575)(25 - j782.215)}{(25 + j782.215)(25 - j782.215)}$$

$$\therefore Z_{COMB1} = \frac{(2499.922 - j79.575)(25 - j782.215)}{25^2 + 782.215^2}$$

$$\therefore Z_{COMB1} = \frac{(2499.922 \times 25) + (2499.922 \times -j782.215) + (-j79.575 \times 25) + (-j79.575 \times -j782.215)}{25^2 + 782.215^2}$$

$$\therefore Z_{COMB1} = \frac{62498.05 - j1955476.487 - j1989.375 + j^2 62244.759}{612485.306}$$

$$\therefore Z_{COMB1} = \frac{253.291 - j1957465.862}{612485.306}$$

$$\therefore Z_{COMB1} = 4.135E^{-4} - j3.196 \, \Omega$$

CHAPTER 8   AC ANALYSIS

As 4.135E-4 is very small, and quite close to 0, we can say:

$$Z_{Comb1} = 0 - j3.196 \, \Omega$$

We now have to add the value of Z_3 to this result to determine Thevenin's impedance, Z_{THEV}:

$$Z_{THEV} = Z_{COMB1} + Z_3$$

$$\therefore Z_{THEV} = (4.135E^{-4} - j3.196) + (10 + j314.159)$$

$$\therefore Z_{THEV} = 10.0004 + j310.963 \, \Omega$$

In polar format:

$$Z_{THEV} = 311.124 \langle 88.158 \rangle \, \Omega$$

Now we need to calculate Thevenin's voltage V_{THEV}, which is the voltage that would appear at the output terminals of the circuit with the load removed. This is sometimes referred to as the *open circuit voltage*.

With this circuit, as the load is removed, no current flows through Z_3 and so V_{THEV} is simply the voltage across Z_2. This can be calculated using the voltage divider rule:

$$V_{THEV} = \frac{V_1 Z_2}{Z_1 + Z_2}$$

We need to convert the 120V peak to RMS as it is normal to calculate all values in their RMS.

$$Vrms = \frac{Vpk}{\sqrt{2}}$$

$$V_{1rms} = \frac{120}{\sqrt{2}} = 84.853v$$

445

CHAPTER 8   AC ANALYSIS

Using this value and knowing that the supply voltage will be the reference, V_{THEV} can be calculated as follows:

$$V_{THEV} = \frac{V_1 Z_2}{Z_1 + Z_2} = \frac{(84.853\langle 0°\rangle)(3.183\langle -90°\rangle)}{(25 + j785.398) + (0 - j3.183)} = \frac{270.087\langle -90°\rangle}{25 + j782.215} = \frac{270.087\langle -90°\rangle}{782.6144\langle 88.169\rangle} = 345.109E^{-3}\langle -178.169°\rangle v$$

$$V_{THEV} = 345.109E^{-3}\langle -178.169°\rangle v$$

Thevenin's equivalent circuit is shown in Figure 8-15.

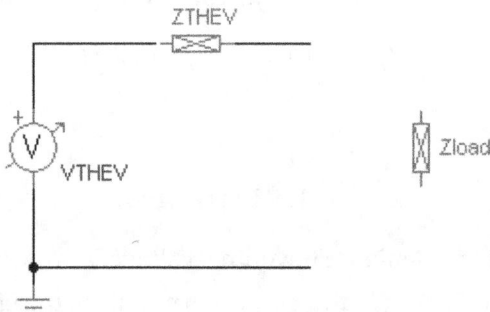

Figure 8-15. *Thevenin's Equivalent Circuit*

Thevenin's circuit shows V_{THEV} with Z_{THEV} in series with it. Note that Z_{THEV} is the source impedance of the circuit supplying the load impedance. For maximum power, the first idea is that, as with the DC circuits, the impedance of the load should equal this source impedance. We will see later if this is correct. This means for maximum power.

$$Z_{LOAD} = Z_{THEV}$$

$$\therefore Z_{LOAD} = 10.0004 + j310.963 \, \Omega$$

It is now a simple matter to calculate the current flowing through the load, as follows:

$$i = \frac{V_{TH}}{Z_{TH} + Z_{LOAD}}$$

CHAPTER 8   AC ANALYSIS

We will do this by converting to polar when we need to. However, we should add Z_{THEV} to Z_{LOAD} first. This is done as follows:

$$Z_{THEV} + Z_{LOAD} = (10.0004 + j310.963) + (10.0004 + j310.963) = 20.0008 + j621.926$$

Now convert this to polar, which gives this:

$$Z_{THEV} + Z_{LOAD} = 622.248 \langle 88.158° \rangle \, \Omega$$

Now we can carry out the division:

$$i = \frac{345.109E^{-3} \langle -178.169° \rangle}{622.248 \langle 88.158° \rangle} = 554.616E^{-6} \langle -266.33° \rangle \, Amps$$

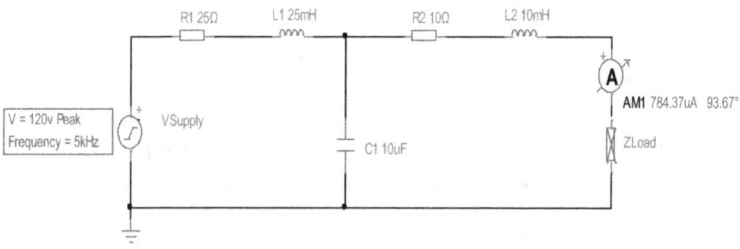

Figure 8-16. *The Simulated Circuit*

Figure 8-16 shows the current flowing through the load of the original circuit when the load impedance was set to Thevenin's impedance. The AM1 shows a peak current of 784.37µA with an angle of 93.67°. The 93.67° is rotating in the normal anticlockwise direction, whereas the -266.33 in the calculation is rotating in the clockwise direction. They will position the phasor for the current in the same place in the second quadrant. Therefore, the angles are the same. The RMS is 554.633µA. This agrees with the calculation using the converting to polar method.

CHAPTER 8   AC ANALYSIS

The Power in the Load

Looking for the maximum power in the load, we know that power is only dissipated in the resistor. With the present load impedance, are we saying that to get the maximum power in the load, we should set the resistance to 10Ω? There is some more maths we can do, involving differentiating a quadratic to calculate the max and min turning points. I leave this maths to my second book on electrical analysis. However, using that approach we can show that for maximum power the resistance in the load can be set using:

$$R_{Load} = \sqrt{R_{TH}^2 + (X_{TH} + X_{Load})^2}$$

This means that we should make the resistance of the load equal to:

$$R_{Load} = \sqrt{10^2 + (310.963 + 310.963)^2} = 622.006 \, \Omega$$

We can investigate this concept by determining the power in the load for various values of resistance in the load. First, we calculate the power in the load when R_{Load} is 10.0004 Ω using this:

$$P = i^2 R_{Load}$$

Therefore:

$$P = 554.633E^{-62} \times 10.004 = 3.076E^{-6} W$$

$$Power = 3.076 \, \mu W$$

When R_{Load} equals 622.006Ω, we get this:

$$i = \frac{V_{TH}}{Z_{TH} + Z_{LOAD}}$$

Putting the values in, we get this:

$$i = \frac{345.109 E^{-3} \langle 181.83^o \rangle}{(10.0004 + j310.963) + (622.006 + j310.963)}$$

Therefore:

$$i = \frac{345.109 E^{-3} \langle 181.83^o \rangle}{632.0064 + j621.926} = \frac{345.109 E^{-3} \langle 181.83^o \rangle}{886.693 \langle 44.539^o \rangle}$$

Therefore:

$$i = 389.21 E^{-6} \langle 137.29^o \rangle \, Amps$$

We can now calculate the power in the load as follows:

$$|P| = (389.21 E^{-6})^2 \times 622.06 = 94.232 E^{-6} \, W$$

When $R_{Load} = 1k$ the current will be as follows:
Putting the values in we get:

$$i = \frac{345.109 E^{-3} \langle 181.83^o \rangle}{(10.0004 + j310.963) + (1000 + j310.963)}$$

Therefore:

$$i = \frac{345.109 E^{-3} \langle 181.83^o \rangle}{1010 + j621.926} = \frac{345.109 E^{-3} \langle 181.83^o \rangle}{1186.125 \langle 31.623^o \rangle} = 290.96 E^{-3} \langle 150.207^o \rangle \, A$$

Using just the magnitude of the current the power in the load can be calculated as follows:

$$|P| = (290.96 E^{-6})^2 \times 1 E^3 = 84.654 E^{-6} W$$

CHAPTER 8   AC ANALYSIS

When the R_{Load} was set to 500Ω the magnitude current was measured at 429.079mA. Using this value, the magnitude power in the load was:

$$|P| = (429.079E^{-6})^2 \times 500 = 92.955E^{-6}W$$

This suggests that the maximum power in the load was 94.232µW when R_{Load} was 622.006Ω. So this confirms that we should use the expression for calculating the value of the load resistance.

Example 8.5

Consider the circuit shown in Figure 8-17.

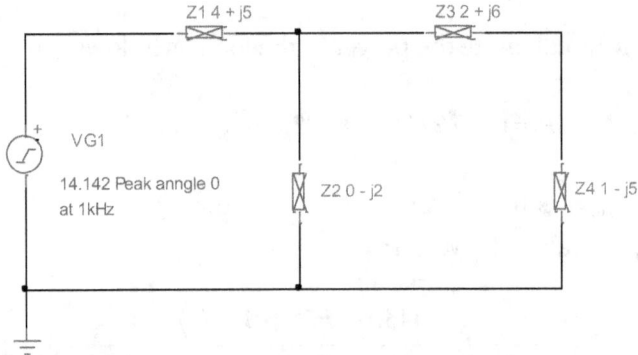

Figure 8-17. *The Circuit for Example 8.5*

We will create Thevenin's equivalent circuit using the impedance Z_4 as the load. Determine the power dissipated in the load and determine if the resistance of the load, Z_4, is the correct value for maximum power in the load. If need be, we will change the resistance to the required value for maximum power and calculate the power in the load with that value of resistance.

CHAPTER 8   AC ANALYSIS

Before we start, it is always good practice to state the impedances and sources in rectangular and polar formats as follows:

$$Z_1 = 4 + j5 = 6.403 \langle 51.34° \rangle \Omega$$

$$Z_2 = 0 - j2 = 2 \langle -90° \rangle \Omega$$

$$Z_3 = 2 + j6 = 6.325 \langle 71.565° \rangle \Omega$$

$$Z_4 = 1 - j5 = 5.099 \langle -78.69° \rangle \Omega$$

$$V_{Supply\,1} = 10 + j0 = 10 \langle 0° \rangle v$$

We are using the RMS value of the supply voltage, as we should. First, remove the load and replace the voltage source with a short circuit. This is shown in Figure 8-18.

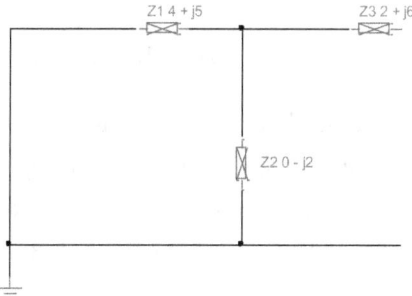

Figure 8-18. *The Circuit with Z_{Load} Removed and the Voltage Source Replaced*

Thevenin's impedance will be Z_3 in series with the parallel combination of Z_1 and Z_2. Therefore, calculate Z_{COMB1} as the parallel combination of Z_1 and Z_2. This gives the following:

$$Z_{COMB1} = \frac{(6.403 \langle 51.34° \rangle)(2 \langle -90° \rangle)}{(4 + j5) + (0 - j2)} = \frac{12.806 \langle -38.66° \rangle}{4 + j3}$$

451

CHAPTER 8 AC ANALYSIS

Therefore:

$$Z_{COMB1} = \frac{12.806\langle -38.66^\circ \rangle}{5\langle 36.87^\circ \rangle} = 2.561\langle -75.53^\circ \rangle \, \Omega$$

We need to convert this to rectangular format so that we can add it to Z_3. Therefore:

$$Z_{COMB1} = 2.561\cos(-75.53^\circ) + j2.561\sin(-75.53^\circ)$$

$$Z_{COMB1} = 0.64 - j2.48 \, \Omega$$

Therefore:

$$Z_{THEV} = Z_{COMB1} + Z_3 = (0.64 - j2.48) + (2 + j6) = 2.64 + j3.52 \, \Omega$$

In polar format:

$$Z_{THEV} = 4.4\langle 53.13^\circ \rangle \, \Omega$$

We now need to calculate Thevenin's voltage. If we examine Figure 8-17, I hope you can see that Thevenin's voltage is simply the voltage dropped across Z_2 as Z_4 is removed. Z_3 plays no part in the circuit. Therefore, we can use the voltage divider rule to determine V_{THEV} as follows:

$$v_{THEV} = \frac{v_{Supply1} Z_2}{Z_1 + Z_2}$$

Therefore:

$$V_{THEV} = \frac{(10\langle 0^\circ \rangle)(2\langle -90^\circ \rangle)}{(4+j5)+(0-j2)} = \frac{20\langle -90^\circ \rangle}{5\langle 36.87^\circ \rangle} = 4\langle -126.87^\circ \rangle \, v$$

Thevenin's equivalent circuit is shown in Figure 8-19.

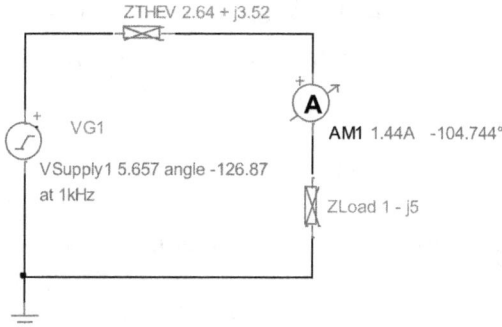

Figure 8-19. *Thevenin's Equivalent Circuit with the Load Impedance*

We can calculate the current flowing in the load as follows:

$$i_{Load} = \frac{v_{THEV}}{Z_{Thev} + Z_{Load}}$$

Therefore:

$$i_{Load} = \frac{4\langle -126.87°\rangle}{(2.64 + j3.52) + (1 - j5)}$$

Therefore:

$$i_{Load} = \frac{4\langle -126.87°\rangle}{3.64 - j1.48} = \frac{4\langle -126.87°\rangle}{3.929\langle -22.126°\rangle} = 1.018\langle -104.744°\rangle \, A$$

If we compare this with the measured current in the load then after dividing the measured current by $\sqrt{2}$, we can see that they agree very closely with each other.

We can calculate the power in the load using this:

$$P = |i|^2 R$$

CHAPTER 8 AC ANALYSIS

Note, we are placing the I between two parallel lines to indicate we are only concerned with the magnitude of the current with this expression. Therefore, we get this:

$$P = 1.018^2 \times 1 = 1.036 \, W$$

We can use an alternative expression for power, such as:

$$P = vi\cos(\theta)$$

Where θ is the angle of the current with respect to the voltage. This would give the following:

$$P = 4 \times 1.018 \times \cos(104.744^\circ) = 1.036 \, W$$

Again, we only use the magnitudes.

Now we can determine the value of resistance for maximum power using this:

$$R_{Load} = \sqrt{R_{TH}^2 + (X_{TH} + X_{Load})^2}$$

Where:

$$R_{THEV} = 2.64$$

$$X_{THEV} = 3.52$$

$$X_{Load} = -5$$

Putting these values in, gives the following:

$$R_{Load} = \sqrt{2.64^2 + (3.52 - 5)^2}$$

Therefore:

$$R_{Load} = \sqrt{6.97 + 2.1904} = 3.0266 \, \Omega$$

CHAPTER 8 AC ANALYSIS

If we use this value for the resistance of the load, then the load impedance would change to this:

$$Z_{Load} = 3.0266 - j5 = 5.845 \langle -58.813° \rangle \, \Omega$$

This means that the current in the load would change to this:

$$i_{Load} = \frac{4\langle -126.87° \rangle}{(2.64 + j3.52) + (3.0266 - j5)}$$

Therefore:

$$i_{Load} = \frac{4\langle -126.87° \rangle}{5.667 - j1.48} = \frac{4\langle -126.87° \rangle}{5.857\langle -14.637° \rangle} = 682.943E^{-3}\langle -112.233° \rangle \, A$$

We can calculate the new power in the load using this:

$$P = (682.943E^{-3})^2 \times 3.0266 = 1.412 \, W$$

Just to check that this gives the maximum power in the load, we will change the resistance to 2.5 Ω and then 4.5 Ω.

When R = 2.5 Ω:

$$Z_{Load} = 2.5 - j5 = 5.59\langle -63.435° \rangle \, \Omega$$

This means that the current in the load would change to:

$$i_{Load} = \frac{4\langle -126.87° \rangle}{(2.64 + j3.52) + (2.5 - j5)}$$

Therefore:

$$i_{Load} = \frac{4\langle -126.87° \rangle}{5.14 - j1.48} = \frac{4\langle -126.87° \rangle}{5.349\langle -16.063° \rangle} = 747.803E^{-3}\langle -110.807° \rangle \, A$$

455

CHAPTER 8   AC ANALYSIS

We can calculate the new power in the load using this:

$$P = \left(747.803E^{-3}\right)^2 \times 2.5 = 1.398\,W$$

When R = 4.5Ω:

$$Z_{Load} = 4.5 - j5 = 6.727\langle -48.013°\rangle\,\Omega$$

This means that the current in the load would change to this:

$$i_{Load} = \frac{4\langle -126.87°\rangle}{(2.64 + j3.52) + (4.5 - j5)}$$

Therefore:

$$i_{Load} = \frac{4\langle -126.87°\rangle}{7.14 - j1.48} = \frac{4\langle -126.87°\rangle}{7.292\langle -11.711°\rangle} = 548.546E^{-3}\langle -115.159°\rangle\,A$$

We can calculate the new power in the load using this:

$$P = \left(548.546E^{-3}\right)^2 \times 4.5 = 1.354\,W$$

This would suggest that the value of 3.0266Ω for R_{load} produces the maximum power in the load. Therefore, the method is correct.

The Superposition Theory

We have used this rule with DC circuits, so now let's see how it works with AC circuits.

Example 8.6

Consider the circuit shown in Figure 8-20.

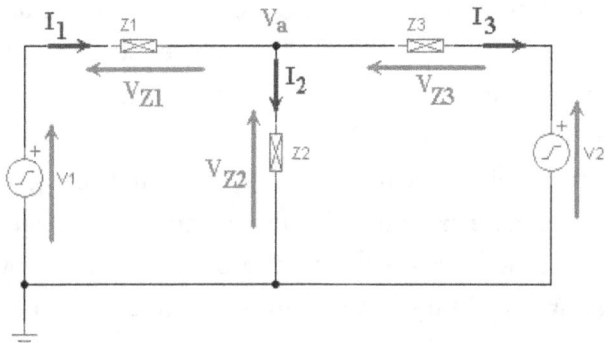

Figure 8-20. *The Circuit for Example 8.6*

We need to be able to calculate all the currents flowing in the circuit so that we can determine the correct wattage rating for the components. This method is based on an interpretation of Ohm's Law:

$$\text{The Current Flowing Through a Component} = \frac{\text{The Voltage at One End} - \text{The Voltage at The Other End}}{\text{The Impedance of The Component}}$$

If this is applied to the three currents flowing in the circuit shown in Figure 8-20, then the following can be said:

$$I_1 = \frac{V_1 - V_a}{Z_1}$$

$$I_2 = \frac{V_a - 0}{Z_2}$$

$$I_3 = \frac{V_a - V_2}{Z_3}$$

Note the three expressions assume that the direction of the current is clockwise, as shown in Figure 8-20. If this assumption is wrong, then the

CHAPTER 8   AC ANALYSIS

results will be negative, or 180° out of phase with what we have calculated, which means the current actually flows in the opposite direction. You have to start somewhere, so you need to assume a direction of current flow.

Before we can us the three expressions, we need to calculate the voltage (v_a) at the junction of all three impedance. This voltage will be due to the two sources in the circuit—V_1 and V_2. To determine this voltage, the superposition theory can be used.

The basic principle of the theory is that the actual voltage in any point of a circuit can be calculated by determining the voltage due to the sources, one at a time with the other sources being replaced by their ideal internal impedances. Then all results are added to give the final value of the voltage.

This means that we need to calculate the voltage v_a due to V_1 with V_2 replaced by a short circuit. Then calculate the voltage v_a due to V_2 with V_1 replaced by a short circuit. Then finally add the two results to determine the voltage, v_a. As is normal, we should state all the impedances and sources in both rectangular and polar format. Therefore, we have the following:

$$V_1 = 10 + j0\,v = 10\langle 0°\rangle v$$
$$V_2 = 20 - j20\,v = 28.284\langle -45°\rangle v$$
$$Z_1 = 5 + j10\,\Omega = 11.18\langle 63.435°\rangle \Omega$$
$$Z_2 = 5 - j20\,\Omega = 20.616\langle -75.964°\rangle \Omega$$
$$Z_3 = 5 + j12\,\Omega = 13\langle 67.38°\rangle \Omega$$

Again, we are using impedance, not actual components, so the frequency used in the circuit is irrelevant.

CHAPTER 8   AC ANALYSIS

The Voltage Va Due to V_1

The voltage source V_2 must be replaced with a short circuit. This is shown in Figure 8-21.

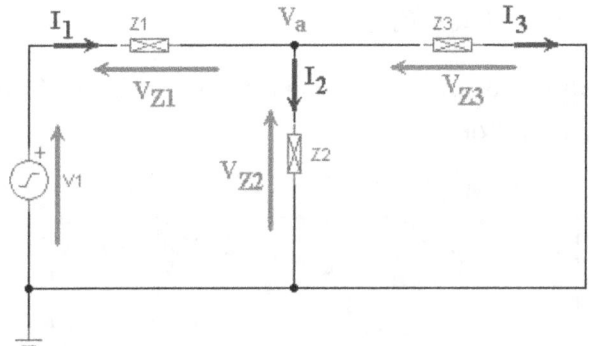

Figure 8-21. *The Circuit to Calculate v_a Due to V1*

Note that Z_2 and Z_3 are in parallel so we can calculate v_a due to V_1 using the voltage divider rule. We start by calculating Z_2 in parallel with Z_3 as follows:

$$\frac{Z_2 Z_3}{Z_2 + Z_3} = Z_{Comb1}$$

$$Z_{Comb1} = \frac{(20.616 \langle -75.964^o \rangle)(13 \langle 67.38^o \rangle)}{(5-j20)+(5+j12)} = \frac{268.008 \langle -8.584^o \rangle}{10-j8} = \frac{268.008 \langle -8.584^o \rangle}{12.806 \langle -38.66^o \rangle}$$

$$Z_{Comb1} = 20.928 \langle 30.076^o \rangle \, \Omega = 18.092 + j10.52 \, \Omega$$

Now complete the calculation of v_a due to V_1 as follows:

$$\text{Va Due To } V_1 = \frac{V_1 Z_{Comb1}}{Z_1 + Z_{Comb1}} = \frac{(10 \langle 0^o \rangle)(20.928 \langle 30.076^o \rangle)}{(5+j10)+(18.092+j10.52)} = \frac{209.28 \langle 30.076^o \rangle}{23.092+j20.52}$$

459

CHAPTER 8 AC ANALYSIS

$$\therefore \text{Va Due To V}_1 = \frac{209.28 \langle 30.076° \rangle}{30.892 \langle 41.625° \rangle} = 6.775 \langle -11.549° \rangle v = 6.638 - j1.356\, v$$

The Voltage Va Due to V₂

Figure 8-22 shows the circuit to calculate v_a due to V_2. The V_1 supply has been replaced by a short circuit.

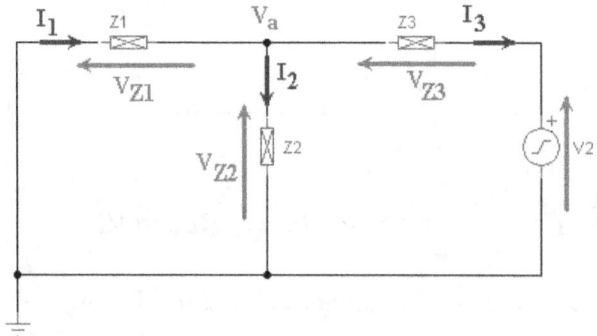

Figure 8-22. *The Circuit to Calculate v_a Due to V2*

Figure 8-22 shows that v_a due to V_2 can be calculated in the same way as v_a due to V_1 except that Z_1 and Z_2 are in parallel. We start by calculating Z_{Comb2}, which is Z_1 in parallel with Z_2:

$$Z_{Comb2} = \frac{(11.18\langle 63.435°\rangle)(20.616\langle -75.964°\rangle)}{(5+j10)+(5-j20)} = \frac{230.487\langle -12.529°\rangle}{10-j10} = \frac{230.487\langle -12.529°\rangle}{14.142\langle -45°\rangle}$$

$$Z_{Comb2} = 16.298\langle 32.471°\rangle\,\Omega = 13.75 + j8.75\,\Omega$$

Therefore, we have the following:

$$\text{Va Due To V}_2 = \frac{V_2 Z_{Comb2}}{Z_3 + Z_{Comb2}} = \frac{(28.284\langle -45°\rangle)(16.298\langle 32.471°\rangle)}{(5+j12)+(13.75+j8.75)}$$

$$\text{Va Due To } V_2 = \frac{460.973\langle -12.529\rangle}{18.75 + j20.75}$$

$$\text{Va Due To } V_2 = \frac{V_2 Z_{Comb2}}{Z_3 + Z_{Comb2}} = \frac{460.973\langle -12.529^o\rangle}{27.966\langle 47.899^o\rangle}$$

$$\text{Va Due To } V_2 = 16.483\langle -60.428^o\rangle v = 8.135 - j14.336\,v$$

The Complete Voltage Va

To calculate the actual voltage at v_a we simply need to add the two results, as follows:

$$V_a = V_a \text{ due to } V_1 + V_a \text{ due to } V_2$$

$$\therefore V_a = (6.638 - j1.356) + (8.135 - j14.336)$$

$$\therefore V_a = 14.773 - j15.692\,v$$

$$\therefore V_a = 21.55\langle -46.7^o\rangle v$$

The Three Currents Flowing in the Circuit

We can now calculate the three currents.
The current i_1 can be calculated as follows:

$$i_1 = \frac{V_1 - V_a}{Z_1}$$

$$\therefore i_1 = \frac{(10 + j0) - (14.773 - j15.692)}{5 + j10} = \frac{-4.773 + j15.692}{5 + j10}$$

$$i_1 = \frac{16.402\langle -73.082^o\rangle}{11.18\langle 63.435^o\rangle} = 1.467\langle -136.517^o\rangle \text{ Amps} = -1.064 - j1.01\,Amp$$

461

CHAPTER 8 AC ANALYSIS

Similarly, the current i_2 can be calculated as follows:

$$i_2 = \frac{V_a}{Z_2} = \frac{14.773 - j15.692}{5 - j20} = \frac{21.55\langle -46.7°\rangle v}{20.616\langle -75.964°\rangle}$$

$$i_2 = 1.045\langle 29.264\rangle \ Amps = 911.634E^{-3} + j510.832E^{-3} \ Amps$$

Finally, the current i_3 can be calculated as follows:

$$i_3 = \frac{V_a - V_2}{Z_3} = \frac{(14.776 - j15.685) - (20 - j20)}{5 + j12}$$

$$i_3 = \frac{-5.224 + j4.315}{13\langle 67.38°\rangle}$$

$$i_3 = \frac{6.776\langle -39.557°\rangle}{13\langle 67.38°\rangle} = 521.23E^{-3}\langle -106.937°\rangle \ Amps$$

In rectangular format, this is:

$$i_3 = -151.81E^{-3} - j498.517E^{-3} \ Amps$$

If we use the complex conjugate to calculate i_3, we get the following:

$$\therefore i_3 = \frac{-5.225 + j4.315}{5 + j12} = \frac{(-5.225 + j4.315)(5 - j12)}{(5 + j12)(5 - j12)}$$

$$\therefore i_3 = \frac{25.659 + j84.27}{169}$$

$$\therefore i_3 = 0.152 + j0.499 \ A$$

$$\therefore i_3 = 0.521\langle 73.065°\rangle A$$

The two methods give the same result. It is up to you which method you use.

CHAPTER 8   AC ANALYSIS

A simulation can be used to verify the results, as shown in Figure 8-23.

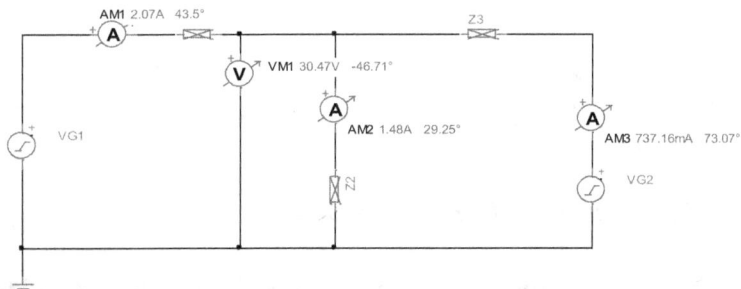

Figure 8-23. *The Simulation for Example 8.6 with the Measured Results*

When we use the RMS values of the meter readings shown in Figure 8-23, we see that they all agree with our calculations. The only difference is the phase angle for the current i_1. The simulation shows an angle of 43.5° whereas our calculations give the angle -136.517°. This is a difference 180°, which suggests that our assumed direction of current was wrong.

Using Thevenin's Theory to Confirm the Result

We may not have any ECAD software to confirm the calculation. However, you should always check your work. Once you sign off your design, you are responsible for it. We will use Thevenin's theory to confirm the work. We will use the impedance Z_2 as our load and create our Thevenin's equivalent circuit. We must remove the load and replace both voltage sources with their ideal internal impedance, as a short circuit. This will create the circuit shown in Figure 8-24.

463

CHAPTER 8 AC ANALYSIS

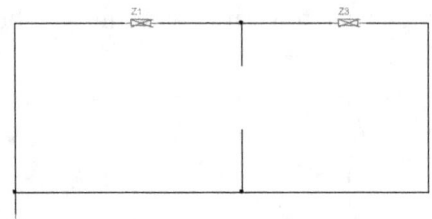

Figure 8-24. *Thevenin's Impedance Z_{THEV}*

Note that, because the two tops of Z_1 and Z_3 are connected and the two bottoms are connected, we can say this:

$$Z_{THEV} = \frac{Z_1 Z_3}{Z_1 + Z_3}$$

Therefore:

$$Z_{THEV} = \frac{(11.18 \langle 63.435 \rangle)(13 \langle 67.38 \rangle)}{(5+j10)+(5+j12)}$$

Therefore:

$$Z_{THEV} = \frac{(145.34 \langle 130.815 \rangle)}{(10+j22)} = \frac{(145.34 \langle 130.815 \rangle)}{(24.1661 \langle 65.556 \rangle)}$$

Therefore:

$$Z_{THEV} = 6.014 \langle 65.259° \rangle = 2.517 + j5.462 \, \Omega$$

We now need to calculate V_{THEV} due to the two voltage sources. We can calculate V_{THEV} due to V_1 using the circuit shown in Figure 8-25.

CHAPTER 8   AC ANALYSIS

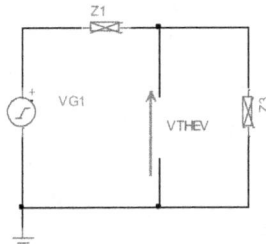

Figure 8-25. *The Circuit to Calculate V_{THEV} due to V_1*

We can use the voltage divider rule to calculate this voltage, as V_{THEV} is simply the voltage across Z_3. Therefore, we can say:

$$V_{THEV\,Due\,To\,V1} = \frac{V_1 Z_3}{Z_1 + Z_3}$$

Therefore,

$$V_{THEV\,Due\,To\,V1} = \frac{(10\langle 0\rangle)(13\langle 67.38\rangle)}{(5+j10)+(5+j12)} = \frac{130\langle 67.38\rangle}{10+j22}$$

Therefore,

$$V_{THEV\,Due\,To\,V1} = \frac{130\langle 67.38\rangle}{24.166\langle 65.556\rangle} = 5.379\langle 1.824\rangle v$$

In rectangular format.

$$V_{THEV\,Due\,To\,V1} = 5.376 + j171.21E^{-3}$$

We can now calculate V_{THEV} due to V_2 using the circuit shown in Figure 8-26.

465

CHAPTER 8   AC ANALYSIS

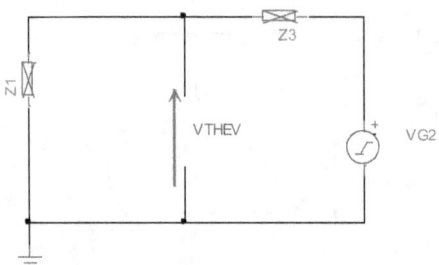

Figure 8-26. *The Circuit to Calculate V_{THEV} Due to V_2*

We can use the voltage divider rule to calculate this voltage. Therefore, we can say.

$$V_{THEV\ Due\ To\ V2} = \frac{V_2 Z_1}{Z_1 + Z_3}$$

Therefore,

$$V_{THEV\ Due\ To\ V2} = \frac{(28.284\langle-45\rangle)(11.18\langle63.435\rangle)}{(5+j10)+(5+j12)}$$

$$V_{THEV\ Due\ To\ V2} = \frac{316.215\langle18.435\rangle}{10+j22}$$

Therefore,

$$V_{THEV\ Due\ To\ V2} = \frac{316.215\langle18.435\rangle}{24.166\langle65.556\rangle} = 13.085\langle-47.121\rangle v$$

In rectangular format.

$$V_{THEV\ Due\ To\ V2} = 8.904 - j9.589$$

466

We now need to add these to get V_{THEV} as follows.

$$V_{THEV} = (5.376 + j171.21E^{-3}) + (8.904 - j9.589)$$

Therefore,

$$V_{THEV} = 14.28 - j9.417 = 17.1055 \langle -33.403 \rangle v$$

The Thevenin's equivalent circuit is shown in Figure 8-27.

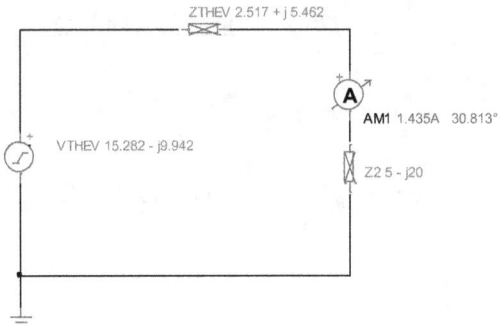

Figure 8-27. *Thevenin's Equivalent Circuit*

We can calculate the current through Z_2 as follows.

$$i_{Z2} = \frac{V_{THEV}}{Z_{THEV} + Z_2} = \frac{17.1055 \langle -33.403 \rangle}{(2.517 + j5.462) + (5 - j20)}$$

$$i_{Z2} = \frac{17.1055 \langle -33.403 \rangle}{(7.517 - j14.538)} = \frac{17.1055 \langle -33.403 \rangle}{16.3664 \langle -62.658 \rangle}$$

Therefore,

$$i_{Z2} = 1.045 \langle 29.255 \rangle A$$

This calculation agrees with the simulated result shown in Figure 8-27 and close to the results shown in Figure 8-23.

CHAPTER 8 AC ANALYSIS

Example 8.7

We will use the superposition theory to calculate the current flowing in the circuit shown in Figure 8-28. We should start by expression the phasor quantities for the sources and impedances in both rectangular and polar formats.

$$Z_1 = 5 + j10 = 11.18 \langle 63.435^o \rangle \Omega$$

$$Z_2 = 2 + j20 = 20.0998 \langle 78.69^o \rangle \Omega$$

$$Z_3 = 0 - j20 = 20 \langle -90^o \rangle \Omega$$

$$Z_4 = 5 + j15 = 15.811 \langle 71.565^o \rangle \Omega$$

$$Z_5 = 15 + j25 = 29.155 \langle 59.036^o \rangle \Omega$$

As there are three separate currents in the circuit, we will create the three equations, one for each current, as follows:

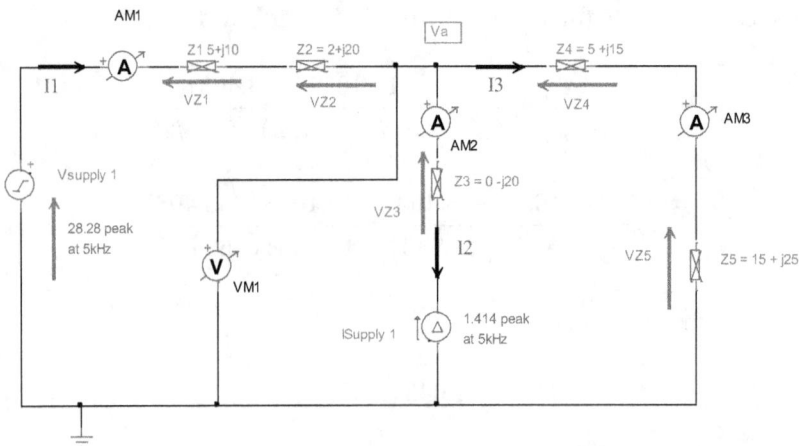

Figure 8-28. *The Circuit for Example 8.7 with the Voltage Source VSupply1 and the Current Source ISupply1*

468

CHAPTER 8   AC ANALYSIS

The three expressions are as follows:

$$i_1 = \frac{v_{Supply1} - v_a}{Z_1 + Z_2}$$

$$i_2 = \frac{v_a}{Z_3}$$

However, we must appreciate that the current source will not allow any current flow through it. The only purpose of the current source is to force current to flow into the circuit. The value of the current from the current source flows up through Z_3 into the rest of the circuit. Therefore, the current i_2 is simply the current from the current source:

$$i_3 = \frac{v_a}{Z_4 + Z_5}$$

We can calculate $Z_1 + Z_2$ as follows:

$$Z_1 + Z_2 = (5 + j10) + (2 + j20) = 7 + j30\, \Omega$$

Also:

$$Z_4 + Z_5 = (5 + j15) + (15 + j25) = 20 + j40\, \Omega$$

It is useful to express these in their polar format, which gives:

$$Z_1 + Z_2 = 30.806 \langle 76.866^o \rangle \Omega$$

$$Z_4 + Z_5 = 44.721 \langle 63.435^o \rangle \Omega$$

We now need to calculate the voltage at v_a. As there are two sources, we need to use the superposition rule. We will calculate v_a due to $v_{Supply1}$ first. We must replace the current source with an open circuit. This gives us the circuit shown in Figure 8-29.

469

CHAPTER 8   AC ANALYSIS

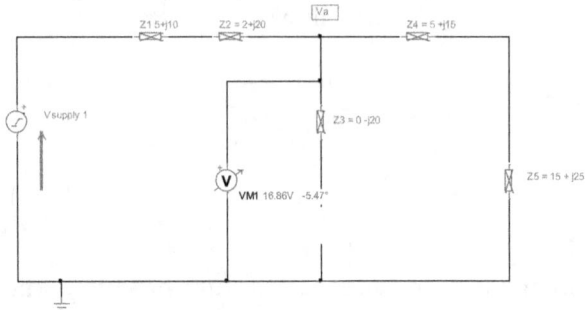

Figure 8-29. *The Circuit to Help Calculate v_a Due to vSupply1*

I hope you can see that, as no current flows through Z_3, it plays no part in the circuit. Also, I hope you can see that V_a is simply the volt drop across Z_4 and Z_5. We can use the voltage divider rule to calculate V_a due to $v_{Supply1}$ as follows:

$$v_a \text{ due to } v_{Supply1} = \frac{v_{Supply1}(Z_4 + Z_5)}{Z_1 + Z_2 + Z_4 + Z_5}$$

We can calculate $Z_1+Z_2+Z_4+Z_5$ as follows:

$$Z_1 + Z_2 + Z_4 + Z_5 = (7 + j30) + (20 + j40) = 27 + j70 \, \Omega$$

In polar format, this is:

$$Z_1 + Z_2 + Z_4 + Z_5 = 75.027 \langle 68.908 \rangle \, \Omega$$

Therefore:

$$v_a \text{ due to } v_{Supply1} = \frac{(20 \langle 0° \rangle)(44.721 \langle 63.435° \rangle)}{75.027 \langle 68.908° \rangle} = 11.921 \langle -5.473° \rangle v$$

If we divide the 16.86V, shown in Figure 8-29, by $\sqrt{2}$ we get the RMS voltage of 11.921. The angle is the same as that displayed by VM1 in

CHAPTER 8 AC ANALYSIS

Figure 8-29. We need to express this in rectangular format, because we will be adding it later. In rectangular format, we get the following:

$$v_a \text{ due to } v_{Supply1} = 11.921Cos\langle-5.473°\rangle + j11.921Sin\langle-5.473°\rangle$$
$$= 11.867 - j1.137\ v$$

Now we need to calculate v_a due to $i_{Supply1}$. We need to replace $v_{Supply1}$ with a short circuit. That gives the circuit shown in Figure 8-30.

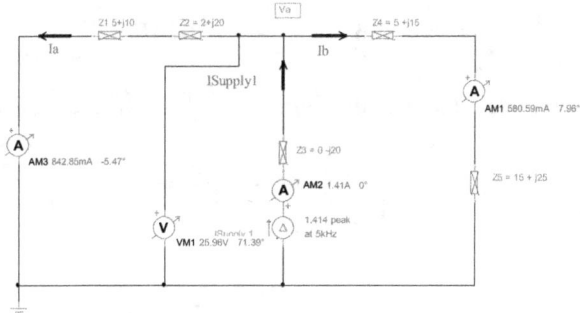

Figure 8-30. *The Circuit to Help Calculate v_a Due to iSupply1*

We can see that when the current reaches the node at v_a it will divide into the two currents, I_a and I_b. We can also see that the voltage v_a is the volt drop across Z_4 and Z_5. This is due to the current I_b flowing through them. We can use the current divider rule to calculate this current, I_b, as follows:

$$I_b = \frac{(i_{Supply})(Z_1 + Z_2)}{Z_1 + Z_2 + Z_4 + Z_5}$$

Putting the values in, we get the following:

$$I_b = \frac{(1\langle 0°\rangle)(30.806\langle 76.866°\rangle)}{75.027\langle 68.908°\rangle} = 410.599E^{-3}\langle 7.958°\rangle\ A$$

471

CHAPTER 8   AC ANALYSIS

If we divide the ammeter reading, shown in Figure 8-30, by $\sqrt{2}$, we get the RMS reading of 410.539mA. The angle is 7.96. These values agree with the calculation for I_b. However, if we don't have access to an ECAD software, we could use KCL to confirm our calculations. This means we need to express I_b in rectangular format, which is as follows:

$$I_b = 410.599E^{-3}Cos(7.958°) + j410.599E^{-3}Sin(7.958°)$$

$$I_b = 406.6445E^{-3} + j56.846E^{-3}$$

Now we must use the current divider rule to calculate I_a, as follows:

$$I_a = \frac{(i_{Supply})(Z_4 + Z_5)}{Z_1 + Z_2 + Z_4 + Z_5}$$

Putting the values in, we get the following:

$$I_a = \frac{(1\langle 0°\rangle)(44.721\langle 63.435°\rangle)}{75.027\langle 68.908°\rangle} = 596.065E^{-3}\langle -5.473°\rangle\ A$$

We need to express I_a in rectangular format, which is the following:

$$I_a = 596.065E^{-3}Cos(-5.473°) + j596.065E^{-3}Sin(-5.473°)$$

This gives us this:

$$I_a = 593.348E^{-3} - j56.851E^{-3}\ A$$

Using KCL, we can say this:

$$i_{current\ source} = I_a + I_b$$

$$= (593.348E^{-3} - j56.851E^{-3}) + (406.6445E^{-3} + j56.846E^{-3})$$

$$i_{current\ source} = 1 + j4.735E^{-6}$$

This confirms that our calculations for I_a and I_b are correct. We can also see that the AM1 meter reading in Figure 8-30 agrees with the calculation for I_b once we use the rms value.

We can now calculate v_a due to $i_{CurrentSource}$ as follows.

$$v_a\ Due\ to\ i_{current\ source} = i_b \times (z_4 + z_5)$$
$$v_a\ Due\ to\ i_{current\ source} = (410.599E^{-3}\ \langle 7.958 \rangle)(44.721\langle 63.435 \rangle)$$

$$= 18.362\langle 71.393 \rangle v$$

We need to express this in rectangular format to that we can add it to v_a due to $v_{Supply1}$. This gives.

$$v_a\ Due\ to\ i_{current\ source} = 18.362Cos(71.393) + j18.362\ Sin(71.393)$$

$$= 5.859 + j17.402\ v$$

We can now calculate v_a as follows.

$$v_a = (11.867 - j1.137) + (5.859 + j17.402) = 17.726 + j16.265v$$

We need to express this in polar format which gives.

$$v_a = 24.057\langle 42.539 \rangle v$$

We can now use this voltage to calculate the three currents as follows. The current i_1 is.

$$i_1 = \frac{v_{Supply1} - v_a}{Z_1 + Z_2}$$

CHAPTER 8 AC ANALYSIS

Putting the values in, we get the following:

$$i_1 = \frac{(20+j0)-(17.726+j16.265)}{7+j30} = \frac{2.275-j16.265}{7+j30}$$

Converting to polar so we can complete the calculation gives us this:

$$i_1 = \frac{16.423\langle -82.038^o \rangle}{30.806\langle 76.866^o \rangle} = 533.11E^{-3}\langle -158.904^o \rangle \, A$$

The current i_2.

This is simply the value of the current source; therefore, it will be:

$$1\langle 0^o \rangle \, A$$

The ammeter AM1 shows this as follows:

$$1\langle 180^o \rangle \, A$$

This is because the initial assumption of current flow is in the opposite direction.

The current i_3 is as follows:

$$i_3 = \frac{v_a}{Z_4+Z_5} = \frac{24.057\langle 42.539^o \rangle}{44.721\langle 63.435^o \rangle} = 537.935E^{-3}\langle -20.896^o \rangle \, A$$

This agrees with the RMS readings of the ammeter shown in Figure 8-28.

CHAPTER 8   AC ANALYSIS

Splitting a Circuit into Different Sections
Example 8.8

In this example we look at a larger circuit where it might be useful to split the circuit into easier smaller sections. We use Thevenin's theory to determine the current in Z_5 in the following circuit and then confirm the results by comparison with the meter readings.

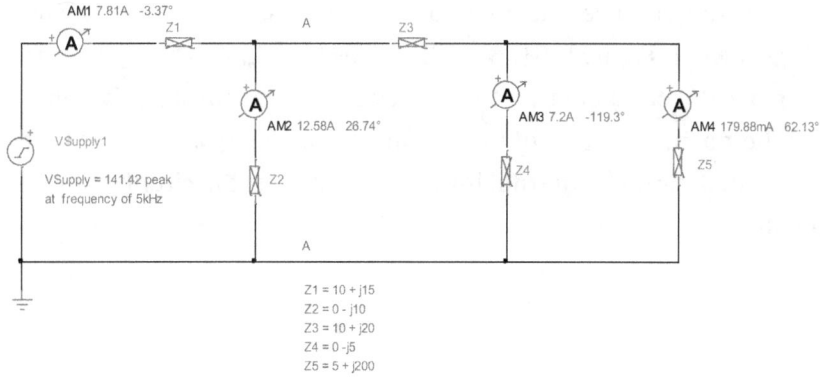

Figure 8-31. *The Circuit for Example 8.8*

We need to list the impedances and the sources in both complex formats, as follows:

$$Z_1 = 10 + j15\,\Omega = 18.028\langle 56.31°\rangle\,\Omega$$

$$Z_2 = 0 - j10\,\Omega = 10\langle -90°\rangle\,\Omega$$

$$Z_3 = 10 + j20\,\Omega = 22.361\langle 63.435°\rangle\,\Omega$$

$$Z_4 = 0 - j5\,\Omega\,5\langle -90°\rangle\,\Omega$$

$$Z_5 = 5 + j200\,\Omega = 200.062\langle 88.568°\rangle\,\Omega$$

$$V_{Supply} = 100 + j0\,v = 100\langle 0°\rangle\,v$$

475

CHAPTER 8   AC ANALYSIS

There are various ways we can analyse this circuit, but we will use Thevenin's approach. We could start anywhere in the circuit, but we will use the theory to determine the current flowing through the impedance Z_5. This means that we could remove this impedance and replace the circuit looking back into it from where Z_5 has been removed. It should not be too difficult to calculate Thevenin's impedance, Z_{TH}, but there may be some issues when calculating Thevenin's voltage, V_{TH}. To make it easier, we can try to split the circuit into smaller sections and replace the section with their Thevenin's equivalent circuit as we progress. Starting with section A-A, as shown in Figure 8-31, we will remove the Z_3, Z_4, and Z_5 impedances and replace the circuit to the left of A-A with a Thevenin's equivalent circuit. Removing this part of the circuit and replacing all sources that are left with their ideal internal impedance gives us the circuit shown in Figure 8-32.

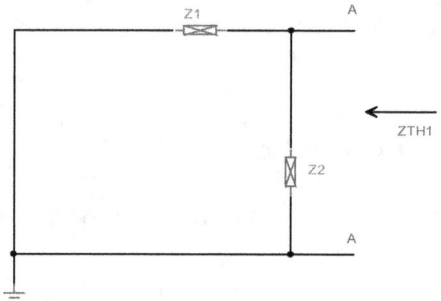

Figure 8-32. *The First Section of the Example 8.1 Circuit*

Figure 8-32 should show us that Z_{THEV1} is simply the parallel combination of Z_1 and Z_2. Therefore:

$$Z_{THEV1} = \frac{Z_1 Z_2}{Z_1 + Z_2} = \frac{(18.028\langle 56.31°\rangle)(10\langle -90°\rangle)}{(10+j15)+(0-j10)} = \frac{180.28\langle -33.69°\rangle}{10+j5} = \frac{180.28\langle -33.69°\rangle}{11.18\langle 26.565°\rangle}$$

476

Therefore:

$$Z_{THEV1} = 16.125 \langle -60.255° \rangle \, \Omega = 8.0003 - j14.0004 \, \Omega$$

We can use the voltage divider rule, as V_{THEV1} is the voltage across Z_2. Therefore, we can say this:

$$V_{THEV1} = \frac{V_{Supply} Z_2}{Z_1 + Z_2} = \frac{(100 \langle 0° \rangle)(10 \langle -90° \rangle)}{(10 + j15) + ((0 - j10))} = \frac{1000 \langle -90° \rangle}{11.18 \langle 26.565° \rangle} = 89.445 \langle -116.565° \rangle \, v$$

$$V_{THEV1} = 89.445 \langle -116.565° \rangle \, v = -40.001 - j80.002 \, v$$

We can now replace the section to the left of A-A with Thevenin's equivalent circuit for that section. Thevenin's circuit is shown in Figure 8-33.

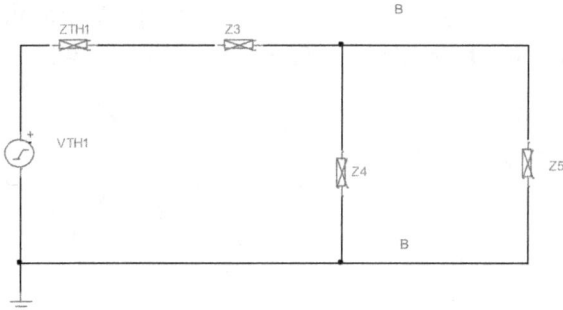

Figure 8-33. *The Rest of the Circuit Being Fed from the First Thevenin's Equivalent Circuit*

By inspecting Figure 8-33, we can see that if we remove Z_5 at Section B-B, we can calculate Thevenin's impedance, Z_{THEV2}, as we have Z_4 in parallel with the series combination of Z_{THEV1} and Z_3. Therefore, we can say that:

$$Z_{THEV2} = \frac{(Z_{THEV1} Z_3) Z_4}{(Z_{THEV1} + Z_3) + Z_4}$$

477

CHAPTER 8   AC ANALYSIS

$$Z_{THEV2} = \frac{(5\langle-90°\rangle) \times ((8.0003 - j14.0004) + (10 + j20))}{(8.0003 - j14.0004) + (10 + j20) + (0 - j5)} = \frac{(5\langle-90°\rangle) \times (18 + j6)}{18 + j1}$$

$$Z_{THEV2} = \frac{(5\langle-90°\rangle)(18.974\langle 18.435°\rangle)}{18.028\langle 3.18°\rangle} = 5.262\langle-74.745°\rangle \Omega = 1.385 + j - 5.077\,\Omega$$

From the inspection of Figure 8-33, with Z_5 removed, we can see that the open circuit voltage V_{THEV2} will be the voltage across the Z_4 impedance. This can be calculated using the voltage divider rule, as follows:

$$V_{THEV2} = \frac{V_{THEV1} Z_4}{Z_{THEV1} + Z_3 + Z_4} = \frac{(89.445\langle-116.565°\rangle)(5\langle-90°\rangle)}{(18.028\langle 3.18°\rangle)} = 24.807\langle-209.745°\rangle\,v$$

This means that we can now replace the complete circuit with this new Thevenin's equivalent circuit. This is shown in Figure 8-34.

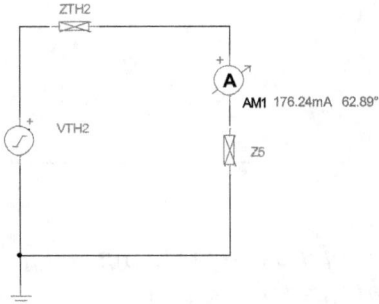

Figure 8-34. *The Completed Thevenin's Equivalent Circuit*

We can now calculate the current flowing through Z_5 as follows:

$$i_{Z5} = \frac{V_{THEV2}}{Z_{THEV2} + Z_5} = \frac{24.807\langle-209.745°\rangle}{(1.385 + j - 5.077) + (5 + j200)} = \frac{24.807\langle-209.745°\rangle}{6.385 + j194.923}$$

478

CHAPTER 8   AC ANALYSIS

Therefore:

$$i_{Z5} = \frac{24.807 \langle -209.745^o \rangle}{195.028 \langle 88.124^o \rangle} = 127.197 E^{-3} \langle -297.869^o \rangle \, Amps$$

This is very close to the RMS value of the peak current measured by AM1 in Figure 8-1 and the angle of -297.869° is at the same point on the phasor diagram as the angle of 62.89°. This confirms that we can apply Thevenin's theory to a circuit with more than one loop in it. You just have to take your time and check your work as you go from one stage to the next. The maths is not too complicated, even though we are using complex numbers. There is just a lot of it. However, electrical engineers must calculate the current flowing through any component in the circuit so that they can use the correct wattage rating for the component. If they don't, they risk causing a fire, which could be considered criminal negligence. Therefore, you must take your time and work everything out carefully before you build and sell your designs.

An Alternative Approach

I have said before that you should always check your work using different approaches. Also, you won't always have access to an ECAD software. If we look at the circuit shown in Figure 8-31, we can see that it is really a circuit that is a combination of series and parallel impedances. This means that we should be able to combine the impedances so that we will have just one impedance, which would be the total impedance Z_T for the whole circuit. We will use an approach that is similar to the analysis we did with the DC circuits in Chapter 2 to confirm the current flowing through Z_5.

CHAPTER 8 AC ANALYSIS

First, we must combine the impedances farthest away from the supply. This would be Z_4 in parallel with Z_5. Therefore, using the product over sum method, we can say this:

$$Z_{COMB1} = \frac{(Z_4)(Z_5)}{(Z_4)+(Z_5)} = \frac{(5\langle-90°\rangle)(200.062\langle 88.568°\rangle)}{(0-j5)+(5+j200)}$$

$$Z_{COMB1} = \frac{1000.31\langle-1.432°\rangle}{195.064\langle 88.531°\rangle} = 5.128\langle-89.963°\rangle\,\Omega$$

In rectangular format, we have the following:

$$Z_{COMB1} = 3.285E^{-3} - j5.128\,\Omega$$

We can now combine this impedance with Z_3. Because as they are in series, this would give the following:

$$Z_{COMB2} = Z_3 + Z_{COMB1} = (10+j20)+(3.285E^{-3}-j5.128)\,\Omega$$

Therefore, we have the following:

$$Z_{COMB2} = 10.003 + j14.872\,\Omega$$

In polar format, we have the following:

$$Z_{COMB2} = 17.923\langle 56.074°\rangle\,\Omega$$

Next, we can calculate Z_{COMB3}, as this is the parallel combination of Z_2 and Z_{COMB2}. Therefore, we can say this:

$$Z_{COMB3} = \frac{(Z_{COMB2})(Z_2)}{(Z_{COMB2})+(Z_2)} = \frac{(17.923\langle 56.074°\rangle)(10\langle-90°\rangle)}{(10.003+j14.872)+(0-j10)}$$

CHAPTER 8 AC ANALYSIS

This gives us this:

$$Z_{COMB3} = \frac{179.23\langle -33.926^o \rangle}{11.126 \langle 25.969^o \rangle} = 16.109 \langle -59.895^o \rangle \, \Omega$$

In rectangular format, we have the following:

$$Z_{COMB3} = 8.08 - j13.935 \, \Omega$$

Finally, we can now calculate the total impedance by adding Z_1 to Z_{COMB3}, as they are in series:

$$Z_T = Z_1 + Z_{COMB3} = (10 + j15) + (8.08 - j13.935) = 18.08 + j1.065 \, \Omega$$

In polar format, we have the following:

$$Z_T = 18.111 \langle 3.37^o \rangle \, \Omega$$

Now we can calculate the current that the circuit will take from the supply as follows:

$$i_{Supply} = \frac{V_{Supplyrms}}{Z_T} = \frac{100 \langle 0^o \rangle}{18.111 \langle 3.37^o \rangle} = 5.522 \langle -3.37^o \rangle \, A$$

In rectangular format, we have the following:

$$i_{Supply} = 5.512 - j0.325 \, A$$

We can calculate the current that would flow through Z_2 using Ohm's Law, as follows:

$$i_{Z2} = \frac{v_{Z2}}{Z_2}$$

481

CHAPTER 8 AC ANALYSIS

The voltage across Z_2 is the supply voltage minus the volt drop across Z_1. We can calculate the volt drop across Z_2 using this:

$$v_{Z1} = i_{Supply} Z_1 = \left(5.522 \langle -3.37° \rangle\right)\left(18.028 \langle 56.31° \rangle\right) = 99.551 \langle 52.94° \rangle v$$

In rectangular format, this is as follows:

$$v_{Z1} = 59.995 + j79.442 \, v$$

We can now calculate the voltage across Z_2 as follows:

$$v_{Z2} = v_{Supplyrms} - v_{Z1} = (100 + j0) - (59.995 - j79.442) = 40.005 - j79.442 \, v$$

In polar format, we have the following:

$$v_{Z2} = 88.946 \langle -63.27° \rangle v$$

We can now calculate the current flowing though Z_2 as follows:

$$i_{Z2} = \frac{v_{Z2}}{Z_2} = \frac{88.946 \langle -63.27° \rangle}{10 \langle -90° \rangle} = 8.8846 \left(26.73°\right) A$$

In rectangular format, we have the following:

$$i_{Z2} = 7.935 + j3.996 \, A$$

We can use the KCL rule to calculate the current flowing through Z_3 as follows:

$$i_{Z3} = 1_{Supply} - i_{Z2} = (5.512 - j0.325) - (7.935 + j3.996) = -2.423 - j4.321 \, A$$

In polar format, we have the following:

$$i_{Z3} = 4.954 \langle -119.28° \rangle A$$

CHAPTER 8   AC ANALYSIS

Note that I subtracted 180° from the angle the calculator gave us because this phasor is in the third quadrant—that is, -a-jb format.

This means we can now calculate the volt drop across Z_3 as follows:

$$v_{Z3} = i_{Z3} Z_3 = \left(4.954 \langle -119.28° \rangle\right)\left(22.361 \langle 63.435° \rangle\right) = 110.777 \langle -55.845° \rangle v$$

In rectangular format, we have the following:

$$v_{Z3} = 62.194 - j91.67 \, v$$

We can now calculate the voltage across Z_4 and Z_5 as follows:

$$v_{Z4} = v_{Z2} - v_{Z3} = (40.005 - j79.442) - (62.194 - j91.67) = -22.189 + j12.228 \, v$$

In polar format, this would give us:

$$v_{Z4} = 25.335 \langle 151.141° \rangle v$$

Note that I added 180° to the angle that the calculation gave us, as the phasor is in the second quadrant—that is, -a+jb format.

As Z_4 is in parallel with Z_5, $v_{Z5} = v_{Z4}$. Therefore, we can calculate the current flowing through Z_5 as follows:

$$i_{Z5} = \frac{v_{Z5}}{Z_5} = \frac{25.335 \langle 151.141° \rangle}{200.062 \langle 88.568° \rangle} = 126.636 E^{-3} \langle 62.573° \rangle A$$

This value agrees with the simulated result shown in Figure 8-31 and the result of Thevenin's approach. I appreciate that there has been a lot of work in both methods, but the examples have shown us how to apply all the theories we have covered in this book to date. The examples also show how useful these complex numbers are when it comes to analysing AC electrical circuits.

483

CHAPTER 8   AC ANALYSIS

Converting a Complex Number into Components

When we first used impedance expressed as complex numbers in Example 8.1, I said I would explain how complex numbers relate to real components. It is not essential that we can do this, as the ECAD software TINA can cope quite easily with impedances expressed as complex numbers. However, it is interesting to see how the impedance can be related to actual components.

To do this, we need to apply a set frequency to the circuit. From Figure 8-1, we can see we have set frequency to 5kHz. We will start by looking at the impedance, Z_1. This states that:

$$Z_1 = 10 + j15 \, \Omega$$

The impedance is made up of a real term, the 10, and a j term, the 15. The real term of all impedances is a resistor, so Z_1 has a resistance of 10Ω.

The j term is the reactive component, which for positive values of j is an inductor, whilst for negative j indicates a capacitor. Therefore, Z_1 is +j15, which means this is made up of an inductor L that has an impedance of 15Ω. This means that we can say this:

$$X_L = 15 \, \Omega$$

This means that:

$$2\pi f L = 15 \, \Omega$$

Therefore:

$$L = \frac{15}{2\pi f} = \frac{15}{2\pi \times 5E^3} = 477.465E^{-6} = 447.465 \, \mu H$$

CHAPTER 8 AC ANALYSIS

This means that we can say Z_1 is made up of a 10Ω resistor in series with a 447.465 µH inductor.

We can do the same for Z_2, as follows:

$$Z_2 = 0 - j10 \, \Omega$$

The real term is 0, which means that there is no resistance associated with Z_2. The j term is negative, which means it is a capacitor with an impedance of 10Ω. This means we can say this:

$$X_C = 10 \, \Omega$$

Therefore, we can say this:

$$\frac{1}{2\pi fC} = 10 \, \Omega$$

Therefore, we can say this:

$$C = \frac{1}{2\pi f 10} = \frac{1}{20\pi \times 5E^3} = 3.183E^{-6} = 3.183 \, \mu F$$

This means that Z_2 is simply a capacitor with a value of 3.183 µF.

Exercise 8.1

See if you can confirm the remaining impedances.

- Z_3 is a 10Ω resistor in series with a 63.662mH
- Z_4 is capacitor of 6.366 µF
- Z_5 is a 5Ω resistor in series with a 6.366mH inductor

485

CHAPTER 8 AC ANALYSIS

Norton's Theory

Example 8.9

I personally prefer Thevenin's theory over Norton's, but for completeness we will use Norton's theory to confirm the calculations in Example 8.5. The circuit in Example 8.5 is shown again in Figure 8-35. However, we will use Z_3 as the load. The process is the same as with a DC circuit; we must remove the load and determine Norton's impedance, looking back into the circuit from where the load has been removed. We must also replace the sources with their ideal internal impedances. This means we should have the circuit shown in Figure 8-35.

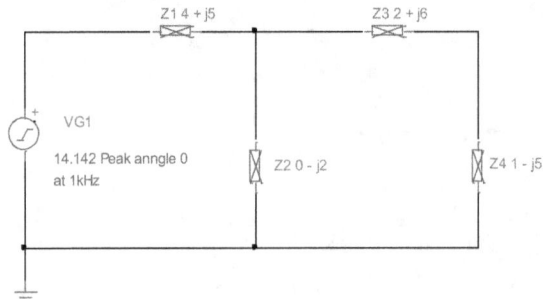

Figure 8-35. *The Circuit for Examples 8.5 and 8.9.*

The component values are as follows:

$$V_1 = 10 + j0\,v = 10\langle 0°\rangle v$$

$$Z_1 = 4 + j5 = 6.403\langle 51.34°\rangle \Omega$$

$$Z_2 = 0 - j2 = 2\langle -90°\rangle \Omega$$

$$Z_3 = 2 + j6 = 6.325\langle 71.565°\rangle \Omega$$

$$Z_4 = 1 - j5 = 5.099\langle -78.69°\rangle \Omega$$

CHAPTER 8 AC ANALYSIS

The circuit to help us calculate Z_{Nort} is shown in Figure 8-36.

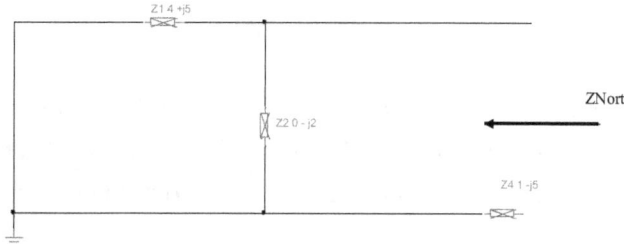

Figure 8-36. *The Circuit to Calculate Z_{NORT}*

From Figure 8-36, we can see that Z_{NORT} is simply the parallel combination of Z_1 and Z_2. It's in series with Z_4. We need to calculate Z_{COMB1}, which is the parallel combination of Z_1 and Z_2. Therefore, we can say this:

$$Z_{COMB1} = \frac{Z_1 Z_2}{Z_1 + Z_2} = \frac{(6.403 \langle 51.34° \rangle)(2 \langle -90° \rangle)}{(4+j5)+(0-j2)}$$

This then gives us this:

$$Z_{COMB1} = \frac{12.806 \langle -38.66° \rangle}{4+j3} = \frac{12.806 \langle -38.66° \rangle}{5 \langle 36.87° \rangle} = 2.561 \langle -75.53° \rangle \, \Omega$$

In rectangular format, this as follows:

$$Z_{COMB1} = 639.925E^{-3} - j2.48 \, \Omega$$

Therefore:

$$Z_{Nort} = Z_{COMB1} + Z_4 = (639.925E^{-3} - j2.48) + (1-j5) = 1.6399 - j7.48 \, \Omega$$

487

CHAPTER 8 AC ANALYSIS

In polar format, we have the following:

$$Z_{Nort} = 7.658 \angle (-77.634°) \, \Omega$$

We need to calculate Norton's current, which will be the current that will flow through a short circuit across where the load, Z_3, had been removed. The circuit shown in Figure 8-37 should help us with that.

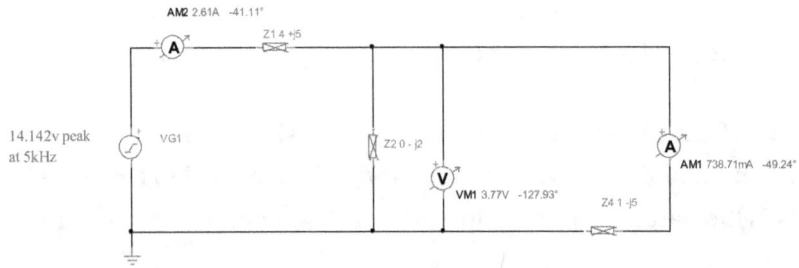

Figure 8-37. *The Circuit to Help Calculate i_{Nort}*

The ammeter AM1 is measuring the short circuit current, which is i_{Nort}. To calculate this current, we need to combine Z_2 and Z_4 in parallel to create Z_{COMB2} as follows:

$$Z_{COMB2} = \frac{(Z_2)(Z_4)}{(Z_2)+(Z_4)} = \frac{(2\angle -90°)(5.099 \angle -78.69°)}{(0-j2)+(1-j5)}$$

$$Z_{COMB2} = \frac{10.198 \angle -168.69°}{7.071 \angle -81.87°} = 1.442 \angle (-86.82°) \, \Omega$$

In rectangular format, we have the following:

$$Z_{COMB2} = 0.08 - j1.44 \, \Omega$$

We can now calculate the current flowing through Z_4 using this:

$$i_{Z4} = \frac{v_{Z4}}{Z_4}$$

488

CHAPTER 8   AC ANALYSIS

From Figure 8-37, we can see that:

$$v_{Z4} = v_{ZCOMB2}$$

We can calculate the voltage V_{ZCOMB2} as follows:

$$v_{ZCOMB2} = \frac{v_{Supply} Z_{COMB2}}{Z_{COMB2} + Z_1} = \frac{(10\langle 0°\rangle)(1.442\langle -86.82°\rangle)}{(0.08 - j1.44) + (4 + j5)}$$

$$v_{ZCOMB2} = \frac{14.42\langle -86.82°\rangle}{5.415\langle -41.106°\rangle} = 2.6631\langle -127.926°\rangle v$$

Finally, we can calculate Norton's current as follows:

$$i_{NORT} = i_{Z4} = \frac{2.6631\langle -127.926°\rangle}{5.099\langle -78.69°\rangle} = 522.3E^{-3}\langle -49.236°\rangle A$$

In rectangular format, we have the following:

$$i_{Nort} = 341.033E^{-3} - j395.593E^{-3} \ A$$

We can now create Norton's equivalent circuit. This is shown in Figure 8-38.

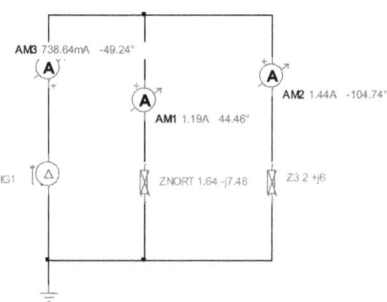

Figure 8-38. *Norton's Equivalent Circuit*

489

CHAPTER 8   AC ANALYSIS

The circuit in Figure 8-38 shows Norton's circuit with Z_3 placed in parallel with it. We can use the current divider rule to calculate the current flowing through Z_3, as follows:

$$i_{Z3} = \frac{i_{NORT} Z_{Nort}}{Z_{Nort} + Z_3} = \frac{\left(522.3E^{-3} \langle -49.236°\rangle\right)\left(7.658 \langle -77.634°\rangle\right)}{(1.6399 - j7.48) + (2 + j6)}$$

$$i_{Z3} = \frac{4.0 \langle -126.87°\rangle}{3.6399 - j1.48} = \frac{4.0 \langle -126.87°\rangle}{3.929 \langle -22.127°\rangle} = 1.018 \langle -104.743°\rangle \, A$$

This agrees with the simulated result. Also, when we compare the results with the calculated current for i_{Z4}, in Example 8.5, when using Thevenin's approach, we can see that they do match. This is because in the real circuit Z_3 and Z_4 are in series with each other.

One thing that these examples have shown is that with an AC circuit, some of the currents and voltages can be larger than expected. This is because a capacitor can become a temporary source of energy.

Exercise 8.2

This exercise uses the circuit shown in Figure 8-39.

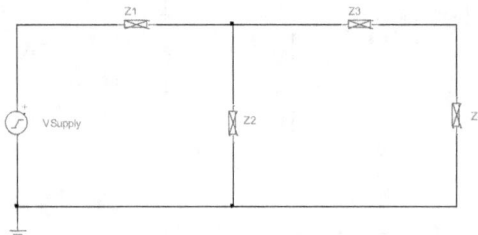

Figure 8-39. *The Circuit for Exercise 8.2*

CHAPTER 8 AC ANALYSIS

Q1

Using the two sets of component values, use Thevenin's theory to determine the value of the current flowing through the impedance Z_4. Then confirm your answers using Norton's theory.

Set A:

$$v_{Supply} = 25 + j0 \; v \; rms$$

$$Z_1 = 5 + j20 \; \Omega$$

$$Z_2 = 0 - j12 \; \Omega$$

$$Z_3 = 10 + j35 \; \Omega$$

$$Z_4 = 3 - j8 \; \Omega$$

Set B:

$$v_{Supply} = 20 + j10 \; v \; rms$$

$$Z_1 = 15 + j30 \; \Omega$$

$$Z_2 = 0 - j25 \; \Omega$$

$$Z_3 = 8 + j24 \; \Omega$$

$$Z_4 = 1 - j11 \; \Omega$$

CHAPTER 8   AC ANALYSIS

Q2

With respect to the circuit shown in Figure 8-39, use Thevenin's theory to determine the initial impedance for maximum power in the load, assuming Z_4 was the load. Then determine the correct value of resistance for maximum power in the load. Use the values for set A only.

Exercise 8.3

Q1

Using the circuit shown in Figure 8-40, calculate the current flowing through Z_2.

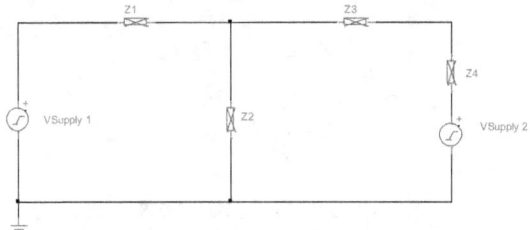

Figure 8-40. The Circuit for Exercise 8.3 Q1

Complete the exercise using the two sets of values of A and B.
Set A:

$$v_{Supply1} = 15 + j0\, v\, rms$$

$$v_{Supply2} = 10 + j10\, v\, rms$$

$$Z_1 = 15 + j20\, \Omega$$

$$Z_2 = 0 - j10\, \Omega$$

$$Z_3 = 20 + j35\,\Omega$$

$$Z_4 = 0 - j8\,\Omega$$

Set B:

$$v_{Supply\,1} = 25 + j0\,v\,rms$$

$$v_{Supply\,2} = 30 - j10\,v\,rms$$

$$Z_1 = 5 + j20\,\Omega$$

$$Z_2 = 0 - j20\,\Omega$$

$$Z_3 = 12 + j45\,\Omega$$

$$Z_4 = 0 - j8\,\Omega$$

Q2

If the $V_{Supply\,2}$ voltage source was replaced by a current source pushing a 500mA rms with an angle of 0°, current upwards through Z_4, calculate all the currents flowing in the circuit, assuming $V_{Supply\,1}$ and all four impedances were unchanged. Use set A values.

Exercise 8.4

Q1

With respect to the circuit shown in Figure 8-41, use two methods to calculate the current flowing through Z_5. Use the values for the components as listed.

CHAPTER 8   AC ANALYSIS

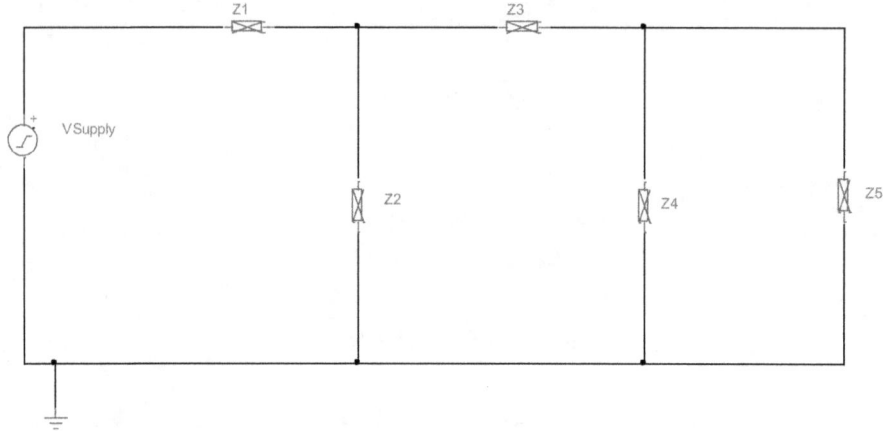

Figure 8-41. *The Circuit for Exercise 8.4 Q1*

The component values are as follows:

$$V_1 = 15 + j0 \; v \; rms$$

$$Z_1 = 14 + j15 \, \Omega$$

$$Z_2 = 0 - j12 \, \Omega$$

$$Z_3 = 12 + j16 \, \Omega$$

$$Z_4 = 0 - j15 \, \Omega$$

$$Z_5 = 5 + j11 \, \Omega$$

The answers to these exercises are listed after the summary.

CHAPTER 8   AC ANALYSIS

Summary

In this chapter we have applied Thevenin's Norton's theories as well as the Superposition rule to ac circuits. We have experienced how the use of complex numbers can be used to analyse ac circuits. I hope, that through the use of these examples you have learnt how to apply your understanding how parts of the circuit are connected together in analysing ac circuits and you have learnt how to use the different theorems with ac circuits.

In the next chapter we will look at how electrical engineers can attempt to create one of nature's most hidden but effective forces that of magnetism. We will study how we can represent magnetic systems as a magnetic circuit.

Answers to Exercise 8.2

Ex2 Q1 Set A.

$$Z_{Thev} = 20.691 \langle 29.0697 \rangle \, \Omega$$

$$i_{Z4} = 1.5 \langle -153.563 \rangle \, A$$

Set B

$$i_{Z4} = 601.657 E^{-3} \langle -80.651 \rangle \, A$$

Q2

$$Z_{THEV} = 18.099 + j10.0562 \, \Omega$$

For maximum power R should be 27.051Ω.

CHAPTER 8 AC ANALYSIS

Answers to Exercise 8.3

Set A

$$i_{Z2} = 1.56 \langle 8.495 \rangle \, A$$

Set B

$$i_{Z2} = 3.4457 \langle 55.748 \rangle \, A$$

Q2

$$i_{Z1} = 877.1E^{-3} \langle -15.255 \rangle \, A$$

$$i_{Z2} = 1.365 \langle -9.7276 \rangle \, A$$

$$i_{Z3} = i_{z4} = 500E^{-3} \langle 180 \rangle \, A$$

Answers to Exercise 8.4

$$i_{Z5} = 588.3E^{-3} \langle -163.61 \rangle \, A$$

CHAPTER 9

Magnetism, the Electromagnet, and the Inductor

In this chapter, we learn about magnetism and how we create it with electromagnetism. We learn about flux and flux density. We also learn about magnetic cores and how we use them to create an electromagnet.

After reading this chapter, you will:

- Understand what reluctance is and the difference between mmf and magnetising force, H.

- Be able to use a B/H curve to determine how different materials can be used for different purposes.

- Understand how to create magnetic circuits and use them to determine the energy drops in circuits.

Magnetism

Magnetism is one of the most formidable forces that exist in the world, or even the universe, even if it seems manmade or natural. It accounts for the tides that wash upon our shores and it is responsible for keeping

CHAPTER 9   MAGNETISM, THE ELECTROMAGNET, AND THE INDUCTOR

the solar system and its planets in place. It may even be linked to the way humans behave. For a long time, engineers have been able to produce magnetism and use it in many applications. Indeed, it has been one of the most important finds of engineering technology, as its uses range from the production of electricity, that keeps society running, to the microscopic storage of a single bit on a computer's hard drive. It is therefore essential that the engineer of today has a fundamental understanding of magnetism.

Michael Faraday: 1791 to 1867

Michael Faraday was an English scientist who made significant contributions to the study of electricity and magnetism. He found that when a length of wire is moved through a magnetic field, a voltage can be induced across it and if the wire makes up a complete circuit, then a current can be made to flow through it. The discovery of this phenomenon, which is called *electromagnetic induction,* contributed to the development of Maxwell's equations and led to the invention of the electric generator.

Electromagnetism

When a current is forced to pass through a conductor, a magnetic field is set up around it. Experiments have shown that the magnetic field orbits the conductor in circular paths perpendicular to the length of the conductor. The direction of rotation of the flux around the conductor is dependent upon direction of current passing through the conductor. The corkscrew rule helps us determine the direction of the flux around the conductor. To help use the rule, the direction of the current flow through the conductor is symbolised in Figure 9-1.

CHAPTER 9   MAGNETISM, THE ELECTROMAGNET, AND THE INDUCTOR

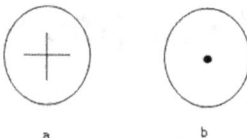

Figure 9-1. The Direction of Current Through a Conductor

In Figure 9-1, the direction of current flow in conductor a is into the paper; in conductor b the flow is out of the paper. A way of remembering this is to picture a crosshead screw; how you see the screw when you are screwing it in and then what it would look like coming out of the other side of the paper.

The magnetic flux orbits the conductors in circular paths, as shown in Figure 9-2.

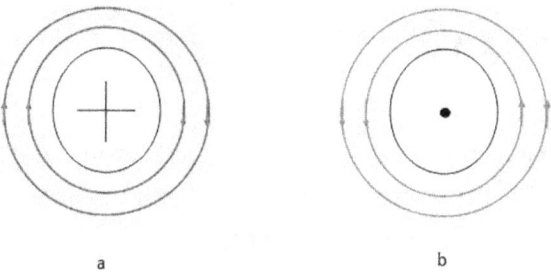

Figure 9-2. The Direction of Flux Around a Current Carrying Conductor

We can continue the screw analogy to remember the direction of the flux flow around the current carrying conductor. Figure 9-2a shows the current flowing into the paper. Therefore, to screw a screw into anything, we would have to turn the normal screw clockwise. This is the direction in which the flux flows around the conductor, as indicated by the four small arrows in the Figure 9-2a. Similarly, we have to turn the screw anticlockwise to draw it out of the paper and so the flux flows in an anticlockwise direction, as shown by the small arrows in Figure 9-2b.

499

CHAPTER 9　MAGNETISM, THE ELECTROMAGNET, AND THE INDUCTOR

The Magnetomotive Force (F)

The force that creates the magnetic field is the current. Therefore, if we consider this as the force that motivates the magnetic field, we can say we have a magnetomotive force, abbreviated to *mmf*, which is proportional to the current flowing through a coil of wire. Also, the greater the number of turns the current flows through, the greater the flux created. This means that the expression for this mmf given the symbol F is simply:

$$F = IN$$

The units are simply Ampere Turns. However, some might say that as turns N does not have any units, the units for mmf should be just amps.

Flux Density (B)

Flux is a difficult quantity to grasp, as it is invisible. Indeed, flux can only be shown to exist by the effect that it has on its surrounding area and the objects nearby. Bring two magnets together and you will experience the effect of the flux, but you won't see the flux. That is one reason that engineers use the measure of the density of the flux to quantify this magnetic effect. The symbol for flux density is B and this is a measure of the amount of flux in an area. The symbol for flux is ϕ and the symbol for area is A then the expression for flux density B is as follows:

$$B = \frac{\Phi}{A}$$

CHAPTER 9 MAGNETISM, THE ELECTROMAGNET, AND THE INDUCTOR

Nikola Tesla: 1856 to 1943

Tesla was an Austrian scientist who developed much of the early work on three-phase generation. If you read about his life, you will be very impressed by his dedication, vision, and work. Because of his contribution to the work with magnetic fields, the units for flux density are named after him.

The units for flux ϕ are Webers, or Wbs, and so the units for flux density B is Weber's/m². This is a difficult unit to state, therefore engineers use another term to describe the units of flux density, in recognition of the work of Nikola Tesla—the Tesla.

Therefore, the units for flux density B is the Tesla, T.

Note One Tesla is defined as 1 Weber of flux existing in an area of 1m².

One Tesla of flux density is a very large value, as is 1 Weber of flux. More usual values are 100mT and 100mWbs. There is a laboratory in Cheshire, England, where engineers have managed to create a flux density of 3 Tesla. This is at Darsby Labs, and they have created a Stonehenge arrangement of electromagnetic coils that has been used to split the atom, which requires an incredible force.

CHAPTER 9   MAGNETISM, THE ELECTROMAGNET, AND THE INDUCTOR

Flux, Flux Density, and the Coil

Engineers create much smaller electromagnetic coils and the way we create them is investigated here. With electromagnetism, a current is used to produce the flux. It can be shown that, to a certain limit, the greater the current flowing, the greater the flux created. To increase the flux more turns are added to the coil. This could be viewed as having a long length of wire made to occupy a small space, however, there is slightly more to it as we will see. Indeed, electromagnets are basically coils of wire wound on a former called a core. It has been shown that the flux will emanate radially away from the conductor or coil. The flux that is too far away from the coil is of little use. The flux, which is of most use, is the flux inside the confines of the coil. Indeed, engineers must do all they can to ensure as much of the flux as possible flows through the confines of the core.

Figure 9-3 shows a coil cut through the centre of the coils. The conductors on the left side carry the current into the coil and it passes around the coil coming out on the right side to carry on and enter the coil again on the left side. The current passes around the turns of the coil used to make up the electromagnet. Figure 9-2 shows how the flux rotates around the current carrying conductors, so I hope you can see why, with the conductors on the left side, the flux is rotating in a clockwise direction, whilst with the conductors on the right side, the flux flows in an anticlockwise direction. This means that the flux flows down the centre of the coil in the direction from top to bottom, as shown in Figure 9-3.

CHAPTER 9   MAGNETISM, THE ELECTROMAGNET, AND THE INDUCTOR

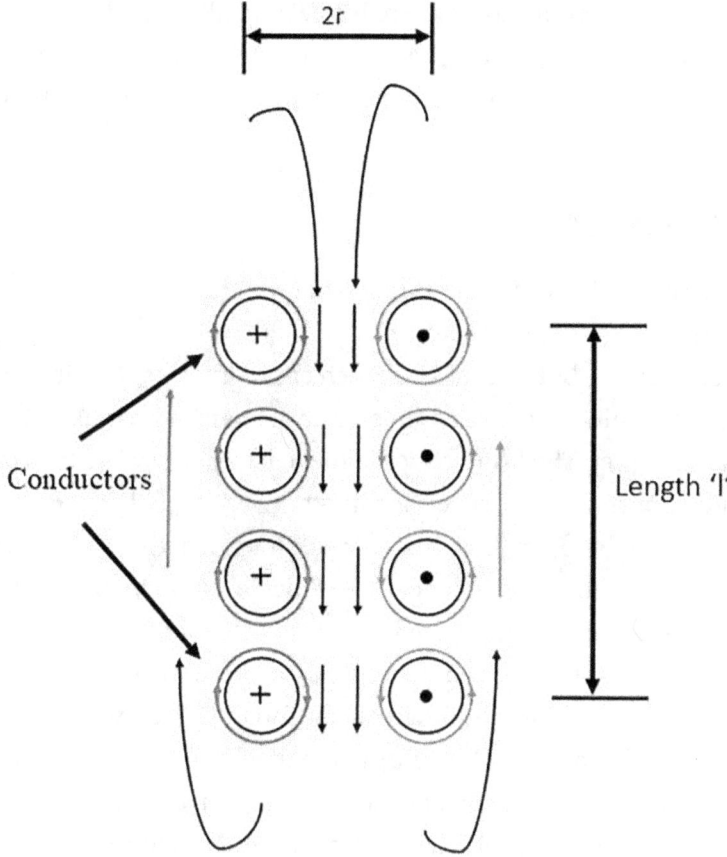

Figure 9-3. The Inside of a Coil of Current Carrying Wire

The convention for the flow of flux from a magnet is that flux flows out of the North Pole and re-enters in at the South Pole. This means that with respect to Figure 9-3, we have created an electromagnet that has a South Pole at the top and a North Pole at the bottom. If we reversed the direction of current through the coils, we would create an electromagnet with the North Pole at the top and the South Pole at the bottom.

It can be seen from Figure 9-3 that the flux inside the coil is more uniform than the flux outside the coil. This in turn means that the flux density will be greatest inside the coil. Note ALL the flux created *must* flow

CHAPTER 9   MAGNETISM, THE ELECTROMAGNET, AND THE INDUCTOR

through the inside of the coil. One point I would like to make is that with Figure 9-3 we are using a DC voltage to force the current through the coil. Transformers use AC supplies, which we will look at in another book.

Permeability

Figure 9-3 shows the basic construction of the electromagnet, but we have left out one parameter. We could wind the coil just by coiling it up like a piece of rope, but it would be much easier is we could wind the coil on a bobbin within which we could place a former which makes up the core of the magnet. The bobbin would make it easier to wind the coil on but, more importantly if we use a former then we would have the facility to concentrate where the flux flows. If we don't place a former inside the bobbin then the flux that exits the North Pole flows everywhere through space before re-entering the magnet at the South Pole. This is a waste as it takes a lot of effort, known as magnetising force, to create the flux and a lot of the flux risks being lost as it flows all around the coil. It would be much better if we could capture all the flux and make it flow back into the magnet at the south pole. Just as a current can flow easier in different materials, that is, through materials with less resistance, then so flux can flow easier in different materials. Also, just as current tries to find the easiest path to go from the positive terminal to the negative terminal of the supply, then so flux will also find the easiest path to go from the North Pole to the South Pole of the magnet. The parameter which relates how flux flows through different materials is called *permeability*.

Permeability is the ease with which the material permits or allows flux to flow through it. If we don't use a former, or core, as in an air cored coil or transformer, the flux will flow through air, or free space. If we use a core, then hopefully the flux will find it easier to flow through the core

CHAPTER 9   MAGNETISM, THE ELECTROMAGNET, AND THE INDUCTOR

than through free space. Engineers need to relate the permeability of the different materials to a benchmark, or reference figure. The benchmark used is, the permeability of *free space* given this symbol:

$$\mu_o.$$

It has been found experimentally that the permeability of free space μ_o has a value of:

$$\mu_0 = 4\pi E^{-7}$$

The units are Henry/Metre, which is quite a strange unit. However, we use the "Henry" as really, we are creating inductance which has the units of Henry, named after the American scientist Jospeh Henry for his work in electromagnet induction around 1831. This does give you some idea of how old the study of electricity is.

Most materials will allow flux to flow through them easier than free space and so the factor that relates the permeability of the different materials, to that of free space is a multiplying factor called the *relative permeability* of the material given the symbol:

$$\mu_r$$

The product of the two terms produces the term called the *absolute permeability* of the material. This is given the symbol:

$$\mu_a$$

The expression for μ_a is therefore:

$$\mu_a = \mu_0 \mu_r$$

If we use a former, or core, we must increase the amount of flux used within the coil, and this must increase the flux density B. That being the case most electromagnets are manufactured in this way.

CHAPTER 9   MAGNETISM, THE ELECTROMAGNET, AND THE INDUCTOR

The Magnetising Force (H)

This is used to distinguish magnetomotive force, mmf, which simply creates the magnetic field around the coil, which is used to create the electromagnet. It basically introduces the concept that engineers can force the magnetic field to flow through a circuit of their choice. This is done by introducing a core with a high permeability into the manufacture. Without a core we have what we call an air-cored electromagnet and this in one in which a lot of the flux is left to flow outwards from the coil covering a far too large a distance before it re-enters into the electromagnet at the south pole. When we introduce a core into the manufacture, we create an easier path for the flux to flow from the North Pole to the South Pole. This is because the core has a better permeability than air. This increases the flux density of the electromagnet and so creates a better electromagnet. This means we have better control over the length of the path the flux must pass through. We will have made it much shorter. However, the length of the magnetic path does affect the amount of magnetism. Taking all this into account the expression for magnetising force H is as follows:

$$H = \frac{IN}{l}$$

Where IN is the mmf and l is the length of the path the flux is made to flow through.

The units for H abbreviated to mf are Ampere Turns per metre. However, as the term "turns" has no units then engineering does use the units of A/m, however, when we are calculating the value for H, we multiply the current by the number of turns before we divide it by the length of the magnetic path. Therefore, I think we should use the units of AT/m. It is your choice.

CHAPTER 9   MAGNETISM, THE ELECTROMAGNET, AND THE INDUCTOR

A Basic Electromagnet

The simplest method might be to wind the coil on a toroid. One such example is shown in Figure 9-4.

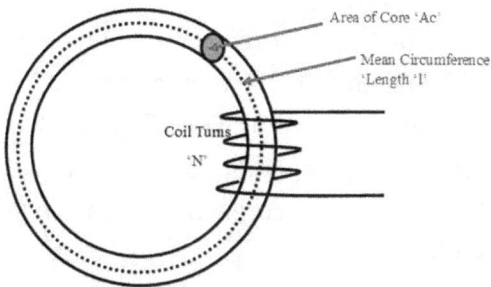

Figure 9-4. *A Basic Toroid Electromagnet*

Using the expressions we have derived, we must be able to calculate the flux ϕ and the flux density B for a given circuit. The specification for the toroid is as follows:

- N is the number of turns on the coil. In this case, N = 400.

- I is the current flowing in the coil. In this case, I = 400mA.

- The relative permeability of the material μr is in this case μr = 800.

- The radius of the mean circumference is 50mm.

- The radius of the cross-sectional area of the core is 25mm.

We can start by calculating the length l that the flux flows through within the toroid. With respect to Figure 9-4, l is the mean circumference of the toroid core. Therefore, l can be calculated as follows:

$$l = 2\pi r = 2\pi \times 50E^{-3} = 314.16 mm$$

507

CHAPTER 9   MAGNETISM, THE ELECTROMAGNET, AND THE INDUCTOR

The number of coils is 400 and the current flowing through the coils is 400mA. Putting these values into the expression for H gives this:

$$H = \frac{400 \times 400E^{-3}}{314.16E^{-3}} = 509.296 \; AT/m$$

I use the units for H of Amper Turns per meter as NI is amps times turns and we divide the result by the length in meters.

This magnetising force will create a flux ϕ that will flow through the toroid. The amount of flux will depend upon the permeability of the core and the cross-sectional area of the core. The expression for ϕ that relates it to these terms is as follows:

$$\phi = \mu_a HA$$

From this we can say:

$$\phi = \frac{\mu_0 \mu_r NIA}{l}$$

The cross-sectional area A is that of the core and so it can be calculated as follows:

$$A = \pi r^2 = \pi \times (25E^{-3})^2 = 1.963E^{-3} \; m^2$$

Putting all the values into express we get this:

$$\phi = \frac{4\pi E^{-7} \times 800 \times 400 \times 400E^{-3} \times 1.963E^{-3}}{314.16E^{-3}} = 1.005mWbs$$

You might find it difficult to enter πE^{-7} into your calculator. If you do, you could enter $4\pi E^{-7}$ as $4E^{-7} \times \pi$ this will work just as well.

All this flux is forced into the cross-sectional area of the core A and so the flux density B can be calculated using this expression:

$$B = \frac{\Phi}{A} = \frac{1.005E^{-3}}{1.963E^{-3}} = 512mT$$

CHAPTER 9   MAGNETISM, THE ELECTROMAGNET, AND THE INDUCTOR

We can use the expression for flux ϕ and flux density B to show how flux density is related to the magnetizing force H as follows:

$$\phi = \frac{\mu_0 \mu_r NIA}{l}$$

$$B = \frac{\Phi}{A}$$

However:

$$H = \frac{NI}{l}$$

Therefore, we can replace this in the expression for ϕ as follows:

$$\Phi = \mu_0 \mu_r HA$$

If we now divide both sides by A we get this:

$$\frac{\Phi}{A} = \mu_0 \mu_r H$$

This means we can say:

$$B = \mu_0 \mu_r H$$

Example 9.1

Another common type of core is a rectangular shape as shown in Figure 9-5.

CHAPTER 9   MAGNETISM, THE ELECTROMAGNET, AND THE INDUCTOR

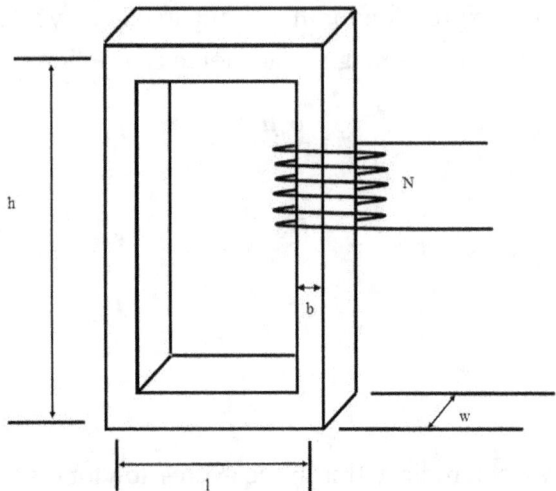

Figure 9-5. *An Example of a Rectangular Core*

The specification for this example is:

- The number of turns N is 400.

- The current I, flowing into the coil is 4mA.

- The relative permeability of the core material is 5000.

- The width of the core w is 30mm.

- The mean hight of the core h is 100mm.

- The mean length of the core l is 50mm.

- The thickness of the core b is 15mm.

We can calculate the flux using:

$$\phi = \frac{\mu_a NIA}{l}$$

CHAPTER 9   MAGNETISM, THE ELECTROMAGNET, AND THE INDUCTOR

The cross-sectional area A is that of the core and so it can be calculated as follows:

$$A = b \times w = 15E^{-3} \times 30E^{-3} = 450 mm^2 = 450E^{-6}$$

We can calculate the length l of the flux path as follows:

$$l = 2l + 2h = 2 \times 50E^{-3} + 2 \times 100E^{-3} = 300 mm$$

Putting all the values into expression for φ we get this:

$$\phi = \frac{4\pi E^{-7} \times 5000 \times 400 \times 4E^{-3} \times 450E^{-6}}{300E^{-3}} = 15.08 \mu Wbs$$

This means that the flux density B can be calculated as follows:

$$B = \frac{\Phi}{A} = \frac{15.08E^{-6}}{450E^{-6}} = 33.51 mT$$

We can calculate the magnetizing force H as follows:

$$H = \frac{NIA}{l} = \frac{400 \times 4E^{-3}}{300E^{-3}} = 5.333 \ AT/m$$

Using this value for H, we can say:

$$B = 4\pi E^{-7} \times 5000 \times 5.333 = 33.49 mT$$

The small difference is due to rounding errors.

The Magnetic Circuit

We can also use two U type cores to wind the coils on with one side of the joining of the cores creating an air gap through which the flux must still flow. This creates a magnetic circuit which we can analyse in a similar fashion as we do with electrical circuits. An example of this type of core is shown in Figure 9-6.

CHAPTER 9   MAGNETISM, THE ELECTROMAGNET, AND THE INDUCTOR

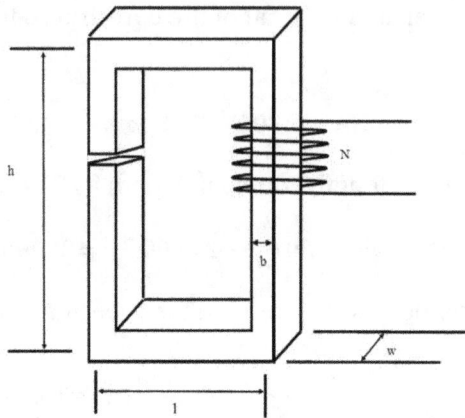

Figure 9-6. *An Example of a U-Cored Electromagnet*

This magnetic arrangement can be analysed by creating an equivalent magnetic circuit. This circuit is shown in Figure 9-7.

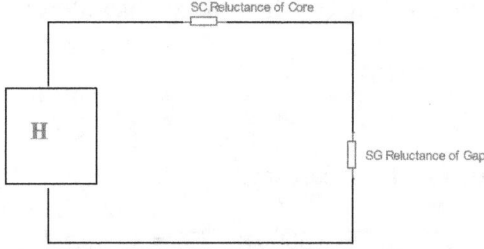

Figure 9-7. *The Magnetic Circuit for the Electromagnet Shown in Figure 9-6*

There is no ground in the circuit as this is not an electrical circuit. The two components are not resistors, but they are used to represent the two reluctances of the magnetic circuit. The H is magnetising force created by the current flowing through the coil of the electromagnet. Before we go too far into the analysis of the magnetic circuit, we should look at what reluctance is.

512

CHAPTER 9   MAGNETISM, THE ELECTROMAGNET, AND THE INDUCTOR

Reluctance

This is the magnetic equivalent of resistance in electrical circuits. Reluctance is a measure of how reluctant a material is to allow flux to flow or pass through it. In this way it is the inverse of permeability. If a material was made longer the reluctance would increase. Therefore, reluctance is proportional to the length l of the material. If the cross-sectional area of the material was made bigger, it would be easier for the flux to flow through the material. Therefore, we can say reluctance is proportional to length but inversely proportional to the cross-sectional area A of the material. Reluctance is given the symbol S and we can state that reluctance S is as follows:

$$S \propto \frac{l}{A}$$

The proportional term $\propto$ can be replaced by a constant of proportionality. The only parameter that is constant for any material is the materials absolute permeability. Note the length can be varied and the cross-sectional area can be varied. We can combine all these parameters of length, cross-sectional area, and permeability to show that the expression for reluctance S of magnetic materials is as follows:

$$S = \frac{l}{\mu_a A}$$

We can also relate this term reluctance to the magnetomotive force mmf and the amount of flux ϕ flowing around the circuit. The relationship gives us this expression:

$$S = \frac{mmf}{\Phi}$$

It is always good to have two different expressions for any quantity we want to calculate so that we can check our work. Using this expression for reluctance we state that units for reluctance are Amps/Wbs, or AmpTurns/

CHAPTER 9   MAGNETISM, THE ELECTROMAGNET, AND THE INDUCTOR

Wbs depending on whether you give the number of turns a unit. However, some engineers give this unit as the inverse of the magnetizing force H. Therefore, we could use H^{-1} as the units for reluctance. I will leave the units up to you and just use the numerical value of the reluctance.

Of the two reluctances S_c, is the reluctance of the core, and S_g is the reluctance of the gap, in the magnetic circuit shown in Figure 9-7. The reluctance of the gap S_g would have the greatest reluctance as the core is made of a metal with a high permeability whereas the gap is filled with air, which will have a lower permeability. We will go through an example that will determine the reluctances of the electromagnet shown in Figure 9-6. The specification for the electromagnet is as follows:

$N = 300$

$\mu_r = 2700$

$I = 100mA$

$h = 32.4mm$

$l = 18.1mm$

$b = 5mm$

$w = 6.05mm$

air gap = 1mm

The lengths are the means.

Using that specification, we can calculate the mean path length that the flux will flow through, as follows:

$$Mean\ Length = 2h + 2l = 2 \times 32.4 + 2 \times 18.1 = 101 mm$$

Similarly, the mean cross-sectional area is as follows:

$$Mean\ Area = b \times w = 5E^{-3} \times 6.05E^{-3} = 30.25E^{-6}\ m^2$$

CHAPTER 9 MAGNETISM, THE ELECTROMAGNET, AND THE INDUCTOR

The parameters—mf the magnetising force H, the flux ɸ, the flux density B, and the reluctances S_c and S_g—can now be calculated.

The mf H

This can be calculated using this formula:

$$H = \frac{NI}{l}$$

Therefore, putting the values in, we get this:

$$H = \frac{300 \times 100E^{-3}}{101E^{-3}}$$

$$H = 297.03 \, \text{AT/m}$$

The Flux ɸ

We can calculate the flux ɸ using the analogy to Ohm's Law:

$$\Phi = \frac{H}{S_T}$$

Where S_T is the total reluctance in the circuit. Again, if we liken the two reluctances to two resistors in series we can say:

$$S_T = S_C + S_G$$

This means we must first calculate the two reluctances, S_c and S_g.

The Reluctance of the Core.

The parameters for the core are as follows:

- The mean length is 100mm
- The mean cross-sectional area is $30.25E^{-6}$
- The relative permeability μ_r is 2700

Note with the length of the core we must subtract the 1mm of the gap as this would be a parameter for the reluctance of the gap S_G.

CHAPTER 9 MAGNETISM, THE ELECTROMAGNET, AND THE INDUCTOR

Then we use this:

$$S = \frac{l}{\mu_a A}$$

Note that $\mu_a = \mu_0\mu_r$:

$$S = \frac{l}{\mu_0\mu_r A}$$

$$S = \frac{100E^{-3}}{4\pi E^{-7} \times 2700 \times 30.25E^{-6}}$$

This gives a value for the reluctance of the core of:

$$S_C = 974.32 \text{ k AT/wbs}$$

The Reluctance of the Air Gap S_g

Similarly, the reluctance of the air gap can now be calculated. Using this:

$$S_G = \frac{l}{\mu_a A}$$

Note for air $\mu r = 1$ ∴ for the air gap $\mu a = \mu o$.
Therefore:

$$S_G = \frac{1E^{-3}}{4\pi E^{-7} \times 30.25E^{-6}}$$

$$S_g = 26.307 \text{ M AT/wbs}$$

Knowing the two reluctance values, the value of S_T the total reluctance is as follows:

$$S_T = S_C + S_G = 974.32\text{k} + 26.307 \text{ M} = 27.28\text{M AT/wbs}$$

CHAPTER 9 MAGNETISM, THE ELECTROMAGNET, AND THE INDUCTOR

From this, we can calculate the flux flowing in the circuit as follows:

$$\Phi = \frac{H}{S_T}$$

Putting the values in, we have:

$$\Phi = \frac{297.03}{27.28E^6} = 10.9E^{-6} = 10.9\,\mu Wbs$$

If we tried to use the expression for flux from Example 9.1, we would not get the same result:

$$\phi = \frac{\mu_a NIA}{l}$$

$$\Phi = \frac{4\pi E^{-7} \times 2700 \times 300 \times 100E^{-3} \times 30.25E^{-6}}{101E^{-3}} = 30.492\,\mu Wbs$$

However, this expression does not consider the air gap that we now have in this example. The air gap reduces the amount of flux in the circuit.

The Flux Density, B

We can now calculate the flux density B in the coil. Using flux density:

$$B = \frac{\Phi}{A}$$

Putting the values in gives us this:

$$B = \frac{10.9E^{-6}}{30.25E^{-6}} = 360.33\,mT$$

CHAPTER 9   MAGNETISM, THE ELECTROMAGNET, AND THE INDUCTOR

The Energy Drops Around the Circuit

We can now calculate where the energy drops are around the magnetic circuit in the same way as we would calculate the voltage drops around an electrical circuit.

The Energy Across S_C the Reluctance of the Core

Using the same concept as for the volt drops in the electrical circuit the expression for the energy drop across S_C is as follows:

$$\text{Energy drop in the core} = \Phi S_C = 10.9E^{-6} \times 974.32^3 = 10.62 \ AT/m$$

The Energy Drop Across the Air Gap

Similarly, this can be calculated as follows:

$$\text{Energy drop in the gap} = \Phi S_G = 10.9E^{-6} \times 26.396^6 = 287.716 \ AT/m$$

By the analogy with voltage and therefore Kirchhoff's Voltage Law, the sum of these two energy drops must equal the total energy supplied to the circuit, which means:

$$H = \phi \, S_C + \phi \, S_G$$

Putting the two energy values in, we get:

$$H = 10.62 + 287.716 = 298.34 \ AT/m$$

This agrees with the first value for H.

Comparisons Between Magnetic and Electrical Circuit

Whilst analysing the electromagnet shown in Figure 9-6, we have made some analogies to electrical circuits. These various comparisons are summed up in Table 9-1.

CHAPTER 9 MAGNETISM, THE ELECTROMAGNET, AND THE INDUCTOR

Table 9-1. Comparison of Magnetic and Electrical Properties

Magnetic				Electrical			
Parameter	Symbol	Expression	Units	Parameter	Symbol	Expression	Units
mf	H	$H = \dfrac{NI}{l}$	AT/m	Voltage	V	$V = IR$	Volt
Flux	Φ	$\Phi = \dfrac{H}{S_T}$	Wbs	Current	I	$I = \dfrac{V}{R}$	Amp
Reluctance	S	$S = \dfrac{l}{\mu_a A}$	A/Wbs	Resistance	R	$R = \dfrac{\rho l}{A}$	Ohm
Energy Drop	H	$H = \Phi S$	AT/m	Volt Drop	V	$V = IR$	Volts

CHAPTER 9   MAGNETISM, THE ELECTROMAGNET, AND THE INDUCTOR

The B/H Curve

A magnetic field will be created when a force is exerted on a material. This force can be a natural force as with a permanent magnet or an electrical force as with an electromagnet. This force is called a magnetising force or mf for short, and it is given the symbol H. As engineers we need to appreciate how different materials will react to this magnetizing force. To do this we use graphs that show how the material reacts. As these graphs plot flux density B against magnetizing force H then they are called B/H curves. A typical B/H curve is shown in Figure 9-8.

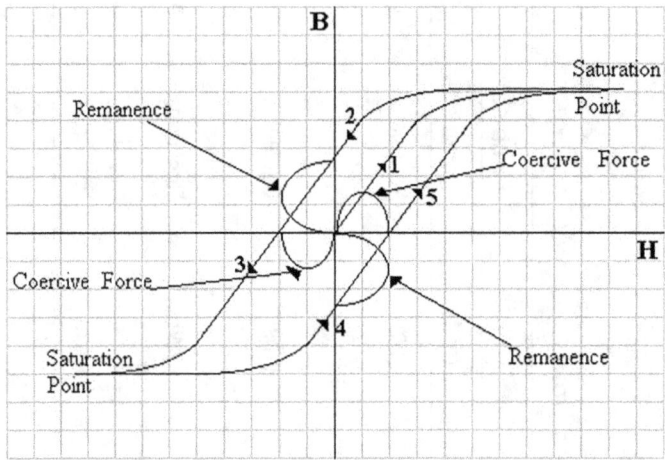

Figure 9-8. A Typical B/H Curve

From the graph we can see that as H rises from 0 the flux density B starts to rise. Initially the rise in flux density follows the line marked 1. It is also linear at the beginning. However, there comes a point where the same increase in H produces a smaller increase in B. The relationship between B and H is now non-linear. As the value of H is increased even more there comes a point where any further increase in H does not produce any increase in the flux density B. This is the point of *saturation.*

520

CHAPTER 9   MAGNETISM, THE ELECTROMAGNET, AND THE INDUCTOR

If we now start to reduce the mf H the flux density B starts to reduce but it does not follow the original curve. The fall in B is shown by Curve 2. It can be seen from this curve that when H has been reduced to 0 there is still some flux density B left in the magnet. This means that there is some flux in the core and the material has not been fully de-magnetised. The flux density value that is left when the mf H has been reduced to 0 is called the *remanence* of the material.

It can also be seen, from the graph, that we need to take the mf H negative to bring the value of B back down to 0. The amount of mf needed to reduce the flux density to 0 is called the *coercive force* as it is the force needed to coerce the flux density back to 0.

Further variation in the mf produces Curves 3, 4, and 5, producing similar saturation points and values of remanence and coercive force as before. If we now vary the mf H form its maximum positive to its maximum negative the flux density value B will follow the outer loop described by Lines 2, 3, 4, and 5. This is then called the B/H loop or the *hysteresis* loop for the material. Different materials will produce different hysteresis loops but they will all follow the same basic pattern. The loop is called a hysteresis loop because even when the mf is reduced to 0, the material will still have some flux left in it (i.e., it still remembers something of what it was, a magnet).

Absolute Permeability of the Material

If we look at the B/H curve we can see that the gradient of the curve for the Loops 2, 3, 4, and 5, is not constant. Indeed, the value of the gradient at the saturation point is 0. As the mf goes towards 0 the gradient of the curve goes to a maximum. The gradient of the B/H curve varies for different materials, and this suggest that the gradient of the curve tells us something about the material. To find out what it tells us we must determine what the gradient of the curve is. From basic interpretation of graphs, we can say that the gradient of the curve is the change in the vertical axis divided by the change in the horizontal axis. This means that the gradient of the B/H curve is as follows:

$$gradient = \frac{\text{change in } B}{\text{change in } H}$$

Earlier we expressed B and H as follows:

$$B = \frac{\Phi}{A}$$

$$H = \frac{NI}{l}$$

Therefore, the gradient is as follows:

$$\frac{\Phi}{A} \div \frac{NI}{l}$$

As this is a fraction divided by another fraction which we do by inverting and multiplying. This then means that the expression for the gradient can be rewritten as follows:

$$gradient = \frac{\Phi l}{ANI}$$

The gradient of the B/H curve can be denoted as $\frac{dB}{dH}$ and so we can write the expression for this as follows:

$$\frac{dB}{dH} = \frac{\phi l}{ANI} = \phi \times \frac{l}{ANI}$$

If this expression for $\frac{dB}{dH}$ is compared with the expression for ϕ then as follows:

$$\Phi = \frac{\mu_0 \mu_r NIA}{l}$$

CHAPTER 9 MAGNETISM, THE ELECTROMAGNET, AND THE INDUCTOR

Then if we replace the term ϕ with the above expression, the gradient can now be expressed as follows:

$$\frac{dB}{dH} = \frac{\mu_r \mu_o NIA}{l} \times \frac{l}{ANI}$$

$$\therefore \frac{dB}{dH} = \mu_r \mu_o = \mu_a$$

This means that the gradient of the B/H curve is the actual value of the absolute permeability, μ_a, of the material. Note, for all materials, except that of free space, the gradient of the B/H curve will not be a constant. It will go from an infinite value when H = 0 down to 0 when the saturation point has been reached.

The units for the gradient are Wbs/AT/m.

The B/H curve for different materials can tell the engineer a lot about the possible use for the material. A material that has a fat or broad B/H curve will have a high degree of remanence. This means that the material would be able to have some memory as it can retain some magnetism even when the magnetising force has been removed. Therefore, this type of material could be used for magnetic tapes to store digital data or the coating on a CD for the same purpose. Materials with a narrow B/H curve will have very little remanence and so they could be used with electromagnets that will lose their magnetism when the current has been switched off. Therefore, a material with a very narrow B/H curve could be used for an electromagnet as in a crane used to lift and move metal items as in a scrap yard.

Relays

One of the most common uses of electromagnetism with DC is the relay. These are basically switches, but there are used in an indirect approach. Imagine you want your garage door to open when it sensed your car was

CHAPTER 9   MAGNETISM, THE ELECTROMAGNET, AND THE INDUCTOR

coming up the drive. The motor that would start to open the garage door could easily take some 20Amps of current or more. However, the switching part of the sensor that sensed your car could only safely pass a small amount of current say 50mA. That's where a relay could help. The relay would use that small current from the sensor to close the contacts of a larger switch that could easily pass the 20A demanded by the motor.

Figure 9-9 shows the relay, which is an electromagnet called a *solenoid*, that is being used to force the larger contacts of the switch in the motor circuit to close when the small 50mA of current is allowed to flow through the coil of the solenoid.

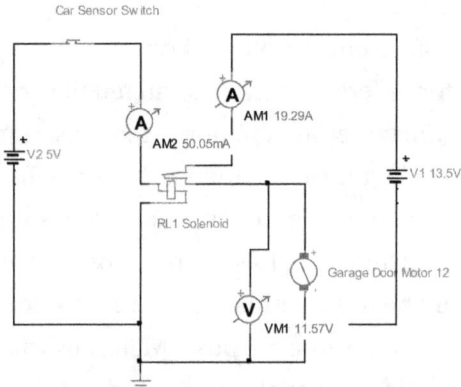

Figure 9-9. *The Relay Circuit for the Garage Door*

Magnetic Calculations Examples

Now that you have some idea about how magnetic circuits work, you can apply this understanding to some example situations.

CHAPTER 9   MAGNETISM; THE ELECTROMAGNET, AND THE INDUCTOR

Example 9.2

The flux φ in the poles of an electromotor is 50μWbs. If the cross-sectional area of the poles is 200mm² calculate the flux density B
Using:

$$B = \frac{\Phi}{A}$$

We should appreciate that 200mm² can be written as follows:

$$200E^{-6}$$

Putting the values in, we get this:

$$B = \frac{50E^{-6}}{200E^{-6}} = 250mT$$

Example 9.3

A relay solenoid can create a flux density of 75mT. If the dimensions of the core of the solenoid are 15mm by 10mm, calculate the amount of flux created in the solenoid.
The area can be calculated as follows:

$$A = lb = 15E^{-3} \times 10E^{-3} = 15mm \times 10mm = 150mm^2$$

We should appreciate that 150mm² can be written as follows:

$$150E^{-6}.$$

Using:

$$B = \frac{\Phi}{A}$$

We can transpose this for φ as follows:

$$\Phi = BA = 75E^{-3} \times 150E^{-6} = 11.25\mu Wb$$

CHAPTER 9   MAGNETISM, THE ELECTROMAGNET, AND THE INDUCTOR

Example 9.4

The flux density of the primary coil in a transformer is 0.25T. If the flux in the coil is 575µWbs, calculate the cross-sectional area of the former the primary coil is wound upon.

Using:

$$B = \frac{\Phi}{A}$$

We can transpose this for A as follows:

$$A = \frac{\Phi}{B} = \frac{575E^{-6}}{0.25} = 0.0023 m^2$$

Example 9.5

An iron toroid core has an outer radius of 120mm and an inner radius of 100mm. A coil of 450 turns is wound on it and a flux of 50µWbs is produced when a 10A current flows through the coil. Determine the flux density and the magnetising force.

The flux density B can be calculated using this expression:

$$B = \frac{\Phi}{A}$$

We know the flux ϕ but we need to calculate the area A. As the core is a toroid then the area A will be the cross-sectional area of the toroid. We can calculate it using this expression:

$$A = \pi r^2$$

The average diameter of the toroid will be the difference between the outer and inner radius of the toroid. This means that the radius of the cross-section of the toroid will be half this diameter. Therefore, the radius r can be calculated as follows:

CHAPTER 9 MAGNETISM, THE ELECTROMAGNET, AND THE INDUCTOR

$$r = \frac{120mm - 100mm}{2} = 10mm$$

Therefore, the cross-sectional area is as follows:

$$A = \pi\left(10E^{-3}\right)^2 = 314.16E^{-6} \ m^2$$

We can now calculate the flux density B as follows:

$$B = \frac{50E^{-6}}{314.16E^{-6}} = 159.15mT$$

To calculate the magnetising force H, we use this:

$$H = \frac{NI}{l}$$

We need to determine the length l. This will be the mean circumference of the toroid. To calculate the circumference C we use:

$$C = 2\pi r$$

Where r is the mean radius of the toroid. This will be the inner radius plus half the difference of the two radii. This means that the mean radius of the toroid is as follows:

$$Mean\ radius = 100mm + \frac{120mm - 100mm}{2} = 110mm.$$

This means that the mean circumference is as follows:

$$C = 2\pi \times 110E^{-3} = 691.15mm$$

We can now calculate the magnetising force H as follows:

$$H = \frac{450 \times 10}{691.15E^{-3}} = 6510.884 \frac{AT}{m}$$

CHAPTER 9 MAGNETISM, THE ELECTROMAGNET, AND THE INDUCTOR

Example 9.6

A toroid has a coil with 300 turns on it. When a current of 7.5A flows through it a magnetising force of 5400 AT/m is produced. Calculate the mean radius of the toroid.

Using the expression:

$$H = \frac{NI}{l}$$

We know H and we know N and I so we can transpose the expression for the unknown parameter l. This would be:

$$l = \frac{NI}{H}$$

Putting the values in, we get this:

$$l = \frac{300 \times 7.5}{5400} = 416.667 mm$$

As this length is the mean circumference of a toroid, then the mean radius r can be calculated as follows:

$$r = \frac{C}{2\pi} = \frac{416.667 E^{-3}}{2 \times \pi} = 66.315 mm$$

Example 9.7

A toroid has a mean circumference of 550mm and a radius of 10mm in the core material. There is a 1mm gap in the core opposite a coil of 300 turns. The relative permeability of the core is 4500. If a current of 6A flows through the coil, determine the following:

1. The flux created
2. The reluctance of the core

CHAPTER 9 MAGNETISM, THE ELECTROMAGNET, AND THE INDUCTOR

3. The reluctance of the gap
4. The magnetising force created

We can use the following expression to calculate the flux:

$$\Phi = \frac{H}{S_T}$$

This means we must calculate the total reluctance and then the magnetising force before we can calculate the flux. The total reluctance is simply the sum of the reluctance of the core and the reluctance of the gap.
The reluctance of the core can be calculated as follows:

$$S_C = \frac{l}{\mu_0 \mu_r A}$$

The length of the core will be 1mm less than the mean circumference of the toroid which means it will be 549mm. To calculate the area of the core material we will use the radius of the core material, which is 10mm. Therefore, the area A can be calculated as follows:

$$A = \pi r^2 = \pi \left(10E^{-3}\right)^2 = 314.159E^{-6} \, m^2$$

We can now calculate the reluctance of the core S_C as follows:

$$S_C = \frac{549E^{-3}}{4\pi E^{-7} \times 4500 \times 314.159E^{-6}} = 309.03E^3$$

The reluctance of the gap can be calculated as follows:

$$S_G = \frac{1E^{-3}}{4\pi E^{-7} \times 314.159E^{-6}} = 2.533E^6$$

We can now calculate the total reluctance in the toroid using this:

$$S_T = S_C + S_G = 309.03E^3 + 2.533E^6 = 2.842E^6$$

CHAPTER 9 MAGNETISM, THE ELECTROMAGNET, AND THE INDUCTOR

We can calculate the mF H using this:

$$H = \frac{NI}{l}$$

Therefore:

$$H = \frac{300 \times 6}{550E^{-3}} = 3272.727$$

Therefore:

$$\Phi = \frac{3272.727}{2.842E^{6}} = 1.152 mWbs$$

Inductance and Magnetism

Inductance is related to the ability of an electrical component to induce a voltage. The main device used by engineers to induce a voltage is coil of wire known as an inductor. It is the main component in a generator. The principle that the generator uses is Faraday's Law.

Michael Faraday discovered that, if a wire was passed through a magnetic field such that the wire cut the magnetic field, then a voltage would be induced across the wire. It was also found that the faster the wire was passed through or cut the magnetic field then the greater the voltage would be that was induced. We can term this passing the wire through the field as making the flux around the wire change. For example, when the wire is outside the magnetic field there is no flux around it. As it approaches the magnetic field the flux increases until it reaches the middle of the field. When it does the flux will be at a maximum. As the wire starts to exit the magnetic field so the flux starts to diminish until it becomes 0

CHAPTER 9 MAGNETISM, THE ELECTROMAGNET, AND THE INDUCTOR

again when the wire leaves the magnetic field. In this way we can say that the wire experiences a change in flux across it. This rate of change of flux can be expressed using the letter d to denote change as follows:

$$\text{rate of change of flux} = \frac{d\phi}{dt}$$

With a generator a wire is wound into a coil that is wound on a rotor. The rotor is then forced to turn inside a magnetic field. The force used to make the rotor turn is produced by a steam turbine that is connected to the rotor in the generator, so the rotor also turns. The heat required to produce the steam can be produced via simply coal furnaces, or gas furnaces or even nuclear fusion.

The voltage induced in the generator can be increased by turning the rotor faster, as this increases the rate of change of the flux across the rotor. The voltage can also be increased by increasing the number of turns N on the coil. The generators for the UK all turn at 3000 rpm, which produces one cycle of the mains voltage every 50th of a second—that is, every 20ms. Hence the mains frequency is 50Hz or 50 cycles per second. The units for frequency f used to be "cycles per second," which I think describes the units perfectly. However, we now use the units of "Hertz" in respect of the German physicist Heinrich Hertz. It was adopted as the SI unit for frequency.

As the voltage, termed *EMF* (E), the *electromotive force*, is proportional to the number of turns N and the rate of change of the flux, $\frac{d\phi}{dt}$, then we can express the relationship between; E, N and $\frac{d\phi}{dt}$ as follows:

$$EMF(E) = \frac{Nd\varphi}{dt}$$

This is a very basic expression for the induced voltage in a coil.

CHAPTER 9 MAGNETISM, THE ELECTROMAGNET, AND THE INDUCTOR

The Impedance of a Coil

When a current is passed through a length of wire a magnetic field is set up around the wire or coil. We need to understand how this current sets up the magnetic field around the coil. All metals have what are termed *magnetic domains* within them. They can be viewed simplistically as small magnets inside the material. However, the material does not display any magnetic properties such as North and South poles, as these domains are all facing in different orientations, and so their overall effect is zero. However, when we try to force a current to flow through the material the current will try to align all these domains into facing the same direction. When the current eventually achieves this the material can then display the North and South poles of a magnet and so act as a magnet. I say try and eventually, as the current finds it hard to flow through the material, even though we have applied a voltage across it, until the current has aligned all the domains in the same direction. Then the current can flow easily through the coil. This is why, when we apply a voltage across a coil, the current lags behind, as it takes time to build up to its peak value of current.

In this way then we could say that the coil greatly impedes the flow of current the instant we apply the voltage across the coil, but then, after some time, the impedance falls to 0. Well, that is the case with a DC voltage, as we saw in Chapter 4. However, if we apply a voltage that changes polarity, as with an AC voltage, then we are constantly changing the direction of current flowing through the coil. This in turns means that we will be constantly changing the alignment of the domains to face in one direction then, as the direction of current changes, we force the domains to face in the opposite direction. It is not too hard to see that the inductor will not like that and so it will be impeding this change of direction. Also, the faster we try to change the direction of current by increasing the frequency of the AC voltage, the greater will be the impedance of the inductor. Also,

CHAPTER 9   MAGNETISM, THE ELECTROMAGNET, AND THE INDUCTOR

it should be obvious that the larger the coil or inductor then the greater the number of domains to align and so the greater the impedance of the inductor. These considerations allow us to develop an expression for the impedance of an inductor. We can say that:

$$X_L \text{ is proptional to } L \text{ and } f$$

Note X_L is the symbol we use for inductive impedance.

L is the label we give to the inductor; it's not that we can't spell, but it's because we use I for current. We don't use C for current, as C is for Coulombs or Capacitance.

f is the label for frequency.

We can summarise the expression for X_L as follows:

$$X_L \propto fL$$

However, through empirical experiments we can replace the proportional term $\propto$ with a constant of proportionality which is 2π. This gives us the expression for inductive impedance of:

$$X_L = 2\pi fL$$

Another consequence of this impedance is that the current in the coil lags the voltage across the coil by 90°. In fact, if we applied a sine waveform voltage across the coil the current would be a cosine waveform. As cosine is the differential of sine then we can see that the current in a coil will be the differential of the voltage across it. Conversely, if we force a current to

CHAPTER 9   MAGNETISM, THE ELECTROMAGNET, AND THE INDUCTOR

flow through the coil then the voltage induced across the coil will be the differential of the current. This means we can express the voltage, or EMF, across the coil in relation to the current as follows:

$$EMF \propto \frac{di}{dt}$$

where $\propto$ is the proportional sign, $\frac{di}{dt}$ is the differential of the current. The proportional sign can be replaced by a constant of proportionality which with inductors is L, where L is the value of inductance.

Therefore, we have this:

$$EMF = L\frac{di}{dt}$$

This is the second most basic expression concerning the voltage induced across a coil. The two expressions are so important they are worth rewriting now; they are as follows:

$$EMF = N\frac{d\Phi}{dt}$$

And:

$$EMF = L\frac{di}{dt}$$

Lenz's Law

Faraday's Law shows how the EMF generated across a coil is related to the flux change around the coil. However, in 1833 a German scientist called Heinrich Lenz took this law a step further. He realised that if the coil, in which the EMF, formed a closed loop, or circuit, then a current would be set up in the coil. This current would be related to the voltage induced across the coil which in turn is related the change of flux around the coil.

However, this current, flowing through the coil, would create its own magnetic field around it. The direction of the magnetic field around the coil, due to this current flow, would depend on the direction the current is flowing through the coil. We can get an idea of what Lenz looked at if we consider the diagrams shown in Figures 9-10, 9-11, and 9-12.

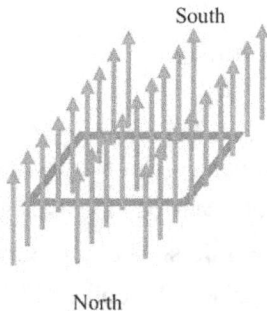

Figure 9-10. *A Single Coil of Wire Within a Magnetic Field*

We need to assume that the flux f has gone through a change in a shortchange of time. This will have induced an EMF across the coil shown as the blue rectangle in Figure 9-10. The flux is depicted as the orange arrows, and it flows from the North to the South pole. The coil will have a small value of resistance as it is made of copper wire. We know that due to the voltage induced across the coil and the fact that it makes a closed circuit, then a current will flow through the coil. The question is in what direction would the current flow in the coil. It could flow through the coil in a clockwise direction or an anticlockwise direction. We know that this current would set up a magnetic field around the wire of the coil. Figure 9-11 shows how the magnetic field would set up if the current flowed in a clockwise direction through the coil.

CHAPTER 9   MAGNETISM, THE ELECTROMAGNET, AND THE INDUCTOR

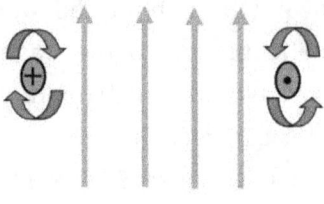

The current flowing clockwise around the coil

Figure 9-11. *The Flux Around the Coil with a Clockwise Current Flow*

Figures 9-11 and 9-12 show a cross-sectional view of the coil of wire within the magnetic field. With a clockwise current in the coil, the conductor at the right side would see current flowing out of the paper. The magnetic field around that part of the coil would flow in an anticlockwise direction around the wire. With the left-hand side of the coil the magnetic field would rotate in a clockwise direction around the coil. The magnetic fields around the coil oppose the changing magnetic field that induced the EMF across the coil in the first place.

We can use Figure 9-12 to see what would happen if the current in the coil flowed in an anticlockwise direction.

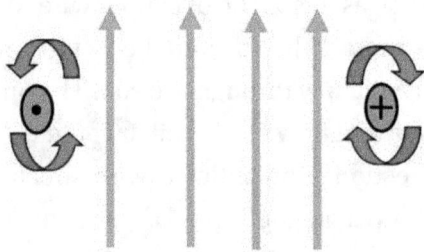

The current flowing anti-clockwise around the coil

Figure 9-12. *The Flux Around the Coil with an Anticlockwise Current Flow*

536

The direction of flux around the conductors of the coil is now in the opposite direction. This means that the flux around the conductors assists the flux change that created the EMF and so created the current. If this situation happened then this means that the coil has a greater flux change across it. This means the EMF induced across the coil would increase. The current flowing through the coil would increase, which would mean that the flux set up around the conductors of the coil would also increase. This would then increase the flux change across the coil, which would increase the EMF induced across the coil. If the current flowed in an anticlockwise direction, a runaway situation would ensue and the current would snowball. This is not possible as all energy must come from somewhere and the only real source of energy is the original magnetic field from the North and South Poles of the magnetic force.

Henrich Lenz said that this shows that you can predict which direction the current would flow through and that the current would flow in a direction that would create a magnetic field around the coil that would oppose the magnetic field that induced the EMF which created the current flow in the first place. This is why some text show the expressions for the EMF with a minus sign in front of them. I prefer not to include a minus sign as I think it is confusing. However, we must remember that Lenz's Law tells us that the current set up in a coil will create a magnetic field around the coil that opposes the magnetic field that induced the voltage across the coil in the first place.

The Induced Voltage Across an Inductor

It is quite hard to use TINA to simulate a change in flux across a coil. This means that we cannot easily consider the first expression for the EMF:

$$EMF = N \frac{d\Phi}{dt}$$

CHAPTER 9   MAGNETISM, THE ELECTROMAGNET, AND THE INDUCTOR

However, we should be able to set up an experiment to show that the second expression is true:

$$EMF = L\frac{di}{dt}$$

The first circuit we will use is shown in Figure 9-13.

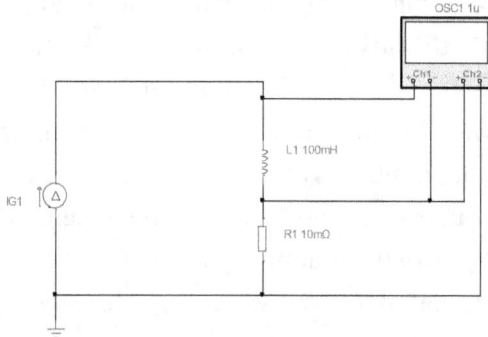

Figure 9-13. *The Test Circuit to Prove the Expression* $EMF = L\frac{di}{dt}$

The IG1 component is a current generator as we want to force a known current through an inductor. We are using the oscilloscope to measure the voltage across the inductor. We have shown the resistance of the inductor as a separate resistor so that we can measure the voltage across the resistor with the oscilloscope. In this way, we can interpret the voltage across the resistor to show the current flowing in the circuit by dividing the peak voltage by the value of the resistor. The waveforms obtained from the simulation are shown in Figure 9-14.

CHAPTER 9   MAGNETISM, THE ELECTROMAGNET, AND THE INDUCTOR

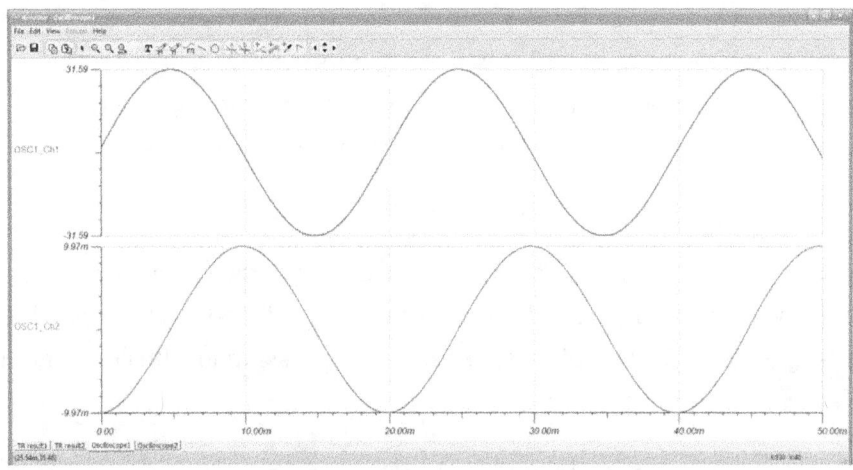

Figure 9-14. *The Waveforms from the Test Circuit Shown in Figure 9-13*

The Channel 1 trace shows the voltage across the inductor and the Channel 2 trace shows the voltage across the resistor. If we divide the voltage across the resistor by the resistance value, we can interpret this trace as showing how the current in the circuit changes. We can see that the peak voltage across the resistor is shown as 9.97mv. If we divide this by 0.01 or 10m, the value of the resistor, we get a peak current of 997mA, which is practically the correct current in the circuit as the current source was set to a peak of 1A at a frequency of 50Hz. Given that the voltage developed across the inductor will be the differential of the current waveform multiplied by the value of the inductance, we need to state the expression for the current waveform so that we can differentiate it. The current waveform is simply a sine wave, and it can be expressed as follows:

$$i = A\sin(\theta)$$

CHAPTER 9 MAGNETISM, THE ELECTROMAGNET, AND THE INDUCTOR

Where A is the peak value of the current which was set to 1Amp. The angle θ can be expressed with a variety of units such as degrees, radians or time. We will use the units of time to express that the angle varies with time. That being the case, we can express the angle as follows:

$$\theta = 2\pi ft$$

The variable is time t and once we have set the frequency for the current waveform the 2πf will be a constant. For this test circuit, we will set the frequency to 50Hz. This means that the expression for the current is as follows:

$$i = 1\sin(100\pi t) = 1\sin(314.16t)$$

Using the standard differentials we have:

$$a\sin(nx) \text{ differentiates to } na\cos(nx)$$

This means:

$$1\sin(314.16t)$$

This differentiates to this:

$$314.16 \times 1\cos(314.16t) = 314.16\cos(314.16t)$$

We know that when passing a current through an inductor the voltage across the inductor can be expressed as follows:

$$V_L = L\frac{di}{dt}$$

This means that with respect to our test circuit the voltage across the inductor will be:

$$V_L = 100E^{-3} \times 314.16\cos(314.16t)$$

CHAPTER 9 MAGNETISM, THE ELECTROMAGNET, AND THE INDUCTOR

Therefore, we can say:

$$V_L = 31.42 \cos(314.16t)\, v$$

If we look at the Channel 1 trace, we can see that it is the voltage across the inductor peaks at 31.57v. This is very close to what we expect. If we consider the time difference between the peaks of the voltage and the current waveforms, we can see that the voltage waveform peaks at around 5ms before the current waveform. We can convert this time difference into a phase shift using this:

$$\text{Phase Shift 'P'} = \text{Time Difference 'TD'} \times \text{frequency} \times 360$$

Putting the values in, we get this:

$$PS = 5E^{-3} \times 50 \times 360 = 90^\circ$$

This confirms that the voltage waveform is a cosine, as a cosine wave is 90° ahead of a sine wave.

We can investigate the concept that the voltage across the inductor is the differential of the current multiplied by the value of the inductance, with a second test circuit, as shown in Figure 9-15.

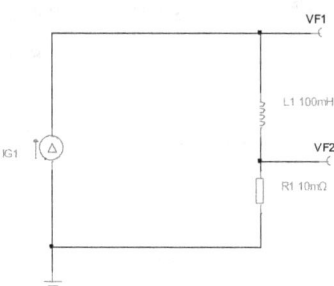

Figure 9-15. *The Second Test Circuit*

CHAPTER 9   MAGNETISM, THE ELECTROMAGNET, AND THE INDUCTOR

This is the same circuit as before except that the current waveform is now a simple pulse rising from 0 to 1Amp with a rise and fall time of 1ms. The current stays high at 1 Amp for 50ms and then returns to 0. The waveforms obtained from the transient analysis are shown in Figure 9-16.

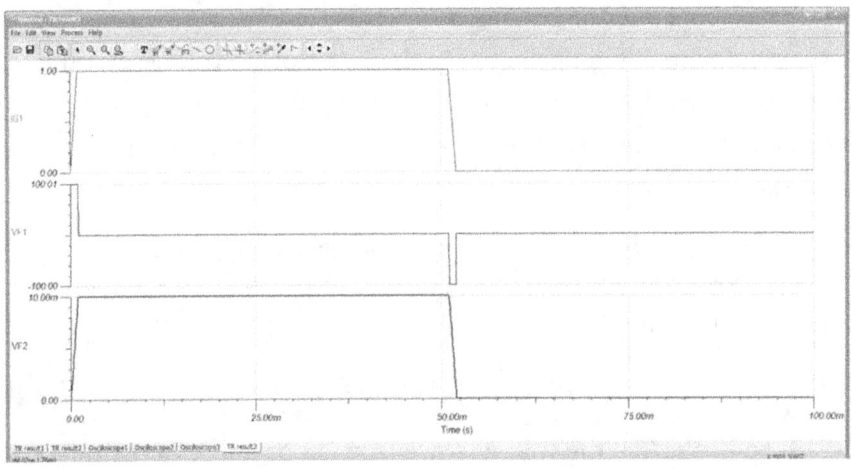

Figure 9-16. *The Waveforms for the Second Test Circuit*

The current source IG1 waveforms and the voltage across the resistor VF2 are as expected. A peak of 10mv divided by the 10m Ohm resistance gives the peak current of 1A, which is the current from the source IG1. The voltage waveform for across the inductor is shown as the VF1 trace. We need to understand what is going on to appreciate how the voltage waveform is produced. The expression for the voltage across the inductor is as follows:

$$V_L = L\frac{di}{dt}$$

The term $\frac{di}{dt}$ relates to the gradient of the waveform as that is what differentiation is, it is the act of determining the expression for the gradient of the waveform. Looking at the two current waveforms, the gradient is

CHAPTER 9 MAGNETISM, THE ELECTROMAGNET, AND THE INDUCTOR

constant at 0most of the time (i.e., from time 1ms to time 51ms). During 0s to 1ms, the gradient is positive at the following:

$$gradient = \frac{1}{1E^{-3}} = 1000$$

Then during the time from 51ms to 52ms, the gradient is negative at the following:

$$gradient = -\frac{1}{1E^{-3}} = -1000$$

Therefore, we can say that during time is from 0 to 1ms, the voltage across the inductor will be:

$$V_L = 100E^{-3} \times 1000 = 100v$$

During the time from 51ms to 52ms, the voltage across the inductor will be:

$$V_L = -100E^{-3} \times 1000 = -100v$$

During all the rest of the time, because the gradient of the current waveform is 0, the voltage across the inductor will also be 0. If we look at the voltage waveform, VF1, shown in Figure 9-16, we can see that it agrees with these calculations. In this way we have confirmed that when a current is forced to flow through an inductor, the voltage across the inductor can be expressed as follows:

$$V_L = L\frac{di}{dt}$$

CHAPTER 9 MAGNETISM, THE ELECTROMAGNET, AND THE INDUCTOR

The Current Flowing Through an Inductor

It is more usual to apply a voltage across an inductor and then see what current flows through it. We can transpose the expression we got for the voltage across the inductor for an expression for the current as follows:

First divide both sides by L. This gives:

$$\frac{V_L}{L} = \frac{di}{dt}$$

If we now integrate both sides with respect to time we get:

$$i = \int \frac{V_L}{L} dt$$

We need to appreciate that integration is the mathematical opposite of differentiation. We can take the constant of $\frac{1}{L}$ out of the integral; this gives the expression for the current i as follows:

$$i = \frac{1}{L} \int V_L \, dt$$

We can test this concept by simulating the circuit shown in Figure 9-17.

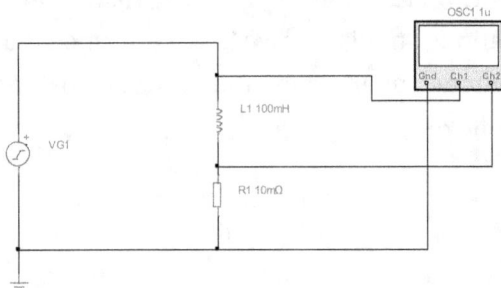

Figure 9-17. *The Test Circuit to Show the Current Flowing Through an Inductor*

CHAPTER 9   MAGNETISM, THE ELECTROMAGNET, AND THE INDUCTOR

The supply to the circuit is now a voltage set to the following voltage:

$$V_{supply} = 2\sin(314.16t)$$

We need to integrate this to develop the expression for the current flowing through the inductor. We can use standard integral tables to show that this:

$$a\sin(nx)$$

Which integrates to this:

$$\frac{-a\cos(nx)}{n}$$

We don't need to concern ourselves with any limits of integration as we are trying to develop and expression for the current flowing through the inductor. Therefore, carrying out the integration we get:

$$integral = \frac{-2\cos(314.16t)}{314.16} = -6.366E^{-3}\cos(314.16t)$$

We now need to divide this by the value of the inductor to obtain the expression for the current flowing through the inductor as follows:

$$I_L = \frac{-6.366E^{-3}\cos(314.16t)}{100E^{-3}} = -63.66E^{-3}\cos(314.26t)$$

When we simulate the circuit, the waveforms obtained from the oscilloscope are as shown in Figure 9-18.

545

CHAPTER 9   MAGNETISM, THE ELECTROMAGNET, AND THE INDUCTOR

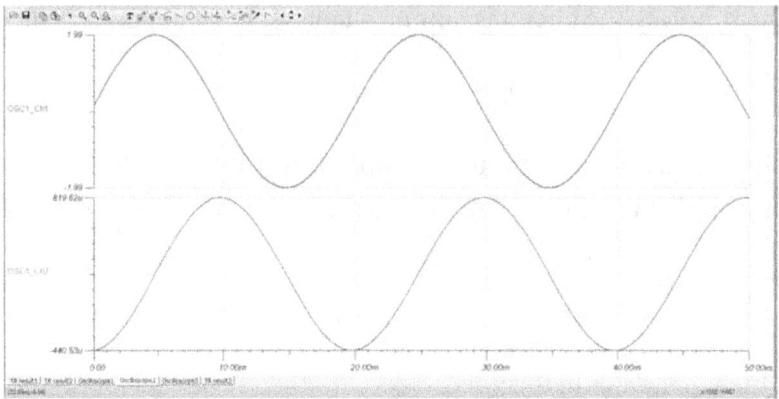

Figure 9-18. *The Oscilloscope Waveforms for the Test Circuit Shown in Figure 9-17*

The Channel 1 trace is the supply voltage, and we can see that it peaks at 1.99V which is what we expect. The Channel 2 trace shows the voltage across the 10mΩ resistor. We can see that the total peak to peak is the 819.62µv + 440.53µv. This gives a total peak to peak of 1.260mv. If we divide this by 2, we get a peak voltage of 630.075mv. If we divide this voltage by the 10mΩ value of the resistor this gives us a value of 63.007mA for the current flowing through the inductor. This is the peak value we expect. How do we confirm that the current flowing through the inductor follows the expression:

$$i = -63.66E^{-3}\cos(314.26t)$$

We must appreciate that a cosine cycles 90° ahead of a sine wave. However, the expression for the current has a minus sign in front of it. This means that there is a full 180° phase shift between cosine and minus cosine. This means that the current should be 90° behind or lagging the voltage. If we look at the Channel 2 trace shown in Figure 9-18, we can see that it peaks 4.99ms later than the voltage waveform on the Channel 1 trace. We have already shown that at a frequency of 50Hz this 4.99ms

CHAPTER 9   MAGNETISM, THE ELECTROMAGNET, AND THE INDUCTOR

time delay equates to 90°. This means that the current waveform shown as the Channel 2 trace on Figure 9-18 does agree with the expression for the current i_L flowing through the inductor.

The Expressions for Inductance (L)

We have determined the main expressions for the EMF across a coil of wire. We will now use these expressions to develop an expression for inductance, L.

As the EMFs are the same, then we must be able to say that:

$$N\frac{d\Phi}{dt} = L\frac{di}{dt}$$

If we multiply both sides by dt, we get:

$$Nd\Phi = Ldi$$

If we now integrate both sides, we get:

$$N\Phi = Li$$

We have already shown that:

$$\Phi = \frac{\mu_0 \mu_r NiA}{l}$$

So, we can say this:

$$\frac{N^2 \mu_0 \mu_r iA}{l} = Li$$

If we now divide both sides by i, we get:

$$L = \frac{N^2 \mu_0 \mu_r A}{l} = \frac{N^2 \mu_a A}{l}$$

547

We can also say:

$$S = \frac{l}{\mu_a A}$$

Therefore, we can say:

$$\frac{\mu_a A}{l} = \frac{1}{S}$$

Putting this into the expression for L, we get:

$$L = N^2 \times \frac{1}{S}$$

Therefore, we can say:

$$L = \frac{N^2}{S}$$

This gives us two fundamental expressions for inductance L, which are as follows:

$$L = \frac{N^2 \mu_0 \mu_r A}{l}$$

And:

$$L = \frac{N^2}{S}$$

This shows that the inductance of a coil depends upon the relative permeability of the material the coil is wound upon—that is, the permeability of the material of the core. However, there is one important aspect of these expressions and that is they are only usable if we are in the linear aspect of the B/H curve for the inductor.

CHAPTER 9   MAGNETISM, THE ELECTROMAGNET, AND THE INDUCTOR

Magnetic Fields and Motors

The next aspect of magnetism we will look at is how to use magnetism to create a motor. A motor is basically a rotor, which in most cases, is a coil wound on a former, that resides inside a magnetic field. If we force a current to flow through the coil, the magnetic field that is created around the coil creates an interaction between the two magnetic fields.

We know that a magnet can create a force that will either push another magnet away from it (like poles repel) or pull the magnet towards it (unlike poles attract). We should also realise that it is the magnetic flux, which creates this force. Magnetic flux exits around a magnet and if we can increase or decrease the flux then we can then increase or decrease the force. We can increase or decrease the flux electrically by changing the current flowing in the circuit.

Flux is a vector quantity, which means it has magnitude and direction. This means that if two vectors, or phasors, of flux exist in the same direction they will add together and so increase the net flux. Alternatively, if the two fluxes exist in the opposite directions to each other, then the flux will subtract from each other and so reduce the net flux. This is the principle on which the DC motor works. Figure 9-19 shows how this net reduction and net increase of flux is obtained.

CHAPTER 9   MAGNETISM, THE ELECTROMAGNET, AND THE INDUCTOR

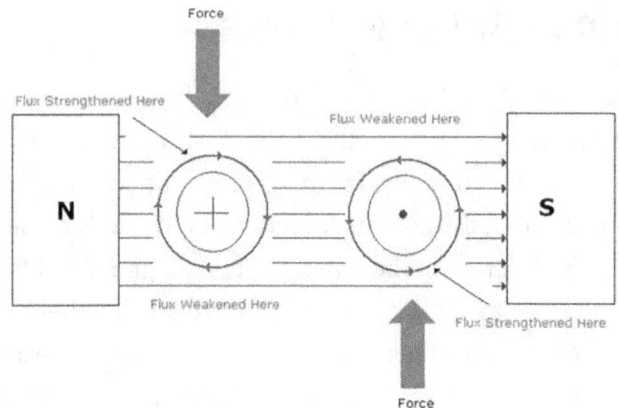

Figure 9-19. *The Forces on a Current Carrying Conductor Inside a Magnetic Field*

In Figure 9-19, we can see that the flux flowing around the conductor on the left flows in the same direction as the flux from the permanent magnet, at the top of the conductor, but in the opposite direction at the bottom of the conductor. This means that the flux at the top of the conductor is strengthened but at the bottom of the conductor the flux is weakened. This difference between the flux levels means a force is created on the conductor acting in a downward direction. If we consider the conductor on the right side, we see the opposite occurs and the force is acting upwards on the conductor.

Note that the two circles symbolising conductors are the same conductor, as it simply makes up a coil with current flowing into the paper on the left side and flowing out on the right side. These two forces on the conductor or coil mean that the coil will start to turn in an anticlockwise direction.

The next stage to consider is when the coil has turned just beyond 90°, as shown in Figure 9-20.

CHAPTER 9   MAGNETISM, THE ELECTROMAGNET, AND THE INDUCTOR

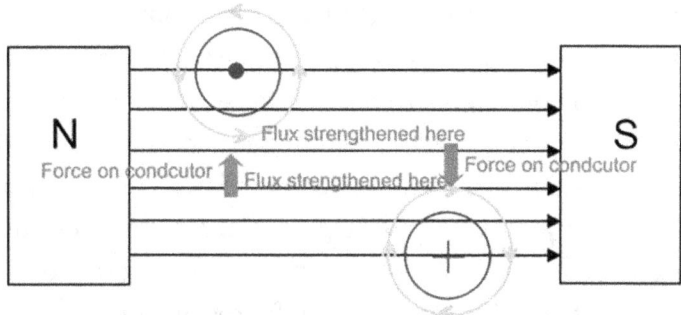

Figure 9-20. *The Coil Moving Anticlockwise Has Just Passed 90⁰*

The momentum of the coil will be sufficient to make the coil reach this point. However, at this point the forces on the coil are such that the coil will now start to turn clockwise instead of continuing in its original anticlockwise direction. This means that the coil may start to oscillate. If we do nothing, the coil will soon come to rest in the position shown in Figure 9-21.

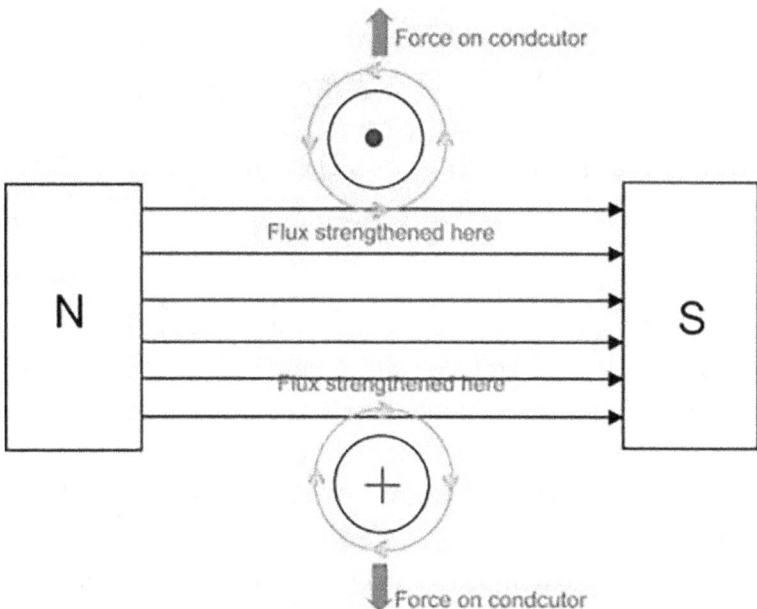

Figure 9-21. *The Coil Comes to Rest at the Vertical After Moving Through 90⁰*

551

CHAPTER 9 MAGNETISM, THE ELECTROMAGNET, AND THE INDUCTOR

In this situation, the forces are acting vertically outwards in opposite directions. This means that the coil will become stationary and stay in this vertical position. Something must be done to keep the motor turning.

We change the direction of the current flowing through the coil when the coil just passes the horizontal, as shown in Figure 9-20. This changes the direction of flux around the coil. Figure 9-22 shows what would happen if, with the coil moving initially anticlockwise, we change the direction of the current when the coil has just past 90° for the first time.

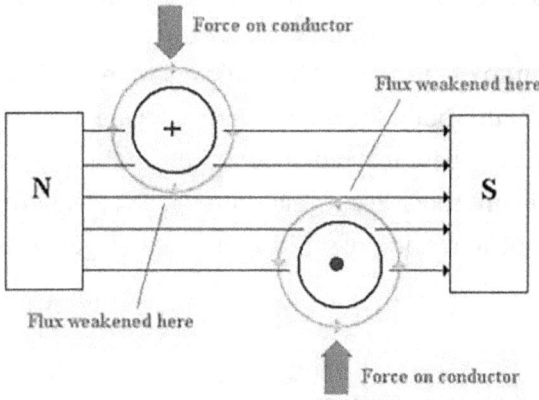

Figure 9-22. *Changing the Direction of Current When the Coil Reaches 90° the First Time*

The forces will now keep the coil rotating in the anticlockwise direction. This change in the direction of current is brought about by the act of commutation action on the connection of the supply to the coil. If this commutation is brought about every 180° then the coil will keep rotating correctly.

I restrict my analysis to the motors in Figures 9-19 to 9-22. This is because motors, both DC and AC, are a field of electrical engineering that require a book on their own. What I wanted to introduce to you was the concept of the BIL and BLU laws and the simple DC motor is a good application of the BIL law.

CHAPTER 9   MAGNETISM, THE ELECTROMAGNET, AND THE INDUCTOR

The BIL and BLU Laws

We will start with the BIL law. With this introduction to the DC motor, we have shown that when a current carrying conductor is placed within a magnetic field, a force is experienced by the conductor. The force on the conductor must depend upon the amount of flux around the coil—that is, the flux density, B. It must also depend upon the flux around the conductor, which in turn depends upon the current I that flows through the conductor. Finally, it must depend upon the length l of the conductor that is inside the permanent magnetic field. All these terms are put together in the expression for the force F, where we have:

$$F = BIl \quad \text{Newtons N}$$

We can use this expression to calculate the force that would be placed on a current carrying conductor that lies within a magnetic field.

Example 9.8

If a 0.5m length of a conductor carrying 2.5A of current lies in a magnetic field of 500mT, calculate the force on the conductor.

Use this:

$$F = BIl \ \text{N}$$
$$\therefore F = 500E^{-3} \times 2.5 \times 0.5$$
$$\therefore F = 0.625N$$
$$\therefore F = 625mN$$

This example used a conductor, which was at right angles to the magnetic field. This concept is shown in Figure 9-23.

CHAPTER 9   MAGNETISM, THE ELECTROMAGNET, AND THE INDUCTOR

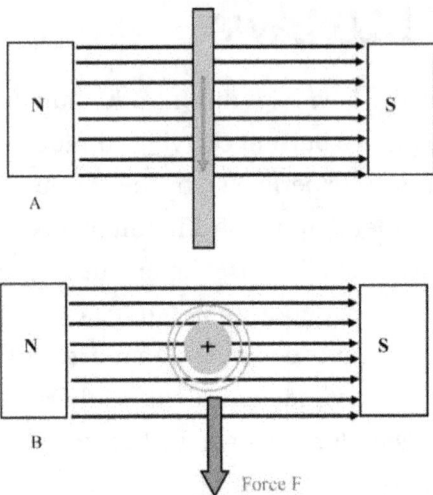

Figure 9-23. *A Current Carrying Conductor that Lies Perpendicular to a Magnetic Field*

The view A in Figure 9-23 is from above the conductor and B is an end-on view. In both views, the conductor is at right angles to the magnetic field. I hope you can see from Figure 9-23B that the flux is increased on the top of the conductor and weakened at the bottom. This forces the conductor to move downwards, as shown on Figure 9-23B.

Consider the situation the conductor is not perpendicular to the magnetic field. This is shown in the Figure 9-24.

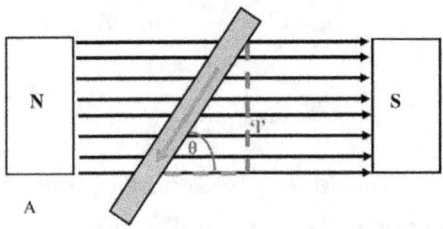

Figure 9-24. *A Current Carrying Conductor at Some Angle θ to the Magnetic Field*

554

CHAPTER 9 MAGNETISM, THE ELECTROMAGNET, AND THE INDUCTOR

Here, the conductor is at some angle θ to the magnetic field. This means now that the useful length of the conductor inside the magnetic field is no longer the same as actual length of the conductor. This is because the most force would be applied to the component of the conductor that is perpendicular (at right angles) to the magnetic field. When using the expression for the force on the conductor, we should always use the component of length of the conductor that lies at right angles to the magnetic field. We will denote this length by using the small letter l, and this is shown as the dotted vertical line in Figure 9-24A. This means that the complete expression for the force on a conductor is as follows:

$$F = BIlSin(\theta)$$

B is the flux density, I is the current flowing through the conductor, and l is the actual length of conductor that is inside the magnetic field, even though it is not perpendicular to the magnetic field. Note that θ is the angle of the conductor with respect to the magnetic field.

Example 9.9

If the half meter length of wire in Example 9.8 was lying at an angle of 35°, similar to the one shown in Figure 9-24, calculate the new force that would be applied to the conductor.

We need to use this expression:

$$F = BIl\sin(\theta)$$

Putting the values in, we get:

$$F = 500E^{-3} \times 2.5 \times 0.5 \times \sin(35) = 358.49 mN$$

CHAPTER 9   MAGNETISM, THE ELECTROMAGNET, AND THE INDUCTOR

Example 9.10

If a current carrying conductor of 0.5m in length experiences a force of 2N when lying at right angles to a magnetic field with a flux density of 1.25T, calculate the current that would be flowing through the conductor.

Because the conductor lies at right angles to the magnetic field, we can use this expression:

$$F = BIl$$

This can be transposed for the current I as follows:

$$I = \frac{F}{Bl}$$

Putting the values in, we get:

$$I = \frac{2}{1.2 \times 0.5} = 3.333 A$$

We now need to consider the direction in which the conductor will be moved due to the force exerted on it. This will depend on the direction of the current flowing through the conductor and the direction of flow of the flux between the two magnetic poles. We will assume that the direction of flux flow is from left to right, with the North pole of the magnet on the left and the South pole on the right. This is as shown in all the figures in this section. This means that the direction of the force is dependent upon the direction of current flow through the conductor.

We can use Fleming's left-hand rule to determine the direction of the force that will make the conductor move. This uses the idea that we place the first finger in the direction of the flux flow—that is, the magnetic field. Then we place the second in the direction of the current flow through the conductor. Then whilst ensuring the thumb, the first finger, and the second finger are all at right angles to each other, the thumb indicates the direction of motion of the conductor and so the direction that the force will act in. The principle of Fleming's left-hand rule for motors is shown in Figure 9-25.

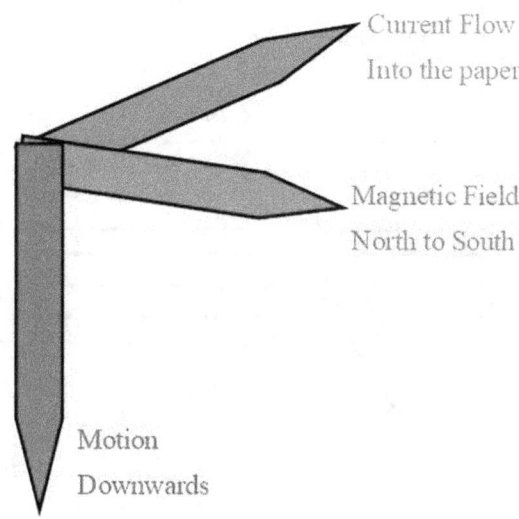

Figure 9-25. *Fleming's Left-Hand Rule*

If we apply Fleming's left-hand rule to the situation in Figure 9-23B, we can see that the first finger is pointing from left to right. The second finger is pointing into the paper, which means the thumb must be pointing downwards, as all three digits are at right angles to each other. This agrees with the force arrow in Figure 9-23B, as it is pointing downwards.

Generating a Voltage Across a Conductor

We have seen that when a current carrying conductor resides within a magnetic field, it will be forced to move through the field. We will now look at what happens if we physically move a conductor through a magnetic field. Fleming showed us that if a conductor experienced a flux change across it, then a voltage could be induced across it. As it is easier to move

CHAPTER 9   MAGNETISM, THE ELECTROMAGNET, AND THE INDUCTOR

the conductor through a magnetic field than make the flux across the conductor to change. The principle of moving the conductor through a magnetic field is the one that is used in generating a voltage across the conductor. We will consider a conductor being forced to move through a magnetic field, as shown in Figure 9-26.

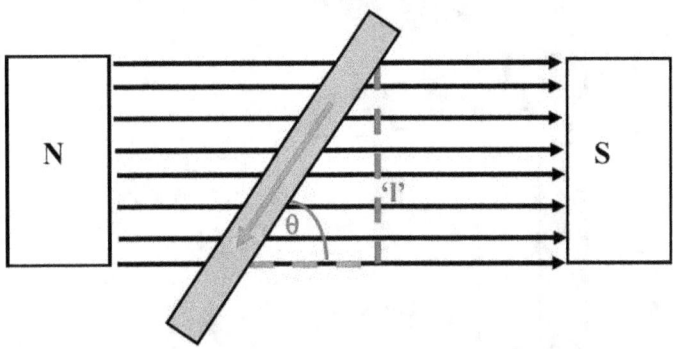

Figure 9-26. Moving a Conductor Through a Magnetic Field

Figure 9-26 shows the conductor being forced to move through a magnetic field at some angle θ. From our work with the DC motor, we know it is the perpendicular component of the length of the conductor with respect to the magnetic field that is important. If the angle θ was 90° then we could say that the conductor is passing through the magnetic field at right angles to it. Recall that the greater the flux density B and the perpendicular length l, the greater the induced voltage. The other parameter that affects the induced voltage across the conductor is the velocity u at which the conductor is forced to pass through the magnetic field. That being so, the expression for the induced EMF is as follows:

$$emf = Blu \times sin(\theta)$$

The sin(θ) is there to relate the actual length of the conductor within the magnetic field to the perpendicular length l.

CHAPTER 9   MAGNETISM, THE ELECTROMAGNET, AND THE INDUCTOR

Example 9.11

The conductor shown in Figure 9-26 has an actual length of 20cm and the angle it is forced to move through the field is perpendicular to the field. The flux density of the magnetic field is 1.1T. If the rate at which it is forced to move through the field is 10m/s, calculate the EMF developed across the conductor.

As the conductor is perpendicular to the field, θ is 90° and sin (θ) = 1. This means that we can use this:

$$emf = Blu$$

Putting the values in, we get:

$$emf = 1.1 \times 20E^{-2} \times 10 = 200mV$$

Example 9.12

If a train has an axle width of 1.4m and it is travelling perpendicular to the Earth's magnetic field, which has a flux density of approximately 40μT, calculate the induced EMF in the axle if the train is travelling at 80km/h.

As the axel is moving perpendicular to the flux field, we can calculate the EMF induced using this:

$$emf = Blu$$

We need to convert the speed of 80km/h to m/s. This is done by dividing the speed by 3600, as there are 3600 seconds in one hour. This mean the value for u is as follows:

$$u = \frac{80000}{3600} = 22.2 m/s$$

CHAPTER 9   MAGNETISM, THE ELECTROMAGNET, AND THE INDUCTOR

Therefore, we can calculate the EMF as follows:

$$emf = 40E^{-6} \times 1.4 \times 22.2 = 1.244 mv$$

Example 9.13

An aeroplane with a wingspan of 12m is travelling at a speed of 375mph and flying perpendicular to the Earth's magnetic field that has a flux density of 40µT. Calculate the voltage induced across the wingspan of the plane.

Knowing 1mile is 1.609km, 375mph is 603.375kph. We need to convert this to m/s, which is done as follows:

$$u = \frac{603.75E^3}{3600} = 167.604 m/s$$

We can now calculate the EMF using this:

$$emf = Blu = 40E^{-6} \times 12 \times 167.604 = 80.45 mV$$

Fleming's Right-Hand Rule

We used Fleming's left-hand rule to show how a current carrying conductor would be forced to move through a magnetic field. We can use Fleming's right-hand rule to show the direction the current would flow through a conductor as it is forced to move through a magnetic field. This assumes that the voltage induced across the conductor can force a current to flow. Figure 9-27 is a representation of Fleming's right-hand rule.

CHAPTER 9 MAGNETISM, THE ELECTROMAGNET, AND THE INDUCTOR

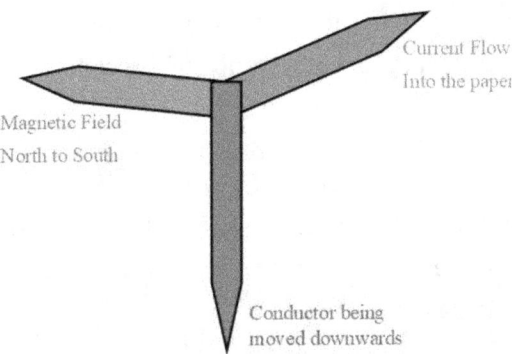

Figure 9-27. *Fleming's Right-Hand Rule*

One way that might help you remember which of Fleming's rules to use is that the G in right is for generators. This leaves left for motors.

Exercises for Chapter 9

Here are some exercises for you to try with respect to magnetism and magnetic circuits.

Exercise 9.1

1. A magnetic circuit creates a flux density of 75mT. If the cross-sectional area is 0.75m^2, calculate the flux that the circuit creates.

   (56.25mWbs)

2. Two U-cores are used to create a magnetic circuit. There is a gap in the joint opposite the coil. If the cross-sectional area of the air gap is 300mm^2, calculate the amount of flux required to create a flux density of 800mT.

   (240µWbs)

CHAPTER 9 MAGNETISM, THE ELECTROMAGNET, AND THE INDUCTOR

3. If the actual gap in the U-core in Question 2 is 2.5mm, calculate the reluctance of the gap.

   (6.631E⁶)

4. The mean circumference of a toroid is 750mm. If a current of 3.5A flows through a coil of 250 turns, calculate the magnetomotive force, F, and the magnetizing force, H.

   (F = 875, H = 1166.667)

5. A toroid has a coil of 350 turns wound on one side of it. The mean radius of the toroid is 100mm and the cross-sectional area is 400 mm². When a current of 7.5A flows through the coil, a flux of 30μWbs is created. Calculate the flux density, the magnetomotive force F, and the magnetizing force, H.

   [B = 75mT, F = 2625, H = 4177.82]

6. A rectangular piece of iron has a cross-sectional area of 40mm². It is bent to form a circular path of 250mm in length. When a current of 3.5A is passed through a coil of 400 turns wound on one side of the iron bar, a flux of 15μWbs is produced. Calculate the relative permeability of the iron. Note that we have shown that:

$$B = \mu_0 \mu_r H$$

   (53.288)

CHAPTER 9   MAGNETISM, THE ELECTROMAGNET, AND THE INDUCTOR

Exercise 9.2

With reference to Figure 9-28a, determine the direction the conductor will move through the magnetic field.

With reference to Figure 9-28b, determine the direction of current flowing through the conductor.

With reference to Figure 9-28c, determine which are the North and South Poles of the magnet.

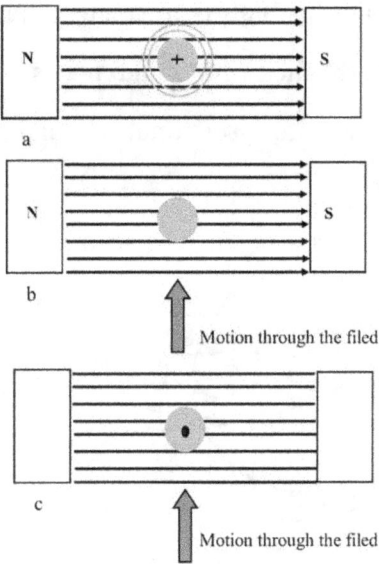

Figure 9-28. *The Magnetic Figures for Exercise 9.2*

Exercise 9.3

With respect to the toroid shown in Figure 9-29, calculate the following.

- The flux created in the toroid
- The magnetomotive force

CHAPTER 9   MAGNETISM, THE ELECTROMAGNET, AND THE INDUCTOR

- The magnetizing force
- The flux density
- The reluctance of the toroid

Use the following parameters for the toroid:

- N (the number of turns on the coil) is 450.
- The current flowing in the coil is 750mA.
- The relative permeability of the material μr is 500.
- The radius of the mean circumference is 75mm.
- The radius of the cross-sectional area of the core is 35mm.

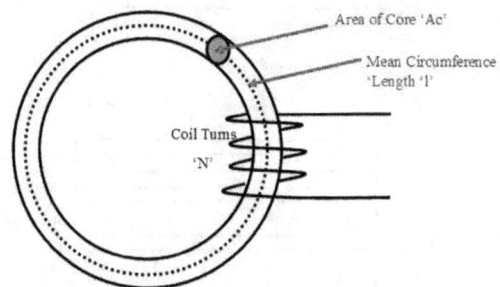

Figure 9-29. *The Toroid for Exercise 9.3*

$$[\Phi = 1.732 mWbs,\ F = 337.5\ AT,\ H = 716.197\ AT/m,\ B = 450 mT,\ S = 413.555 E^3]$$

CHAPTER 9   MAGNETISM, THE ELECTROMAGNET, AND THE INDUCTOR

Exercise 9.4

With respect to the two U-cores used to create the electromagnet shown in Figure 9-30, complete the following:

1. Create a magnetic circuit to represent the electromagnet.
2. Calculate the magnetomotive force.
3. Calculate the magnetizing force.
4. Calculate the total reluctance of the magnetic circuit.
5. Calculate the flux in the circuit.
6. Calculate the flux density of the electromagnet.
7. Calculate the energy drops around the circuit and use them to confirm you are correct.
   N = 350
   μ_r = 2200
   I = 50mA
   h = 34mm
   l = 19mm
   b = 5mm
   w = 6mm
   air gap = 1.5mm

CHAPTER 9   MAGNETISM, THE ELECTROMAGNET, AND THE INDUCTOR

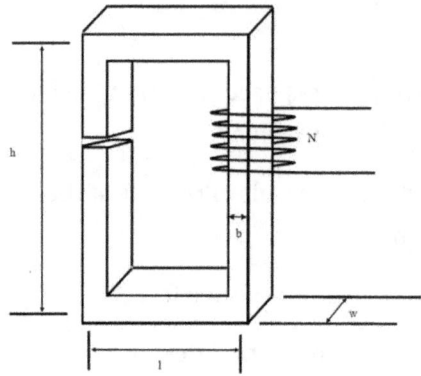

Figure 9-30. *The Magnet for Exercise 9.4*

Here are the answers:

$$[\text{mmf} = 17.5 \text{ AT, mf } H = 165.094 \text{ AT/m, ST} = 41.049 \text{M}\Omega,$$

$$\text{The flux } \Phi = 4.022 \mu Wbs, B = 134.067 mT,$$

$$H = 5.068 + 160.031 = 165.1 \ AT/m]$$

Summary

In this chapter, we looked at what magnetism is and how we can create it with electromagnets. We studied the main parameters of magnetism such as flux, flux density, the magnetomotive force, and the magnetizing force. We studied the B/H curve and the relationship between permeability and inductance. We learnt how to analyse magnetic circuits and how to use Fleming's left-hand and right-hand rules.

This is the last aspect of electrical analysis we will study in this book. I hope you have found the book useful, interesting, and informative. In my next book, *Mastering AC Analysis of Electrical Circuits*, we move on to two port analysis and look at filters and transmission lines and look at three

CHAPTER 9 MAGNETISM, THE ELECTROMAGNET, AND THE INDUCTOR

phase AC systems and ABCD parameters. Together, my four books on electrical engineering will provide you with an essential reference that will support you on your advancement in your career as an electrical engineer. Thank you for reading them.

The final chapter in this book shows you how to use the ECAD software TINA, which I have used throughout this book.

CHAPTER 10

Using TINA 12

In this chapter we look at how to use the ECAD software TINA 12. As we work through the book, we use this software to simulate the circuits so that we can test the theories that are covered in this book. This chapter will help you learn how to use some of the basic aspects of this software, and we will also look at some of the more specialised aspects that we use in this book. This chapter is not intended to be a complete manual for using TINA, but after reading this chapter, you should be able to carry out all the simulations discussed in this book. The following is a reference to a book that might help with using TINA.

   Title: *Electric and Electronic Circuit Simulation using TINA-TI*
   Author: Farzin Asadi

What Are ECAD and TINA 12?

ECAD stands for Electronic Computer Aided Design and TINA 12 is one of many pieces of software you can use when designing electrical and electronic circuits. I am not saying it is the best software, as there are pros and cons of all software. However, I have used TINA whilst teaching electrical and electronic engineering, and I found it more than sufficient for every aspect of what I was trying to teach. At around £100 for the basic software, it is one of the more affordable pieces of software, whilst giving you more than enough to start your career as an engineer. Even the demo version, which is free, is enough for you to use alongside most, if not all, the simulations in this book. With the demo version, you are allowed 31

CHAPTER 10   USING TINA 12

runs of the software, on separate days, before you need to buy it. There are no major restrictions in what it can do except there is a limitation on the number of nodes in the circuits you can simulate. This will mean that some of the larger circuits won't run in the demo software. You also can't save your files. However, you should be able to simulate most of the circuits and get a good appreciation of what the book is about.

Having TINA 12 at your disposal is simply like having a full electrical and electronics lab at your disposal. You can have almost any component you want at any value. You also have any piece of test equipment you could ever want at your disposal. You even have some specialist analysis tool that would be difficult to have anywhere else. However, to be fair, this is only what you would expect from any industrial standard ECAD software.

The other ECAD software programs I have used are PROTEUS and Multisim. These are very good ECAD programs, but they come at a price. It is up to you what software you eventually end up buying. However, as this book uses TINA 12 to simulate all the circuits in this book, I show you how to use its most common aspects.

Running the Software

The software can be downloaded from the www.tina.com. You must register your request for the demo version. Assuming you have successfully downloaded the software, you need to click the Tina icon shown in Figure 10-1.

Figure 10-1. *The Program Icon for Tina*

570

CHAPTER 10   USING TINA 12

You may be presented with a registration window or run as a demo. You may have to choose to run the software as the administrator. The program should then open to the main editing window, as shown in Figure 10-2.

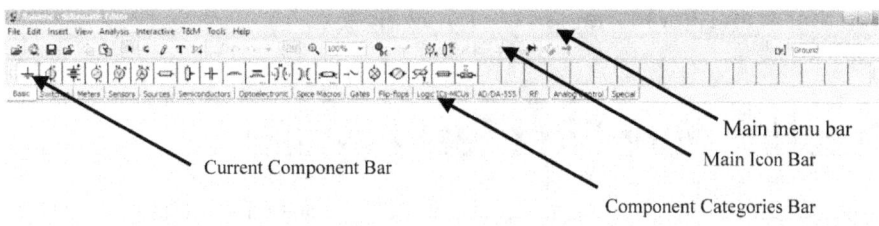

Figure 10-2. The Opening Screen

There are four toolbars on the main working window of TINA. These are identified in Figure 10-2 as follows:

- The main menu bar, which is where we can select the File, Edit, Insert, View, Analysis, Interactive, T&M Tools, and Help options.

- The main icon bar, which has some graphical icons for the commands, such as Open, Save, and so on.

- The Current Component bar. TINA splits the different components that you can use into different categories. When a category has been selected, the components in that category are shown in this menu bar.

- The Component Categories bar. This is where TINA allows you to select one of the many component categories that TINA uses.

Note that these are my names that I have given to the menu bars. This is so that I can refer to them in the following text.

Creating Your First Test Circuit

The first circuit we create is the simple CR high pass filter. I use this test circuit to show you how to run an AC analysis to produce a *bode plot*. The first thing we do is find the two components. This is in the Basic component category for TINA. Therefore, you must click Basic on the Component Categories bar. The Current Category bar will change to that shown in Figure 10-3.

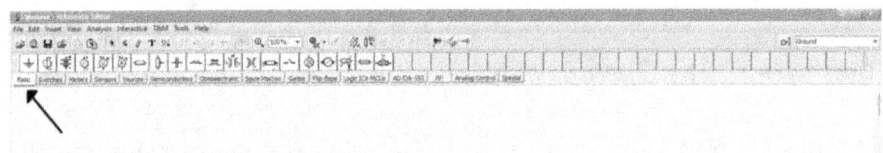

Figure 10-3. The Basic Current Category Menu Bar

The resistor symbol is the seventh icon on the Current Category bar.

TINA allows you to choose from two sets of symbols for the components you use. You can choose USA ANSII or European Din. I prefer the European Din set of symbols. To choose the set of symbols you want, click the Vie tab from the main menu bar. When you do that, a menu will drop down, and you must select the Options command from it, as shown in Figure 10-4.

CHAPTER 10   USING TINA 12

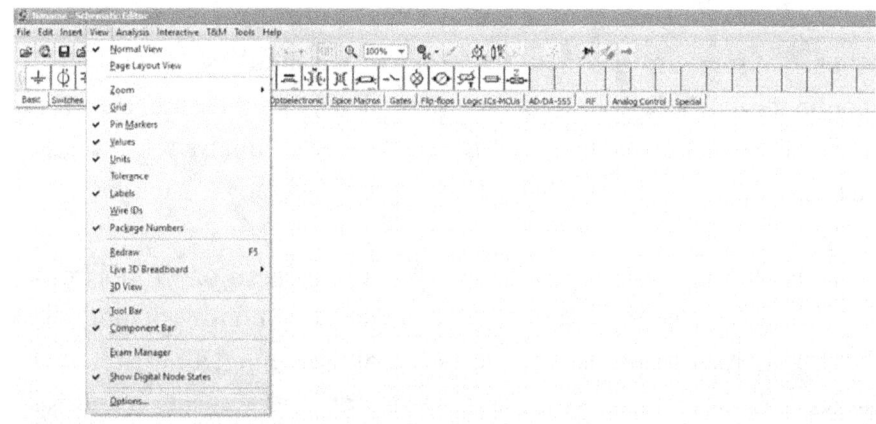

Figure 10-4. *The Drop-Down Menu from the View Tab*

When you select the Options command, the Editor Options window will appear, as shown in Figure 10-5.

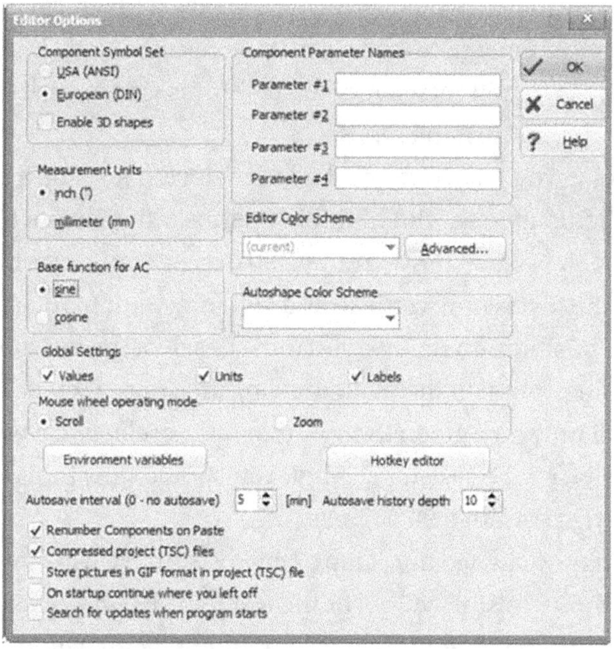

Figure 10-5. *The Editor Options Window*

573

You will be able to see the Component Symbol Set in the top-left corner. Whilst we are looking at this window, we should set the Base function for AC. It defaults to the mathematical base of cosine. However, I use the sine function as the base function for my AC analysis, so I suggest you change it to sine here. Click OK when you are ready to save your changes.

If you click the resistor icon, you will select the resistor symbol from the Current Component menu bar. If you move the mouse, you don't have to click and drag the mouse, you will see that the symbol for the resistor follows the mouse around the main drawing area. Now, with the mouse in a suitable position, simply click and the resistor will be dropped, in the place the mouse is pointing to when you clicked it. You should see that the resistor is still red, which means it is still selected. If the resistor turned green, it's deselected, but don't worry; it just means you clicked the mouse too many times.

Now we want to rotate the resistor to place it in a vertical orientation. To do this, we simply right-click whilst the resistor is still highlighted red, which means it is still selected. If the resistor is green, click the resistor using the left button of the mouse.

Assuming you have right-clicked the selected resistor, a drop-down window should appear with multiple options. Click Rotate Right. When you do this, the screen move through 90 degrees, into a vertical position. However, the text is now vertical, and you may want to rotate it into a horizontal position. To do this, you must deselect the resistor by simply clicking somewhere on the main drawing area of the screen. The resistor symbol will now turn green to show that it is deselected. Now right-click the text only, not the resistor symbol. You should now be able to rotate the text to the right through 90 degrees.

We will now change the value of the resistor. We can either double-click the whole resistor symbol or the text for the component. When you do either of those procedures, the component flyout window appears, as shown in Figure 10-6.

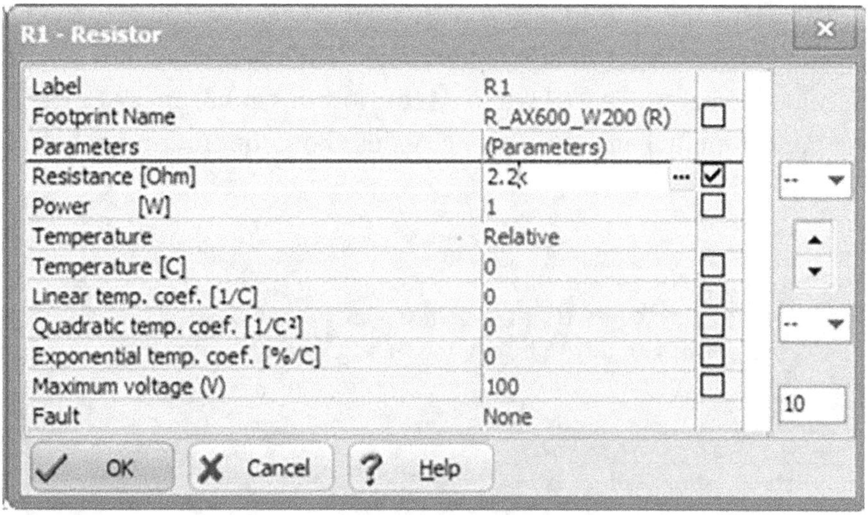

CHAPTER 10 USING TINA 12

R1 - Resistor			
Label	R1		
Footprint Name	R_AX600_W200 (R)	☐	
Parameters	(Parameters)		
Resistance [Ohm]	2.2k	... ☑	-- ▼
Power [W]	1	☐	
Temperature	Relative		▲ ▼
Temperature [C]	0	☐	
Linear temp. coef. [1/C]	0	☐	
Quadratic temp. coef. [1/C²]	0	☐	-- ▼
Exponential temp. coef. [%/C]	0	☐	
Maximum voltage (V)	100	☐	10
Fault	None		
✓ OK ✗ Cancel ? Help			

Figure 10-6. *The Component Value Window*

From this window you can change the value of the component. You can also change the label if you want to. There are various other parameters you can change for a more detailed simulation. You can also add a fault such as an open circuit or a short circuit. Change the value to 2.2k, as shown in Figure 10-6. Once you are happy with your settings, click OK to close the window; you will return to the main drawing area.

Now you need to add the capacitor. This is done in the same way as adding the resistor except that the capacitor is the ninth symbol on the Current Component menu bar. We can keep the default horizontal orientation and the default value of 1μF. Now we need to add the earth or ground. We must do this for all our circuits, as voltage needs a reference. The normal reference for any circuit is ground, or earth, or 0V. The earth symbol is the first one on the Current Component menu bar. I normally place this on the bottom-left corner of the circuit. You can see this in Figure 10-8.

575

CHAPTER 10   USING TINA 12

The next item we need to add is the signal generator. This is used to apply a variety of input voltage to the circuit. The signal generator is called the voltage generator in TINA, and it is the fourth symbol on the Current Component menu bar. I normally place this above the ground symbol; see Figure 10-7.

Figure 10-7. *The Wire Tool*

TINA provides a grid to help align the components we use. If the grid is not present in the main drawing area, click View from the main menu bar. A drop-down menu will appear. If you now select the word GRID the tick should appear, and the grid will be turned on to your main drawing area. The grid can help you align the components as you place them.

The next thing we need to do is wire the components together. To start the wire, select the wire tool, as shown in Figure 10-7. Then move the wire symbol, which looks like a soldering iron, to where you want to start the wire. Then click the mouse button to connect the tool and drag it around the circuit, whilst keeping the mouse button pressed, to where you want to end the wire. Then click again to fasten the end of the wire at the required

CHAPTER 10 USING TINA 12

position. You should be able to move to the end of another component and start wiring again. However, you may now need to select the wire tool again to complete the wiring of the components.

When you have wired the circuit completely, it should look like the circuit shown in Figure 10-8.

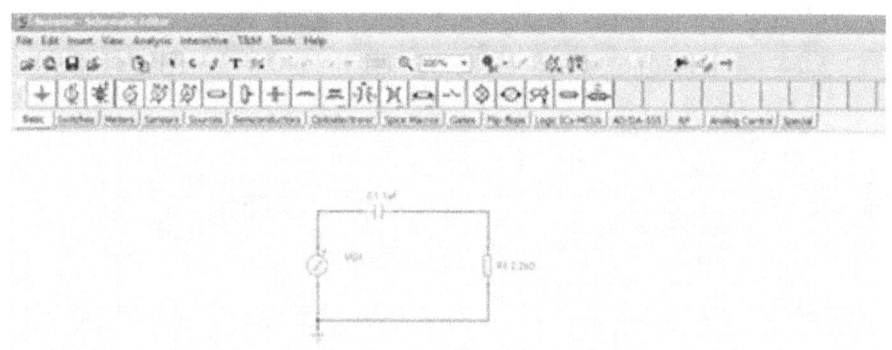

Figure 10-8. *The Circuit Wired Completely*

We need to identify where we want to monitor what the circuit will do in the simulated analysis. There are a variety of ways we can identify the point of the circuit. I inserted outputs, as shown in Figure 10-9.

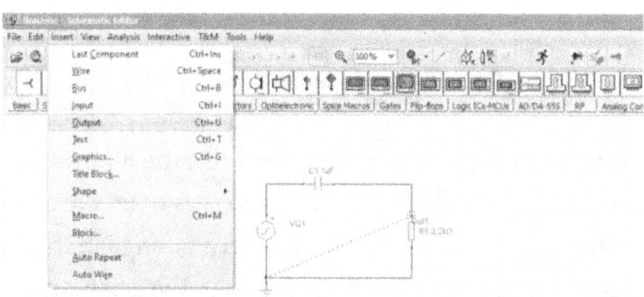

Figure 10-9. *Using the Insert Output to Add a Monitoring Point on the Circuit*

577

However, I find that I sometimes have to move the out wire slightly to ensure that it makes a connection. An alternative approach is to add a voltage pin, as shown in Figure 10-10.

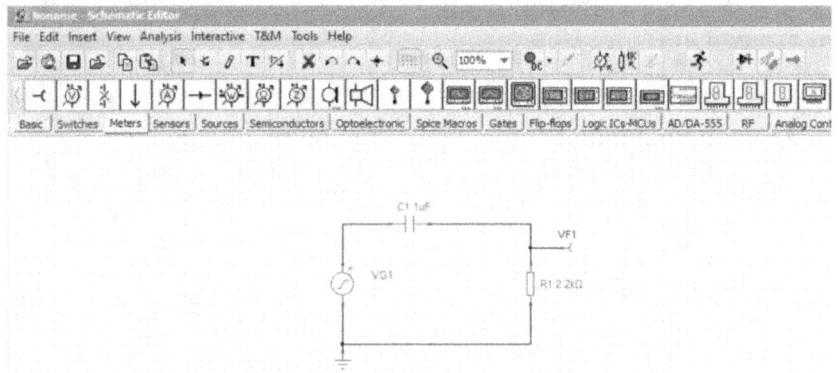

Figure 10-10. Using the Voltage Pin

To select a voltage pin, you must first change the component categories tab to Meters (click the Meters tab). The voltage pin is the first symbol on the now changed Current Component bar. We simply place the voltage pin in the same way as any component and use the wire tool to connect it to where we want to monitor the voltage.

Running the AC Analysis

We are now ready to simulate the circuit and run the analysis. This will be an AC transfer characteristic. This will allow us to create a bode plot to show how the gain of the circuit varies with a change in frequency. To select this type of analysis, we firstly click the Analysis tab on the main menu bar. Then we select the AC Analysis option from the drop-down menu that appears. Finally, we select the AC Transfer Characteristics from the flyout menu that appears. This is shown in Figure 10-11.

CHAPTER 10   USING TINA 12

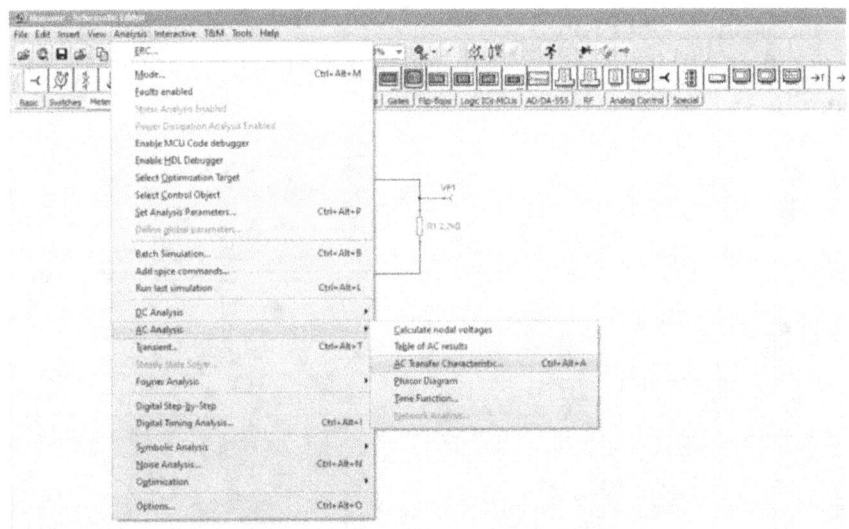

Figure 10-11. The AC Transfer Characteristics Option

When we select AC Transfer Characteristics, the AC Transfer Characteristics window appears. I changed the number of points to 1000 but kept everything else as the defaults. This is shown in Figure 10-12.

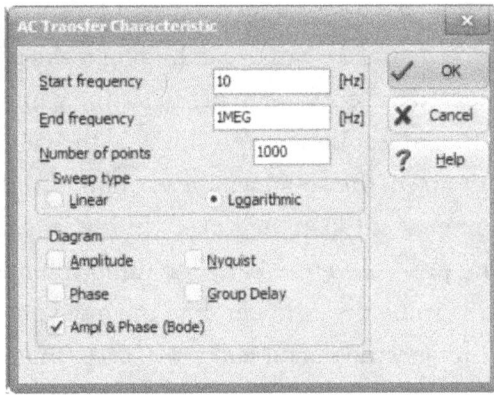

Figure 10-12. The AC Transfer Characteristics Window

579

CHAPTER 10 USING TINA 12

Once you are happy with the settings, click the OK button. The circuit will simulate and the bode plot will appear on the screen. This is shown in Figure 10-13.

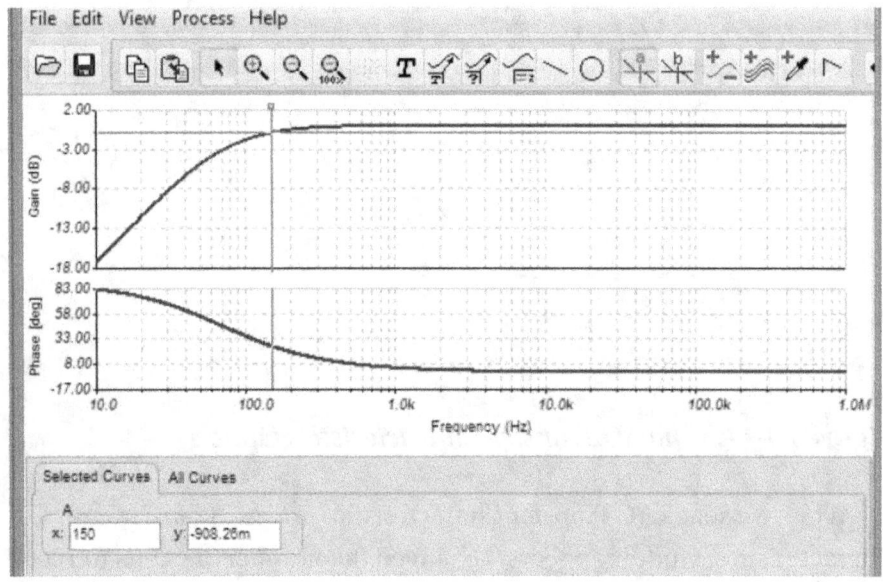

Figure 10-13. *The Bode Plot*

There are two cursors we can use to highlight the plot at a particular value. I have selected the cursor a to highlight the gain value, in dBs, of the plot at a particular frequency. You can type the value that you are interested in into one of the small windows on the display. In this case, I entered the frequency of 150 in the x axis window; the cursor goes to that frequency when I press the Enter key. One thing you need to remember is to always type in a value that is lower than the one you want so that when you press the Enter key the cursor can move up to that value.

CHAPTER 10   USING TINA 12

Transient Analysis

Another useful analysis used in the book is transient analysis. This looks at how the voltage or current at different points in the circuit changes over time. This is especially useful to see what happens in the first few milliseconds after a change has occurred within the circuit, such as being switched on. It enables the software to act like a storage scope. We will use this type of analysis to examine the voltage rise across a capacitor and confirm the time constant of the DC CR circuit. We will firstly create the circuit, which is like the first circuit we created. We will select the components in the same way and wire them up as before to create the circuit shown in Figure 10-14.

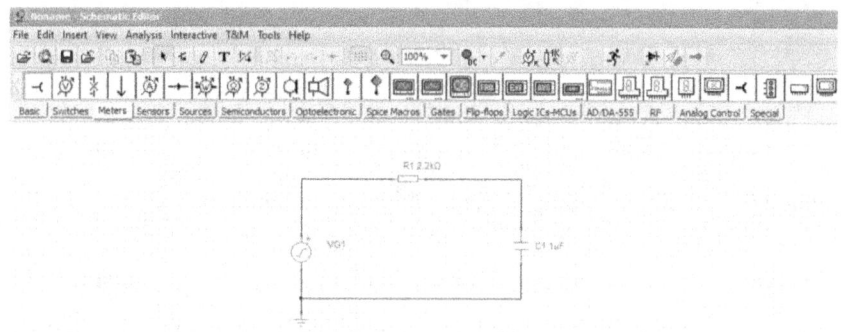

Figure 10-14. The RC Circuit for the DC Transient Analysis.

We need to set up the input signal to apply the DC wave that will stay high for enough time for the capacitor to charge up fully and then go to 0V, where it will stay low long enough for the capacitor to discharge. This means we must have an idea of how long it will take the capacitor to charge up and discharge. The theory states that it will take 5 tau (i.e., five-time constants) for this to happen. The RC circuit one-time constant is equal to RC seconds. In this circuit, the time constant, Toa, is as follows:

$$Toa = \tau = CR \; seconds = 1E^{-6} \times 2.2E^{3} = 2.2ms$$

581

CHAPTER 10   USING TINA 12

Therefore, five-time constants will equal 11ms. This means that we need to create a voltage that stays high for 11ms and then low for 11ms. It will then repeat the cycle. In TINA, this is a general waveform. To create it we need to click VG1, the voltage generator symbol in the circuit. This will open the Voltage Generator window shown in Figure 10-15.

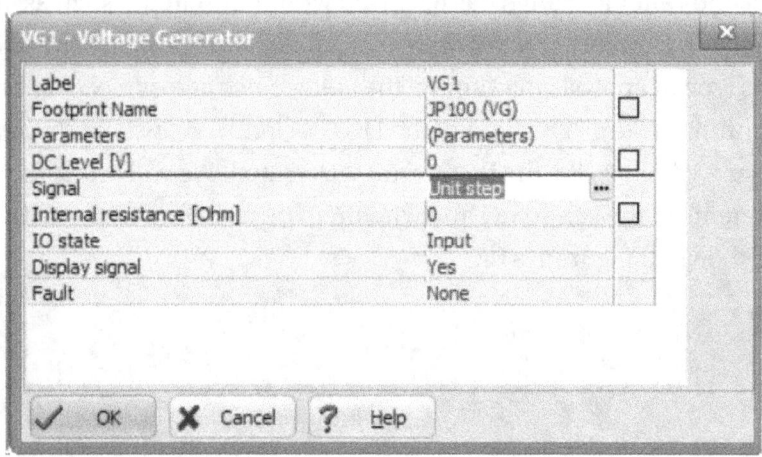

Figure 10-15. The Voltage Generator Window

The default signal is the Unit Step. To change this, click the small three dots. This will open the Signal Editor window, shown in Figure 10-16.

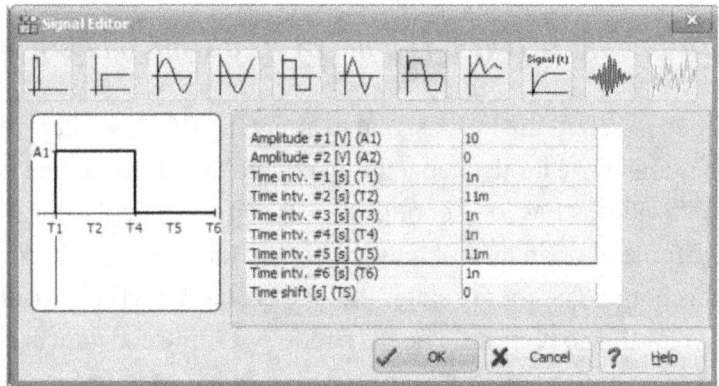

Figure 10-16. The Signal Editor Window

582

We want the seventh signal type, which has been selected here. We need to set the following time settings:

- The amplitude the signal should rise to. I set it to 10V.
- The amplitude the signal should fall to. I set it to 0V.
- The (T1) which is the rise time of the signal. I left this at 1ns.
- The (T2) which is the time the signal stays high. This is set to 11ms.
- The (T3) which is the fall time of the signal. I left this at 1ns.
- The (T4) which is the second rise time of the signal. I have left this at 1ns.
- The (T5) which is the time the signal stays low. This is set to 11ms.
- The (T6) which is the second fall time. This has been left at 1ns.
- The (Ts) which is a delay time you might want to introduce into the starting of the signal waveform. This has been left at 0.

As you enter these settings, the waveform will be shown in the preview window. When you are happy with the settings, simply click OK and the window will close. Then click OK again to close the Voltage Generator window.

We now need to add a voltage pin and place it above the top of the capacitor. This will allow us to monitor the voltage across the capacitor over time.

CHAPTER 10   USING TINA 12

We also need to set up the transient analysis. To do this, click the Analysis tab on the main menu bar and select Transient from the drop-down menu that appears. The Transient Analysis window will appear, as shown in Figure 10-17.

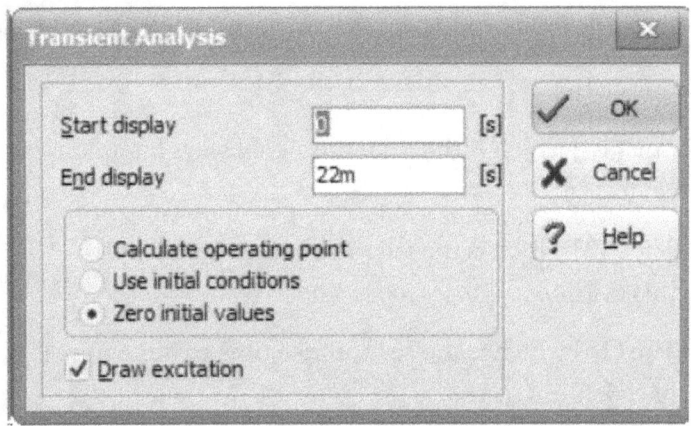

Figure 10-17. *The Transient Analysis Window*

We need to change the settings to those as shown in Figure 10-17. Make sure you select the Zero Initial Values option. When you are happy with the settings, click OK.

CHAPTER 10   USING TINA 12

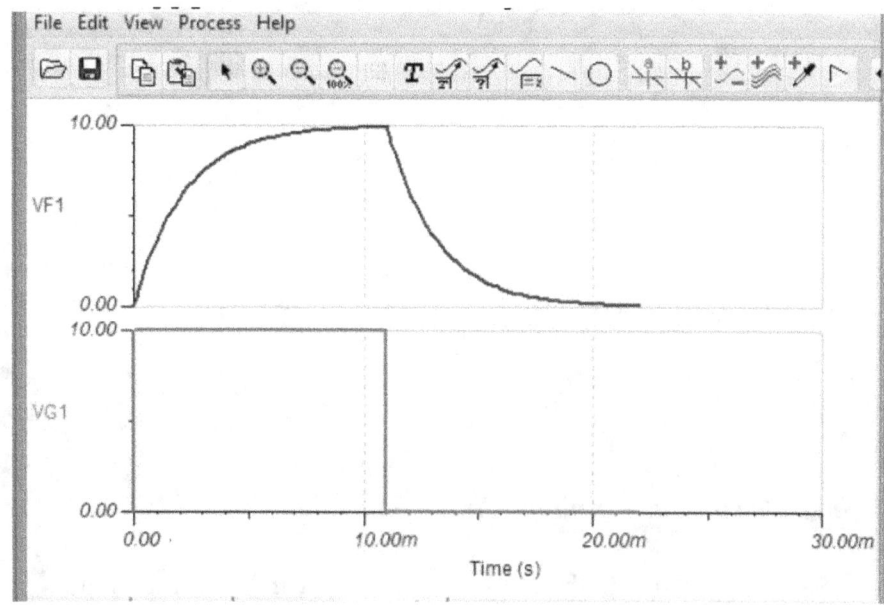

Figure 10-18. *The TR Results Window*

The default view shows the curves on top of each other. To separate them, click the View option on the menu bar and then select Separate Curves. The display will change to that shown in Figure 10-18.

Using the Oscilloscope

We will use the oscilloscope to monitor the input and output of amplifiers in the book. We will create a class A stabilised amplifier to show how to use the oscilloscope. The circuit uses four resistors, one capacitor, and a voltage generator. The circuit will need a DC supply for the VCC; the simplest is a battery. This is the third symbol on the Basic Component Category bar. Placing the battery in the circuit and changing the voltage to 15V gives the circuit shown in Figure 10-19.

585

CHAPTER 10   USING TINA 12

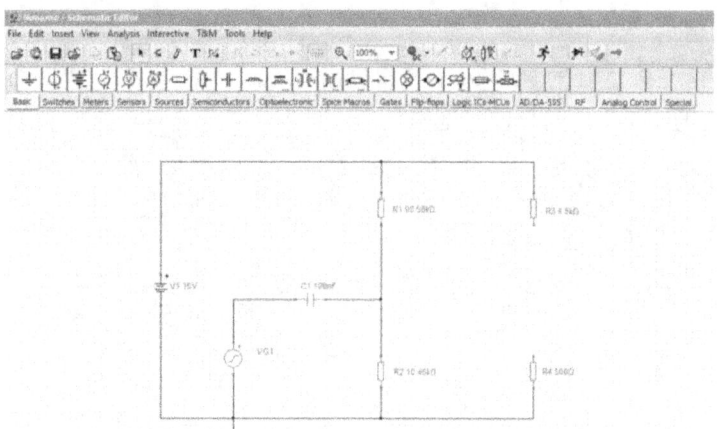

Figure 10-19. *The Amplifier Circuit So Far*

We now need to add the BJT transistor. This can be found on the Semiconductor menu, which is the eighth symbol on that menu bar. We want the NPN transistor. You can place it on the circuit and when you double-click the transistor, the NPN Bipolar Transistor window will appear, as shown in Figure 10-20.

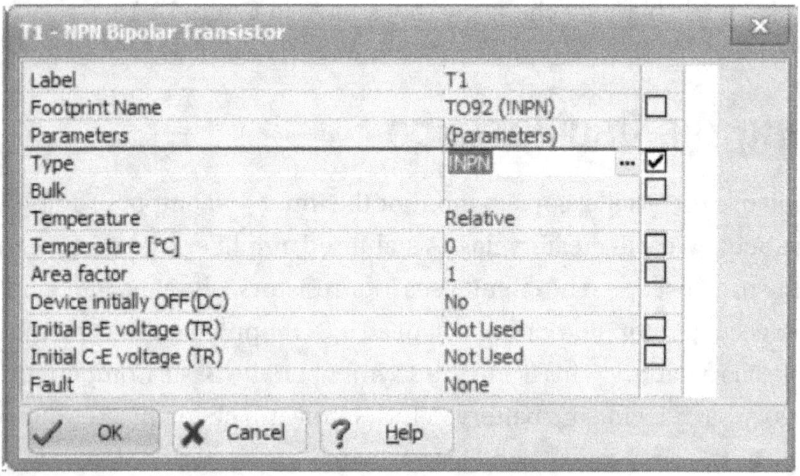

Figure 10-20. *The NPN Bipolar Transistor Window*

CHAPTER 10   USING TINA 12

If we click the three dots, the Catalog Editor window will appear, as shown in Figure 10-21.

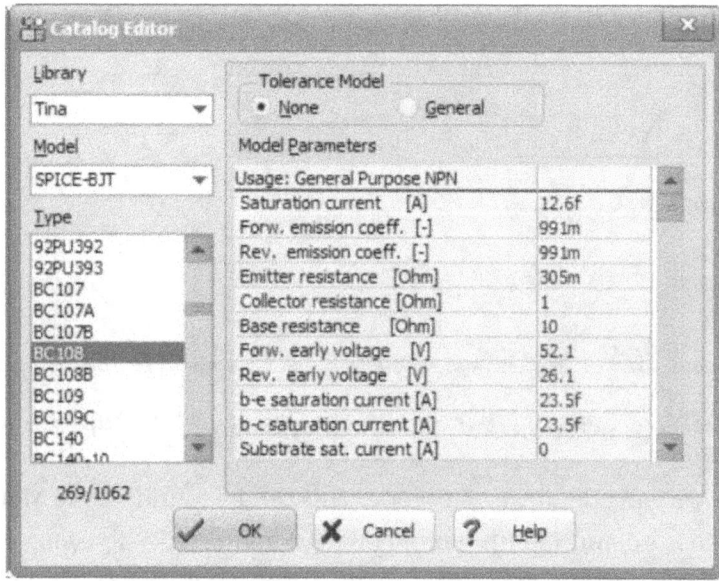

Figure 10-21. The Transistor Catalog Editor Window

We can use this window to change the transistor type. I selected the BC108 transistor here. We can use this window to change the various parameters of the transistor, such as the beta and internal capacitance values. Once you are happy with your settings, click OK to close this window and click OK again to close the first window.

We must change the input signal to a sine wave. To do this, we need to open the Signal Editor window and select the sine wave. Set the parameters as shown in Figure 10-22.

587

CHAPTER 10   USING TINA 12

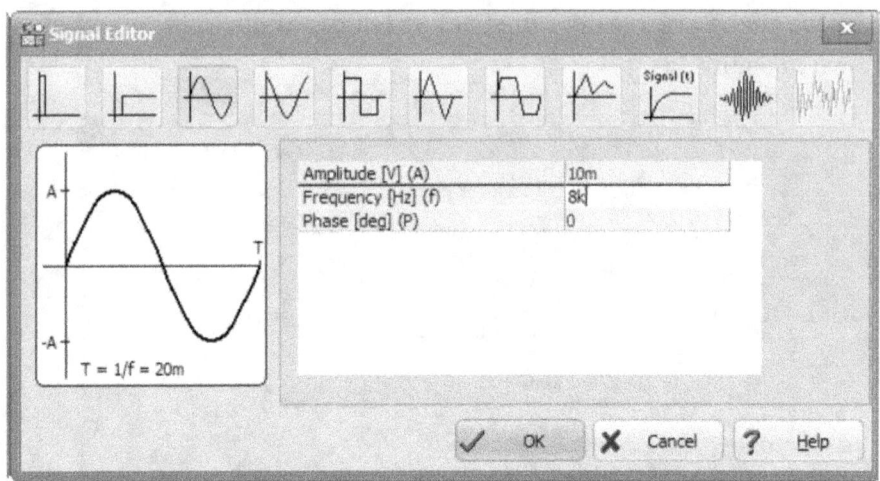

Figure 10-22. *Setting Up a Sine Wave Voltage at the Input*

Now we will add the oscilloscope. This can be found on the Meters tab, which is the fourteenth symbol on that menu bar. When you click on the Oscilloscope, select the three-terminal option and place it somewhere convenient on the screen. Connect the oscilloscope, as shown in Figure 10-23.

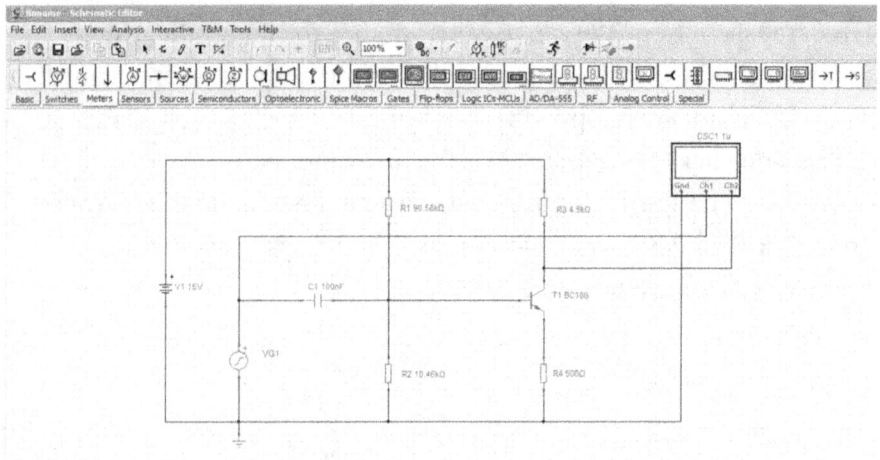

Figure 10-23. *Connecting the Oscilloscope*

CHAPTER 10   USING TINA 12

We must now set the oscilloscope up and run the simulation. We need to click the T&M option on the main menu bar. Then select the Oscilloscope option from the drop-down menu that appears. This will open the Oscilloscope window, as shown in Figure 10-24.

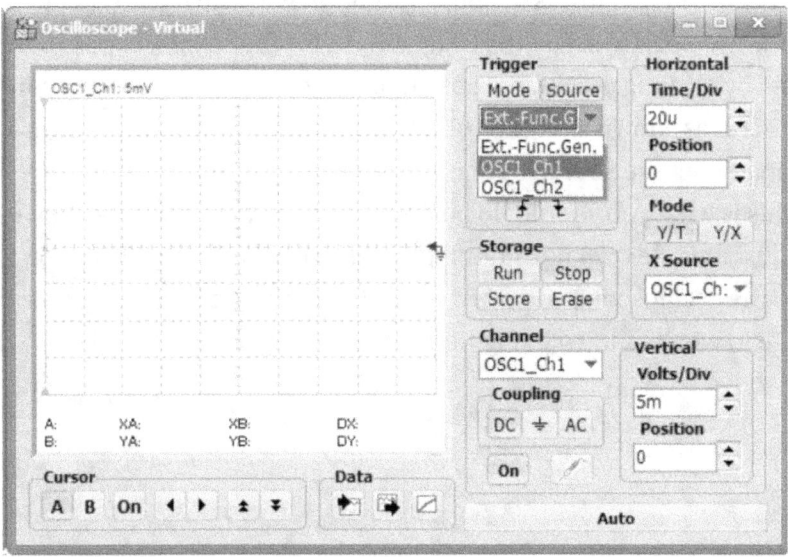

Figure 10-24. The Oscilloscope Window

We need to set up the Time/Div and Volts/Div options. With respect to the Time/Div, we should try to display two cycles of the waveform we are measuring. This means we need to display two times the periodic time on the screen. We know that the horizontal width of the screen has ten divisions. Knowing this we can set the Time/Div using this:

$$\frac{Time}{Div} = \frac{2}{10f}$$

When f = 8kHz, we have the following:

$$\frac{Time}{Div} = \frac{2}{10 \times 8E^{3}} = 25E^{-6} = 25\mu s$$

589

CHAPTER 10   USING TINA 12

We do not have this setting on the oscilloscope so we will set the Time/Div to 50µs.

As to the Volts/Div, we know the peak of the input is 10mv and we have four divisions to display this on the vertical. Therefore, we must set the volts/div to 5mV, as this is the best resolution we have in that order.

Now we need to select the trigger input for the oscilloscope. This is done by clicking the Source option on the oscilloscope and selecting Channel 1, as shown in Figure 10-24.

Finally, set the Source option to Normal.

This is what you should do before you use any oscilloscope; however, most just twiddle the knobs until they get a steady picture. Once you have set up the oscilloscope correctly, press the Run button. The display will change to what's shown in Figure 10-25.

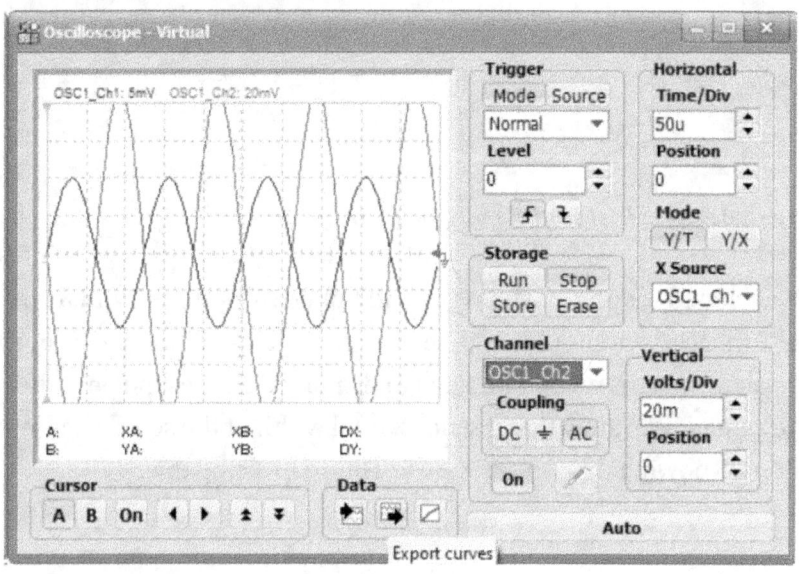

Figure 10-25. *The Oscilloscope Display*

CHAPTER 10   USING TINA 12

Once you are happy with the display, click the Stop button and the display should freeze. Now you can clock the second data arrow to export the display to a graph you can use and save for later.

Summary

This chapter looked at using some options available to you within the TINA 12 ECAD software. We will go through these and some more in the book as we use them. I hope you find this software useful in your design work and that you do enjoy using it.

This chapter was not intended to provide you with a complete manual on how to use TINA. It was only meant as an introduction into how you can use TINA to create and simulate the circuits in this book.

Appendix 1

Common Useful Formulas

Rules of Indices

$$x^a \times x^b = x^{a+b}$$

$$\frac{x^a}{x^b} = x^{a-b}$$

$$y = (x^a)^b$$

then

$$y = x^{a \times b}$$

$$y = x^{\frac{a}{b}}$$

is the same as

$$y = \sqrt[b]{x^a}$$

Sine Rule $\quad \dfrac{a}{\sin A} = \dfrac{b}{\sin B} = \dfrac{c}{\sin C}$

Cosine Rule $\quad a^2 = b^2 + c^2 - 2bc\cos A$

Common Standard Differentials

y or $f(x)$	$\dfrac{dy}{dx}$ or $f'(x)$
ax^n	nax^{n-1}
$a\sin(nx)$	$na\cos(nx)$
$a\cos(nx)$	$-na\sin(nx)$

APPENDIX 1

$a\sin(nx+\alpha)$	$na\cos(nx+\alpha)$
$a\cos(nx+\alpha)$	$-na\sin(nx+\alpha)$
$a\tan(nx)$	$na\sec^2(nx)$
$a\tan(nx+\alpha)$	$na\sec^2(nx+\alpha)$
$\log_e(x)$ or $\ln(x)$	$\dfrac{1}{x}$
ae^{nx}	nae^{nx}
$a\text{Sinh}(nx)$	$na\text{Cosh}(nx)$
$a\text{Cosh}(nx)$	$na\,\text{Sinh}(nx)$
$a\tanh(nx)$	$na\,\text{Sech}^2(nx)$
$\sin^{-1}(nx)$	$\dfrac{n}{\sqrt{1-(nx)^2}}$
$\cos^{-1}(nx)$	$\dfrac{-n}{\sqrt{1-(nx)^2}}$
$\tan^{-1}(nx)$	$\dfrac{n}{1+(nx)^2}$

note 'a' and 'n' are constants

Function of Function Rule:

$$\frac{dy}{dx} = \frac{dy}{du} \times \frac{du}{dx}$$

Product Rule:

$$\frac{dy}{dx} = v\frac{du}{dx} + u\frac{dv}{dx}$$

Quotient Rule:

$$\frac{dy}{dx} = \frac{v\dfrac{du}{dx} - u\dfrac{dv}{dx}}{v^2}$$

APPENDIX 1

Differential of Inverse Trig Relationships:

$$y = \sin^{-1}\left(\frac{x}{a}\right) \qquad \frac{dy}{dx} = \frac{1}{\sqrt{a^2 - x^2}}$$

$$y = \sin^{-1} f(x) \qquad \frac{dy}{dx} = \frac{f'(x)}{\sqrt{1 - [f(x)]^2}}$$

$$y = \cos^{-1}\left(\frac{x}{a}\right) \qquad \frac{dy}{dx} = \frac{-1}{\sqrt{a^2 - x^2}}$$

$$y = \cos^{-1} f(x) \qquad \frac{dy}{dx} = \frac{-f'(x)}{\sqrt{1 - [f(x)]^2}}$$

$$y = \tan^{-1}\left(\frac{x}{a}\right) \qquad \frac{dy}{dx} = \frac{a}{a^2 + x^2}$$

$$y = \tan^{-1} f(x) \qquad \frac{dy}{dx} = \frac{f'(x)}{1 + [f(x)]^2}$$

$$y = \sec^{-1}\left(\frac{x}{a}\right) \qquad \frac{dy}{dx} = \frac{a}{x\sqrt{x^2 - a^2}}$$

$$y = \sec^{-1} f(x) \qquad \frac{dy}{dx} = \frac{f'(x)}{f(x)\sqrt{[f(x)]^2 - 1}}$$

$$y = \operatorname{cosec}^{-1}\left(\frac{x}{a}\right) \qquad \frac{dy}{dx} = \frac{-a}{x\sqrt{x^2 - a^2}}$$

$$y = \operatorname{cosec}^{-1} f(x) \qquad \frac{dy}{dx} = \frac{-f'(x)}{f(x)\sqrt{[f(x)]^2 - 1}}$$

$$y = \cot^{-1}\left(\frac{x}{a}\right) \qquad \frac{dy}{dx} = \frac{-a}{a^2 + x^2}$$

$$y = \cot^{-1} f(x) \qquad \frac{dy}{dx} = \frac{-f'(x)}{1 + [f(x)]^2}$$

APPENDIX 1

Common Standard Integrals:

function of x $f(x)$	Integral $\int f(x)dx$
ax^n	$\dfrac{ax^{n+1}}{n+1} + C$
$a\sin(nx)$	$\dfrac{-a\cos(nx)}{n} + C$
$a\cos(nx)$	$\dfrac{a\sin(nx)}{n} + C$
ae^{nx}	$\dfrac{ae^{nx}}{n} + C$
$x^{-1} = \dfrac{1}{x}$	$\log_e x + C$
$\tan(nx)$	$\dfrac{1}{n}\ln(\sec(nx)) + C$
$\sec(nx)$	$\dfrac{1}{n}\ln(\sec(nx) + \tan(nx)) + C$
$a\sec^2(nx)$	$\dfrac{a\tan(nx)}{n} + C$
$\cosh(nx)$	$\dfrac{1}{n}\sinh(nx) + C$
$\sinh(nx)$	$\dfrac{1}{n}\cosh(nx) + C$
$\dfrac{1}{x^2 + a^2}$	$\dfrac{1}{a}\tan^{-1}\dfrac{x}{a} + C \quad$ for $a \rangle 0$
$\dfrac{1}{x^2 - a^2}$	$\dfrac{1}{2a}\ln\left(\dfrac{x-a}{x+a}\right) + C \quad$ for $|x|\rangle a\rangle 0$

Extra Integrals:

$$a\sec^2(nx) = \dfrac{1}{n}\tan(nx) + C$$

$$a\operatorname{cosec}^2(nx) = -\dfrac{1}{n}\cot(nx) + C$$

APPENDIX 1

$$a\cosec(nx) = -\frac{1}{n}\cosec(nx) + C$$

$$a\sec(nx)\tan(nx) = \frac{1}{n}\sec(nx) + C$$

Integration By Parts:

$$I = [uv]_a^b - \int_a^b v\frac{du}{dx}dx$$

Mean:

$$mean = \frac{1}{b-a}\int_a^b f(x)\,dx$$

Root Mean Square (RMS):

$$rms = \sqrt{\frac{1}{b-a}\int_a^b (f(x))^2\,dx}$$

Some Common Trig Identities:

$$\tan\theta = \frac{\sin\theta}{\cos\theta}$$

$$\cot\theta = \frac{1}{\tan\theta} = \frac{\cos\theta}{\sin\theta}$$

$$\sec\theta = \frac{1}{\cos\theta}$$

$$\cosec\theta = \frac{1}{\sin\theta}$$

$$\sec^2\theta = 1 + \tan^2\theta$$

$$\cos^2\theta + \sin^2\theta = 1$$

$$\cosec^2\theta = 1 + \cot^2\theta$$

APPENDIX 1

The Double Angle Formula

$$\sin^2 A + \cos^2 A = 1$$

$$\frac{\sin A}{\cos A} = \tan A$$

$$\sin(A+B) = \sin A \cos B + \sin B \cos A$$

$$\sin(A-B) = \sin A \cos B - \sin B \cos A$$

$$\cos(A+B) = \cos A \cos B - \sin A \sin B$$

$$\cos(A-B) = \cos A \cos B + \sin A \sin B$$

$$\sin 2A = 2 \sin A \cos A$$

$$\cos 2A = 1 - 2\sin^2 A$$

$$\cos 2A = 2\cos^2 A - 1$$

$$\cos 2A = \cos^2 A - \sin^2 A$$

$$\tan(A+B) = \frac{\tan A + \tan B}{1 - \tan A \tan B}$$

$$\tan(A-B) = \frac{\tan A - \tan B}{1 + \tan A \tan B}$$

$$\sin^2 A = (\sin A)^2$$

$$\cos^2 A = (\cos A)^2$$

$$\tan 2A = \frac{2 \tan A}{1 - \tan^2 A}$$

Converting Products of sin and cos into Sums and Differences:

$$\sin A \cos B = \frac{1}{2}\left[\sin(A+B) + \sin(A-B)\right]$$

$$\cos A \sin B = \frac{1}{2}\left[\sin(A+B) - \sin(A-B)\right]$$

$$\cos A \cos B = \frac{1}{2}\left[\cos(A+B) + \cos(A-B)\right]$$

$$\sin A \sin B = -\frac{1}{2}\left[\cos(A+B) - \cos(A-B)\right]$$

APPENDIX 1

Converting Sums and Differences of sin and cos into Products:

$$\sin X + \sin Y = 2\sin\left(\frac{X+Y}{2}\right)\cos\left(\frac{X-Y}{2}\right)$$

$$\sin X - \sin Y = 2\cos\left(\frac{X+Y}{2}\right)\sin\left(\frac{X-Y}{2}\right)$$

$$\cos X + \cos Y = 2\cos\left(\frac{X+Y}{2}\right)\cos\left(\frac{X-Y}{2}\right)$$

$$\cos X - \cos Y = -2\sin\left(\frac{X+Y}{2}\right)\sin\left(\frac{X-Y}{2}\right)$$

Common Partial Fractions:

$$\frac{f(x)}{(x+a)(x+b)} \equiv \frac{A}{x+a} + \frac{B}{x+b}$$

$$\frac{f(x)}{(x+a)^2} \equiv \frac{A}{x+a} + \frac{B}{(x+a)^2}$$

$$\frac{f(x)}{(ax^2+bx+c)(x+d)} \equiv \frac{Ax+B}{ax^2+bx+c} + \frac{C}{x+d}$$

$$Sin^n(x) = (Sin(x))^n$$
$$Cos^n(x) = (Cos(x))^n$$
$$\frac{1}{\cos(x)} = \sec(x)$$

Basic Hyperbolic Equations:

$$\sinh(x) = \frac{e^x - e^{-x}}{2}$$

$$\cosh(x) = \frac{e^x + e^{-x}}{2}$$

$$\tanh(x) = \frac{e^x - e^{-x}}{e^x + e^{-x}}$$

APPENDIX 1

$$\operatorname{cosech}(x) = \frac{2}{e^x - e^{-x}}$$

$$\operatorname{sech}(x) = \frac{2}{e^x + e^{-x}}$$

$$\coth(x) = \frac{e^x + e^{-x}}{e^x - e^{-x}}$$

Differentials of Hyperbolic Expressions:

$$y = a\sinh(nx) \qquad \frac{dy}{dx} = na\cosh(nx)$$

$$y = a\cosh(nx) \qquad \frac{dy}{dx} = na\sinh(nx)$$

$$y = a\tanh(nx) \qquad \frac{dy}{dx} = na\operatorname{sech}^2(nx)$$

$$y = a\operatorname{sech}(nx) \qquad \frac{dy}{dx} = -na\operatorname{sech}(nx)\tanh(nx)$$

$$y = a\operatorname{cosech}(nx) \qquad \frac{dy}{dx} = -na\operatorname{cosech}(nx)\coth(nx)$$

$$y = a\coth(nx) \qquad \frac{dy}{dx} = -na\operatorname{cosech}^2(nx)$$

$$\cos\theta = \frac{1}{2}\left(e^{j\theta} + e^{-j\theta}\right)$$

$$\sin\theta = \frac{1}{2j}\left(e^{j\theta} - e^{-j\theta}\right)$$

$$\cos j\theta = \cosh\theta$$
$$\sin j\theta = \sinh\theta$$
$$\cosh^2\theta - \sinh^2\theta = 1$$
$$\cos^2 j\theta + \sin^2 j\theta = 1$$
$$\cosh j\theta = \cos\theta$$

APPENDIX 1

$\sinh j\theta = j\sin\theta$

$\tanh j\theta = j\tan\theta$

$\coth^2\theta - 1 = \text{cosech}^2\theta$

$\cosh A - \cosh B = 2\sinh\left(\dfrac{A+B}{2}\right)\sinh\left(\dfrac{A-B}{2}\right)$

Differentials of Inverse Hyperbolic Expressions:

$y = \sinh^{-1}\left(\dfrac{x}{a}\right) \qquad \dfrac{dy}{dx} = \dfrac{1}{\sqrt{x^2 + a^2}}$

$y = \sinh^{-1} f(x) \qquad \dfrac{dy}{dx} = \dfrac{f'(x)}{\sqrt{[f(x)]^2 + 1}}$

$y = \cosh^{-1}\left(\dfrac{x}{a}\right) \qquad \dfrac{dy}{dx} = \dfrac{1}{\sqrt{x^2 - a^2}}$

$y = \cosh^{-1} f(x) \qquad \dfrac{dy}{dx} = \dfrac{f'(x)}{\sqrt{[f(x)]^2 - 1}}$

$y = \tanh^{-1}\left(\dfrac{x}{a}\right) \qquad \dfrac{dy}{dx} = \dfrac{a}{a^2 - x^2}$

$y = \tanh^{-1} f(x) \qquad \dfrac{dy}{dx} = \dfrac{f'(x)}{1 - [f(x)]^2}$

$y = \sec h^{-1}\left(\dfrac{x}{a}\right) \qquad \dfrac{dy}{dx} = \dfrac{-a}{x\sqrt{a^2 - x^2}}$

$y = \sec h^{-1} f(x) \qquad \dfrac{dy}{dx} = \dfrac{-f'(x)}{f(x)\sqrt{1 - [f(x)]^2}}$

$y = \text{cosech}^{-1}\left(\dfrac{x}{a}\right) \qquad \dfrac{dy}{dx} = \dfrac{-a}{x\sqrt{x^2 + a^2}}$

$y = \text{cosech}^{-1} f(x) \qquad \dfrac{dy}{dx} = \dfrac{-f'(x)}{f(x)\sqrt{[f(x)]^2 + 1}}$

APPENDIX 1

$$y = \coth^{-1}\left(\frac{x}{a}\right) \qquad \frac{dy}{dx} = \frac{a}{a^2 - x^2}$$

$$y = \coth^{-1} f(x) \qquad \frac{dy}{dx} = \frac{f'(x)}{1 - [f(x)]^2}$$

Vector Equations:

$$\text{given } \overline{OP} = ai + bj + ck$$

$$\text{then length or magnitude or } norm = |OP| = \sqrt{a^2 + b^2 + c^2}$$

$$\text{also argument or angle} = \theta = \cos{-1}\left[\frac{a_1 b_1 + a_2 b_2 + a_3 b_3}{\sqrt{(a_1^2 + a_2^2 + a_3^2)}\sqrt{(b_1^2 + b_2^2 + b_3^2)}}\right]$$

Laplace Transforms

Function f(t)	Transform $L\{f(t)\}\int_0^\infty e^{-st}f(t)dt = \overline{f}(s)$	
1	$\dfrac{1}{s}$	
t	$\dfrac{1}{s^2}$	
t^n	$\dfrac{n!}{s^{n+1}}$	n = a positive integer
e^{-at}	$\dfrac{1}{s+a}$	
te^{-at}	$\dfrac{1}{(s+a)^2}$	

(continued)

APPENDIX 1

Function f(t)	Transform $L\{f(t)\}\int_0^\infty e^{-st}f(t)dt = \bar{f}(s)$	
$t^n e^{-at}$	$\dfrac{n!}{(s+a)^{n+1}}$	n = a positive integer
$\sin\omega t$	$\dfrac{\omega}{S^2+\omega^2}$	
$\cos\omega t$	$\dfrac{S}{S^2+\omega^2}$	
$t\sin\omega t$	$\dfrac{2\omega S}{(S^2+\omega^2)^2}$	
$t\cos\omega t$	$\dfrac{S^2-\omega^2}{(S^2+\omega^2)^2}$	
$\sin\omega t - \omega t\cos\omega t$	$\dfrac{2\omega}{(S^2+\omega^2)^2}$	?
$\sinh\omega t$	$\dfrac{\omega}{S^2-\omega^2}$	
$\cosh\omega t$	$\dfrac{S}{S^2-\omega^2}$	
$e^{-at}\sin\omega t$	$\dfrac{\omega}{(S+a)^2+\omega^2}$	

(*continued*)

APPENDIX 1

Function f(t)	Transform $L\{f(t)\}\int_0^\infty e^{-st}f(t)dt = \bar{f}(s)$
$e^{-at}\cos\omega t$	$\dfrac{S+a}{(S+a)^2+\omega^2}$
$e^{-at}\sinh\omega t$	$\dfrac{\omega}{(S+a)^2-\omega^2}$
$e^{-at}\cosh\omega t$	$\dfrac{S+a}{(S+a)^2-\omega^2}$
Unit Impulse S(t)	1
S(t-a)	e^{-sa}
$e^{-at}f(t)$	$\bar{f}(s+a)$
tf(t)	$\dfrac{-d}{ds}\bar{f}(s)$
f(t - a)H(t - a)	$e^{-sa}\bar{f}(s)$
$\dfrac{dx}{dt}$	$s\bar{x}-x_0$
$\dfrac{d^2x}{dt^2}$	$s^2\bar{x}-sx_0-x_1$

(continued)

APPENDIX 1

Function f(t)	Transform $L\{f(t)\}\int_0^\infty e^{-st}f(t)dt = \bar{f}(s)$
$\dfrac{d^3x}{dt^3}$	$s^3\bar{x} - s^2x_0 - sx_1 - x_2$
$\int_0^t f(t)\,dt$	$\dfrac{1}{s}\bar{f}(s)$
$\bar{x} = L\{x\},\ .x_0 = x_{(t=0)} = x(0)$	
$.x_1 = \dfrac{dx}{dt}_{(t=0)} = x'(0)$	
$.x_2 = \dfrac{d^2x}{dt^2}_{(t=0)} = x''(0)$	

Index

A

AA/AAA batteries, 10
Absolute permeability, 505, 521–523
AC analysis
    alternative approach, 479–483
    converting complex number into components, 484, 485
    exercise, 485–494
    maximum power in load, 440, 441
    power in load, 448–456
    splitting circuit into sections, 475–479
    straightforward circuit, 427–431
    superposition theory, 456–463
    Thevenin's equivalent circuit, 432–440
    Thevenin's theory, 463–474
    transfer characteristics option, 373
    Z_{THEV}, 441–447
AC voltage
    adding volt drops, 329–333
    and angles, 281
    argand diagrams, 300–303
    calculating current and volt drops, 305–307
    calculating RMS waveform, 291, 293
    calculating Z_T using trigonometry, 303, 305
    circumference of circle, 282, 283
    complex conjugate, 334–340
    complex numbers, 313–318
    complex numbers to phasor quantities, 308
    converting rectangular to polar and polar to rectangular formats, 321–328
    current flowing through R1, 288–290
    cycles per second, 283
    description, 275
    distributing 144W of power DC, cable of 10Ω resistance, 276
    distribution system, 279
    frequency calculation, 289
    graph of voltage supply, 287
    horizontal axis, 282
    impedance, 297–299
    j means moving through 90°, 311–313
    magnetic flux, 280
    radians, 282, 284
    RC circuit, 342

INDEX

AC voltage (*cont.*)
    rectification (*see* Rectification)
    resistance of load, 276
    resistor capacitor
        circuit, 318–321
    RL circuit, 341
    RMS of sine wave, 293–297
    RMS values, 288
    rotating coil inside a magnetic
        field, 279, 280
    $\sin(\theta)$ expression, 280
    smoothing, 349–353
    time t, 285, 286
    transformer, 277–279
    transmission line, 277, 278
    value of j, 308, 310, 311
    values, 288
Admittance, 49–52
Alternating current (AC), 275
    analysis (*see* AC analysis)
    defined, 23
    periodic time, 24
    polarity, 24
    typical voltage, 23
    See also AC voltage
AM, *see* Amplitude
    modulation (AM)
Ampere, defined, 17
Amplitude modulation (AM), 416
Argand diagrams, 300–303
Argument, 301
Audio system, 361, 362

B

Bandwidth of the circuit, 378
BC108 transistor, 587
B/H curves, 520–523
B/H loop, 521
BIL law, 553–557
BLU law, 553–557
Bridge rectifier, 348, 349

C

Calculus, 171, 244, 247
Capacitance, 208–210, 212
Capacitors, 134
    calculations, 254, 255, 257
    charge, 215–221
    charge Q, 231–234
    CR transient, 222–231
    current and voltage
        waveforms, 216
    defined, 208
    dielectric effect, 211
    discharging, 250–257
    electrostatic effect, 208
    free space constant, 209
    impedance, 222
    measurements, 217, 218
    microfarads, 210
    parallel plate, 212
    proportionality, 209
    series, 212–215
    simulated experiments, 217

INDEX

Carbon film resistors, 29
Car ignition circuit, 192–198
Chemical energy, 15, 16
Coercive force, 521
Complex numbers, 308, 313–318, 323, 331, 335
Compound fraction, 146, 241, 243
Conductor, 5, 557–560
Constant of permittivity, 209
Conventional current flow, 6, 7
Core, 502, 504–511
Current divider rule, 73, 74, 116, 119, 121
    Norton's equivalent circuit, 440, 490
    Thevenin's theory, 471
Current flow, 5–7, 17
Cycles per second, 24, 283, 531

D

-3dB point, 377
DC, *see* Direct current (DC)
DC analysis
    circuit redrawn with R_{COMB1}, 97
    converting from Thevenin's to Norton's theorem, 124–126
    ideal internal resistance
        current source, 96
        voltage source, 94–96
    Kirchhoff's mesh
        currents, 81–89
    load current, 111
    maximum power transfer theorem, 100, 101
    Norton's theorem, 118–124
    open circuited voltage, 110
    short circuit replacing $V_{Supply\,1}$, 98
    short circuit replacing $V_{Supply\,2}$, 97
    superposition theorem, 93, 94
    Thevenin's theorem, 102–106
    two circuits, 99, 100
    voltage V_A due to $V_{Supply\,1}$, 96, 97
    voltage V_A due to $V_{Supply\,2}$, 98, 99
    V_{THEV} due to current source I_{S1}, 108–111
    V_{THEV} due to voltage source V_1, 107, 108
DC transients in CR circuits
    calculated and measured results, 267
    capacitor (*see* Capacitors)
    current, 234–237
    current flowing, 257
    exercises, 269–271
    initial conditions, 258–261
    irregular waveform
        current flowing during first discharge period, 264
        first charge-up period, 263
        first discharge period, 263, 264
        intial 2ms time period, 262
        second charge-up period, 265

INDEX

DC transients in CR circuits (*cont.*)
    second discharge period, 266–269
    Laplace transforms, 237–247
    periods of growth, 248–250
    resistor and current waveforms, 250
    voltage and current traces, 268
    waveforms, 230

DC transients in LR circuits
    capacitors, 134
    car ignition circuit, 192–198
    component properties, 137
    current flowing through R1 and voltage across C1, 196
    current growth expression, 199–202
    current lag in inductor, 134–136
    current waveform, 202
    decaying current, 158–164
    exercises, 202–204
    growth and decay waveforms, 184
    inductors, 132–134
    irregular supply, 185–190
    Laplace transforms, 141
    measurements, 180
    power and energy in inductor, 190–192
    resistor and inductor, 181, 182
    RL circuit with initial conditions, 164–171
    settings, 139
    signal editor window, 138
    simulation, 139, 171–180
    steady state zero conditions, 137
    supply voltage and current, 188
    test circuit, 136
    time circuit is switched on
        algebraic equations, 142
        applied voltage V_{Supply}, 142
        differential of current i, 143–145
        Laplace transforms, 141
        partial fractions, 146–155
        resistor VR, 143
        using iR, current i, 142
    time constant, 140, 141
    TINA, 155–158
    transients and transient analysis, 133, 134
    VG1 voltage generator parameter window, 138
    voltage expressions during decay, 182, 184, 185
    voltage generator component, 138

Differential of inverse trig relationships, 595

Differentials of hyperbolic expressions, 600

Differentials of inverse hyperbolic expressions, 601

Direct current (DC)
    analysis (*see* DC analysis)
    concept, 8

INDEX

dry cell, 9, 10
primary and secondary cells, 10
series parallel combination circuit, 53
simple cell, PD and voltage, 8, 9
single cell with internal resistance, 12
wet cell, 8
Dry cell, 9–10
Dynamic impedance (Z_D), 390–401

E

ECAD, *see* Electronic computer aided design (ECAD)
Electrical charge, 4
Electrical circuits
  AC, 23, 24
  amp/ampere, 17
  current and charge calculations, 21, 22
  current flow and amp, 15, 16
  DC, 8–10
  EMF *vs*. PDs/voltage, 11, 12
  exercises, 34–36
  operation, 2–7
  power, 27–29
  resistance and resistivity, 17–20
  resistor types, 29–33
  RMS, 24–27
  series and parallel cells, 13–15
  series with current of 2A, 14
  series with no load current, 13
  voltage, 15
Electricity, 2, 5, 38, 498, 505
Electrolyte, 8, 9
Electromagnetic coils, 502–504
Electromagnetic induction, 498, 505
Electromagnetism, 565
  construction, 504
  defined, 498
  direction of current through conductor, 498, 499
  direction of flux around current carrying conductor, 499
  flux density, 509
  magnetic circuit, 512
  rectangular core, 509–511
  toroid, 507
  U-cored, 512
Electro-motive force (EMF), 8, 10, 11, 531, 534, 547, 559
  vs. PDs/voltage, 11, 12
Electron flow, 6, 7
Electronic circuits, 89, 569
Electronic computer aided design (ECAD), 12, 44, 63, 92, 247, 569
Electrons
  charge C, 3, 4
  concept, 2, 3
  movement of, 5
EMF, *see* Electro-motive force (EMF)
Energy storage devices, 197, 362
Engineering numbers, 54–57

611

INDEX

Exponential decay, 149–151, 153, 163, 235
Extra integrals, 596–597

F, G

Faraday, Michael, 498, 530
Faraday's Law, 530, 534
First-order differential equation, 158, 225, 238
Fleming's left-hand rule, 557
Fleming's right-hand rule, 560, 561
Flux
   air gap, 511
   anticlockwise current flow, 536
   calculation, 515
   clockwise current flow, 536
   and coil, 502–504
   magnetic field, 530
   materials, 504, 505
   rotor, 531
   units, 501
   vector quantity, 549
Flux density, 501, 503, 509
   calculation, 517
   defined, 500
   electromagnet, 506
   magnetic field, 556, 559, 560
   outer loop, 521
   primary coil, 526
   symbol, 500
Frequency of oscillation, 364, 365, 368, 401, 412

Full-wave rectification
   bridge rectifier, 348, 349
   defined, 347
   drawbacks, 347
   power supply, 353, 355, 356
   smoothing capacitor, 355
   specifications, 357
   voltage waveforms, 348
Function rule, 594

H

Half-wave rectification, 347
Hertz, Heinrich, 531
High-tension circuit, 192, 198
Hyperbolic equations, 599–600
Hysteresis loop, 521

I, J

Ideal internal resistance
   circuit redrawn with load and sources, 112
   current source, 96
   voltage source, 94–96
Ignition coil, 192
Impedance, 428, 479
   AC voltage, 297–299
   capacitors, 222
   coil, 532–534
   inductor and capacitor, 366
   parallel circuit, 394
   phasor diagram, 366, 367, 388
   phasor quantities, 301

INDEX

Inductance, 132, 134, 530, 531, 541
   differential of current
      waveform, 539
   expressions, 547, 548
Inductive impedance, 135, 136, 301, 367, 533
Inductors, 134
   current flowing, 544–547
   current lag, 134–136
   defined, 132, 530
   impedance, 532
   induced voltage, 537–543
   magnetic field, 132
   phase shift, 135
   power and energy, 190–192
   and resistor, 181, 182
   second test circuit, 541, 542
   series and parallel, 132, 133
   test circuit, 538
   units, 132
   waveforms, 539
Insulators, 5
Inverse Laplace transforms, 145, 171
I^2R losses, 28, 277, 279

K

KCL, *see* Kirchhoff's Current Law (KCL)
KE, *see* Kinetic energy (KE)
Kinetic energy (KE), 3, 16
Kirchhoff's Current Law (KCL), 7, 47–53, 66, 84, 409, 410, 422

Kirchhoff's Laws
   defined, 38
   series circuits, 38–40
   volt drops, 40, 41
Kirchhoff's mesh currents
   ammeter readings, 87
   circuit, 81, 82
   clockwise and anticlockwise direction, 82
   equations, 84, 85
   examples, 89–93
   expression, 83
   KVL applied to loop 1, 88
   KVL applied to loop 2, 88, 89
   voltage arrows
      redrawn, 87, 88
   voltage sources, 82
Kirchhoff's Voltage Law, 39, 40, 63, 66, 83, 140, 518

L

Laplace transforms, 141, 237–247, 253, 602
Law of conservation of energy, 15, 16
Leclanché cell, 9, 10
Lenz, Heinrich, 534, 537
Lenz's Law, 534–537
Load impedance, 428, 431, 440, 446, 448, 453, 455
Low-tension circuit, 192, 197
Low-tension coil, 192

613

INDEX

M

Magnetic calculations
examples, 524–530
Magnetic circuit, 511–512, 561, 563
Magnetic domains, 135, 532
Magnetic field, 520, 535, 537
  current carrying conductor, 553, 554
  current carrying conductor at angle θ, 554
  forces on current carrying conductor, 550
  and motor, 549–552
  moving conductor, 558
  orbits, 498
  rotor, 531
  single coil of wire, 535
Magnetic flux, 280, 499, 549
Magnetic *vs.* electrical circuit, 518, 519
Magnetising force, 504, 506, 509, 520
Magnetism, 140, 497, 498, 530, 531, 549
Magnetomotive force, 500, 506, 513, 531, 562
Maximum power transfer theorem, 100–101
Maxwell's equations, 498
Mercury cell, 10
Motors, 189, 549–552
Multisim, 570

N

Napierian/exponential logs, 162
No load potential/voltage, 11
Norton's equivalent circuit, 120, 125, 126, 489
  ammeter readings, 439
  calculations, 437
  current divider rule, 440
  currents, 438
  load connected, 439
  load Z3 replaced with short circuit, 438
Norton's resistance, 119
Norton's theory
  current, 119–122
  current due to I_{S1}, 123, 124
  current due to V1, 122
  defined, 118
  example, 122

O

Ohm's Law, 11, 27, 34, 62, 83, 109, 234, 290, 306, 324, 355, 395, 457, 481, 515
  defined, 38
  expression, 40, 93
  load resistance, 120
  resistance R, 41, 42, 44
  resistance value, 181
  series circuit, 43, 44

INDEX

transposition, 62
voltage divider rule, 64, 65
Open circuit voltage, 103, 107, 109, 114, 115, 445
Oscilloscope, 298
   amplifiers, 585, 586
   connecting, 588
   display, 590, 591
   inductor, 538
   measurement, 289
   NPN bipolar transistor window, 586
   series RL, 299
   sine wave voltage, 587, 588
   sinusoidal wave, 289
   traces, 320, 345, 346
   transistor catalog editor window, 587
   waveform cycles, 589
   waveforms, 545, 546
   window, 589

P

Parallel plate capacitor, 212
Parallel RLC circuit, 390
   alternative expression Z_T, 417–423
   currents, 390
   currents flowing
      calculated *vs.* simulated results, 410
      capacitor (i_c), 408
      current i_1, 409

   impedances in parallel, 402
   impedances Z_1, 403, 404
   impedances Z_2, 405–408
   magnitude and phase, 411
   defined, 390
   exercise, 423
   expression, 401
   phasor/argand diagram
      high frequencies, 392
      low frequencies, 391
      resonance, 392, 393
   procedures, 399
   Q factor, 414, 416
   resonant frequency, 396
   simulated circuit with R changed to 50Ω, 413
   Tan ratio, 395
   trigonometry, 394
   tuned amplifiers, 416
Partial fractions, 146–155, 599
PD, *see* Potential difference (PD)
PE, *see* Potential energy (PE)
Peak inverse voltage, 351
Permeability, 504, 505, 514, 548
Phase difference, 307
Phase shift, 541
Phasor diagram, 322, 479
   current, 391
   impedances, 365–367, 388
   low/high frequency, 391
   phasor of magnitude 1, 311
   phasor quantities, 301
   resistance, 301
   RL circuit, 300

INDEX

Phasor diagram (*cont.*)
   series RLC circuit, 393
   voltage, 389
   VR + VL, 328
Phasor quantities, 299, 301, 306, 308, 427
Potential difference (PD), 8, 11, 12
Potential energy (PE), 3
Power, defined, 27–29
Power supply unit (PSU), 95
Product rule, 594
PROTEUS, 570
PSU, *see* Power supply unit (PSU)
Pythagoras theorem, 303

Q

Quality (Q) factor
   parallel RLC circuit, 414, 416
   series RLC circuit
      AC transfer characteristics, 380
      bandwidth, 383
      defined, 379
      proportional sign, 384
      resistance increased to 45Ω, 382
      resistance reduced to 5Ω, 381
      simulation, 380
      voltage magnification, 382
      volt drops, 380
      waveforms, 380
Quotient rule, 594

R

Rationalizing complex number, 338
Reactive power, 72
Rectification
   AC voltage waveform, 344
   defined, 343
   full-wave, 347–349
   half-wave, 347
   negative half-cycle, 345
   oscilloscope traces, 345–347
   semiconductor material, 345
Relative permeability, 505, 528
Relative permittivity, 210, 211
Relays, 523–524
Reluctance, 513–518, 529
Remanence, 521, 523
Resistivity, 17–20
Resistor capacitor circuit, 318–321
Resistors
   carbon film, 29
   colour coding, 30–32
   E12 series, 29
   exercise, 36
   four-band, 33
   packages, 30
   parallel expression, 60
   tolerance and temperature band colours, 32
   usage, 32, 33
   wattage ratings, 29
Resonant frequency, 197, 362–372, 380, 381, 385, 403
RMS, *see* Root mean square (RMS)

INDEX

Root mean square (RMS), 24–27, 597
Rules of indices, 173, 228, 593

S

Saturation, 520
Sea of free electrons, 5
Series RLC circuit, 298, 390
   components, 369
   exercise, 424, 425
   first circuit in audio system, 361, 362
   impedance phasor, 397, 398
   phasor diagram, 366, 367, 393
   quality factor, 379–389
   resonant frequency, 362–372
   selectivity and bandwidth
      AC transfer characteristics, 372–374
      concept, 372
      default display, AC transfer simulation, 374, 375
      default setting. linear-dB, 376
      half power points, 377
      high *vs.* low frequency, 377
      maximum current value, 377
      resistance reduced to 5Ω, 378
      set axis window, 375
      signal analyser, 373
      sufficient strength, 377
      supply current against frequency, 376
      simulation, 371
      statements, 371
      typical, 362
      values, 365
      waveforms, 198
   See also Parallel RLC circuit
Series RL circuit, 150, 298, 394
Smoothing, 349–353
Solenoid, 524, 525
Standard differentials, 540, 593
Standard integrals, 161, 226, 295, 596
Superheterodyne receiver, 416
Superposition theorem, 93, 94
Superposition theory, 434, 468
   circuit, 457
   complete voltage v_a, 461
   currents flowing through component, 457
   expressions, 458
   principle, 458
   simulation results, 463
   three currents flowing in circuit, 461–463
   voltage v_a due to V_1, 459
   voltage v_a due to V_2, 460
Supply current, 57–63, 392, 408
Switch mode power supplies (SWMPS), 356
SWMPS, *see* Switch mode power supplies (SWMPS)

INDEX

T

Tesla, Nikola, 501
Thevenin's equivalent circuit, 104, 106, 110, 125, 431, 446, 450, 467, 477, 478
  example, 106, 107, 111–118, 432
  impedance, 432
  load impedance, 453
  load resistor, 112
  R_{Load} changed to 10.55Ω, 116
  R_{Load} set to 10.5Ω, 117
  R_{THEV} calculation, 113, 114
  simulated result, 436, 437
  sources, 433
  voltage divider rule, 435
  voltage (v_{THEV}), 434–436
  V_{THEV} due to I_{S1}, 115
  V_{THEV} due to V1, 114
  Z_{THEV} calculation, 113, 433
Thevenin's impedance (Z_{THEV}), 451, 464
  parallel impedance, 443
  polar format, 442, 443
  redrawn circuit, 441
  RMS, 445
  simulated circuit, 447
  three impedances circuit, 441
  value of Z_3, 445
  voltage divider rule, 445
  Z_{Comb1} calculation, 443
Thevenin's resistance, 103, 106, 107
Thevenin's theory, 102–106, 428, 432, 479

ammeter reading, 472, 473
current divider rule, 471
current flow assumption, 474
equations, 468
expressions, 469
phasor quantities, 468
simulated result, 467
v_a due to iSupply1, 471
v_a due to VSupply1, 469, 470
voltage divider rule, 465, 466, 470
voltage sources, 463, 464
voltage source VSupply1 and current source ISupply1, 468
V_{THEV} due to V_1, 465
V_{THEV} due to V_2, 465, 466
Three-phase generation, 501
Times decay, 175
TINA 12
  AC transfer characteristics, 579
  bode plot, 580
  creating first test circuit
    bode plot, 572
    capacitor, 575
    circuit wired completely, 577
    component value window, 574, 575
    current category menu bar, 572
    drop-down menu, 572, 573
    editor options window, 573
    grid, 576
    inserted outputs, 577

INDEX

    parameters, 575
    resistor, 574
    voltage pin, 578
    wire tool, 576
defined, 569, 570
opening screen, 571
oscilloscope, 585–591
program icon, 570
running AC analysis, 578, 580
running software, 570–572
toolbars, 571, 572
transient analysis, 581–585
TINA simulation circuit, 44–47
Toroid, 507, 526–528, 563, 564
Transformers, 192, 277–279, 351
Transient analysis, 133, 134, 155–158, 188, 542
    circuit changes, 581
    RC circuit, 581
    results, 585
    set up, 584
    signal editor window, 582
    time constants, 582
    time settings, 583
    voltage generator window, 582
Trig identities, 294, 597
Trigonometry, 303, 305
Tuned amplifiers, 416

U

U-cored electromagnet, 512
Unidirectional current (UDC), 8

V

Valence shell, 5
Vector equations, 602
Voltage divider rule, 115, 434
    ammeter measurement, 70
    circuit diagram, 64
    current flowing through components, 72
    final redrawn circuit, 68
    high wattage rating, 73
    Ohm's Law, 64, 65
    product over sum approach, 67
    R_{COMB1} inserted, 67
    reduced circuit, 68
    resistor values, 65
    separate loops, 70, 71
    supply current, 69
    test circuit, 63, 64
    Thevenin's equivalent circuit, 435
    Thevenin's theory, 465, 466, 470
    V_{THEV}, 452
    Z_{THEV}, 445
Voltage generator, 138, 576, 582
Voltage phasor diagram, 359, 389
Voltaic pile, 15

W, X, Y, Z

Wet cell, 8–10, 16

GPSR Compliance

The European Union's (EU) General Product Safety Regulation (GPSR) is a set of rules that requires consumer products to be safe and our obligations to ensure this.

If you have any concerns about our products, you can contact us on

ProductSafety@springernature.com

In case Publisher is established outside the EU, the EU authorized representative is:

Springer Nature Customer Service Center GmbH
Europaplatz 3
69115 Heidelberg, Germany

www.ingramcontent.com/pod-product-compliance
Lightning Source LLC
LaVergne TN
LVHW021954060526
838201LV00048B/1571